TALES, 1812

AND OTHER SELECTED POEMS

GEORGE CRABBE

TALES, 1812
AND OTHER SELECTED POEMS

EDITED WITH AN INTRODUCTION BY

HOWARD MILLS

Lecturer in English Literature, University College of South Wales and Monmouthshire, Cardiff

CAMBRIDGE
AT THE UNIVERSITY PRESS
1967

Published by the Syndics of the Cambridge University Press
Bentley House, 200 Euston Road, London, N.W.1
American Branch: 32 East 57th Street, New York, N.Y. 10022

Library of Congress Catalogue Card Number: 67–10348

Printed in Great Britain
at the University Printing House, Cambridge
(Brooke Crutchley, University Printer)

PREFACE

This book aims to provide the student and the general reader with as large as possible a selection of Crabbe. It prints all the *Tales* of 1812, two-thirds of *The Parish Register* and nearly half *The Borough*, besides other poems—in all, a good third of Crabbe's prolific work. It is thus the fullest selection in print. It should meet a serious need, for no complete edition is in print, and because of this the vicious circle of taste is excluding Crabbe from study. When he *is* studied, it is usually with reference to a handful of poems imposed by thin, cramped selections.

This volume avoids that restriction. It aims, first, to show the range of Crabbe's powers over forty years in subjects, styles and moods. Hence, partly, the large selection from *The Borough* and the inclusion of two interesting if imperfect experiments *The World of Dreams* and *In a Neat Cottage*. More generally, while including 'the best of Crabbe' I have tried to avoid the impression of a severely restricted canon, and to include enough borderline cases to give the reader room to manœuvre, so that he feels free to make his own selection of the best and distinguish it from the merely competent. For this reason I have printed complete one volume of tales as Crabbe himself selected and published it: here the reader has complete independence of judgement. (It should be added that my own 'best of Crabbe' would in any case include fifteen or more of these *Tales* of 1812, and few more than the present four *Tales of the Hall.*) Similarly the Introduction is not an attempt at a definitive assessment of Crabbe but tries to raise as many critical issues as possible.

This edition owes a special debt to the late Douglas Brown, who was to have prepared a selection for the Cambridge University Press. He died suddenly in 1964, before being able to carry out this plan. While my selection differs from the one he would have made, I feel very indebted to him for having first interested the Press in reprinting Crabbe.

I wish to express my thanks to the friends, past teachers and present students who have discussed Crabbe with me and have helped to improve the choice of poems. I am particularly grateful to Mr Charles Page for the friendly advice and stimulation that has helped to develop my interest in Crabbe from the first, and has mitigated in this volume the shortcomings for which I alone am responsible.

I am grateful to Mr Benjamin Britten for permission to reproduce the picture of Aldeburgh Beach in 1812 used on the cover, and to Faber and Faber Ltd for the loan of the print.

1967 H.M.

CONTENTS

TABLE OF LIFE AND WORKS

1755 1 January, born at Aldeburgh, Suffolk, son of a collector of salt-duties.

c. 1762 Went to school at Bungay, Suffolk.

1766 Went to school at Stowmarket, Suffolk.

1768 Apprenticed to a surgeon-apothecary at Wickham Brook, near Bury St Edmunds. Began frequent writing of verse.

1771 Apprenticed to a surgeon at Woodbridge, Suffolk.

1772 Met and became engaged to Sarah Elmy. Published verse in *Wheble's Magazine.*

1775 *Inebriety* published anonymously. Returned to Aldeburgh and worked as a warehouseman on Slaughden quay before setting up practice as a surgeon.

1776 Went to London to 'pick up a little surgical knowledge'.

1777 Resumed practice in Aldeburgh.

1780 Went to London with £5, to seek living as a writer. Unsuccessful appeals for patronage. Witnessed Gordon Riots. (See *Journal to Mira* printed in *Life* by his son.) *The Candidate, A Poetical Epistle* published.

1781 Successfully appealed to Edmund Burke for patronage (letter printed in *Life* by son). *The Library* published. Stayed with Burke: met Charles James Fox and Sir Joshua Reynolds. Ordained as a deacon.

1782 Returned to Aldeburgh as curate. Ordained priest and appointed chaplain to Duke of Rutland at Belvoir Castle.

1783 Met Dr Johnson who read, praised and slightly 'corrected' *The Village*, which was published in May. Married Sarah Elmy.

1785 Became curate at Stathern, Leicestershire. Studied botany and entomology; acted as doctor to poor of the parish. *The Newspaper* published.

1789 Took up the living of Muston, Leicestershire, which he kept until 1814. (Lived there until 1792.)

c. 1790 Began taking opium on medical advice. Took 'a constant but slightly increasing dose' for rest of his life.

1792 Moved to Suffolk.

1795 *An Account of the Natural History of the Vale of Belvoir* published.

1796 Third son died: wife's manic-depressive fits began, and continued until her death.

1801–2 Wrote and destroyed three novels.

1802 Began *The Parish Register.*

1804 Began *The Borough.*

1805 Laws against absentee clergy made him return to Muston.

1807 *The Parish Register*, *Sir Eustace Grey* and *The Hall of Justice* published in *Poems*, which also collected earlier poems.

1810 *The Borough* published.

1812 *Tales* published.

1813 Wife died; Crabbe dangerously ill.

1814 Moved to Trowbridge, Wiltshire as rector. Brief engagement to Charlotte Ridout.

1816 *Infancy—A Fragment* written.

1817 First of several visits to London, where he met Campbell, Moore, Rogers, and (later) Wordsworth and Southey. (*London Journal* of 1817 printed in *Life* by son.) Son became curate at Trowbridge. *The World of Dreams* written *c.* 1817.

1819 *Tales of the Hall* published.

1822 Visited Sir Walter Scott in Edinburgh. *In A Neat Cottage* written.

1823 *Works* published (a collected edition in 5- and 8-volume formats).

1832 Died at Trowbridge, aged 77.

1834 *The Poetical Works*, 8 vols., published. Contained *Life* by son (vol. I) and *Posthumous Tales* (vol. VIII).

INTRODUCTION

> The reader, I believe, is seldom pleased to find his opinion anticipated; it is natural to delight more in what we find or make, than in what we receive. Judgment, like other faculties, is improved by practice, and its advancement is hindered by submission to dictatorial decisions, as the memory grows torpid by the use of a table-book. Some initiation is however necessary; ...I have, therefore, shown as much as may enable the candidate of criticism to discover the rest.
>
> Johnson, *Preface to Shakespeare*[1]

CRABBE IN THE REGENCY, AND LATER

When the author of *Tales 1812* re-emerged in London in the Regency decade of the 1810s, he struck people as an incongruous figure, a survival of an earlier age. He was, after all, now sixty, and had last been in literary society thirty years earlier when, after his youth in East Anglia, he had won Burke as patron, who had had *The Village* looked over and commended by Dr Johnson and published in 1783. Crabbe had taken holy orders and married, then vanished again into provincial life and published nothing for twenty-two years. 'By God, he was as like Parson Adams as twelve to a dozen'[2]—Lord Thurlow's parallel must have occurred to the younger Regency writers. A parson-poet was an outmoded figure among the new-style poets, the 'banker-poet' Rogers, the 'noble poet' Byron and professionals like Moore. As outmoded was his appearance, 'dressed as he was in rather an old-fashioned style of clerical propriety', and with his 'apparent simplicity of look and manners'.[3] His talk, too, seemed simple and narrow, unquickened by the great events of the time and of the last twenty years: he confessed he preferred talking to the ladies, with an old-fashioned courtesy they found sugary and the men alarming: 'Damme, Sir, the very first time Crabbe dined at my house, he made love to my sister.' But exactly as Jeffrey noted in the poet 'the sure and profound sagacity with which he...startles us in the midst of very unambitious discussions',[4] so in the man

[1] *Works* (1825), vol. v, p. 145.

[2] See *The Life of George Crabbe*, by his son, ed. E. M. Forster (Worlds Classics, Oxford University Press, 1932), p. 117.

[3] *Ibid.* p. 263. This—Lockhart on Crabbe in Edinburgh—sums up London's impressions.

[4] *Edinburgh Review*, vol. XXXII, p. 119.

one would have been too apt to forget what lurked beneath that good-humoured, unpretending aspect, but that every now and then he uttered some brief pithy remark, which showed how narrowly he had scrutinised into whatever might be said or done before him, and called us to remember, with some awe, that we were in the presence of the author of *The Borough*.[1]

They respected Crabbe as a link with the age of Johnson, Burney and Burke—as Campbell put it, with 'the giants before the flood'.

But the Regency found it more complicated to place Crabbe the poet. When he published again in 1807, Jeffrey for instance greeted him as a forgotten friend from 'the old poetical establishment' and contrasted him with Wordsworth's 'new system of feeling and writing'. But in the same breath he called Crabbe 'the most original writer who has ever come before us' and spoke of the 'novelty of his style'.[2] And this paradox was common with the readers who made Crabbe 'one of the most popular and admired of our living poets'.[3]

More simple and abrupt was the hostility of the Romantics. Wordsworth thought Crabbe, like Jane Austen, could make 'an admirable copy of life', but 'unless the truth of nature were presented to him clarified, as it were, by the pervading light of the imagination, it had scarce any attractions in his eyes'.[4] One motive was pique: Wordsworth was stung by Jeffrey's comparison of himself and Crabbe into trying to outdo Crabbe on his own ground in the later books of *The Excursion* (1814).[5] But Coleridge and De Quincey were just indifferent to Crabbe, and listlessly echoed Wordsworth's terms 'unpoetical', 'unimaginative'. There is, as often with this trio, strong evidence of price-fixing: they offer suspiciously close estimates and similarly worded tenders.[6] Even their friend Crabb Robinson, usually the 'common reader' in his unprejudiced and wide tastes, echoes them in a revealing diary-entry. Generalising entirely, as he admits, from distant memories of *The Village*,

I take no pleasure in his unpoetical representations of human life...he ...could faithfully portray what he saw, yet he had an eye only for the sad realities of life... Indeed this impression is so strong that I have

[1] Lockhart in *Life*, by son (ed. Forster), p. 266.
[2] *Edinburgh Review*, vol. xii, p. 151; vol. xvi, p. 31; vol. xx, p. 304.
[3] W. Hazlitt, *The Spirit of the Age* (1825); Everyman (1922), p. 330.
[4] M. L. Peacock (ed.), *The Critical Opinions of Wordsworth* (1950), p. 179.
[5] See J. S. Lyon, *The Excursion: A Study* (Yale, 1950), pp. 37–46.
[6] See J. E. Jordan, *Thomas de Quincey, Literary Critic* (California University Press, 1952), esp. p. 205.

never read his later works—I know little about them—I feel infinite respect for Crabbe and may read some two or three of his poems that I may have something like an idea of him.[1]

What we have traced so far were spontaneous reactions, not considered critical appraisals—excitement or boredom, not insight or obtuseness. We expect indifference to Crabbe's lesser creative advances in those who found Wordsworth and Coleridge the exciting 'fine points of consciousness'[2] in the age, to read whom 'had... the effect that arises from the turning up of fresh soil, or of the first welcome breath of spring',[3] 'the greatest event in the unfolding of my own mind...an absolute revelation of untrodden worlds'.[4] The real harm began when literary maps of the period were made, history solidified and simplified, and the Romantic poets appeared the *only* creative advance from the eighteenth century. In place of Jeffrey's closer and sharper view and mixed response, the modern historian's distant view blurs together all Crabbe's work (fifty years' work and over fifty pieces) into a lowest common denominator 'Crabbe poem', and pushes him back into a mythically uniform eighteenth century. And the poet whom Jeffrey found 'shocking' is reduced to a tame parson-coupleteer. This view can be traced from Leslie Stephen's essay of 1876, through Huchon's study of 1907 (one of the first modern mindless card-index biography doctorates) to the latest *Oxford Literary History*.[5] Admittedly nobody takes the Oxford Histories seriously. But in Crabbe's case historians do matter because there is little real criticism and because the poems themselves are out of print, making people rely on hearsay.

It is hoped that this selection will lead many to follow Crabb Robinson and 'read some...poems that I may have something like an idea of him'. The aim of this Introduction is to break open the simplifications about Crabbe, and so spread the reader's attention over a variety of critical approaches and the variety of his work.

[1] *On Books and their Writers*, ed. E. J. Morley (1938), vol. II, p. 472.
[2] The phrase is F. R. Leavis's, who after highly praising Crabbe, writes this suggestive and metaphorical remark: 'Crabbe, however, was hardly at the fine point of consciousness in his time. His sensibility belongs to an order that those who were most alive to the age—who had the most sensitive antennae—had ceased to find sympathetic' (*Revaluation* (1936), p. 128).
[3] De Quincey, *Reminiscences of the English Lake Poets*, ed. J. E. Jordan (1961), p. 1.
[4] Hazlitt, *Works*, ed. P. P. Howe (1932), vol. XVII, p. 117.
[5] W. L. Renwick, *English Literature 1789–1815* (1963).

POETIC DEVELOPMENT AND PERSONAL EXPERIENCE

One key to Crabbe is the change in his art from the mode of *The Village* to that of *The Tales*, and in the experience behind that change. And here, straightaway, the reader can be forced back on his own perceptions. For the historian's simple picture is an obvious fraud when juxtaposed with the deep and varied figure in the *Life of Crabbe* by his son. This, the best book on Crabbe, knows his 'essential biography' and leads us to corresponding poems.

The historian finds 'no...change or development either in spirit, thought, or manner'.[1] All this means surely is that 'the impression of *The Village* is so strong that I have never read his later works'. For as he moves from section to section of this volume a reader can't miss the change Crabbe's son notes in all three respects:

> There was but little in the earlier series that could have led to the expectation of such a performance as *The Parish Register*. In former works, a few minute descriptions had been introduced—but here there was nothing but a succession of such descriptions; in them there had been no tale—this was a chain of stories; they were didactic—here no moral influence is directly inculcated... Thus differing from his former self, his utter dissimilarity to any other author then enjoying public favour was still more striking.[2]

Equally striking is the evolution of the new form through the central collections of 1807–12. *The Register* (1807) tries out a remarkable variety of modes—the Dryden epigram-character (for example, *Collett*, 3, l. 75), the skeletal life-history (for example, *Monday*, 1, l. 688), and others that rely completely on the character's speech. *The Borough* (1810) reverts partly to the general survey. But as early as letter 3 comes the sketch of the vicar. Here the form is more fluid: it isn't the eighteenth-century epigram–couplet bricklaying of a preconceived character, but builds up touches with something like Chaucer's apparent inconsequentiality, returning, as one's mind does when thinking about people, to dominant or puzzling traits. The irony too is like Chaucer's, more delicate here than Crabbe's earlier heavy sarcasm. But how far, again, this sketch is from the tales at the other end of *The Borough*: *Peter Grimes* (22) leads directly into *Tales, 1812*.

The historian's Crabbe is a figure of sloth who having won a

[1] Renwick, *op. cit.* p. 109.
[2] *Life*, by son (ed. Forster), p. 176.

position idled away twenty-two years—'the incentive was lacking' until he published to finance his son's education.[1] But that son tells us of those years:

As the chief characteristic of his heart was benevolence, so that of his mind was a buoyant exuberance of thought and perpetual exercise of intellect. Thus he had an inexhaustible resource within himself...I never saw him...doing nothing. Out of doors he had always some object in view...and in the house, if he was not writing, he was reading.

...He was all that time busily engaged in composition. Numberless were the manuscripts which he completed; and not a few of them were never destined to see the light. I can well remember more than one grand incremation—not in the chimney, for the bulk of paper to be consumed would have endangered the house—but in the open air.[2]

These manuscripts included three novels, as well as poems.

This confirms that the Rip-Van-Winkle notion won't do: one could not suddenly wake up and write three great and varied collections such as those of 1807–12 like some intellectual sleeping beauty. Nor could they come from an uneventful 'emotional' life, for the poems progress in depth as well as assurance of form. One is not surprised to find the historian—'The general character of his stories is obvious enough...*having an assured status, a good wife*, and a well-doing family, he was sorry for lonely men and deserted women'[3]—proved wrong again:

He always seemed to shrink from going into oral details on the subject. The numberless allusions to the nature of a literary dependant's existence in a great lord's house, which occur in my father's writings, and especially in the tale of *The Patron*, [show] that the situation he filled at Belvoir was attended with many painful circumstances, and productive in his mind of some of the acutest sensations of wounded pride that have ever been traced by any pen.[4]

My mother was attacked, on the death of her son Edmund, by a nervous disorder; and it proved of an increasing and very lamentable kind; for, during the latter months of the year, she was oppressed by the deepest dejection of spirits I have ever witnessed in anyone, and this circumstance alone was sufficient to undermine the happiness of so feeling a mind as my father's.[5]

Passages like these (there are others) touch the quick of Crabbe's life and his poetry. These experiences became traumas. That term is used not melodramatically but in the strict sense of emotional

[1] Renwick, *op. cit.* p. 109.
[2] *Life* by son (ed. Forster), p. 127.
[3] Renwick, *op. cit.* (my italics).
[4] *Life* by son (ed. Forster), p. 108.
[5] *Ibid.* p. 155.

wounds that never healed. Like Dickens' traumas of blacking factory and debtors' prison, they obsessed Crabbe's mind. Like Dickens, he would 'shrink' from talking of them: and like Dickens's again, they pushed their way up, often despite himself, into tale after tale, into even the most unexpected contexts. Scholars who say Crabbe's life was 'uneventful' don't understand where the real 'events' of life occur. Crabbe was not a Romantic poet: his mode was dramatic fiction: but like them he had his experiences to work out, sicknesses to shed, in his poems.

THE SOCIAL ELEMENT

The radical change his son notes in the poetry makes it unfair to judge Crabbe by *The Village* and the mode of 'social survey' it represents—the mode unfairly called 'versified blue-books'.[1] However, it over-simplifies the other way to say that in his Regency poems Crabbe's interest was 'psychological...rather than sociological'.[2] Great fiction never excludes like that. It is therefore worth weighing, first, the part 'social description' plays in that transitional work, *The Borough*, and then the way social insights come through the medium of the psychological tale.

The aim of *The Borough*—a Fielding-like panorama—comes out in the full list of contents, from which this selection takes nearly half:

General Description; the Church; the Vicar, Curate, etc.; Sects and Professions in Religion; Elections; Professions—Law, Physic; Trades; Amusements; Clubs and Social Meetings; Inns; Players; The Alms-House and Trustees; Inhabitants of the Almshouse—Blaney, Clelia, Benbow; the Hospital and Governors; The Poor and their Dwellings; the Poor of the Borough—The Parish Clerk, Ellen Orford, Abel Keene, Peter Grimes; Prisons; Schools.

But behind this facade, we are curious at how much of England around 1810 Crabbe misses out. His borough certainly belongs 'before the flood' of changes in industry, trade and communications. Even for the provinces Aldeburgh was a backwater that was to be left behind by those changes, never to recover: and Crabbe didn't feel obliged to tamper much with recollections of his home town years earlier so as to make his borough a significant point of growth in English life. In contrast, Galt's roughly contemporary

[1] See Hazlitt, *The Spirit of the Age* and Stephen, *Hours in a Library*.
[2] L. Haddakin, *The Poetry of Crabbe* (1955), p. 46.

Annals of the Parish, although dull and perfunctory, does register the reverberations of distant shocks and developments. With the setting up of a cotton-mill and of an industrial New Town, 'we were become part of the great web of commercial reciprocities, and felt in our corner and extremity every touch or stir that was made on any part of the texture'.[1] Whereas Crabbe's letter 8 on *Trades* begins airily

> Of manufactures, trade, inventions rare,
> Steam-powers and looms, you'd know our Borough's share—
> 'Tis small...

and so quickly on to leisure—a butterfly-collecting weaver—and a story about the death of feeling. Again, Galt's parish, helped by the new wave of literacy, newsprint and communications, does feel the flood of war and political unrest: 'mankind read more, and the spirit of reflection and reasoning was more awake...There was a handsome bookseller's shop...with not only a London newspaper daily, but magazines, and reviews, and other new publications.'[2] But not Aldeburgh: in the fascinating letter 10 on Reading (and other) Clubs, provincial society is bored, boorish and uninquisitive. Books are tumbled, but cards and booze soon take over, and the loutish outsider pushes in and destroys serious talk.

But if *The Borough* doesn't touch on the provincial growth-points of the early 1800s, it does convey the variety and interdependence of a community. The *General Description* weaves the contrasts of workers and leisured or rich (with the detail of the shivering oyster-fisher and his roasting customers); the different and exchanged produce of village, port and surrounding country; the various characters of villager and sailor (with the 'sons of the ocean' showing off in front of overawed village-boys); the evils of Enclosure; and the relaxations of Sunday. And note the artistic ease of Crabbe's transitions and of his weaving-in the seascapes and landscapes.

The most vivid 'social description' comes from the mouth of Benbow (16), old drunkard mourning 'Old England' and Squire Asgill—

> No pride had he, and there was difference small
> Between the master's and the servants' hall.

Tenants and tradesmen were well-oiled, guests 'tippled till they slept', poachers had the freedom of the park and the squire ('him-

[1] *Works of John Galt*, ed. D. Storrar Meldrum (1895): *Annals of the Parish*, vol. II, p. 57.
[2] *Ibid.* p. 30.

self a poacher, though at different game') had the freedom of the village-girls. Leslie Stephen rightly traces this thirty or forty years back from 1810, to Crabbe's father and his cronies and to Mrs Crabbe's uncle Mr Tovell. It was a social order, a 'coarse, hearty, patriarchal way of life' that survived, in isolated parts of England like those Crabbe lived in until the 1810s: but 'to get a realistic picture of country life as Crabbe saw it, we must go back to Squire Western or to some of the roughly-hewn masses of flesh who sat to Hogarth'.[1]

But you can't push Crabbe back to the age of Fielding. He is aware of change: Squires Asgill and Western are dead and gone. Women and prudery rule the big houses now; the gentry, more unsure of their position and function, are more on their dignity and reserve.

> The father dead, the son has found a wife,
> And lives a formal, proud, unsocial life...
> The lands are now enclosed; the tenants all,
> Save at a rent-day, never see the hall...
> [Asgill's ghost would] see a pale old hag preside,
> A thing made up of stinginess and pride;
> Who carves the meat, as if the flesh could feel...

Crabbe touches on the effects of 'improvement' and enclosure—both of agricultural land and of parks that became self-contained rather than merging into the surrounding country. It was a sign of meanness and isolation, and led to the separation of classes.

> He never planted nor inclosed—his trees
> Grew like himself, untroubled and at ease:
> Bounds of all kinds he hated, and had felt
> Chok'd and imprison'd in a modern belt,
> Which some rare genius now has twined about
> The good old house, to keep old neighbours out.

Elsewhere, too, Crabbe registers the social and psychological effects of enclosure that touched Clare so strongly.[2]

So Crabbe isn't altogether behind the times in what he sees. Nor is his response to change simple or conservative. In the dramatic

[1] Stephen, *Hours in a Library*, ser. II, pp. 40–2.

[2] In the year of *The Borough* enclosure was in progress on the other side of the fens from Aldeburgh, at Clare's Helpston. Clare too writes of 'petty minds' as well as the material hardships of the change. Both poets note in land-clearing the loss of trees which were embodiments of feelings—of personal memories and those of the whole village. More personally, enclosure came to symbolise for Clare the restriction of hopes, disconnection from his childhood, and the final mental enclosure of his madness.

context, this is an old soak's lament for free liquor up at the hall; but that Fielding world appeals strongly to the 'masculine generosity' and 'buoyant exuberance' in Crabbe. His attitude complicates over the squire's mistresses. He hates Methodism and Moral Reform, but knows the prickly role of chaplain in such a house—Crabbe's own position at Belvoir, and the chaplain's in the later tale *The Squire and the Priest.* Crabbe's uneasy balance of tolerance and disapproval is conveyed brilliantly through tone, through chinks in Benbow's bland picture of innocence. Through the park the girls 'take their pleasant rambles in the dark', and maybe call in the House for a nightcap. Prudes disapprove,

> But better natures saw, with much delight,
> The different orders of mankind unite;
> 'Twas schooling pride to see the footman wait,
> Smile on his sister and receive her plate.

As for the chaplain, it's cutting your own throat to attack your superiors and lose your audience. Luckily Asgill took the sermons like a gentleman—'he only swore and smiled'. This whole episode ruins Stephens's idea that Crabbe's irony is simple in intention and heavy in style—'ramming a joke into clodhoppers'.

The Borough is a transitional work, starting with general social surveys and ending with studies of individuals that lead us directly into the later collections of *Tales.* By 1812 'Crabbe the Social Critic' is a misleading approach. However a good half of the *Tales* deliberately invite us to consider them as 'social criticism' in that they appraise, in terms of individuals, nonconformism and 'Freethinkers'.

On the whole, the subject of 'Freethinkers' is where we feel the constriction of the dog-collar. Crabbe's blanket term for all shades of agnostics, social theorists and revolutionaries, used with the vagueness and animus of the contemporary term 'Jacobins', was as old-fashioned by the Regency as the books he cites. Gibbon, Hume, Voltaire and Bolingbroke were not 'guides of *this* enquiring age'[1] but of Johnson's or even Pope's age. In any case Crabbe deals only with cases like *The Learned Boy,* village-idiot turned village-atheist who parrots the ideas learned from office-boy agnostics. Crabbe's reaction is contempt and his cure a whipping:

> Till all the panting flesh was red and raw,
> And every thought was turned to fear and awe.

[1] See *The Gentleman Farmer.*

This horrible passage is the only point where Crabbe shocks us—shocks us not with what he shows of others but of himself, his alien bigotry.

It is the bigotry and contempt of ignorance. Compare the account of restless aimless study in the openings of *Edward Shore* and Rochester's *A Satyr Against Mankind.* The latter's violent metaphors and rhythms convey bitter personal disillusion, whereas Crabbe's sequence of abstractions denotes hearsay. Shore, trusting to 'reason' alone to guide his life and misled by his friend's liberal ideas, seduces that friend's wife and goes mad with remorse. The story has curious parallels with a contemporary incident. In 1811 Shelley's Oxford friend Hogg, impressed by Bysshe's Godwinian notions of free love, tried to seduce Harriet (unlike Shore's friend, Shelley was furious: and unlike Shore, Hogg felt little remorse and tried again later with Mary Shelley). A specific case like this jerks one into seeing that here Crabbe is of an age earlier than Shelley's: unlike Peacock, Crabbe could not diagnose the romanticism that fuses with individual character and directs one's life.

On freethinkers there is professional complacency; on nonconformists, professional pique. For in 1805 half Crabbe's congregation and servants had been abducted by a touring ploughman-turned-Methodist-preacher. As with his deeper traumas, Crabbe compulsively picks at this wound in tale after tale. Yet here is more fairness. In *The Squire and the Priest* as in *Benbow*, his discriminations are subtler because two of his strongest feelings cross tracks: the wound of the ploughman and the embarrassment of Belvoir. He weighs the old squire's laxities and young evangelical's severities, but weighs also the latter's sincerity against the social disaster of a parish split by his spiritually self-important parrots.

What impresses is how many of the age's religious strands the tales interpret, grasping them in their material and domestic context. *The Convert* shows typically how a human story carries a general social theme: this individual, caught in the context of trade, breathes life into the themes Religion and the Rise of Capitalism, Puritanism and the Individual Conscience. The finest example of insight and respect is *The Frank Courtship*, which takes an older sect, the Independents or Saints, which had lived on as a self-contained community since Cromwell's time. Their representative impresses: Jonas Kindred

> Was six feet high, and look'd six inches higher;
> Erect, morose, determined, solemn, slow.

Crabbe first describes the home in all its 'decent gloom', then focuses on a devastating detail: Kindred's friends admiring the portrait of their 'patron saint' Cromwell, in all 'his stern, strong features',

> Drawn in that look with which he wept and swore,
> Turn'd out the members, and made fast the door,
> Ridding the house of every knave and drone,
> Forced, though it grieved his soul, to rule alone.
> The stern still smile each friend approving gave,
> Then turn'd the view, and all again were grave.

This touch of Crabbe's genius makes our eyes jump from picture to viewers. Cromwell dismisses parliament and 'rules alone': so in this house 'Jonas ruled unquestion'd and alone'. And despite their stress on individual conscience the Independents are driven by the urge to control or willingness to be spiritually bullied. Nevertheless the reader who follows the tale through will feel respect for that community as a lifelong formative influence, affecting and involving the whole character, utterly different from the Methodism whose converts suddenly assume a manner, the 'solemn tone, the lengthened face of care, the low and inward groan'.[1] The outcome of the story, and the upshot of Crabbe's appraisal, is a union of two very different strengths. An intelligent but strict Saint marries Kindred's daughter, who in herself unites all her father's will-power with a wider experience and freer manner. And their mutual criticism and 'drawn battle' typifies the mode of the *Tales*: it is intensely personal and dramatic, yet socially representative.

THE MORAL ELEMENT

Moral Tales, Versified, by the Rev. G. Crabbe, LL.B. is a common distortion of his work, encouraged by Jeffrey's comment that many of the 1812 Tales 'may be ranked by the side of the inimitable tales of Miss Edgeworth'.[2]

Which is, happily, just what they can't. Hannah More and Maria Edgeworth wrote moral tales to illustrate the strictly practical precepts of their previous didactic treatises. With Crabbe curiosity about people came first, and his tale-form evolved from this. Critics who claim the tales are extensions of his sermons are the first to point out elsewhere that Crabbe was bored by the sermons themselves: he had a stock which he read in rota, each coming up

[1] *The Convert*, lines 79–80.
[2] *Edinburgh Review*, vol. xx, p. 279.

every three years. As over the years, so is the order of interests in the individual tale. While he may clutter up the opening with the sort of commentary he learnt (unfortunately) from his favourite novelist, Fielding, nevertheless curiosity about individual behaviour came first, and the generalisations clearly arise from the drama, as something seen about individuals. After all, Jeffrey recognised the drama by calling the poems 'shocking', 'painful', 'very powerfully represented'. Whereas all that could be said for tediously instructive dogmatic commentary and black-and-white characters of the moral tale proper was that 'if it were not too dull to be read, it might do a great deal of good'.[1]

Nor does Crabbe's import boil down to the *triste utilité*[2] of practical lessons and useful knowledge, which have 'little connection with the heart, and rarely leading to any difficult or important efforts of virtue'.[3] In Crabbe, the notion of 'heart', and the deeper struggles of motive and conscience, are as central as in Jane Austen.

One might feel one has caught Crabbe at it in *The Widow's Tale*: it is instructive to see how the tale walks off with the moral nail. A farmer's daughter home from boarding-school is nauseated by farm-life and turns for sympathy to a refined widow, who however persuades her to forget her squeamishness and marry a young farmer. The moral lessons come explicitly in the widow's speeches against 'romantic' love—'passion' versus 'reason', 'love uncheck'd by prudence'. But life breaks through when Crabbe concentrates on the personal experience of the story—for instance, on Nancy's nausea at feeding-time in the farmhouse:

> Us'd to spare meals, dispos'd in manner pure,
> Her father's kitchen she could ill endure;
> Where by the steaming beef he hungry sat,
> And laid at once a pound upon his plate;
> Hot from the field, her eager brother seiz'd
> An equal part, and hunger's rage appeas'd...
> The swelling fat in lumps conglomerate laid,
> And fancy's sickness seiz'd the loathing maid...
> [She] Rein'd the fair neck, and shut th' offended eye;
> She minc'd the sanguine flesh in frustrums fine.

The poetry makes this as revolting (to us, not just to false-refinement) and as disconcerting to conventional moralisings about one's home and family as Jane Austen's prose makes Fanny Price's home at Portsmouth. Working his way through the selection, the

[1] *Quarterly Review*, vol. II, p. 153.
[2] Mme de Staël's phrase.
[3] *Quarterly Review*, vol. II, p. 148.

reader will find this typical of the way didactic elements are overwhelmed by a poem's sheer fictional life.

But a more particular worry may remain. Many readers are afraid of finding the kind of morality-riddled interest and limited knowledge of sexual relations that one would expect from a vicar—what Shelley speaking of the Reverend Mr Malthus called 'a priest, [and therefore] a eunuch and a tyrant'.[1] 'What's he know of the distresses of the poor musing over a snug coal fire in his parsonage-box', asked John Clare of Crabbe; 'if I had an enemy I could wish to torture...my worst wish should be a week's confinement in some vicarage to hear an old parson and his lecture on the wants and wickednesses of the poor.'[2] But Jeffrey pointed out the incongruity of Crabbe's position in *The Parish Register*, by saying of Old Gaffer Kirk's marriage with a young girl that 'The Reverend Mr Crabbe is very facetious on this match; and not very scrupulously delicate.'[3] The same could be said of the ribald similes on 'th' indecent fondling' of the senile newlyweds (*Old Lodge*, *P.R.* 2):

So two dried sticks, all fled the vital juice,
When rubb'd and chaf'd, their latent heat produce...
  So two cold limbs, touch'd by Galvani's wire,
Move with new life, and feel awaken'd fire;
Quivering awhile, their flaccid forms remain,
Then turn to cold torpidity again.

'Crabbe was not so "excellent" (in the goody sense) as Stephen seems to intimate', commented Fitzgerald.[4] But Crabbe's period was, and he had to bowdlerise both passages in later editions.[5] (The Rev. Dr Thomas Bowdler published his doctored Shakespeare in these years.) Both matches, like most incidents in the *Register*, are versions of common folk-tales, and Crabbe feels quite at ease in their atmosphere. Rather than playing the vicar he errs in the other direction, content to join in the sly and ribald village gossip about the bastards and forced marriages that make up half his business.

In the *Tales* there is a more positive side to the way moralisings are kept at a distance. The very themes of some, like *The Lover's Journey* and *The Parting Hour*, make it obvious that Crabbe's

[1] *A Philosophical View of Reform : Political Tracts*, ed. R. J. White (Cambridge, 1953), p. 239.
[2] *Letters*, ed. J. W. and A. Tibble (1951), p. 75.
[3] *Edinburgh Review*, vol. XII, p. 144.
[4] *Letters* (1894), vol. II, p. 209.
[5] The original passages can be read in the variants at the back of Ward's edition, vol. I.

impulse is a disinterested and penetrating curiosity about people. Elsewhere (for example, *Squire Thomas* and *The Convert*) he deliberately excludes a moral reaction, until the characters are first established and their spirit felt from the inside. Where moral comments *are* in place (for example, the gypsies in *The Lover's Journey*) Crabbe shows great tact in making us feel that his conclusions arise inevitably out of the facts.

A characteristic of the *Tales* that links them with Jane Austen's novels, is to take up 'immorality' in terms of social situations and effects. When in *The Squire and the Priest* the squire keeps a mistress, it destroys frankness: the priest squirms in a false position, the squire self-consciously bluffs it out. The neighbours of *The Gentleman Farmer* don't know where they stand in relation to his mistress and stop calling, more out of social uneasiness than disapproval. Worse, the couple themselves don't know where *they* stand. A battle of wills develops; he orders her about to make his authority clear to her, to the neighbours—and to himself; she fights because her insecure position makes her over-anxious about her rights. 'Domestic arrangements' (quite literally, not as a euphemism) covers Crabbe's field of criticism, not 'living in sin'. He exposes their liaison first on social, then on psychological, but never on moral grounds.

He is in fact very critical of moral denunciations, aware of the motives behind them and their overlapping with hypocrisy or cant and conventional social disapproval. This is the subject of *Arabella*, as Crabbe's endnote underlines. It also runs through *Procrastination*.

The start of the latter tale may have given Jane Austen an idea for *Persuasion*. Persuaded by the voice of elderly prudence, the young couple postpone marriage: Rupert goes to war in the navy, while Dinah lives with a rich aunt whose property she inherits, and so forgets her lover. Crabbe's key is the 'contending passions' of Love and Avarice. And the key description is of opulence and sterility: at its close the hard jewel movement and face of the clock suggests Dinah's own movements and routine:

> Through the pure chrystal shone th' enamell'd face;
> And while on brilliants moved the hands of steel,
> It click'd from pray'r to pray'r, from meal to meal.

But Crabbe goes further, stressing her isolation from other people and so from ordinary troubles and feelings:

> She knew that mothers grieved, and widows wept,
> And she was sorry, said her prayers, and slept.

It's easy to moralise about life when you don't participate; and so, at the window, Dinah meditates comfortably on what people tell her of the wicked ways of the outside world—

> How tender damsels sail'd in tilted boats,
> And laugh'd with wicked men in scarlet coats.

That couplet has what makes one *warm* to Crabbe: it's a vivid glimpse of real life, pleasure, movement and colour, tempting us through the window from the stifling atmosphere of show and spinsterliness. It catches, too, the extravagant shocked tones of spinsters. But Crabbe doesn't just mock, he condemns. Tender damsels, tilted boats, wicked men and scarlet coats—how sensual, how depraved! But what a voluptuously furnished room in which to criticise the normal human feelings from which they've cut themselves off!—

> Around the room an Indian paper blazed,
> With lively tint and figures boldly raised;
> Silky and soft upon the floor below
> Th' elastic carpet rose with crimson glow.

'Erotic substitute'—the tag of modern jargon springs boldly to life.

The outside world and real feelings burst in, in the shape of *her* sailor, whose impetuous love she greets with a stonewalling of religious cant. The verbal contrast is pressed home by a visual one:

> She ceased; with steady glance, as if to see
> The very root of this hypocrisy,—
> He her small fingers moulded in his hard
> And bronzed broad hand.

—and by the allusion of the final line, when she, going to church, meets Rupert who is now a parish-pauper:

> She cross'd, and pass'd him on the other side.

'Crabbe has a range and a generous masculine strength that bring out by contrast Jane Austen's spinsterly limitations.'[1] *Procrastination*, typically, celebrates human feelings that moral horror is blind to; and, as often, Crabbe associates generosity with the masculine and experienced while the moralist is a 'narrow-gutted spinster'. Not of course that Lawrence's phrase fits Jane Austen: and any definition of *Mansfield Park* as mere 'moral

[1] Leavis, *Revaluation*, p. 125.

severity' 'will only show the narrowness of the definer'.[1] But nor does *Mansfield Park* make Crabbe seem slight. That his generosity is a strength and not moral irresponsibility comes home in an episode in *The Borough*, 11: *Inns*. He treats sexual laxity lightly: James gets Juliet 'I' the way that all the Capulets have been'. Her father talks as cavalierly of the bastard son and of marriage:

> There smiles your bride, there sprawls your new-born son,
> —A ring, a licence, and the thing is done.

But this lightness has no cynicism, it rejoices rather in the blessed facts of sex and marriage, in the tones of that masculine initiative that Jane Austen herself came to celebrate in the sailors of *Persuasion*. And the reconciliation and marriage follow from an appeal to those over-riding human feelings that rightly drown 'moral faults'. In contrast Crabbe saves his moral horror for people like Blaney (*Borough*, 14), the pimp, pornographer and deflowerer whose lust destroys those overriding human feelings.

True, Crabbe's generosity is often too near Fielding's simple sense of forgiveness and red-faced indignation at heartlessness. The suggestive phrase 'generous masculine strength', when thought out in relation to Mozart stands for a more profound spirit, which acknowledges tragic feeling. But—to end this section on a positive note—if true tragic feeling is rare in Crabbe, he never avoids direct treatment of marriage and sexual relations generally, and the intimacies and frictions they involve. Tale after tale uses them as the real test and revelation of character. In this sense the centre of his stories is the place where Jane Austen's usually break off.

LANGUAGE AND THE PRESENTATION OF CHARACTER

The crucial test of a writer's sensibility is, whether he has a creative relation to the language: and one has to admit that Crabbe's is frequently a lazy and inert relation. Anyone who has tried to win him converts by reading aloud knows the queasy experience of having to skip or break off when a good passage crumbles into jingling banality, stock phrases and all the rotting jetsam of eighteenth-century poetic diction, framed by opportunist rhymes ('When boy cannot be made to rhyme with employ, Crabbe is very

[1] Johnson, *Life of Pope: Works*, 1825 (Oxford English Classics), vol. VIII, p. 345.

fond of dragging in a hoy', says Leslie Stephen.) So in *The Borough*, 1 (the following quotations form a consecutive passage) one begins

> ...just the hot and stony beach above,
> Light twinkling streams in bright confusion move;

suppresses the explanation

> (For heated thus, the warmer air ascends,
> And with the cooler in its fall contends)—

braves out

> Then the broad bosom of the ocean keeps
> An equal motion;

and continues in relief with

> swelling as it sleeps,
> Then slowly sinking, curling to the strand,
> Faint, lazy waves o'ercreep the ridgy sand,
> Or tap the tarry boat with gentle blow,
> And back return in silence, smooth and slow.

It is not critical escapism to take up this issue on a larger ground. Otherwise one gets no further than piecemeal comment on small ineptitudes. Such ineptitudes rarely ruin a tale unless some larger blindness or convention is involved. Conversely, when Crabbe is free from such larger conventions, then he is usually free from local linguistic inertia.

The larger convention I discern leads to the centre of his work, and of his mixture of inertia and originality. It is also something in which his links with Johnson can usefully be traced; and it engages with one of the most interesting changes of Crabbe's period. It is a *framework* that underlies most of what was written about people in the eighteenth century, and that the nineteenth found inadequate. This framework can be picked out at its most obvious in Johnson's general analyses of Shakespeare's characters:

> The fiery openness of Othello, magnanimous, artless, and credulous, boundless in his confidence, ardent in his affection, inflexible in his resolution, and obdurate in his revenge; the cool malignity of Iago, silent in his resentment, subtle in his designs, and studious at once of his interest and his vengeance; the soft simplicity of Desdemona, confident of merit, and conscious of innocence, her artless perseverance in her suit, and her slowness to suspect that she can be suspected, are such proofs of Shakespeare's skill in human nature, as, I suppose, it is in vain to seek in any modern writer...Cassio is brave, benevolent, and honest, ruined only by his want of stubbornness to resist an insidious invitation.[1]

[1] *Works* (1825), vol. v, pp. 178–9.

Of course Johnson is only summarising the drama and pinning down the essential facts of the characters: he knows this is only a skeleton, the drama is the flesh and blood. And his analysis has a very original acuteness; this is not a 'sentimentalist's Othello' by anyone's standards. But there is still the eighteenth-century urge to *sum up*, and behind the summary lies the framework. Johnson uses certain plain terms that for him stand adequately for distinct and definable *qualities*—'openness', 'confidence', 'affection', 'brave', 'benevolent', 'honest'. Similarly the feelings or passions are distinct and nameable—'revenge', 'malignity', 'love', 'ambition'. Elsewhere Johnson sees the mind as constituted of various distinct *faculties*—'genius', 'judgement', 'knowledge'. In the *Life of Pope* he compares Dryden and Pope faculty by faculty.

Qualifications crowd in, most of which can be ascribed to Johnson's genius, which could transcend that framework. He never fell for simplifications like Pope's idea of the ruling passion. And, after all, the notes to Shakespeare were the place for summaries, for keys like this: 'This idea of dotage encroaching upon wisdom, will solve all the phenomena of the character of Polonius.'[1] The framework remains in the best *Lives of the Poets*, even on the character and madness of Swift. But there it is transcended with individual life, imagery and unexpected details and connections. The point will be brought out by comparing it with a routine *Rambler*—no. 11 on the character of an angry old man—nominally the same subject but abstracted into the skeletal framework terms.

What matters is that this framework pokes through so much in that century: not only the criticism of lesser minds than Johnson, but even the novelists, where one would expect personality and feeling presented dramatically. Fielding, who stands in many ways behind Crabbe, is full of analyses in terms of the ruling passion: Fanny Burney, who stands behind Jane Austen, states the component parts of her characters as Johnson states Othello's. So does Jane Austen in her early novels. And one can usefully see Crabbe's struggle to originality as an escape from that way of looking at people.

The change between the two centuries that Crabbe spanned can only be asserted here: the reader investigating it might well use as outside markers two passages of 'theory' (this is not to simplify the complicated ground between them). The first is from Johnson's

[1] W. Raleigh (ed.), *Johnson on Shakespeare* (London, 1908), p. 191.

Preface to Shakespeare and lies behind the practice of his character-analyses:

> He has been able to obtain an exact knowledge of many modes of life, and many casts of native dispositions; to vary them with great multiplicity; to mark them by nice distinctions; and to show them...by proper combinations[1] [cf. 'the combinations of concurring [and] the perplexity of contending, passions'[2]].

In the second, George Eliot comments on her 'problem of style' in the famous passage of *Daniel Deronda*, Gwendolen's turmoil of feelings at Grandcourt's proposal:

> The subtly-varied drama between man and woman is often such as can hardly be rendered in words put together like dominoes, according to obvious fixed marks. The word of all work Love will no more express the myriad modes of mutual attraction, than the word Thought can inform you what is passing through your neighbour's mind.[3]

That Crabbe often relaxed into the eighteenth-century habits is clear from surface signs. He is full of summaries like these:

> 'A wife grown feeble, mourning, pining, vex'd.'[4]
>
> 'Jesse with fear, disgust, alarm, surprise.'[5]

Those are words used like dominoes: it is as if George Eliot had merely written 'Gwendolen, with panic, haste, alarm, uncertainty ...' or 'Within her breast contended Fear, Ambition, Love...'

Elsewhere Crabbe extends the habit to make distinctions between aspects of the same general quality:

> ...malicious and yet kind;
> Frank and yet cunning, with a heart to love
> And malice prompt—the serpent and the dove.[5]

This takes us back to Johnson's notes on Shakespeare, with a close parallel (on Juliet's nurse): 'He has, with great subtilty of distinction, drawn her at once loquacious and secret, obsequious and insolent, trusty and dishonest.'[6]

In the tales as a whole the habit comes out in Crabbe's love of untangling motives and qualities beneath manners and self-deceptions. This accounts for the fairly elementary insights of most of *Arabella* and *The Lover's Journey*. Elsewhere an apparently simple diagnosis in framework terms escapes into drama and freer

[1] *Works* (1825), vol. v, p. 192.
[2] *Works* (1825), vol. VII, pp. 139–40 (*Life of Milton*).
[3] Chapter XXVII.
[4] *The Borough*, 3.
[5] *Jesse and Colin*
[6] *Works* (1825), vol. v, p. 176.

insights. It has already been argued that *Procrastination* breaks out of its Humeian-theorising—

> This passion [Avarice] grew, and gain'd at length such sway,
> That other passions shrank to make it way...
> A love of splendour now with av'rice strove...

Again *The Frank Courtship* begins to describe Kindred like this:

> Erect, morose, determined, solemn, slow.

But, even when Kindred is not the centre of interest, the poem is full of touches that light up those general adjectives: for instance his abrupt introduction:

> 'Daughter, my Friend—my Daughter, Friend' he cried,
> And gave a meaning look, and stepp'd aside.

The reader will however want to assess for himself the originality of each tale. It is enough here to consider the extreme, *Peter Grimes*.

The originality of *Peter Grimes* does not lie in a new subject (sadism, nightmare, madness) but a new treatment. Crabbe never 'sums up' Grimes: he avoids analysing motives and impulses, suggesting that his cruelty is inexplicable in those terms and so even more horrifying. Above all he makes us feel, as in a drama, what that person was like, and what it was like to be that person. Thus, in the background of Grimes's tragedy is his relationship with his father, but it is not *defined* as a motive: it is evoked in fleeting scenes in Grimes's memory when, at his father's death

> On an oak-settle, in his maudlin grief,
> This he revolved, and drank for his relief.

It is true that much of the tale is 'narrative', Grimes observed by others. But the inner tragedy is enforced by this outside view, the townsfolk's changing reaction—first indifference, then their awakening conscience and his self-justification, then their outlawing of him, and their final pity. They help awaken *his* conscience; and the outlawing is half the tragedy, for Grimes isn't the Byronic outlaw-hero wronged by or defying society.

However one consecutive passage shows Crabbe's telling transitions from the outside to the inner view. First comes the citizens' cheerful indifference, which adds to the horror:

> None put the question,—'Peter, dost thou give
> The boy his food?—What, man! the lad must live:
> Consider, Peter, let the child have bread,

He'll serve thee better if he's stroked and fed!'
None reason'd thus—and some, on hearing cries,
Said calmly, 'Grimes is at his exercise.'

Immediately Crabbe switches to the boy's feelings and thirdly to Grimes's own:

Pinn'd, beaten, cold, pinch'd, threaten'd, and abused—
His efforts punish'd and his food refused,—
Awake tormented,—soon aroused from sleep,—
Struck if he wept, and yet compell'd to weep,
The trembling boy dropp'd down and strove to pray,
Received a blow, and trembling turn'd away,
Or sobb'd and hid his piteous face;—while he,
The savage master, grinn'd in horrid glee:
He'd now the power he ever loved to show,
A feeling being subject to his blow.

The couplets take on the rhythm of a relentless series of cruelties. ('Horrid glee' lets us down, worthier of the linguistic crudity of Scott, whose *Marmion* stands behind *Grimes*. Crabbe had to struggle free of such *Regency* idiom as well as breathe life into Popeian techniques.)

The outstanding passage breaks radically away from the mode of the Popeian couplet and is utterly different in kind from most of Crabbe's poetry. It describes the scene that both corresponds to and 'nurses' Grimes's feelings as he sits hopeless and lifeless in his boat, despised by the townsfolk and haunted by his victims.

At the same times the same dull views to see,
The bounding marsh-bank and the blighted tree;
The water only, when the tides were high,
When low, the mud half-cover'd and half-dry;
The sun-burnt tar that blisters on the planks,
And bank-side stakes in their uneven ranks;
Heaps of entangled weeds that slowly float,
As the tide rolls by the impeded boat.

The whole passage (lines 171–204) is no vague evocation: it depends on a variety of precisely observed details which build up a set of impressions of dullness, flatness, sterility, lack of motion, purpose or hope. The details are linked by the recurring key words *slow*, *lazy*, *dull*, *sultry*, yet each has its distinct correspondence with Grimes's feelings. Not, however, that the passage is 'precise' in Hazlitt's simple sense, 'an exact *facsimile* of one of the most unlovely parts of the Creation'.[1] While based on an actual fenland

[1] *The Spirit of the Age*, p. 334.

estuary that you can still recognise at Aldeburgh, it is transformed into something strange and remote. It sounds eerily primeval, a featureless, unformed landscape with rudimentary forms of life—shellfish, a few desolate birds, otherwise just weed.

> Where gaping muscles, left upon the mud,
> Slope their slow passage to the fallen flood;—
> Here dull and hopeless he'd lie down and trace
> How sidelong crabs had scrawl'd their crooked race;
> Or sadly listen to the tuneless cry
> Of fishing gull or clanging golden-eye;

It is also like the world after the flood, with the mud, the water draining away and the smelly warmth and decomposition. This corresponds fundamentally to Grimes's slow moral decay and physical torpor. The landscape and his body, the ebbing water in the channels and the sluggish life in his veins—these become hardly distinguishable.

> The dark warm flood ran silently and slow;
> There anchoring, Peter chose from man to hide,
> There hang his head, and view the lazy tide
> In its hot slimy channel slowly glide;...
> And loved to stop beside the opening sluice;
> Where the small stream, confined in narrow bound,
> Ran with a dull, unvaried, sadd'ning sound;

The passage is a key one in the discussion of Crabbe's sensibility. It is wholly free from any eighteenth-century framework, and is the opposite of this kind of description:

> A wife grown feeble, mourning, pining, vex'd.

In *Grimes* Crabbe does not name and illustrate the constituent emotions: he finds images and rhythms to recreate the feel of feelings—the experience itself.

DRAMATIC AND 'ROMANTIC' POETRY

That 'inscape' of Grimes is a rare passage. There is something similar in *Delay Has Danger* (lines 701–24) but these lines revert to a more sedate Augustan decorum. More often the later tales escape from character-summary into drama. *The Patron* is a good example of what Jeffrey once called 'Mr Crabbe's extraordinary powers of giving pain': the theme is distilled into several painful scenes—the young poet abandoned at the country house as the patron and family leave for London; the hours of waiting in hope of an interview in the cold and showiness of the patron's London house; the sense of degradation when he is reduced to work in an office:

> For ever shrinking from the vulgar crew;
> Distaste for each mechanic law and rule,
> Thoughts of past honour, and a patron cool.

—these lines, which summarise what the drama shows, make a link with a similar trauma:

> No words can express the secret agony of my soul as I sunk into this companionship; compared these everyday associates with those of my happier childhood; and felt my early hopes of growing up to be a learned and distinguished man, crushed in my breast...My whole nature was so penetrated with the grief and humiliation...that even now, famous and caressed and happy, I often forget in my dreams that I have a dear wife and children; and wander desolately back to that time of my life.[1]

Crabbe's biography shows that *The Patron* brings together experiences as intense as Dickens's. Yet in one sense Crabbe is the freer man and the freer artist. The rhythm of the passage quoted shows that Dickens, like Grimes, 'nursed' those feelings, and the novels too rarely escape from that horrified, snobbish, self-centred response. So far is Crabbe from mere indulgence that he can enter with sympathy into the feelings of the patron (lines 706–15).

Crabbe also has the advantage over Dickens in using his experiences dramatically and impersonally in a wider sense, in contexts and in moods remote from life. Dealing with a manic-depressive wife wasn't funny: but the poetry can use it almost comically:

> 'Would she some sea-port, Weymouth, Scarborough grace?'—
> 'He knew she hated every watering-place':
> 'The town?'—'What! now 'twas empty, joyless dull?'
> —'In winter?'—'No; she liked it worse when full'.
> She talk'd of building—'Would she plan a room?'—
> 'No! she could live, as he desired, in gloom.'...
> 'My dear, my gentle Dorothea, say,
> Can I oblige you?'—'You may go away'.[2]

There is a double strength. Crabbe's own and his wife's experiences as servants are turned to the comedy of *Squire Thomas*, a study of three distinct styles of flattery in which the biter is twice bitten. Yet the grim experience drawn on guarantees the inwardness of the study: Crabbe tempers a moral reaction to the legacy-hunter with a strong sympathy at the pain and strain involved.

[1] *Dickens: an Autobiographical Fragment.* See J. Forster, *Life of Dickens*, vol. I (1872), p. 33.

[2] *The Mother*, lines 47–61.

Crabbe, it needs stressing, best used his experiences in that *dramatic* way: his strength is not lyrical or directly personal. It is odd that, while we all know how boring other people's dreams usually are, the very word dreams (like madness and opium) makes critics like E. M. Forster shout 'Eureka! Crabbe the Romantic Poet.' But *Sir Eustace Grey* and *The World of Dreams* cannot align Crabbe with Wordsworth or Coleridge merely through a common subject. In fact those interesting experiments are closest to the bad dream poems Byron was writing around the same time, and like them drag themselves free only momentarily from the swamp of routine Regency verse, with all its inert stilted language and clumsy imagery. Ironically it is Coleridge who in *The Pains of Sleep* brings to the 'romantic' subject a strong moral interest and an Augustan restraint and diction.

Crabbe did learn from Wordsworth; or rather, Wordsworth released something in Crabbe himself. *Infancy*, *The Adventures of Richard* and *Silford Hall* are about childhood, memory and 'the growth of a poet's mind'. Allowing for its unrevised notebook state, *In A Neat Cottage* is a good attempt at Wordsworthian blank-verse. But the influence is fruitful because Crabbe assimilates it with his own strength, the narrative tale. He is modest too, knowing he offers something less than a vision or wisdom about childhood and that he must find his own language. So he wrote no monstrosities like Clare's *Pastoral Poesy*, that incoherent imitation rushed down on first reading Wordsworth and Coleridge.

CRABBE AFTER 1812

1812 and just after, where this Introduction took up Crabbe, is the turning-point. The poet scarcely responded to the new experience that fame brought. For this reason the influence of Wordsworth came too late to have major effects.

Crabbe himself was more aware of loneliness than fame. In 1813 his wife died and he suffered a dangerous illness that aged him. The next year he left his sons, friends and East Anglian roots for the distant and at first very hostile parish of Trowbridge in Wiltshire. The letters of the 1810s are filled with cries of loneliness and energyless self-pity—

> Ties cut asunder, and bonds of affection cancelled, and the tenderest associations dissolved and places once endeared...now become the seats and sources of the most poignant grief and mortification...Making

verses is an amusement but is temporary and soon tires: then I am weak and foolish and perhaps vain and want to be loved and that can hardly be.[1]

These images were taken up in *The World of Dreams*: but he was too ashamed to use in later tales his pathetic efforts to satisfy that 'want to be loved'. Most of the letters are such an effort; flirting by post with ladies he had never met and becoming engaged to another. He himself confessed that

The fancied, the visionary love of a man at that period of life for a nymph whom he had not seen, as well as the pre-possession of another nymph for this romantic admirer of her friend, known to her by letters only, and those directed and addrest to another woman, all this forms a tale for an Arabian Night, and is too crazy for sober belief.[2]

The misery numbed Crabbe to wider experiences. His visits to Bath, London and Edinburgh do not colour his later poetry; nor do the size, industries and political liveliness of Trowbridge itself. As he says, poetry did not engage with his life as much as provide an escape, 'by which the mind should be diverted from preying upon itself'.[3] He fixed himself a routine:

July 8th. Thirty lines today; but not yesterday: must work up...
July 10th. Make up my thirty lines for yesterday and today.
July 17th. Wrote my lines today, but no more.[4]

Tales of the Hall do suffer. Many rework old subjects, and their keenest supporter, Edward Fitzgerald, admitted that their main original contribution occurs when Crabbe's acute sense of loss is muted to a sunset glow of nostalgia.[5] Fitzgerald also saw that these tales are too long, and his edition replaces rambling *longueurs* with prose summaries. The present selection prints complete the four most varied tales. The romantic affinities of *Adventures of Richard* have already been mentioned. The comedy *The Preceptor Husband* is swift and light in touch: 'in place of a "Pope in worsted stocking"...we [are] more reminded of a Dryden in a one-horse chaise'.[6] After *Delay Has Danger* comes *The Visit Concluded*, which treats, more vividly than the opening book, the relationship of the two brothers who tell these stories. The volume ends with the prospect of them completely reconciled and living close together. It is the glow of an elderly man's wishful thinking. Knowing his misery in

[1] Broadley and Jerrold, *The Romance of an Elderly Poet* (1913), pp. 79, 120.
[2] *Ibid.* p. 88. [3] *Ibid.* p. 111.
[4] Diary for 1817: *Life* by son, pp. 236–9.
[5] Introduction to *Readings in Crabbe: 'Tales of the Hall'* (1882).
[6] Lockhart in *Quarterly Review*, vol. LII, p. 186.

the 1810s, we do not grudge that glow, although it blurs the sharpness of vision that makes Crabbe's earlier volumes greater.

This Introduction has no conclusion. For its aim is to make the reader reject the 'trenchant ignorance' with which historians jump to conclusions, and make his own way through the poems, exercising only that 'natural selection' Johnson defined: 'Judgment is forced upon us by Experience. He that reads many books must compare one opinion or one style with another; and when he compares, must necessarily distinguish, reject, and prefer.'[1]

THE TEXT

This edition follows the text of the *Works* in five volumes of 1823, which Crabbe himself saw through the press. A. W. Ward's *Poems* (Cambridge, 1905–7) follows the 1823 text but alters the interpunctuation. But his principles, as stated in the Preface to volume I, seem impressionistic. I have found no original reading that makes the sense unclear or the movement uneffective and apart from deleting running quotation marks I have kept strictly to Crabbe's version.

Infancy and *The World of Dreams* were first published in the *Poetical Works* of 1834, from which the present text is taken. *In a Neat Cottage* was edited from a notebook by Arthur Pollard and I am grateful for permission to base the present text on his *New Poems by Crabbe* (Liverpool University Press, 1960). I have however altered many of the over-frequent capitals and exclamation marks to bring it into line with the text of the other poems.

The text prints complete poems or sections (for example, *Parts* of *The Parish Register* and *Letters* of *The Borough*), except that a few lines of the Introduction to *The Register* are included to lead into Part One. Crabbe's routine epigraphs are omitted, but not his carefully chosen Shakespearian quotations for the 1812 *Tales* which are integral and help to interpret the themes. Following Ward I have corrected the sources of these, but not the minor misquotations, which are often intentional and heighten the relevance of epigraph to tale.

The notes are mainly Crabbe's own: even so, some redundant and fussy ones are omitted. Editorial notes have been sacrificed for extra space for the poems themselves, which in any case rarely need factual or textual explanation.

Nobody who has looked for critical help on Crabbe will be surprised by the brevity of the bibliography.

[1] *Works* (1825), vol. VIII, p. 172.

SELECT BIBLIOGRAPHY

COMPLETE EDITIONS

No complete edition is now in print. Most likely to be in a library are:

Poetical Works, 8 vols. (London, 1834).

Poems, edited by A. W. Ward, 3 vols. (Cambridge, 1905–7).

Poetical Works, edited by A. J. and R. M. Carlyle (Oxford, 1908).

These are supplemented by the poems from manuscript in *New Poems by George Crabbe*, edited by A. Pollard (Liverpool University Press, 1960).

BIOGRAPHY AND CRITICISM

The Life of George Crabbe, by his son—the only indispensable work, printed as follows:

Works of Crabbe (1834), vol. I.

Edited with Introduction by E. M. Forster (Oxford, Worlds Classics, 1932).

Edited with Introduction by Edmund Blunden (London, Cresset Press, 1947).

By Crabbe himself

Life by son prints Crabbe's Journals of London—when poor in 1780–1 and when famous in 1817; first letter to Burke; notebook remarks on poems; and letters to Scott and others.

'Biographical Account of the Rev. George Crabbe, LL.B.' (written by himself) in *The New Monthly Magazine*, vol. IV (Jan. 1816). Reprinted in *Souvenir of Bi-Centenary Celebrations and Exhibition* (Aldeburgh, 1954).

'*Bunbury*' *Letter* to Burke, a more trenchant and bitter account of his early life than the previous item or Crabbe's initial letter to Burke. Reprinted in Forster's edition of *Life* by son.

Prefaces of 1810, 1812 and 1819 volumes.

By contemporaries

Life by son prints letters and comments from Scott, Wordsworth and others.

Francis Jeffrey, in *Edinburgh Review*, vol. XII (1808); vol. XVI (1810); vol. XX (1812); vol. XXXII (1819). *Contributions to the Edinburgh Review*, collected in 4 vols. (1844) and 3 vols. (1846).

William Hazlitt, *The Spirit of the Age* (1825), reprinted in Everyman's Library (1922).

J. G. Lockhart, *Quarterly Review*, vol. LII (1834).

William Wordsworth: see M. L. Peacock Jnr. (ed.), *The Critical Opinions of William Wordsworth* (Baltimore, 1950).

P. Hodgart and T. Redpath (editors): *Romantic Perspectives; The Work of Crabbe, Blake, Wordsworth and Coleridge as Seen by Their Contemporaries and Themselves* (London, 1964).

Later writers

Leslie Stephen, *Hours in a Library*, series 2 (London, 1876).

Edward Fitzgerald, *Readings in Crabbe : 'Tales of the Hall'* (London, 1882). Contains introductory essay also reprinted in vol. I of Fitzgerald's *Works* (New York, 1887). See also his *Letters* (London, 1894), *passim.*

A. M. Broadley and W. Jerrold, *The Romance of An Elderly Poet : A Hitherto Unknown Chapter in the Life of George Crabbe* (1913).

Ezra Pound, *The Rev. G. Crabbe, LL.B.* (1917). Reprinted in *Literary Essays*, edited by T. S. Eliot (London, 1954).

F. R. Leavis, *Revaluation* (London, 1936), chapter IV, esp. pp. 124–129.

E. M. Forster, *George Crabbe and Peter Grimes* (1948) in his *Two Cheers for Democracy* (London, 1951).

Arthur Sale, 'The Development of Crabbe's Narrative Art', in *The Cambridge Journal* (May, 1952).

Lilian Haddakin, *The Poetry of Crabbe* (London, 1955).

F. Whitehead, 'George Crabbe', in *From Blake to Byron*, edited by Boris Ford (Pelican, 1957).

NOTE. René Huchon, *George Crabbe and his Times* (1907), should be avoided as a large obstacle only likely to impede one's interest in Crabbe. It corrects the *Life* by Crabbe's son on small factual points, but is critically obtuse.

THE VILLAGE

BOOK I

The Village Life, and every care that reigns
O'er youthful peasants and declining swains;
What labour yields, and what, that labour past,
Age, in its hour of languor, finds at last;
What form the real picture of the poor,
Demand a song—the Muse can give no more.
Fled are those times, when, in harmonious strains,
The rustic poet praised his native plains:
No shepherds now, in smooth alternate verse,
Their country's beauty or their nymphs' rehearse;
Yet still for these we frame the tender strain,
Still in our lays fond Corydons complain,
And shepherds' boys their amorous pains reveal,
The only pains, alas! they never feel.
On Mincio's banks, in Cæsar's bounteous reign,
If Tityrus found the Golden Age again,
Must sleepy bards the flattering dream prolong,
Mechanic echoes of the Mantuan song?
From Truth and Nature shall we widely stray,
Where Virgil, not where Fancy, leads the way?
Yes, thus the Muses sing of happy swains,
Because the Muses never know their pains:
They boast their peasants' pipes; but peasants now
Resign their pipes and plod behind the plough;
And few, amid the rural-tribe, have time
To number syllables, and play with rhyme;
Save honest Duck, what son of verse could share
The poet's rapture, and the peasant's care?
Or the great labours of the field degrade,
With the new peril of a poorer trade?
From this chief cause these idle praises spring,
That themes so easy few forbear to sing;
For no deep thought the trifling subjects ask;
To sing of shepherds is an easy task:
The happy youth assumes the common strain,
A nymph his mistress, and himself a swain;

With no sad scenes he clouds his tuneful prayer,
But all, to look like her, is painted fair.
I grant indeed that fields and flocks have charms
For him that grazes or for him that farms;
But when amid such pleasing scenes I trace
The poor laborious natives of the place,
And see the mid-day sun, with fervid ray,
On their bare heads and dewy temples play;
While some, with feebler heads and fainter hearts,
Deplore their fortune, yet sustain their parts:
Then shall I dare these real ills to hide
In tinsel trappings of poetic pride?
No; cast by Fortune on a frowning coast,
Which neither groves nor happy valleys boast;
Where other cares than those the Muse relates,
And other shepherds dwell with other mates;
By such examples taught, I paint the Cot,
As Truth will paint it, and as Bards will not:
Nor you, ye poor, of letter'd scorn complain,
To you the smoothest song is smooth in vain;
O'ercome by labour, and bow'd down by time,
Feel you the barren flattery of a rhyme?
Can poets soothe you, when you pine for bread,
By winding myrtles round your ruin'd shed?
Can their light tales your weighty griefs o'erpower,
Or glad with airy mirth the toilsome hour?
Lo! where the heath, with withering brake grown o'er,
Lends the light turf that warms the neighbouring poor;
From thence a length of burning sand appears,
Where the thin harvest waves its wither'd ears;
Rank weeds, that every art and care defy,
Reign o'er the land, and rob the blighted rye:
There thistles stretch their prickly arms afar,
And to the ragged infant threaten war;
There poppies nodding, mock the hope of toil;
There the blue bugloss paints the sterile soil;
Hardy and high, above the slender sheaf,
The slimy mallow waves her silky leaf;
O'er the young shoot the charlock throws a shade,
And clasping tares cling round the sickly blade;
With mingled tints the rocky coasts abound,

And a sad splendour vainly shines around.
So looks the nymph whom wretched arts adorn,
Betray'd by man, then left for man to scorn;
Whose cheek in vain assumes the mimic rose,
While her sad eyes the troubled breast disclose;
Whose outward splendour is but folly's dress,
Exposing most, when most it gilds distress.
  Here joyless roam a wild amphibious race,
With sullen wo display'd in every face;
Who, far from civil arts and social fly,
And scowl at strangers with suspicious eye.
  Here too the lawless merchant of the main
Draws from his plough th'intoxicated swain;
Want only claim'd the labour of the day,
But vice now steals his nightly rest away.
  Where are the swains, who, daily labour done,
With rural games play'd down the setting sun;
Who struck with matchless force the bounding ball,
Or made the pond'rous quoit obliquely fall;
While some huge Ajax, terrible and strong,
Engaged some artful stripling of the throng,
And fell beneath him, foil'd, while far around
Hoarse triumph rose, and rocks return'd the sound?
Where now are these?—Beneath yon cliff they stand,
To show the freighted pinnace where to land;
To load the ready steed with guilty haste,
To fly in terror o'er the pathless waste,
Or, when detected, in their straggling course,
To foil their foes by cunning or by force;
Or, yielding part (which equal knaves demand),
To gain a lawless passport through the land.
  Here, wand'ring long, amid these frowning fields,
I sought the simple life that Nature yields;
Rapine and Wrong and Fear usurp'd her place,
And a bold, artful, surly, savage race;
Who, only skill'd to take the finny tribe,
The yearly dinner, or septennial bribe,
Wait on the shore, and, as the waves run high,
On the tost vessel bend their eager eye,
Which to their coast directs its vent'rous way;
Theirs, or the ocean's, miserable prey.

As on their neighbouring beach yon swallows stand,
And wait for favouring winds to leave the land;
While still for flight the ready wing is spread:
So waited I the favouring hour, and fled;
Fled from these shores where guilt and famine reign,
And cried, Ah! hapless they who still remain;
Who still remain to hear the ocean roar,
Whose greedy waves devour the lessening shore;
Till some fierce tide, with more imperious sway,
Sweeps the low hut and all it holds away;
When the sad tenant weeps from door to door,
And begs a poor protection from the poor!
But these are scenes where Nature's niggard hand
Gave a spare portion to the famish'd land;
Hers is the fault, if here mankind complain
Of fruitless toil and labour spent in vain;
But yet in other scenes more fair in view,
Where Plenty smiles—alas! she smiles for few—
And those who taste not, yet behold her store,
Are as the slaves that dig the golden ore,
The wealth around them makes them doubly poor.
Or will you deem them amply paid in health,
Labour's fair child, that languishes with wealth?
Go then! and see them rising with the sun,
Through a long course of daily toil to run;
See them beneath the dog-star's raging heat,
When the knees tremble and the temples beat;
Behold them, leaning on their scythes, look o'er
The labour past, and toils to come explore;
See them alternate suns and showers engage,
And hoard up aches and anguish for their age;
Through fens and marshy moors their steps pursue,
When their warm pores imbibe the evening dew;
Then own that labour may as fatal be
To these thy slaves, as thine excess to thee.
Amid this tribe too oft a manly pride
Strives in strong toil the fainting heart to hide;
There may you see the youth of slender frame
Contend with weakness, weariness, and shame;
Yet, urged along, and proudly loth to yield,
He strives to join his fellows of the field.

Till long-contending nature droops at last,
Declining health rejects his poor repast,
His cheerless spouse the coming danger sees,
And mutual murmurs urge the slow disease.
  Yet grant them health, 'tis not for us to tell,
Though the head droops not, that the heart is well;
Or will you praise that homely, healthy fare,
Plenteous and plain, that happy peasants share!
Oh! trifle not with wants you cannot feel,
Nor mock the misery of a stinted meal;
Homely, not wholesome, plain, not plenteous, such
As you who praise would never deign to touch.
  Ye gentle souls, who dream of rural ease,
Whom the smooth stream and smoother sonnet please;
Go! if the peaceful cot your praises share,
Go look within, and ask if peace be there;
If peace be his—that drooping weary sire,
Or theirs, that offspring round their feeble fire;
Or hers, that matron pale, whose trembling hand
Turns on the wretched hearth th'expiring brand!
  Nor yet can Time itself obtain for these
Life's latest comforts, due respect and ease;
For yonder see that hoary swain, whose age
Can with no cares except his own engage;
Who, propp'd on that rude staff, looks up to see
The bare arms broken from the withering tree,
On which, a boy, he climb'd the loftiest bough,
Then his first joy, but his sad emblem now.
  He once was chief in all the rustic trade;
His steady hand the straightest furrow made;
Full many a prize he won, and still is proud
To find the triumphs of his youth allow'd;
A transient pleasure sparkles in his eyes,
He hears and smiles, then thinks again and sighs:
For now he journeys to his grave in pain;
The rich disdain him; nay, the poor disdain:
Alternate masters now their slave command,
Urge the weak efforts of his feeble hand,
And, when his age attempts its task in vain,
With ruthless taunts, of lazy poor complain.
  Oft may you see him, when he tends the sheep,

His winter-charge, beneath the hillock weep;
Oft hear him murmur to the winds that blow
O'er his white locks and bury them in snow,
When, roused by rage and muttering in the morn,
He mends the broken hedge with icy thorn:—
  'Why do I live, when I desire to be
At once from life and life's long labour free?
Like leaves in spring, the young are blown away,
Without the sorrows of a slow decay;
I, like yon wither'd leaf, remain behind,
Nipp'd by the frost, and shivering in the wind;
There it abides till younger buds come on,
As I, now all my fellow-swains are gone;
Then, from the rising generation thrust,
It falls, like me, unnoticed to the dust.
  'These fruitful fields, these numerous flocks I see,
Are others' gain, but killing cares to me;
To me the children of my youth are lords,
Cool in their looks, but hasty in their words:
Wants of their own demand their care; and who
Feels his own want and succours others too?
A lonely, wretched man, in pain I go,
None need my help, and none relieve my wo;
Then let my bones beneath the turf be laid,
And men forget the wretch they would not aid.'
  Thus groan the old, till, by disease oppress'd,
They taste a final wo, and then they rest.
  Theirs is yon house that holds the parish-poor,
Whose walls of mud scarce bear the broken door;
There, where the putrid vapours, flagging, play,
And the dull wheel hums doleful through the day;—
There children dwell who know no parents' care;
Parents, who know no children's love, dwell there!
Heart-broken matrons on their joyless bed,
Forsaken wives, and mothers never wed;
Dejected widows with unheeded tears,
And crippled age with more than childhood fears;
The lame, the blind, and, far the happiest they!
The moping idiot and the madman gay.
Here too the sick their final doom receive,
Here brought, amid the scenes of grief, to grieve,

Where the loud groans from some sad chamber flow,
Mix'd with the clamours of the crowd below;
Here, sorrowing, they each kindred sorrow scan,
And the cold charities of man to man:
Whose laws indeed for ruin'd age provide,
And strong compulsion plucks the scrap from pride;
But still that scrap is bought with many a sigh,
And pride embitters what it can't deny.
  Say ye, oppress'd by some fantastic woes,
Some jarring nerve that baffles your repose;
Who press the downy couch, while slaves advance
With timid eye, to read the distant glance;
Who with sad prayers the weary doctor tease,
To name the nameless ever-new disease;
Who with mock patience dire complaints endure,
Which real pain and that alone can cure;
How would ye bear in real pain to lie,
Despised, neglected, left alone to die?
How would ye bear to draw your latest breath,
Where all that's wretched paves the way for death?
  Such is that room which one rude beam divides,
And naked rafters form the sloping sides;
Where the vile bands that bind the thatch are seen,
And lath and mud are all that lie between;
Save one dull pane, that, coarsely patch'd, gives way
To the rude tempest, yet excludes the day:
Here, on a matted flock, with dust o'erspread,
The drooping wretch reclines his languid head;
For him no hand the cordial cup applies,
Or wipes the tear that stagnates in his eyes;
No friends with soft discourse his pain beguile,
Or promise hope till sickness wears a smile.
  But soon a loud and hasty summons calls,
Shakes the thin roof, and echoes round the walls;
Anon, a figure enters, quaintly neat,
All pride and business, bustle and conceit;
With looks unalter'd by these scenes of wo,
With speed that, entering, speaks his haste to go,
He bids the gazing throng around him fly,
And carries fate and physic in his eye:
A potent quack, long versed in human ills,

Who first insults the victim whom he kills;
Whose murd'rous hand a drowsy Bench protect,
And whose most tender mercy is neglect.
  Paid by the parish for attendance here,
He wears contempt upon his sapient sneer;
In haste he seeks the bed where Misery lies,
Impatience mark'd in his averted eyes;
And, some habitual queries hurried o'er,
Without reply, he rushes on the door:
His drooping patient, long inured to pain,
And long unheeded, knows remonstrance vain;
He ceases now the feeble help to crave
Of man; and silent sinks into the grave.
  But ere his death some pious doubts arise,
Some simple fears, which 'bold bad' men despise;
Fain would he ask the parish-priest to prove
His title certain to the joys above:
For this he sends the murmuring nurse, who calls
The holy stranger to these dismal walls:
And doth not he, the pious man, appear,
He, 'passing rich with forty pounds a year'?
Ah! no; a shepherd of a different stock,
And far unlike him, feeds this little flock:
A jovial youth, who thinks his Sunday's task
As much as God or man can fairly ask;
The rest he gives to loves and labours light,
To fields the morning, and to feasts the night;
None better skill'd the noisy pack to guide,
To urge their chase, to cheer them or to chide;
A sportsman keen, he shoots through half the day,
And, skill'd at whist, devotes the night to play:
Then, while such honours bloom around his head,
Shall he sit sadly by the sick man's bed,
To raise the hope he feels not, or with zeal
To combat fears that e'en the pious feel?
  Now once again the gloomy scene explore,
Less gloomy now; the bitter hour is o'er,
The man of many sorrows sighs no more.—
Up yonder hill, behold how sadly slow
The bier moves winding from the vale below;
There lie the happy dead, from trouble free,

And the glad parish pays the frugal fee:
No more, O Death! thy victim starts to hear
Churchwarden stern, or kingly overseer;
No more the farmer claims his humble bow,
Thou art his lord, the best of tyrants thou!
  Now to the church behold the mourners come,
Sedately torpid and devoutly dumb;
The village children now their games suspend,
To see the bier that bears their ancient friend:
For he was one in all their idle sport,
And like a monarch ruled their little court;
The pliant bow he form'd, the flying ball,
The bat, the wicket, were his labours all;
Him now they follow to his grave, and stand
Silent and sad, and gazing, hand in hand;
While bending low, their eager eyes explore
The mingled relics of the parish poor:
The bell tolls late, the moping owl flies round,
Fear marks the flight and magnifies the sound;
The busy priest, detain'd by weightier care,
Defers his duty till the day of prayer;
And, waiting long, the crowd retire distress'd,
To think a poor man's bones should lie unbless'd.

BOOK 2

No longer truth, though shown in verse, disdain,
But own the Village Life a life of pain:
I too must yield, that oft amid these woes
Are gleams of transient mirth and hours of sweet repose,
Such as you find on yonder sportive Green,
The 'squire's tall gate and churchway-walk between;
Where loitering stray a little tribe of friends,
On a fair Sunday when the sermon ends:
Then rural beaux their best attire put on,
To win their nymphs, as other nymphs are won;
While those long wed go plain, and by degrees,
Like other husbands, quit their care to please.
Some of the sermon talk, a sober crowd,
And loudly praise, if it were preach'd aloud;

Some on the labours of the week look round,
Feel their own worth, and think their toil renown'd;
While some, whose hopes to no renown extend,
Are only pleased to find their labours end.
  Thus, as their hours glide on, with pleasure fraught,
Their careful masters brood the painful thought;
Much in their mind they murmur and lament,
That one fair day should be so idly spent;
And think that Heaven deals hard, to tithe their store
And tax their time for preachers and the poor.
  Yet still, ye humbler friends, enjoy your hour,
This is your portion, yet unclaim'd of power;
This is Heaven's gift to weary men oppress'd,
And seems the type of their expected rest:
But yours, alas! are joys that soon decay;
Frail joys, begun and ended with the day;
Or yet, while day permits those joys to reign,
The village vices drive them from the plain.
  See the stout churl, in drunken fury great,
Strike the bare bosom of his teeming mate!
His naked vices, rude and unrefined,
Exert their open empire o'er the mind;
But can we less the senseless rage despise,
Because the savage acts without disguise?
  Yet here disguise, the city's vice, is seen,
And Slander steals along and taints the Green:
At her approach domestic peace is gone,
Domestic broils at her approach come on;
She to the wife the husband's crime conveys,
She tells the husband when his consort strays,
Her busy tongue, through all the little state,
Diffuses doubt, suspicion, and debate;
Peace, tim'rous goddess! quits her old domain,
In sentiment and song content to reign.
  Nor are the nymphs that breathes the rural air
So fair as Cynthia's, nor so chaste as fair;
These to the town afford each fresher face,
And the clown's trull receives the peer's embrace;
From whom, should chance again convey her down,
The peer's disease in turn attacks the clown.
  Here too the 'Squire, or 'squire-like farmer, talk,

How round their regions nightly pilferers walk;
How from their ponds the fish are borne, and all
The rip'ning treasures from their lofty wall;
How meaner rivals in their sports delight,
Just rich enough to claim a doubtful right;
Who take a licence round their fields to stray,
A mongrel race! the poachers of the day.
  And hark! the riots of the Green begin,
That sprang at first from yonder noisy inn;
What time the weekly pay was vanish'd all,
And the slow hostess scored the threat'ning wall;
What time they ask'd, their friendly feast to close,
A final cup, and that will make them foes;
When blows ensue that break the arm of toil,
And rustic battle ends the boobies' broil.
  Save when to yonder Hall they bend their way,
Where the grave justice ends the grievous fray;
He who recites, to keep the poor in awe,
The law's vast volume—for he knows the law:—
To him with anger or with shame repair
The injured peasant and deluded fair.
  Lo! at his throne the silent nymph appears,
Frail by her shape, but modest in her tears;
And while she stands abash'd, with conscious eye,
Some favourite female of her judge glides by,
Who views with scornful glance the strumpet's fate,
And thanks the stars that made her keeper great;
Near her the swain, about to bear for life
One certain evil, doubts 'twixt war and wife;
But, while the falt'ring damsel takes her oath,
Consents to wed, and so secures them both,
  Yet why, you ask, these humble crimes relate,
Why make the poor as guilty as the great?
To show the great, those mightier sons of pride,
How near in vice the lowest are allied;
Such are their natures and their passions such,
But these disguise too little, those too much:
So shall the man of power and pleasure see
In his own slave as vile a wretch as he;
In his luxurious lord the servant find
His own low pleasures and degenerate mind:

And each in all the kindred vices trace,
Of a poor, blind, bewilder'd, erring race;
Who, a short time in varied fortune past,
Die, and are equal in the dust at last.
  And you, ye poor, who still lament your fate,
Forbear to envy those you call the great;
And know, amid those blessings they possess,
They are, like you, the victims of distress;
While sloth with many a pang torments her slave,
Fear waits on guilt, and danger shakes the brave.
  Oh! if in life one noble chief appears,
Great in his name, while blooming in his years;
Born to enjoy whate'er delights mankind,
And yet to all you feel or fear resign'd;
Who gave up joys and hopes to you unknown,
For pains and dangers greater than your own:
If such there be, then let your murmurs cease,
Think, think of him, and take your lot in peace.
  And such there was:—Oh! grief, that checks our pride,
Weeping we say there was,—for Manners died:
Beloved of Heaven, these humble lines forgive,
That sing of Thee, and thus aspire to live.
  As the tall oak, whose vigorous branches form
An ample shade and brave the wildest storm,
High o'er the subject wood is seen to grow,
The guard and glory of the trees below;
Till on its head the fiery bolt descends,
And o'er the plain the shatter'd trunk extends;
Yet then it lies, all wond'rous as before,
And still the glory, though the guard no more:
  So THOU, when every virtue, every grace,
Rose in thy soul, or shone within thy face;
When, though the son of Granby, thou wert known
Less by thy father's glory than thy own;
When Honour loved and gave thee every charm,
Fire to thy eye and vigour to thy arm;
Then from our lofty hopes and longing eyes,
Fate and thy virtues call'd thee to the skies;
Yet still we wonder at thy tow'ring fame,
And losing thee, still dwell upon thy name.
  Oh! ever honour'd, ever valued! say,

What verse can praise thee, or what work repay?
Yet verse (in all we can) thy worth repays,
Nor trusts the tardy zeal of future days;—
Honours for thee thy country shall prepare,
Thee in their hearts, the good, the brave shall bear;
To deeds like thine shall noblest chiefs aspire,
The Muse shall mourn thee, and the world admire.
  In future times, when smit with Glory's charms,
The untried youth first quits a father's arms;—
'Oh! be like him,' the weeping sire shall say;
'Like Manners walk, who walk'd in Honour's way;
In danger foremost, yet in death sedate,
Oh! be like him in all things, but his fate!'
  If for that fate such public tears be shed,
That Victory seems to die now THOU art dead;
How shall a friend his nearer hope resign,
That friend a brother, and whose soul was thine?
By what bold lines shall we his grief express,
Or by what soothing numbers make it less?
  'Tis not, I know, the chiming of a song,
Nor all the powers that to the Muse belong,
Words aptly cull'd and meanings well express'd,
Can calm the sorrows of a wounded breast;
But Virtue, soother of the fiercest pains,
Shall heal that bosom, Rutland, where she reigns.
  Yet hard the task to heal the bleeding heart,
To bid the still-recurring thoughts depart,
Tame the fierce grief and stem the rising sigh,
And curb rebellious passion, with reply;
Calmly to dwell on all that pleased before,
And yet to know that all shall please no more;—
Oh! glorious labour of the soul, to save
Her captive powers, and bravely mourn the brave.
  To such these thoughts will lasting comfort give—
Life is not measured by the time we live:
'Tis not an even course of threescore years,
A life of narrow views and paltry fears,
Gray hairs and wrinkles and the cares they bring,
That take from death the terrors or the sting;
But 'tis the gen'rous spirit, mounting high
Above the world, that native of the sky;

The noble spirit, that, in dangers brave,
Calmly looks on, or looks beyond the grave:—
Such Manners was, so he resign'd his breath,
If in a glorious, then a timely death.
 Cease then that grief and let those tears subside;
If Passion rule us, be that passion pride;
If Reason, Reason bids us strive to raise
Our fallen hearts, and be like him we praise;
Or if Affection still the soul subdue,
Bring all his virtues, all his worth in view,
And let Affection find its comfort too:
For how can Grief so deeply wound the heart,
When Admiration claims so large a part?
 Grief is a foe, expel him then thy soul;
Let nobler thoughts the nearer views control!
Oh! make the age to come thy better care,
See other Rutlands, other Granbys there!
And, as thy thoughts through streaming ages glide,
See other heroes die as Manners died:
And from their fate, thy race shall nobler grow,
As trees shoot upwards that are pruned below;
Or as old Thames, borne down with decent pride,
Sees his young streams run warbling at his side;
Though some, by art cut off, no longer run,
And some are lost beneath the summer's sun—
Yet the pure stream moves on, and, as it moves,
Its power increases and its use improves;
While plenty round its spacious waves bestow,
Still it flows on, and shall for ever flow.

THE PARISH REGISTER

1. BAPTISMS

The year revolves, and I again explore
The simple annals of my parish poor;
What infant-members in my flock appear,
What pairs I bless'd in the departed year;
And who, of old or young, or nymphs or swains,
Are lost to life, its pleasures and its pains.

* * *

With evil omen we that year begin:
A Child of Shame,—stern Justice adds, of Sin,
Is first recorded;—I would hide the deed,
But vain the wish; I sigh and I proceed:
And could I well th'instructive truth convey,
'Twould warn the giddy and awake the gay.
Of all the nymphs who gave our village grace,
The Miller's daughter had the fairest face:
Proud was the Miller; money was his pride;
He rode to market, as our farmers ride,
And 'twas his boast, inspired by spirits, there,
His favourite Lucy should be rich as fair;
But she must meek and still obedient prove,
And not presume, without his leave, to love.
A youthful Sailor heard him;—'Ha!' quoth he,
'This Miller's maiden is a prize for me;
Her charms I love, his riches I desire,
And all his threats but fan the kindling fire;
My ebbing purse no more the foe shall fill,
But Love's kind act and Lucy at the mill.'
Thus thought the youth, and soon the chase began,
Stretch'd all his sail, nor thought of pause or plan:
His trusty staff in his bold hand he took,
Like him and like his frigate, heart of oak;
Fresh were his features, his attire was new;
Clean was his linen, and his jacket blue:
Of finest jean, his trowsers, tight and trim,
Brush'd the large buckle at the silver rim.
He soon arrived, he traced the village-green,

There saw the maid, and was with pleasure seen;
Then talk'd of love, till Lucy's yielding heart
Confess'd 'twas painful, though 'twas right to part.
'For ah! my father has a haughty soul;
Whom best he loves, he loves but to control;
Me to some churl in bargain he'll consign,
And make some tyrant of the parish mine:
Cold is his heart, and he with looks severe
Has often forced but never shed the tear;
Save, when my mother died, some drops express'd
A kind of sorrow for a wife at rest:—
To me a master's stern regard is shown,
I'm like his steed, prized highly as his own;
Stroked but corrected, threaten'd when supplied,
His slave and boast, his victim and his pride.'
'Cheer up, my lass! I'll to thy father go,
The Miller cannot be the Sailor's foe;
Both live by Heaven's free gale, that plays aloud
In the stretch'd canvas and the piping shroud;
The rush of winds, the flapping sails above,
And rattling planks within, are sounds *we* love;
Calms are our dread; when tempests plough the deep,
We take a reef, and to the rocking sleep.'
'Ha!' quoth the Miller, moved at speech so rash,
'Art thou like me? then where thy notes and cash?
Away to Wapping, and a wife command,
With all thy wealth, a guinea, in thine hand;
There with thy messmates quaff the muddy cheer,
And leave my Lucy for thy betters here.'
'Revenge! revenge!' the angry lover cried,
Then sought the nymph, and 'Be thou now my bride.'
Bride had she been, but they no priest could move
To bind in law, the couple bound by love.
What sought these lovers then by day, by night?
But stolen moments of disturb'd delight;
Soft trembling tumults, terrors dearly prized,
Transports that pain'd, and joys that agonized:
Till the fond damsel, pleased with lad so trim,
Awed by her parent, and enticed by him,
Her lovely form from savage power to save,
Gave—not her hand—but ALL she could, she gave.

Then came the day of shame, the grievous night,
The varying look, the wandering appetite;
The joy assumed, while sorrow dimm'd the eyes,
The forced sad smiles that follow'd sudden sighs;
And every art, long used, but used in vain,
To hide thy progress, Nature, and thy pain.
Too eager caution shows some danger's near,
The bully's bluster proves the coward's fear;
His sober step the drunkard vainly tries,
And nymphs expose the failings they disguise.
First, whispering gossips were in parties seen;
Then louder Scandal walk'd the village-green;
Next babbling Folly told the growing ill,
And busy Malice dropp'd it at the mill.
'Go! to thy curse and mine,' the Father said,
'Strife and confusion stalk around thy bed;
Want and a wailing brat thy portion be,
Plague to thy fondness, as thy fault to me;—
Where skulks the villain?'—'On the ocean wide
My William seeks a portion for his bride.'—
'Vain be his search! but, till the traitor come,
The higgler's cottage be thy future home;
There with his ancient shrew and care abide,
And hide thy head,—thy shame thou canst not hide.'
Day after day was pass'd in pains and grief;
Week follow'd week,—and still was no relief:
Her boy was born—no lads nor lasses came
To grace the rite or give the child a name;
Nor grave conceited nurse, of office proud,
Bore the young Christian roaring through the crowd:
In a small chamber was my office done,
Where blinks through paper'd panes the setting sun;
Where noisy sparrows, perch'd on penthouse near,
Chirp tuneless joy, and mock the frequent tear;
Bats on their webby wings in darkness move,
And feebly shriek their melancholy love.
No Sailor came; the months in terror fled!
Then news arrived—He fought, and he was DEAD!
At the lone cottage Lucy lives, and still
Walks for her weekly pittance to the mill;
A mean seraglio there her father keeps,

Whose mirth insults her, as she stands and weeps;
And sees the plenty, while compell'd to stay,
Her father's pride, become his harlot's prey.
  Throughout the lanes she glides, at evening's close,
And softly lulls her infant to repose;
Then sits and gazes, but with viewless look,
As gilds the moon the rippling of the brook;
And sings her vespers, but in voice so low,
She hears their murmurs as the waters flow:
And she too murmurs, and begins to find
The solemn wanderings of a wounded mind:
Visions of terror, views of wo succeed,
The mind's impatience, to the body's need;
By turns to that, by turns to this a prey,
She knows what reason yields, and dreads what madness may.
  Next, with their boy, a decent couple came,
And call'd him Robert, 'twas his father's name;
Three girls preceded, all by time endear'd,
And future births were neither hoped nor fear'd:
Bless'd in each other, but to no excess;
Health, quiet, comfort, form'd their happiness;
Love all made up of torture and delight,
Was but mere madness in this couple's sight:
Susan could think, though not without a sigh,
If she were gone, who should her place supply;
And Robert, half in earnest, half in jest,
Talk of her spouse when he should be at rest:
Yet strange would either think it to be told,
Their love was cooling or their hearts were cold.
Few were their acres,—but, with these content,
They were, each pay-day, ready with their rent:
And few their wishes—what their farm denied,
The neighbouring town, at trifling cost, supplied.
If at the draper's window Susan cast
A longing look, as with her goods she pass'd,
And, with the produce of the wheel and churn,
Bought her a Sunday-robe on her return;
True to her maxim, she would take no rest,
Till care repaid that portion to the chest:
Or if, when loitering at the Whitsun-fair,

Her Robert spent some idle shillings there;
Up at the barn, before the break of day,
He made his labour for th'indulgence pay:
Thus both—that waste itself might work in vain—
Wrought double tides, and all was well again.
   Yet, though so prudent, there were times of joy,
(The day they wed, the christening of the boy,)
When to the wealthier farmers there was shown
Welcome unfeign'd, and plenty like their own;
For Susan served the great, and had some pride
Among our topmost people to preside:
Yet in that plenty, in that welcome free,
There was the guiding nice frugality,
That, in the festal as the frugal day,
Has, in a different mode, a sovereign sway;
As tides the same attractive influence know,
In the least ebb and in their proudest flow;
The wise frugality, that does not give
A life to saving, but that saves to live;
Sparing, not pinching, mindful though not mean,
O'er all presiding, yet in nothing seen.
   Recorded next a babe of love I trace!
Of many loves, the mother's fresh disgrace.—
   'Again, thou harlot! could not all thy pain,
All my reproof, thy wanton thoughts restrain?'
   'Alas! your reverence, wanton thoughts, I grant,
Were once my motive, now the thoughts of want;
Women, like me, as ducks in a decoy,
Swim down a stream, and seem to swim in joy;
Your sex pursue us, and our own disdain;
Return is dreadful, and escape is vain.
Would men forsake us, and would women strive
To help the fall'n, their virtue might revive.'
   For rite of churching soon she made her way,
In dread of scandal, should she miss the day:—
Two matrons came! with them she humbly knelt,
Their action copied and their comforts felt,
From that great pain and peril to be free,
Though still in peril of that pain to be;
Alas! what numbers, like this amorous dame,
Are quick to censure, but are dead to shame!

Twin-infants then appear; a girl, a boy,
Th'o'erflowing cup of Gerard Ablett's joy:
One had I named in every year that pass'd
Since Gerard wed! and twins behold at last!
Well pleased, the bridegroom smiled to hear—'A vine
Fruitful and spreading round the walls be thine,
And branch-like be thine offspring!'—Gerard then
Look'd joyful love, and softly said, 'Amen.'
Now of that vine he'd have no more increase,
Those playful branches now disturb his peace:
Them he beholds around his table spread,
But finds, the more the branch, the less the bread;
And while they run his humble walls about,
They keep the sunshine of good-humour out.
Cease, man, to grieve! thy master's lot survey,
Whom wife and children, thou and thine obey;
A farmer proud, beyond a farmer's pride,
Of all around the envy or the guide;
Who trots to market on a steed so fine,
That when I meet him, I'm ashamed of mine;
Whose board is high up-heap'd with generous fare,
Which five stout sons and three tall daughters share:
Cease, man, to grieve, and listen to his care.
A few years fled, and all thy boys shall be
Lords of a cot, and labourers like thee:
Thy girls unportion'd neighb'ring youths shall lead
Brides from my church, and thenceforth thou art freed:
But then thy master shall of cares complain,
Care after care, a long connected train;
His sons for farms shall ask a large supply,
For farmers' sons each gentle miss shall sigh;
Thy mistress, reasoning well of life's decay,
Shall ask a chaise, and hardly brook delay;
The smart young cornet who, with so much grace,
Rode in the ranks and betted at the race,
While the vex'd parent rails at deed so rash,
Shall d—n his luck, and stretch his hand for cash.
Sad troubles, Gerard! now pertain to thee,
When thy rich master seems from trouble free;
But 'tis one fate at different times assign'd,
And thou shalt lose the cares that he must find.

'Ah!' quoth our village Grocer, rich and old,
'Would I might one such cause for care behold!'
To whom his Friend, 'Mine greater bliss would be,
Would Heav'n take those my spouse assigns to me.'
Aged were both, that Dawkins, Ditchem this,
Who much of marriage thought, and much amiss;
Both would delay, the one, till—riches gain'd,
The son he wish'd might be to honour train'd;
His Friend—lest fierce intruding heirs should come,
To waste his hoard and vex his quiet home.
Dawkins, a dealer once, on burthen'd back
Bore his whole substance in a pedler's pack;
To dames discreet, the duties yet unpaid,
His stores of lace and hyson he convey'd:
When thus enrich'd, he chose at home to stop,
And fleece his neighbours in a new-built shop;
Then woo'd a spinster blithe, and hoped, when wed,
For love's fair favours and a fruitful bed.
Not so his Friend;—on widow fair and staid
He fix'd his eye, but he was much afraid;
Yet woo'd; while she his hair of silver hue
Demurely noticed, and her eye withdrew:
Doubtful he paused—'Ah! were I sure,' he cried,
'No craving children would my gains divide;
Fair as she is, I would my widow take,
And live more largely for my partner's sake.'
With such their views some thoughtful years they pass'd,
And hoping, dreading, they were bound at last.
And what their fate? Observe them as they go,
Comparing fear with fear and wo with wo.
'Humphrey!' said Dawkins, 'envy in my breast
Sickens to see thee in thy children bless'd;
They are thy joys, while I go grieving home
To a sad spouse and our eternal gloom:
We look despondency; no infant near,
To bless the eye or win the parent's ear;
Our sudden heats and quarrels to allay,
And soothe the petty sufferings of the day:
Alike our want, yet both the want reprove;
Where are, I cry, these pledges of our love?
When she, like Jacob's wife, makes fierce reply,

Yet fond—Oh! give me children, or I die:
And I return—still childless doom'd to live,
Like the vex'd patriarch—Are they mine to give?
Ah! much I envy thee thy boys, who ride
On poplar branch, and canter at thy side;
And girls, whose cheeks thy chin's fierce fondness know,
And with fresh beauty at the contact glow.'
'Oh! simple friend,' said Ditchem, 'would'st thou gain
A father's pleasure by a husband's pain?
Alas! what pleasure—when some vig'rous boy
Should swell thy pride, some rosy girl thy joy;
Is it to doubt who grafted this sweet flower,
Or whence arose that spirit and that power?
'Four years I've wed; not one has pass'd in vain:
Behold the fifth! behold, a babe again!
My wife's gay friends th'unwelcome imp admire,
And fill the room with gratulation dire:
While I in silence sate, revolving all
That influence ancient men, or that befall;
A gay pert guest—Heav'n knows his business—came;
A glorious boy, he cried, and what the name?
Angry I growl'd,—My spirit cease to tease,
Name it yourselves,—Cain, Judas, if you please;
His father's give him,—should you that explore,
The devil's or yours:—I said, and sought the door.
My tender partner not a word or sigh
Gives to my wrath, nor to my speech reply;
But takes her comforts, triumphs in my pain,
And looks undaunted for a birth again.'
Heirs thus denied afflict the pining heart,
And thus afforded, jealous pangs impart;
Let, therefore, none avoid, and none demand
These arrows number'd for the giant's hand.
Then with their infants three, the parents came,
And each assign'd—'twas all they had—a name;
Names of no mark or price; of them not one
Shall court our view on the sepulchral stone,
Or stop the clerk, th'engraven scrolls to spell,
Or keep the sexton from the sermon bell.
An orphan-girl succeeds: ere she was born
Her father died, her mother on that morn:

1. Baptisms

The pious mistress of the school sustains
Her parents' part, nor their affection feigns,
But pitying feels: with due respect and joy,
I trace the matron at her loved employ;
What time the striplings, wearied e'en with play,
Part at the closing of the summer's day,
And each by different path returns the well-known way—
Then I behold her at her cottage-door,
Frugal of light;—her Bible laid before,
When on her double duty she proceeds,
Of time as frugal—knitting as she reads:
Her idle neighbours, who approach to tell
Some trifling tale, her serious looks compel
To hear reluctant,—while the lads who pass,
In pure respect, walk silent on the grass:
Then sinks the day, but not to rest she goes,
Till solemn prayers the daily duties close.
  But I digress, and lo! an infant train
Appear, and call me to my task again.
  'Why Lonicera wilt thou name thy child?'
I ask'd the Gardener's wife, in accents mild:
'We have a right,' replied the sturdy dame,—
And Lonicera was the infant's name.
If next a son shall yield our Gardener joy,
Then Hyacinthus shall be that fair boy;
And if a girl, they will at length agree,
That Belladonna that fair maid shall be.
  High-sounding words our worthy Gardener gets,
And at his club to wondering swains repeats;
He then of Rhus and Rhododendron speaks,
And Allium calls his onions and his leeks;
Nor weeds are now, for whence arose the weed,
Scarce plants, fair herbs, and curious flowers proceed;
Where Cuckoo-pints and Dandelions sprung,
(Gross names had they our plainer sires among,)
There Arums, there Leontodons we view,
And Artemisia grows, where Wormwood grew.
  But though no weed exists his garden round,
From Rumex strong our Gardener frees his ground,
Takes soft Senicio from the yielding land,
And grasps the arm'd Urtica in his hand.

Not Darwin's self had more delight to sing
Of floral courtship, in th'awaken'd Spring,
Than Peter Pratt, who simpering loves to tell
How rise the Stamens, as the Pistils swell;
How bend and curl the moist-top to the spouse,
And give and take the vegetable vows;
How those esteem'd of old but tips and chives,
Are tender husbands and obedient wives;
Who live and love within the sacred bower,—
That bridal bed, the vulgar term a flower.
Hear Peter proudly, to some humble friend,
A wondrous secret, in his science, lend:—
'Would you advance the nuptial hour, and bring
The fruit of Autumn with the flowers of Spring;
View that light frame where Cucumis lies spread,
And trace the husbands in their golden bed,
Three powder'd Anthers;—then no more delay,
But to the Stigma's tip their dust convey;
Then by thyself, from prying glance secure,
Twirl the full tip and make your purpose sure;
A long-abiding race the deed shall pay,
Nor one unbless'd abortion pine away.'
T' admire their friend's discourse our swains agree,
And call it science and philosophy.
'Tis good, 'tis pleasant, through th'advancing year,
To see unnumber'd growing forms appear;
What leafy-life from Earth's broad bosom rise!
What insect-myriads seek the summer skies!
What scaly tribes in every streamlet move!
What plumy people sing in every grove!
All with the year awaked to life, delight, and love.
Then names are good; for how, without their aid,
Is knowledge, gain'd by man, to man convey'd?
But from that source shall all our pleasures flow?
Shall all our knowledge be those names to know?
Then he, with memory bless'd, shall bear away
The palm from Grew, and Middleton, and Ray:
No! let us rather seek, in grove and field,
What food for wonder, what for use they yield;
Some just remark from Nature's people bring,
And some new source of homage for her King.

Pride lives with all; strange names our rustics give
To helpless infants, that their own may live;
Pleased to be known, they'll some attention claim,
And find some by-way to the house of fame.
The straightest furrow lifts the ploughman's art,
The hat he gain'd has warmth for head and heart;
The bowl that beats the greater number down
Of tottering nine-pins, gives to fame the clown;
Or, foil'd in these, he opes his ample jaws,
And lets a frog leap down, to gain applause;
Or grins for hours, or tipples for a week,
Or challenges a well-pinch'd pig to squeak:
Some idle deed, some child's preposterous name,
Shall make him known, and give his folly fame.
To name an infant meet our village-sires,
Assembled all, as such event requires;
Frequent and full, the rural sages sate,
And speakers many urged the long debate,—
Some harden'd knaves, who roved the country round,
Had left a babe within the parish-bound.—
First, of the fact they question'd—'Was it true?'
The child was brought—'What then remain'd to do?
Was't dead or living?' This was fairly proved,—
'Twas pinch'd, it roar'd, and every doubt removed.
Then by what name th'unwelcome guest to call
Was long a question, and it posed them all;
For he who lent it to a babe unknown,
Censorious men might take it for his own:
They look'd about, they gravely spoke to all,
And not one Richard answer'd to the call.
Next they inquired the day, when, passing by,
Th'unlucky peasant heard the stranger's cry:
This known,—how food and raiment they might give,
Was next debated—for the rogue would live;
At last, with all their words and work content,
Back to their homes the prudent vestry went,
And Richard Monday to the workhouse sent.
There was he pinch'd and pitied, thump'd and fed,
And duly took his beatings and his bread;
Patient in all control, in all abuse,
He found contempt and kicking have their use:

Sad, silent, supple; bending to the blow,
A slave of slaves, the lowest of the low;
His pliant soul gave way to all things base,
He knew no shame, he dreaded no disgrace.
It seem'd, so well his passions he suppress'd,
No feeling stirr'd his ever-torpid breast;
Him might the meanest pauper bruise and cheat,
He was a footstool for the beggar's feet;
His were the legs that ran at all commands;
They used on all occasions Richard's hands:
His very soul was not his own; he stole
As others order'd, and without a dole;
In all disputes, on either part he lied,
And freely pledged his oath on either side;
In all rebellions Richard join'd the rest,
In all detections Richard first confess'd:
Yet, though disgraced, he watch'd his time so well,
He rose in favour, when in fame he fell;
Base was his usage, vile his whole employ,
And all despised and fed the pliant boy.
At length, ''tis time he should abroad be sent,'
Was whisper'd near him,—and abroad he went;
One morn they call'd him, Richard answer'd not;
They deem'd him hanging, and in time forgot,—
Yet miss'd him long, as each, throughout the clan,
Found he 'had better spared a better man.'
  Now Richard's talents for the world were fit,
He'd no small cunning, and had some small wit;
Had that calm look which seem'd to all assent,
And that complacent speech which nothing meant:
He'd but one care, and that he strove to hide,
How best for Richard Monday to provide.
Steel, through opposing plates, the magnet draws,
And steely atoms culls from dust and straws;
And thus our hero, to his interest true,
Gold through all bars and from each trifle drew;
But still more surely round the world to go,
This fortune's child had neither friend nor foe.
  Long lost to us, at last our man we trace,—
Sir Richard Monday died at Monday-place:
His lady's worth, his daughter's we peruse,

And find his grandsons all as rich as Jews:
He gave reforming charities a sum,
And bought the blessings of the blind and dumb;
Bequeathed to missions money from the stocks,
And Bibles issued from his private box;
But to his native place severely just,
He left a pittance bound in rigid trust;—
Two paltry pounds, on every quarter's-day,
(At church produced) for forty loaves should pay;
A stinted gift, that to the parish shows
He kept in mind their bounty and their blows!
  To farmers three, the year has given a son,
Finch on the Moor, and French, and Middleton.
Twice in this year a female Giles I see,
A Spalding once, and once a Barnaby:—
A humble man is he, and, when they meet,
Our farmers find him on a distant seat;
There for their wit he serves a constant theme,—
'They praise his dairy, they extol his team,
They ask the price of each unrivall'd steed,
And whence his sheep, that admirable breed?
His thriving arts they beg he would explain,
And where he puts the money he must gain.
They have their daughters, but they fear their friend
Would think his sons too much would condescend;—
They have their sons who would their fortunes try,
But fear his daughters will their suit deny.'
So runs the joke, while James, with sigh profound,
And face of care, looks moveless on the ground;
His cares, his sighs, provoke the insult more,
And point the jest—for Barnaby is poor.
  Last in my list, five untaught lads appear;
Their father dead, compassion sent them here,—
For still that rustic infidel denied
To have their names with solemn rite applied:
His, a lone house, by Deadman's Dyke-way stood;
And his, a nightly haunt, in Lonely-wood:
Each village inn has heard the ruffian boast,
That he believed 'in neither God nor ghost;
That, when the sod upon the sinner press'd,
He, like the saint, had everlasting rest;

That never priest believed his doctrines true,
But would, for profit, own himself a Jew,
Or worship wood and stone, as honest heathen do;
That fools alone on future worlds rely,
And all who die for faith, deserve to die.'
These maxims,—part th'attorney's clerk profess'd,
His own transcendent genius found the rest.
Our pious matrons heard, and, much amazed,
Gazed on the man, and trembled as they gazed;
And now his face explored, and now his feet,
Man's dreaded foe, in this bad man, to meet:
But him our drunkards as their champion raised,
Their bishop call'd, and as their hero praised;
Though most, when sober, and the rest, when sick,
Had little question whence his bishopric.
But he, triumphant spirit! all things dared,
He poach'd the wood, and on the warren snared;
'Twas his, at cards, each novice to trepan,
And call the wants of rogues the rights of man;
Wild as the winds, he let his offspring rove,
And deem'd the marriage-bond the bane of love.
What age and sickness, for a man so bold,
Had done, we know not;—none beheld him old:
By night, as business urged, he sought the wood,—
The ditch was deep,—the rain had caused a flood,—
The foot-bridge fail'd,—he plunged beneath the deep,
And slept, if truth were his, th'eternal sleep.
These have we named; on life's rough sea they sail,
With many a prosperous, many an adverse gale!
Where passion soon, like powerful winds, will rage,
And prudence, wearied, with their strength engage:
Then each, in aid, shall some companion ask,
For help or comfort in the tedious task;
And what that help—what joys from union flow,
What good or ill, we next prepare to show;
And row, meantime, our weary bark ashore,
As Spenser his—but not with Spenser's oar.

3. BURIALS

There was, 'tis said, and I believe, a time,
When humble Christians died with views sublime;
When all were ready for their faith to bleed,
But few to write or wrangle for their creed;
When lively Faith upheld the sinking heart,
And friends, assured to meet, prepared to part;
When Love felt hope, when Sorrow grew serene,
And all was comfort in the death-bed scene.
  Alas! when now the gloomy king they wait,
'Tis weakness yielding to resistless fate;
Like wretched men upon the ocean cast,
They labour hard and struggle to the last;
'Hope against hope,' and wildly gaze around,
In search of help that never shall be found:
Nor, till the last strong billow stops the breath,
Will they believe them in the jaws of Death!
  When these my records I reflecting read,
And find what ills these numerous births succeed;
What powerful griefs these nuptial ties attend,
With what regret these painful journeys end;
When from the cradle to the grave I look,
Mine I conceive a melancholy book.
  Where now is perfect resignation seen?
Alas! it is not on the village-green:—
I've seldom known, though I have often read
Of happy peasants on their dying-bed;
Whose looks proclaim'd that sunshine of the breast,
That more than hope, that Heaven itself express'd.
  What I behold are feverish fits of strife,
'Twixt fears of dying and desire of life:
Those earthly hopes, that to the last endure;
Those fears, that hopes superior fail to cure;
At best a sad submission to the doom,
Which, turning from the danger, lets it come.
  Sick lies the man, bewilder'd, lost, afraid,
His spirits vanquish'd and his strength decay'd;
No hope the friend, the nurse, the doctor lend—
'Call then a priest, and fit him for his end.'
A priest is call'd; 'tis now, alas! too late,

Death enters with him at the cottage-gate;
Or time allow'd—he goes, assured to find
The self-commending, all-confiding mind;
And sighs to hear, what we may justly call
Death's common-place, the train of thought in all.
'True, I'm a sinner,' feebly he begins,
'But trust in Mercy to forgive my sins:'
(Such cool confession no past crimes excite!
Such claim on Mercy seems the sinner's right!)
'I know, mankind are frail, that God is just,
And pardons those who in his mercy trust;
We're sorely tempted in a world like this,
All men have done, and I like all, amiss;
But now, if spared, it is my full intent
On all the past to ponder and repent:
Wrongs against me I pardon great and small,
And if I die, I die in peace with all.'
His merits thus and not his sins confess'd,
He speaks his hopes, and leaves to Heaven the rest.
Alas! are these the prospects, dull and cold,
That dying Christians to their priests unfold?
Or mends the prospect when th'enthusiast cries,
'I die assured!' and in a rapture dies?
Ah, where that humble, self-abasing mind,
With that confiding spirit, shall we find;
The mind that, feeling what repentance brings,
Dejection's terrors and Contrition's stings,
Feels then the hope, that mounts all care above,
And the pure joy that flows from pardoning love?
Such have I seen in death, and much deplore,
So many dying—that I see no more:
Lo! now my records, where I grieve to trace,
How Death has triumph'd in so short a space;
Who are the dead, how died they, I relate,
And snatch some portion of their acts from fate.
With Andrew Collett we the year begin,
The blind, fat landlord of the Old Crown Inn,—
Big as his butt, and, for the self-same use,
To take in stores of strong fermenting juice.
On his huge chair beside the fire he sate,
In revel chief, and umpire in debate;

Each night his string of vulgar tales he told;
When ale was cheap and bachelors were bold:
His heroes all were famous in their days,
Cheats were his boast and drunkards had his praise;
'One, in three draughts, three mugs of ale took down,
As mugs were then—the champion of the Crown;
For thrice three days another lived on ale,
And knew no change but that of mild and stale;
Two thirsty soakers watch'd a vessel's side,
When he the tap, with dextrous hand, applied;
Nor from their seats departed, till they found
That butt was out and heard the mournful sound.'
  He praised a poacher, precious child of fun!
Who shot the keeper with his own spring-gun;
Nor less the smuggler who the exciseman tied,
And left him hanging at the birch-wood side,
There to expire;—but one who saw him hang
Cut the good cord—a traitor of the gang.
  His own exploits with boastful glee he told,
What ponds he emptied and what pikes he sold;
And how, when bless'd with sight alert and gay,
The night's amusements kept him through the day.
  He sang the praises of those times, when all
'For cards and dice, as for their drink, might call;
When justice wink'd on every jovial crew,
And ten-pins tumbled in the parson's view.'
  He told, when angry wives, provoked to rail,
Or drive a third-day drunkard from his ale,
What were his triumphs, and how great the skill
That won the vex'd virago to his will;
Who raving came;—then talk'd in milder strain,—
Then wept, then drank, and pledged her spouse again.
  Such were his themes: how knaves o'er laws prevail,
Or, when made captives, how they fly from jail;
The young how brave, how subtle were the old:
And oaths attested all that Folly told.
  On death like his what name shall we bestow,
So very sudden! yet so very slow?
Twas slow:—Disease, augmenting year by year,
Show'd the grim king by gradual steps brought near:
'Twas not less sudden; in the night he died,

He drank, he swore, he jested, and he lied;
Thus aiding folly with departing breath:—
'Beware, Lorenzo, the slow-sudden death.'
  Next died the Widow Goe, an active dame,
Famed ten miles round, and worthy all her fame;
She lost her husband when their loves were young,
But kept her farm, her credit, and her tongue:
Full thirty years she ruled, with matchless skill,
With guiding judgment and resistless will;
Advice she scorn'd, rebellions she suppress'd,
And sons and servants bow'd at her behest.
Like that great man's, who to his Saviour came,
Were the strong words of this commanding dame;—
'Come', if she said, they came; if 'go', were gone;
And if 'do this',—that instant it was done:
Her maidens told she was all eye and ear,
In darkness saw and could at distance hear;—
No parish-business in the place could stir,
Without direction or assent from her;
In turn she took each office as it fell,
Knew all their duties, and discharged them well;
The lazy vagrants in her presence shook,
And pregnant damsels fear'd her stern rebuke;
She look'd on want with judgment clear and cool,
She felt with reason and bestow'd by rule;
She match'd both sons and daughters to her mind,
And lent them eyes, for Love, she heard, was blind;
Yet ceaseless still she throve, alert, alive,
The working bee, in full or empty hive;
Busy and careful, like that working bee,
No time for love nor tender cares had she;
But when our farmers made their amorous vows,
She talk'd of market-steeds and patent-ploughs.
Not unemploy'd her evenings pass'd away,
Amusement closed, as business waked the day;
When to her toilet's brief concern she ran,
And conversation with her friends began,
Who all were welcome, what they saw, to share;
And joyous neighbours praised her Christmas fare,
That none around might, in their scorn, complain
Of Gossip Goe as greedy in her gain.

3. Burials

Thus long she reign'd, admired, if not approved;
Praised, if not honour'd; fear'd, if not beloved;—
When, as the busy days of Spring drew near,
That call'd for all the forecast of the year;
When lively hope the rising crops survey'd,
And April promised what September paid;
When stray'd her lambs where gorse and greenweed grow;
When rose her grass in richer vales below;
When pleased she look'd on all the smiling land,
And view'd the hinds, who wrought at her command;
(Poultry in groups still follow'd where she went;)
Then dread o'ercame her,—that her days were spent.
'Bless me! I die, and not a warning giv'n,—
With *much* to do on Earth, and ALL for Heav'n!—
No reparation for my soul's affairs,
No leave petition'd for the barn's repairs;
Accounts perplex'd, my interest yet unpaid,
My mind unsettled, and my will unmade;—
A lawyer haste, and in your way, a priest;
And let me die in one good work at least.'
She spake, and trembling, dropp'd upon her knees,
Heaven in her eye and in her hand her keys;
And still the more she found her life decay,
With greater force she grasp'd those signs of sway:
Then fell and died!—In haste her sons drew near,
And dropp'd, in haste, the tributary tear,
Then from th'adhering clasp the keys unbound,
And consolation for their sorrows found.
Death has his infant-train; his bony arm
Strikes from the baby-cheek the rosy charm;
The brightest eye his glazing film makes dim,
And his cold touch sets fast the lithest limb:
He seiz'd the sick'ning boy to Gerard lent,
When three days' life, in feeble cries, were spent;
In pain brought forth, those painful hours to stay,
To breathe in pain and sigh its soul away!
'But why thus lent, if thus recall'd again,
To cause and feel, to live and die in, pain?'
Or rather say, Why grievous these appear,
If all it pays for Heaven's eternal year;

If these sad sobs and piteous sighs secure
Delights that live, when worlds no more endure?
The sister-spirit long may lodge below,
And pains from nature, pains from reason, know;
Through all the common ills of life may run,
By hope perverted and by love undone;
A wife's distress, a mother's pangs, may dread,
And widow-tears, in bitter anguish, shed;
May at old age arrive through numerous harms,
With children's children in those feeble arms:
Nor till by years of want and grief oppress'd,
Shall the sad spirit flee and be at rest!
Yet happier therefore shall we deem the boy,
Secured from anxious care and dangerous joy?
Not so! for then would Love Divine in vain
Send all the burthens weary men sustain;
All that now curb the passions when they rage,
The checks of youth and the regrets of age;
All that now bid us hope, believe, endure,
Our sorrow's comfort, and our vice's cure;
All that for Heaven's high joys the spirits train,
And charity, the crown of all, were vain.
Say, will you call the breathless infant bless'd,
Because no cares the silent grave molest?
So would you deem the nursling from the wing
Untimely thrust and never train'd to sing;
But far more bless'd the bird whose grateful voice
Sings its own joy and makes the woods rejoice,
Though, while untaught, ere yet he charm'd the ear,
Hard were his trials and his pains severe!
Next died the Lady who yon Hall possess'd;
And here they brought her noble bones to rest.
In Town she dwelt;—forsaken stood the Hall:
Worms ate the floors, the tap'stry fled the wall:
No fire the kitchen's cheerless grate display'd;
No cheerful light the long-closed sash convey'd;
The crawling worm, that turns a summer-fly,
Here spun his shroud and laid him up to die
The winter-death:—upon the bed of state,
The bat shrill-shrieking woo'd his flickering mate;
To empty rooms the curious came no more,

From empty cellars turn'd the angry poor,
And surly beggars cursed the ever-bolted door.
To one small room the steward found his way,
Where tenants follow'd to complain and pay;
Yet no complaint before the Lady came,
The feeling servant spared the feeble dame;
Who saw her farms with his observing eyes,
And answer'd all requests with his replies:—
She came not down, her falling groves to view;
Why should she know, what one so faithful knew?
Why come, from many clamorous tongues to hear,
What one so just might whisper in her ear?
Her oaks or acres, why with care explore;
Why learn the wants, the sufferings of the poor;
When one so knowing all their worth could trace,
And one so piteous govern'd in her place?
  Lo! now, what dismal sons of Darkness come,
To bear this daughter of Indulgence home;
Tragedians all, and well arranged in black!
Who nature, feeling, force, expression lack;
Who cause no tear, but gloomily pass by,
And shake their sables in the wearied eye,
That turns disgusted from the pompous scene,
Proud without grandeur, with profusion, mean!
The tear for kindness past affection owes;
For worth deceased the sigh from reason flows;
E'en well-feign'd passions for our sorrows call,
And real tears for mimic miseries fall:
But this poor farce has neither truth nor art,
To please the fancy or to touch the heart;
Unlike the darkness of the sky, that pours
On the dry ground its fertilizing showers;
Unlike to that which strikes the soul with dread,
When thunders roar and forky fires are shed;
Dark but not awful, dismal but yet mean,
With anxious bustle moves the cumbrous scene;
Presents no objects tender or profound,
But spreads its cold unmeaning gloom around.
  When woes are feign'd, how ill such forms appear;
And oh! how needless, when the wo's sincere.
  Slow to the vault they come, with heavy tread,

Bending beneath the Lady and her lead;
A case of elm surrounds that ponderous chest,
Close on that case the crimson velvet's press'd;
Ungenerous this, that to the worm denies,
With niggard-caution, his appointed prize;
For now, ere yet he works his tedious way,
Through cloth and wood and metal to his prey,
That prey dissolving shall a mass remain,
That fancy loathes and worms themselves disdain.
  But see! the master-mourner makes his way,
To end his office for the coffin'd clay;
Pleased that our rustic men and maids behold
His plate like silver, and his studs like gold,
As they approach to spell the age, the name,
And all the titles of th'illustrious dame.—
This as (my duty done) some scholar read,
A village-father look'd disdain and said:
'Away, my friends! why take such pains to know
What some brave marble soon in church shall show?
Where not alone her gracious name shall stand,
But how she lived—the blessing of the land;
How much we all deplored the noble dead,
What groans we utter'd and what tears we shed;
Tears, true as those, which in the sleepy eyes
Of weeping cherubs on the stone shall rise;
Tears, true as those, which, ere she found her grave,
The noble Lady to our sorrows gave.'
  Down by the church-way walk and where the brook
Winds round the chancel like a shepherd's crook;
In that small house, with those green pales before,
Where jasmine trails on either side the door;
Where those dark shrubs that now grow wild at will,
Were clipp'd in form and tantalized with skill;
Where cockles blanch'd and pebbles neatly spread,
Form'd shining borders for the larkspurs' bed;—
There lived a Lady, wise, austere, and nice,
Who show'd her virtue by her scorn of vice;
In the dear fashions of her youth she dress'd,
A pea-green Joseph was her favourite vest;
Erect she stood, she walk'd with stately mien,
Tight was her length of stays, and she was tall and lean.

There long she lived in maiden-state immured,
From looks of love and treacherous man secured;
Though evil fame—(but that was long before)
Had blown her dubious blast at Catherine's door:
A Captain thither, rich from India came,
And though a cousin call'd, it touch'd her fame:
Her annual stipend rose from his behest,
And all the long prized treasures she possess'd:—
If aught like joy awhile appear'd to stay
In that stern face, and chase those frowns away;
'Twas when her treasures she disposed for view,
And heard the praises to their splendour due;
Silks beyond price, so rich, they'd stand alone,
And diamonds blazing on the buckled zone;
Rows of rare pearls by curious workmen set,
And bracelets fair in box of glossy jet;
Bright polish'd amber precious from its size,
Or forms the fairest fancy could devise:
Her drawers of cedar, shut with secret springs,
Conceal'd the watch of gold and rubied rings;
Letters, long proofs of love, and verses fine
Round the pink'd rims of crisped Valentine.
Her china-closet, cause of daily care,
For woman's wonder held her pencill'd ware;
That pictured wealth of China and Japan,
Like its cold mistress, shunn'd the eye of man.
Her neat small room, adorn'd with maiden-taste,
A clipp'd French puppy, first of favourites, graced:
A parrot next, but dead and stuff'd with art;
(For Poll, when living, lost the Lady's heart,
And then his life; for he was heard to speak
Such frightful words as tinged his Lady's cheek:)
Unhappy bird! who had no power to prove,
Save by such speech, his gratitude and love.
A grey old cat his whiskers lick'd beside;
A type of sadness in the house of pride.
The polish'd surface of an India chest,
A glassy globe, in frame of ivory, press'd;
Where swam two finny creatures; one of gold,
Of silver one; both beauteous to behold:—
All these were form'd the guiding taste to suit;

The beasts well-manner'd and the fishes mute.
A widow'd Aunt was there, compell'd by need
The nymph to flatter and her tribe to feed;
Who, veiling well her scorn, endured the dog,
Mute as the fish and fawning as the dog.
  As years increased, these treasures, her delight,
Arose in value in their owner's sight:
A miser knows that, view it as he will,
A guinea kept is but a guinea still;
And so he puts it to its proper use,
That something more this guinea may produce:
But silks and rings, in the possessor's eyes,
The oft'ner seen, the more in value rise,
And thus are wisely hoarded to bestow
The kind of pleasure that with years will grow.
  But what avail'd their worth—if worth had they,—
In the sad summer of her slow decay?
  Then we beheld her turn an anxious look
From trunks and chests, and fix it on her book,—
A rich-bound Book of Prayer the Captain gave,
(Some Princess had it, or was said to have;)
And then once more, on all her stores, look round,
And draw a sigh so piteous and profound,
That told, 'Alas! how hard from these to part,
And for new hopes and habits form the heart!
What shall I do, (she cried) my peace of mind
To gain in dying, and to die resign'd?'
  'Hear,' we return'd;—'these baubles cast aside,
Nor give thy God a rival in thy pride;
Thy closets shut, and ope thy kitchen's door;
There own thy failings, *here* invite the poor;
A friend of Mammon let thy bounty make;
For widows' prayers, thy vanities forsake;
And let the hungry, of thy pride, partake:
Then shall thy inward eye with joy survey
The angel Mercy tempering Death's delay!'
  Alas! 'twas hard; the treasures still had charms,
Hope still its flattery, sickness its alarms;
Still was the same unsettled, clouded view,
And the same plaintive cry, 'What shall I do?'

Nor change appear'd: for when her race was run,
Doubtful we all exclaimed, 'What has been done?'
Apart she lived, and still she lies alone;
Yon earthy heap awaits the flattering stone,
On which invention shall be long employ'd,
To show the various worth of Catherine Lloyd.
Next to these ladies, but in nought allied,
A noble Peasant, Isaac Ashford, died.
Noble he was, contemning all things mean,
His truth unquestion'd and his soul serene:
Of no man's presence Isaac felt afraid;
At no man's question Isaac look'd dismay'd:
Shame knew him not, he dreaded no disgrace;
Truth, simple truth, was written in his face;
Yet while the serious thought his soul approved,
Cheerful he seem'd, and gentleness he loved:
To bliss domestic he his heart resign'd,
And, with the firmest, had the fondest mind:
Were others joyful, he look'd smiling on,
And gave allowance where he needed none;
Good he refused with future ill to buy,
Nor knew a joy that caused reflection's sigh;
A friend to virtue, his unclouded breast
No envy stung, no jealousy distress'd;
(Bane of the poor! it wounds their weaker mind,
To miss one favour which their neighbours find:)
Yet far was he from stoic pride removed;
He felt humanely, and he warmly loved:
I mark'd his action, when his infant died,
And his old neighbour for offence was tried;
The still tears, stealing down that furrow'd cheek,
Spoke pity, plainer than the tongue can speak.
If pride were his, 'twas not their vulgar pride,
Who, in their base contempt, the great deride;
Nor pride in learning,—though my clerk agreed,
If fate should call him, Ashford might succeed;
Nor pride in rustic skill, although we knew
None his superior, and his equals few:—
But if that spirit in his soul had place,
It was the jealous pride that shuns disgrace;
A pride in honest fame, by virtue gain'd,

In sturdy boys to virtuous labours train'd;
Pride, in the power that guards his country's coast,
And all that Englishman enjoy and boast;
Pride, in a life that slander's tongue defied,—
In fact, a noble passion, misnamed pride.
He had no party's rage, no sect'ry's whim;
Christian and countryman was all with him:
True to his church he came; no Sunday-shower
Kept him at home in that important hour;
Nor his firm feet could one persuading sect,
By the strong glare of their new light, direct;—
'On hope, in mine own sober light, I gaze,
But should be blind and lose it, in your blaze.'
In times severe, when many a sturdy swain
Felt it his pride, his comfort, to complain;
Isaac their wants would soothe, his own would hide,
And feel in that his comfort and his pride.
At length he found, when seventy years were run,
His strength departed, and his labour done;
When he, save honest fame, retain'd no more,
But lost his wife and saw his children poor:
'Twas then, a spark of—say not discontent—
Struck on his mind, and thus he gave it vent:
'Kind are your laws, ('tis not to be denied,)
That in yon house, for ruin'd age, provide,
And they are just;—when young, we give you all,
And for assistance in our weakness call.—
Why then this proud reluctance to be fed,
To join your poor, and eat the parish-bread?
But yet I linger, loth with him to feed,
Who gains his plenty by the sons of need;
He who, by contract, all your paupers took,
And gauges stomachs with an anxious look:
On some old master I could well depend;
See him with joy and thank him as a friend;
But ill on him, who doles the day's supply,
And counts our chances, who at night may die:
Yet help me, Heav'n! and let me not complain
Of what I suffer, but my fate sustain.'
Such were his thoughts, and so resign'd he grew;
Daily he placed the workhouse in his view!

But came not there, for sudden was his fate,
He dropp'd, expiring, at his cottage-gate.
  I feel his absence in the hours of prayer,
And view his seat and sigh for Isaac there:
I see no more those white locks thinly spread
Round the bald polish of that honour'd head;
No more that awful glance on playful wight,
Compell'd to kneel and tremble at the sight,
To fold his fingers, all in dread the while,
Till Mister Ashford soften'd to a smile;
No more that meek and suppliant look in prayer,
Nor the pure faith (to give it force), are there:—
But he is bless'd, and I lament no more
A wise good man contented to be poor.
  Then died a Rambler; not the one who sails
And trucks, for female favours, beads and nails;
Not one, who posts from place to place—of men
And manners treating with a flying pen;
Not he, who climbs, for prospects, Snowden's height,
And chides the clouds that intercept the sight;
No curious shell, rare plant, or brilliant spar,
Enticed our traveller from his home so far;
But all the reason, by himself assign'd
For so much rambling, was, a restless mind;
As on, from place to place, without intent,
Without reflection, Robin Dingley went.
  Not thus by nature;—never man was found
Less prone to wander from his parish-bound:
Claudian's old Man, to whom all scenes were new,
Save those where he and where his apples grew,
Resembled Robin, who around would look,
And his horizon, for the earth's, mistook.
  To this poor swain a keen Attorney came;—
'I give thee joy, good fellow! on thy name;
The rich old Dingley's dead;—no child has he,
Nor wife, nor will; his ALL is left for thee:
To be his fortune's heir thy claim is good;
Thou hast the name, and we will prove the blood.'
  The claim was made; 'twas tried,—it would not stand;
They proved the blood, but were refused the land.
  Assured of wealth, this man of simple heart,

To every friend had predisposed a part:
His wife had hopes indulged of various kind;
The three Miss Dingleys had their school assign'd,
Masters were sought for what they each required,
And books were bought and harpsichords were hired:
So high was hope:—the failure touch'd his brain,
And Robin never was himself again;
Yet he no wrath, no angry wish express'd,
But tried, in vain, to labour or to rest;
Then cast his bundle on his back, and went
He knew not whither, nor for what intent.
Years fled;—of Robin all remembrance past,
When home he wander'd in his rags at last;
A sailor's jacket on his limbs was thrown,
A sailor's story he had made his own;
Had suffer'd battles, prisons, tempests, storms,
Encountering death in all his ugliest forms:
His cheeks were haggard, hollow was his eye,
Where madness lurk'd, conceal'd in misery;
Want, and th'ungentle world, had taught a part,
And prompted cunning to that simple heart:
'He now bethought him, he would roam no more,
But live at home and labour as before.'
Here clothed and fed, no sooner he began
To round and redden, than away he ran;
His wife was dead, their children past his aid:
So, unmolested, from his home he stray'd:
Six years elapsed, when, worn with want and pain,
Came Robin, wrapt in all his rags, again:—
We chide, we pity;—placed among our poor,
He fed again, and was a man once more.
As when a gaunt and hungry fox is found,
Entrapp'd alive in some rich hunter's ground;
Fed for the field, although each day's a feast,
Fatten you may, but never *tame* the beast;
A house protects him, savoury viands sustain;
But loose his neck and off he goes again:
So stole our vagrant from his warm retreat,
To rove a prowler and be deem'd a cheat.
Hard was his fare; for, him at length we saw,
In cart convey'd and laid supine on straw.

His feeble voice now spoke a sinking heart;
His groans now told the motions of the cart;
And when it stopp'd, he tried in vain to stand;
Closed was his eye, and clench'd his clammy hand;
Life ebb'd apace, and our best aid no more
Could his weak sense or dying heart restore:
But now he fell, a victim to the snare,
That vile attorneys for the weak prepare;—
They who, when profit or resentment call,
Heed not the groaning victim they enthrall.
  Then die lamented, in the strength of life,
A valued Mother and a faithful Wife;
Call'd not away, when time had loosed each hold
On the fond heart, and each desire grew cold;
But when, to all that knit us to our kind,
She felt fast-bound, as charity can bind;—
Not when the ills of age, its pain, its care,
The drooping spirit for its fate prepare;
And, each affection failing, leaves the heart
Loosed from life's charm and willing to depart;—
But all her ties the strong invader broke,
In all their strength, by one tremendous stroke!
Sudden and swift the eager pest came on,
And terror grew, till every hope was gone:
Still those around appear'd for hope to seek!
But view'd the sick and were afraid to speak.—
  Slowly they bore, with solemn step, the dead;
When grief grew loud and bitter tears were shed:
My part began; a crowd drew near the place,
Awe in each eye, alarm in every face:
So swift the ill, and of so fierce a kind,
That fear with pity mingled in each mind;
Friends with the husband came their griefs to blend;
For good-man Frankford was to all a friend.
The last-born boy they held above the bier,
He knew not grief, but cries express'd his fear;
Each different age and sex reveal'd its pain,
In now a louder, now a lower strain;
While the meek father, listening to their tones,
Swell'd the full cadence of the grief by groans.
  The elder sister strove her pangs to hide,

And soothing words to younger minds applied:
'Be still, be patient,' oft she strove to say;
But fail'd as oft, and weeping turn'd away.
  Curious and sad, upon the fresh-dug hill,
The village-lads stood melancholy still;
And idle children, wandering to-and-fro,
As Nature guided, took the tone of wo.
  Arrived at home, how then they gazed around,
In every place,—where she—no more, was found;—
The seat at table she was wont to fill;
The fire-side chair, still set, but vacant still;
The garden-walks, a labour all her own;
The latticed bower, with trailing shrubs o'ergrown;
The Sunday-pew she fill'd with all her race,—
Each place of hers, was now a sacred place,
That, while it call'd up sorrows in the eyes,
Pierced the full heart and forced them still to rise.
  Oh sacred sorrow! by whom souls are tried,
Sent not to punish mortals, but to guide;
If thou art mine, (and who shall proudly dare
To tell his Maker, he has had his share?)
Still let me feel for what thy pangs are sent,
And be my guide and not my punishment!
  Of Leah Cousins next the name appears,
With honours crown'd and bless'd with length of years,
Save that she lived to feel, in life's decay,
The pleasure die, the honours drop away;
A matron she, whom every village-wife
View'd as the help and guardian of her life;
Father and sons, indebted to her aid,
Respect to her and her profession paid;
Who in the house of plenty largely fed,
Yet took her station at the pauper's bed;
Nor from that duty could be bribed again,
While fear or danger urged her to remain:
In her experience all her friends relied,
Heaven was her help and nature was her guide.
  Thus Leah lived; long trusted, much caress'd,
Till a Town-Dame a youthful Farmer blessed;
A gay vain bride, who would example give
To that poor village where she deign'd to live;

Some few months past, she sent, in hour of need,
For Doctor Glibb, who came with wond'rous speed:
Two days he waited, all his art applied,
To save the mother when her infant died:—
''Twas well I came,' at last he deign'd to say;
''Twas wond'rous well;'—and proudly rode away.
  The news ran round;—'How vast the Doctor's
    pow'r!
He saved the Lady in the trying hour;
Saved her from death, when she was dead to hope,
And her fond husband had resign'd her up:
So all, like her, may evil fate defy,
If Doctor Glibb, with saving hand, be nigh.'
  Fame (now his friend), fear, novelty, and whim,
And fashion, sent the varying sex to him:
From this, contention in the village rose;
And *these* the Dame espoused; the Doctor *those:*
The wealthier part, to him and science went;
With luck and her the poor remain'd content.
  The matron sigh'd; for she was vex'd at heart,
With so much profit, so much fame, to part:
'So long successful in my art,' she cried,
'And this proud man, so young and so untried!'
  'Nay,' said the Doctor, 'dare you trust your wives,
The joy, the pride, the solace of your lives,
To one who acts and knows no reason why,
But trusts, poor hag! to luck, for an ally?—
Who, on experience, can her claims advance,
And own the powers of accident and chance?
A whining dame, who prays in danger's view,
(A proof she knows not what beside to do;)
What's her experience? In the time that's gone,
Blundering she wrought and still she blunders on:—
And what is Nature? One who acts in aid
Of gossips half asleep, and half afraid:
With such allies I scorn my fame to blend,
Skill is my luck and courage is my friend:
No slave to Nature, 'tis my chief delight
To win my way and act in her despite:—
Trust then my art, that, in itself complete,
Needs no assistance and fears no defeat.'

Warm'd by her well-spiced ale and aiding pipe,
The angry matron grew for contest ripe.
'Can you,' she said, 'ungrateful and unjust,
Before experience, ostentation trust!
What is your hazard, foolish daughters, tell?
If safe, you're certain; if secure, you're well:
That I have luck must friend and foe confess,
And what's good judgment but a lucky guess?
He boasts but what he *can* do:—will you run
From me, your friend! who, all *he* boasts, *have* done?
By proud and learned words his powers are known;
By healthy boys and handsome girls my own:
Wives! fathers! children! by my help you live;
Has this pale Doctor more than life to give?
No stunted cripple hops the village round;
Your hands are active and your heads are sound:
My lads are all your fields and flocks require;
My lasses all those sturdy lads admire.
Can this proud leech, with all his boasted skill,
Amend the soul or body, wit or will?
Does he for courts the sons of farmers frame,
Or make the daughter differ from the dame?
Or, whom he brings into this world of wo,
Prepares he them their part to undergo?
If not, this stranger from your doors repel,
And be content to *be* and to be *well*.'
She spake; but, ah! with words too strong and plain;
Her warmth offended, and her truth was vain:
The *many* left her, and the friendly *few*,
If never colder, yet they older grew;
Till, unemploy'd, she felt her spirits droop,
And took, insidious aid! th'inspiring cup;
Grew poor and peevish as her powers decay'd,
And propp'd the tottering frame with stronger aid,—
Then died!—I saw our careful swains convey,
From this our changeful world, the matron's clay,
Who to this world, at least, with equal care,
Brought them its changes, good and ill to share.
Now to his grave was Roger Cuff convey'd,
And strong resentment's lingering spirit laid.
Shipwreck'd in youth, he home return'd, and found

He was a sober and a comely youth;
He blush'd in meekness as a modest man,
And gain'd attention ere his task began;
When preaching, seldom ventured on reproof,
But touch'd his neighbours tenderly enough.
Him, in his youth, a clamorous sect assail'd,
Advised and censured, flatter'd,—and prevail'd.—
Then did he much his sober hearers vex,
Confound the simple, and the sad perplex;
To a new style his reverence rashly took;
Loud grew his voice, to threat'ning swell'd his look;
Above, below, on either side, he gazed,
Amazing all, and most himself amazed:
No more he read his preachments pure and plain,
But launch'd outright, and rose and sank again:
At times he smiled in scorn, at times he wept,
And such sad coil with words of vengeance kept,
That our best sleepers started as they slept.
'"Conviction comes like lightning," he would cry;
"In vain you seek it, and in vain you fly;
'Tis like the rushing of the mighty wind,
Unseen its progress, but its power you find;
It strikes the child ere yet its reason wakes;
His reason fled, the ancient sire it shakes;
The proud, learn'd man, and him who loves to know
How and from whence these gusts of grace will blow,
It shuns,—but sinners in their way impedes,
And sots and harlots visits in their deeds:
Of faith and penance it supplies the place;
Assures the vilest that they live by grace,
And, without running, makes them win the race."
'Such was the doctrine our young prophet taught;
And here conviction, there confusion wrought;
When his thin cheek assumed a deadly hue,
And all the rose to one small spot withdrew:
They call'd it hectic; 'twas a fiery flush,
More fix'd and deeper than the maiden blush;
His paler lips the pearly teeth disclosed,
And lab'ring lungs the length'ning speech opposed.
No more his span-girth shanks and quiv'ring thighs
Upheld a body of the smaller size;

But down he sank upon his dying bed,
And gloomy crotchets fill'd his wandering head.—
'"Spite of my faith, all-saving faith," he cried,
I fear of worldly works the wicked pride;
Poor as I am, degraded, abject, blind,
The good I've wrought still rankles in my mind;
My alms-deeds all, and every deed I've done,
My moral-rags defile me every one;
It should not be:—what say'st thou? tell me, Ralph."
Quoth I, "Your reverence, I believe, you're safe;
Your faith's your prop, nor have you pass'd such time
In life's good-works as swell them to a crime.
If I of pardon for my sins were sure,
About my goodness I would rest secure."
'Such was his end; and mine approaches fast;
I've seen my best of preachers,—and my last.'—
He bow'd, and archly smiled at what he said,
Civil but sly:—'And is old Dibble dead?'
Yes! he is gone: and WE are going all;
Like flowers we wither, and like leaves we fall;—
Here, with an infant, joyful sponsors come,
Then bear the new-made Christian to its home;
A few short years and we behold him stand,
To ask a blessing, with his bride in hand:
A few, still seeming shorter, and we hear
His widow weeping at her husband's bier:—
Thus, as the months succeed, shall infants take
Their names; thus parents shall the child forsake;
Thus brides again and bridegrooms blithe shall kneel,
By love or law compell'd their vows to seal,
Ere I again, or one like me, explore
These simple annals of the Village Poor.

THE BOROUGH

1. GENERAL DESCRIPTION

'Describe the Borough'—though our idle tribe
May love description, can we so describe,
That you shall fairly streets and buildings trace,
And all that gives distinction to a place?
This cannot be; yet, moved by your request,
A part I paint—let fancy form the rest.
Cities and towns, the various haunts of men,
Require the pencil; they defy the pen:
Could he, who sang so well the Grecian fleet,
So well have sung of alley, lane or street?
Can measured lines these various buildings show,
The Town-Hall Turning, or the Prospect Row?
Can I the seats of wealth and want explore,
And lengthen out my lays from door to door?
Then let thy fancy aid me—I repair
From this tall mansion of our last-year's mayor,
Till we the outskirts of the Borough reach,
And these half-buried buildings next the beach;
Where hang at open doors the net and cork,
While squalid sea-dames mend the meshy work;
Till comes the hour, when fishing through the tide,
The weary husband throws his freight aside;
A living mass, which now demands the wife,
Th' alternate labours of their humble life.
Can scenes like these withdraw thee from thy wood,
Thy upland forest or thy valley's flood?
Seek then thy garden's shrubby bound, and look,
As it steals by, upon the bordering brook;
That winding streamlet, limpid, lingering, slow,
Where the reeds whisper when the zephyrs blow;
Where in the midst, upon her throne of green,
Sits the large lily as the water's queen;
And makes the current, forced awhile to stay,
Murmur and bubble as it shoots away;
Draw then the strongest contrast to that stream,
And our broad river will before thee seem.

With ceaseless motion comes and goes the tide,
Flowing, it fills the channel vast and wide;
Then back to sea, with strong majestic sweep
It rolls, in ebb yet terrible and deep;
Here sampire-banks and salt-wort bound the flood,
There stakes and sea-weeds withering on the mud;
And higher up, a ridge of all things base,
Which some strong tide has roll'd upon the place.
Thy gentle river boasts its pigmy boat,
Urged on by pains, half grounded, half afloat;
While at her stern an angler takes his stand,
And marks the fish he purposes to land;
From that clear space, where, in the cheerful ray
Of the warm sun, the scaly people play.
Far other craft our prouder river shows,
Hoys, pinks and sloops; brigs, brigantines and snows;
Nor angler we on our wide stream descry,
But one poor dredger where his oysters lie;
He, cold and wet, and driving with the tide,
Beats his weak arms against his tarry side,
Then drains the remnant of diluted gin,
To aid the warmth that languishes within;
Renewing oft his poor attempts to beat
His tingling fingers into gathering heat.
He shall again be seen when evening comes,
And social parties crowd their favourite rooms:
Where on the table pipes and papers lie,
The steaming bowl or foaming tankard by;
'Tis then, with all these comforts spread around,
They hear the painful dredger's welcome sound;
And few themselves the savoury boon deny,
The food that feeds, the living luxury.
Yon is our quay! those smaller hoys from town,
Its various wares, for country-use, bring down;
Those laden waggons, in return, impart
The country-produce to the city mart;
Hark! to the clamour in that miry road,
Bounded and narrow'd by yon vessels' load;
The lumbering wealth she empties round the place,
Package, and parcel, hogshead, chest, and case:

While the loud seaman and the angry hind,
Mingling in business, bellow to the wind.
  Near these a crew amphibious, in the docks,
Rear, for the sea, those castles on the stocks:
See! the long keel, which soon the waves must hide;
See! the strong ribs which form the roomy side;
Bolts yielding slowly to the sturdiest stroke,
And planks which curve and crackle in the smoke.
Around the whole rise cloudy wreaths, and far
Bear the warm pungence of o'er-boiling tar.
  Dabbling on shore half-naked sea-boys crowd,
Swim round a ship, or swing upon the shroud;
Or in a boat purloin'd, with paddles play,
And grow familiar with the watery way:
Young though they be, they feel whose sons they are,
They know what British seamen do and dare;
Proud of that fame, they raise and they enjoy
The rustic wonder of the village-boy.
  Before you bid these busy scenes adieu,
Behold the wealth that lies in public view,
Those far-extended heaps of coal and coke,
Where fresh-fill'd lime-kilns breathe their stifling smoke.
This shall pass off, and you behold, instead,
The night-fire gleaming on its chalky bed;
When from the light-house brighter beams will rise,
To show the shipman where the shallow lies.
  Thy walks are ever pleasant; every scene
Is rich in beauty, lively, or serene——
Rich—is that varied view with woods around,
Seen from the seat, within the shrubb'ry bound;
Where shines the distant lake, and where appear
From ruins bolting, unmolested deer;
Lively—the village-green, the inn, the place,
Where the good widow schools her infant race.
Shops, whence are heard the hammer and the saw,
And village-pleasures unreproved by law;
Then how serene! when in your favourite room,
Gales from your jasmine soothe the evening gloom;
When from your upland paddock you look down,
And just perceive the smoke which hides the town;
When weary peasants at the close of day

Walk to their cots, and part upon the way;
When cattle slowly cross the shallow brook,
And shepherds pen their folds, and rest upon their crook.
We prune our hedges, prime our slender trees,
And nothing looks untutor'd and at ease;
On the wide heath, or in the flow'ry vale,
We scent the vapours of the sea-born gale;
Broad-beaten paths lead on from stile to stile,
And sewers from streets, the road-side banks defile;
Our guarded fields a sense of danger show,
Where garden-crops with corn and clover grow;
Fences are form'd of wreck and placed around,
(With tenters tipp'd) a strong repulsive bound;
Wide and deep ditches by the gardens run,
And there in ambush lie the trap and gun;
Or yon broad board, which guards each tempting prize,
'Like a tall bully, lifts its head and lies.'
There stands a cottage with an open door,
Its garden undefended blooms before:
Her wheel is still, and overturn'd her stool,
While the lone widow seeks the neighb'ring pool:
This gives us hope, all views of town to shun—
No! here are tokens of the sailor-son;
That old blue jacket, and that shirt of check,
And silken kerchief for the seaman's neck;
Sea-spoils and shells from many a distant shore,
And furry robe from frozen Labrador.
Our busy streets and sylvan-walks between,
Fen, marshes, bog and heath all intervene;
Here pits of crag, with spongy, plashy base,
To some enrich th'uncultivated space:
For there are blossoms rare, and curious rush,
The gale's rich balm, and sun-dew's crimson blush,
Whose velvet leaf with radiant beauty dress'd,
Forms a gay pillow for the plover's breast.
Not distant far, a house commodious made,
Lonely yet public stands for Sunday-trade;
Thither, for this day free, gay parties go,
Their tea-house walk, their tippling rendezvous;
There humble couples sit in corner-bowers,
Or gaily ramble for th'allotted hours;

Sailors and lasses from the town attend,
The servant-lover, the apprentice-friend;
With all the idle social tribes who seek,
And find their humble pleasures once a week.
  Turn to the watery world!—but who to thee
(A wonder yet unview'd) shall paint—the sea?
Various and vast, sublime in all its forms,
When lull'd by zephyrs, or when roused by storms,
Its colours changing, when from clouds and sun
Shades after shades upon the surface run;
Embrown'd and horrid now, and now serene,
In limpid blue, and evanescent green;
And oft the foggy banks on ocean lie,
Lift the fair sail, and cheat th'experienced eye.
  Be it the summer-noon: a sandy space
The ebbing tide has left upon its place;
Then just the hot and stony beach above,
Light twinkling streams in bright confusion move;
(For heated thus, the warmer air ascends,
And with the cooler in its fall contends)—
Then the broad bosom of the ocean keeps
An equal motion; swelling as it sleeps,
Then slowly sinking; curling to the strand,
Faint, lazy waves o'ercreep the ridgy sand,
Or tap the tarry boat with gentle blow,
And back return in silence, smooth and slow.
Ships in the calm seem anchor'd; for they glide
On the still sea, urged solely by the tide;
Art thou not present, this calm scene before,
Where all beside is pebbly length of shore,
And far as eye can reach, it can discern no more?
  Yet sometimes comes a ruffling cloud to make
The quiet surface of the ocean shake;
As an awaken'd giant with a frown
Might show his wrath, and then to sleep sink down.
  View now the winter-storm! above, one cloud,
Black and unbroken, all the skies o'ershroud;
Th' unwieldy porpoise through the day before
Had roll'd in view of boding men on shore;
And sometimes hid and sometimes show'd his form,
Dark as the cloud, and furious as the storm.

All where the eye delights, yet dreads to roam,
The breaking billows cast the flying foam
Upon the billows rising—all the deep
Is restless change; the waves so swell'd and steep,
Breaking and sinking, and the sunken swells,
Nor one, one moment, in its station dwells:
But nearer land you may the billows trace,
As if contending in their watery chase;
May watch the mightiest till the shoal they reach,
Then break and hurry to their utmost stretch;
Curl'd as they come, they strike with furious force,
And then re-flowing, take their grating course,
Raking the rounded flints, which ages past
Roll'd by their rage, and shall to ages last.
Far off the petrel in the troubled way
Swims with her brood, or flutters in the spray;
She rises often, often drops again,
And sports at ease on the tempestuous main.
High o'er the restless deep, above the reach
Of gunner's hope, vast flights of wild-ducks stretch;
Far as the eye can glance on either side,
In a broad space and level line they glide;
All in their wedge-like figures from the north,
Day after day, flight after flight, go forth.
In-shore their passage tribes of sea-gulls urge,
And drop for prey within the sweeping surge;
Oft in the rough opposing blast they fly
Far back, then turn, and all their force apply,
While to the storm they give their weak complaining cry;
Or clap the sleek white pinion to the breast,
And in the restless ocean dip for rest.
Darkness begins to reign; the louder wind
Appals the weak and awes the firmer mind;
But frights not him, whom evening and the spray
In part conceal—yon prowler on his way:
Lo! he has something seen; he runs apace,
As if he fear'd companion in the chase;
He sees his prize, and now he turns again,
Slowly and sorrowing—'Was your search in vain?'
Gruffly he answers, ''Tis a sorry sight!
A seaman's body: there'll be more to-night!'

1. General Description

Hark! to those sounds! they're from distress at sea:
How quick they come! What terrors may there be!
Yes, 'tis a driven vessel: I discern
Lights, signs of terror, gleaming from the stern;
Others behold them too, and from the town
In various parties seamen hurry down;
Their wives pursue, and damsels urged by dread,
Lest men so dear be into danger led;
Their head the gown has hooded, and their call
In this sad night is piercing like the squall;
They feel their kinds of power, and when they meet,
Chide, fondle, weep, dare, threaten, or entreat.
See one poor girl, all terror and alarm,
Has fondly seized upon her lover's arm;
'Thou shalt not venture;' and he answers 'No!
I will not'—still she cries, 'Thou shalt not go.'
No need of this; not here the stoutest boat
Can through such breakers, o'er such billows float;
Yet may they view these lights upon the beach,
Which yield them hope, whom help can never reach.
From parted clouds the moon her radiance throws
On the wild waves, and all the danger shows;
But shows them beaming in her shining vest,
Terrific splendour! gloom in glory dress'd!
This for a moment, and then clouds again
Hide every beam, and fear and darkness reign.
But hear we now those sounds? Do lights appear?
I see them not! the storm alone I hear:
And lo! the sailors homeward take their way;
Man must endure—let us submit and pray.
Such are our winter-views; but night comes on—
Now business sleeps, and daily cares are gone;
Now parties form, and some their friends assist
To waste the idle hours at sober whist;
The tavern's pleasure or the concert's charm
Unnumber'd moments of their sting disarm;
Play-bills and open doors a crowd invite,
To pass off one dread portion of the night;
And show and song and luxury combined,
Lift off from man this burthen of mankind.
Others advent'rous walk abroad and meet

Returning parties pacing through the street;
When various voices, in the dying day,
Hum in our walks, and greet us in our way;
When tavern-lights flit on from room to room,
And guide the tippling sailor staggering home:
There as we pass, the jingling bells betray
How business rises with the closing day:
Now walking silent, by the river's side,
The ear perceives the rippling of the tide;
Or measured cadence of the lads who tow
Some enter'd hoy, to fix her in her row;
Or hollow sound, which from the parish-bell
To some departed spirit bids farewell!
  Thus shall you something of our Borough know,
Far as a verse, with Fancy's aid, can show;
Of sea or river, of a quay or street,
The best description must be incomplete;
But when a happier theme succeeds, and when
Men are our subjects and the deeds of men;
Then may we find the Muse in happier style,
And we may sometimes sigh and sometimes smile.

3. THE VICAR—THE CURATE, &C.

Where ends our chancel in a vaulted space,
Sleep the departed vicars of the place;
Of most, all mention, memory, thought are past—
But take a slight memorial of the last.
  To what famed college we our Vicar owe,
To what fair county, let historians show:
Few now remember when the mild young man,
Ruddy and fair, his Sunday-task began;
Few live to speak of that soft soothing look
He cast around, as he prepared his book;
It was a kind of supplicating smile,
But nothing hopeless of applause, the while;
And when he finish'd, his corrected pride
Felt the desert, and yet the praise denied.
Thus he his race began, and to the end
His constant care was, no man to offend;

No haughty virtues stirr'd his peaceful mind,
Nor urged the priest to leave the flock behind;
He was his Master's soldier, but not one
To lead an army of his martyrs on:
Fear was his ruling passion; yet was love,
Of timid kind, once known his heart to move;
It led his patient spirit where it paid
Its languid offerings to a listening maid;
She, with her widow'd mother, heard him speak,
And sought awhile to find what he would seek:
Smiling he came, he smiled when he withdrew,
And paid the same attention to the two;
Meeting and parting without joy or pain,
He seem'd to come that he might go again.
The wondering girl, no prude, but something nice,
At length was chill'd by his unmelting ice;
She found her tortoise held such sluggish pace,
That she must turn and meet him in the chase:
This not approving, she withdrew till one
Came who appear'd with livelier hope to run;
Who sought a readier way the heart to move,
Than by faint dalliance of unfixing love.
   Accuse me not that I approving paint
Impatient hope or love without restraint;
Or think the passions, a tumultuous throng,
Strong as they are, ungovernably strong:
But is the laurel to the soldier due,
Who cautious comes not into danger's view?
What worth has virtue by desire untried,
When Nature's self enlists on duty's side?
   The married dame in vain assail'd the truth
And guarded bosom of the Hebrew-youth;
But with the daughter of the Priest of On
The love was lawful, and the guard was gone;
But Joseph's fame had lessen'd in our view,
Had he, refusing, fled the maiden too.
   Yet our good priest to Joseph's praise aspired,
As once rejecting what his heart desired;
'I am escaped,' he said, when none pursued;
When none attack'd him, 'I am unsubdued;'
'Oh pleasing pangs of love,' he sang again,

Cold to the joy, and stranger to the pain.
Ev'n in his age would he address the young,
'I too have felt these fires, and they are strong;'
But from the time he left his favourite maid,
To ancient females his devoirs were paid;
And still they miss him after morning prayer;
Nor yet successor fills the Vicar's chair,
Where kindred spirits in his praise agree,
A happy few, as mild and cool as he;
The easy followers in the female train,
Led without love, and captives without chain.
  Ye lilies male! think (as your tea you sip,
While the town small-talk flows from lip to lip;
Intrigues half-gather'd, conversation-scraps,
Kitchen-cabals, and nursery-mishaps,)
If the vast world may not some scene produce,
Some state where your small talents might have use;
Within seraglios you might harmless move,
'Mid ranks of beauty, and in haunts of love;
There from too daring man the treasures guard,
An easy duty, and its own reward;
Nature's soft substitutes, you there might save
From crime the tyrant, and from wrong the slave.
  But let applause be dealt in all we may,
Our priest was cheerful, and in season gay;
His frequent visits seldom fail'd to please;
Easy himself, he sought his neighbour's ease:
To a small garden with delight he came,
And gave successive flowers a summer's fame;
These he presented with a grace his own
To his fair friends, and made their beauties known,
Not without moral compliment; how they
'Like flowers were sweet, and must like flowers decay.'
  Simple he was, and loved the simple truth,
Yet had some useful cunning from his youth;
A cunning never to dishonour lent,
And rather for defence than conquest meant;
'Twas fear of power, with some desire to rise,
But not enough to make him enemies;
He ever aim'd to please; and to offend
Was ever cautious; for he sought a friend;

Yet for the friendship never much would pay,
Content to bow, be silent, and obey,
And by a soothing suff'rance find his way.
  Fiddling and fishing were his arts: at times
He alter'd sermons, and he aim'd at rhymes;
And his fair friends, not yet intent on cards,
Oft he amused with riddles and charades.
  Mild were his doctrines, and not one discourse
But gain'd in softness what it lost in force:
Kind his opinions; he would not receive
An ill report, nor evil act believe;
'If true, 'twas wrong; but blemish great or small
Have all mankind; yea, sinners are we all.'
  If ever fretful thought disturb'd his breast,
If aught of gloom that cheerful mind oppress'd,
It sprang from innovation; it was then
He spake of mischief made by restless men;
Not by new doctrines: never in his life
Would he attend to controversial strife;
For sects he cared not; 'They are not of us,
Nor need we, brethren, their concerns discuss;
But 'tis the change, the schism at home I feel;
Ills few perceive, and none have skill to heal:
Not at the altar our young brethren read
(Facing their flock) the decalogue and creed;
But at their duty, in their desks they stand,
With naked surplice, lacking hood and band:
Churches are now of holy song bereft,
And half our ancient customs changed or left;
Few sprigs of ivy are at Christmas seen,
Nor crimson berry tips the holly's green;
Mistaken choirs refuse the solemn strain
Of ancient Sternhold, which from ours amain
Comes flying forth from aile to aile about
Sweet links of harmony and long drawn out.'
  These were to him essentials; all things new
He deem'd superfluous, useless, or untrue;
To all beside indifferent, easy, cold,
Here the fire kindled, and the wo was told.
  Habit with him was all the test of truth,
'It must be right: I've done it from my youth.'

Questions he answer'd in as brief a way,
'It must be wrong—it was of yesterday.'
Though mild benevolence our priest possess'd,
'Twas but by wishes or by words express'd:
Circles in water, as they wider flow,
The less conspicuous in their progress grow;
And when at last they touch upon the shore,
Distinction ceases, and they're view'd no more.
His love, like that last circle, all embraced,
But with effect that never could be traced.
Now rests our Vicar. They who knew him best,
Proclaim his life t'have been entirely rest;
Free from all evils which disturb his mind,
Whom studies vex and controversies blind.
The rich approved,—of them in awe he stood;
The poor admired,—they all believed him good;
The old and serious of his habits spoke;
The frank and youthful loved his pleasant joke;
Mothers approved a safe contented guest,
And daughters one who back'd each small request:
In him his flock found nothing to condemn;
Him sectaries liked,—he never troubled them;
No trifles fail'd his yielding mind to please,
And all his passions sunk in early ease;
Nor one so old has left this world of sin,
More like the being that he enter'd in.

* * *

THE CURATE

Ask you what lands our pastor tithes?—Alas!
But few our acres, and but short our grass:
In some fat pastures of the rich, indeed,
May roll the single cow or favourite steed;
Who, stable-fed, is here for pleasure seen,
His sleek sides bathing in the dewy green:
But these, our hilly heath and common wide
Yield a slight portion for the parish-guide;
No crops luxuriant in our borders stand,
For here we plough the ocean, not the land;
Still reason wills that we our pastor pay,

And custom does it on a certain day:
Much is the duty, small the legal due,
And this with grateful minds we keep in view;
Each makes his off'ring, some by habit led,
Some by the thought, that all men must be fed;
Duty and love, and piety and pride,
Have each their force, and for the priest provide.
  Not thus our Curate, one whom all believe
Pious and just, and for whose fate they grieve;
All see him poor, but ev'n the vulgar know
He merits love, and their respect bestow.
A man so learn'd you shall but seldom see,
Nor one so honour'd, so aggrieved as he;—
Not grieved by years alone; though his appear
Dark and more dark; severer on severe:
Not in his need,—and yet we all must grant
How painful 'tis for feeling age to want:
Nor in his body's sufferings; yet we know
Where time has plough'd, there misery loves to sow;
But in the wearied mind, that all in vain
Wars with distress, and struggles with its pain.
  His father saw his powers—'I'll give,' quoth he,
'My first-born learning; 'twill a portion be:'
Unhappy gift! a portion for a son!
But all he had:—he learn'd, and was undone!
  Better, apprenticed to an humble trade,
Had he the cassock for the priesthood made,
Or thrown the shuttle, or the saddle shaped,
And all these pangs of feeling souls escaped.
  He once had hope—hope ardent, lively, light;
His feelings pleasant, and his prospects bright:
Eager of fame, he read, he thought, he wrote,
Weigh'd the Greek page, and added note on note;
At morn, at evening at his work was he,
And dream'd what his Euripides would be.
  Then care began;—he loved, he woo'd, he wed;
Hope cheer'd him still, and Hymen bless'd his bed—
A Curate's bed! then came the woful years;
The husband's terrors, and the father's tears;
A wife grown feeble, mourning, pining, vex'd,
With wants and woes—by daily cares perplex'd;

No more a help, a smiling, soothing aid,
But boding, drooping, sickly, and afraid.
  A kind physician, and without a fee,
Gave his opinion—'Send her to the sea.'
'Alas!' the good man answer'd, 'can I send
A friendless woman? Can I find a friend?
No; I must with her, in her need, repair
To that new place; the poor lie every where;—
Some priest will pay me for my pious pains:'—
He said, he came, and here he yet remains.
  Behold his dwelling; this poor hut he hires,
Where he from view, though not from want, retires;
Where four fair daughters, and five sorrowing sons,
Partake his sufferings, and dismiss his duns;
All join their efforts, and in patience learn
To want the comforts they aspire to earn;
For the sick mother something they'd obtain,
To soothe her grief and mitigate her pain;
For the sad father something they'd procure,
To ease the burthen they themselves endure.
  Virtues like these at once delight and press
On the fond father with a proud distress;
On all around he looks with care and love,
Grieved to behold, but happy to approve.
  Then from his care, his love, his grief he steals,
And by himself an author's pleasure feels;
Each line detains him; he omits not one,
And all the sorrows of his state are gone.—
Alas! ev'n then, in that delicious hour,
He feels his fortune, and laments its power.
  Some tradesman's bill his wandering eyes engage,
Some scrawl for payment thrust 'twixt page and page;
Some bold, loud rapping at his humble door,
Some surly message he has heard before,
Awake, alarm, and tell him he is poor.
  An angry dealer, vulgar, rich, and proud,
Thinks of his bill, and passing, raps aloud;
The elder daughter meekly makes him way—
'I want my money, and I cannot stay:
My mill is stopp'd; what, Miss! I cannot grind;
Go tell your father he must raise the wind:'

Still trembling, troubled, the dejected maid
Says, 'Sir! my father!—' and then stops afraid:
Ev'n his hard heart is soften'd, and he hears
Her voice with pity; he respects her tears;
His stubborn features half admit a smile,
And his tone softens—'Well! I'll wait awhile.'
Pity! a man so good, so mild, so meek,
At such an age, should have his bread to seek;
And all those rude and fierce attacks to dread,
That are more harrowing than the want of bread;
Ah! who shall whisper to that misery peace!
And say that want and insolence shall cease?
'But why not publish?'—those who know too well,
Dealers in Greek, are fearful 'twill not sell;
Then he himself is timid, troubled, slow,
Nor like his labours nor his griefs to show;
The hope of fame may in his heart have place,
But he has dread and horror of disgrace;
Nor has he that confiding, easy way,
That might his learning and himself display;
But to his work he from the world retreats,
And frets and glories o'er the favourite sheets.
But see! the man himself; and sure I trace
Signs of new joy exulting in that face
O'er care that sleeps—we err, or we discern
Life in thy looks—the reason may we learn?
'Yes,' he replied, 'I'm happy, I confess,
To learn that some are pleased with happiness
Which others feel—there are who now combine
The worthiest natures in the best design,
To aid the letter'd poor, and soothe such ills as mine:
We who more keenly feel the world's contempt,
And from its miseries are the least exempt;
Now hope shall whisper to the wounded breast,
And grief, in soothing expectation, rest.
'Yes, I am taught that men who think, who feel,
Unite the pains of thoughtful men to heal;
Not with disdainful pride, whose bounties make
The needy curse the benefits they take;
Not with the idle vanity that knows
Only a selfish joy when it bestows;

Not with o'erbearing wealth, that, in disdain,
Hurls the superfluous bliss at groaning pain;
But these are men who yield such bless'd relief,
That with the grievance they destroy the grief;
Their timely aid the needy sufferers find,
Their generous manner soothes the suffering mind;
Theirs is a gracious bounty, form'd to raise
Him whom it aids; their charity is praise;
A common bounty may relieve distress,
But whom the vulgar succour, they oppress;
This though a favour, is an honour too,
Though mercy's duty, yet 'tis merit's due;
When our relief from such resources rise,
All painful sense of obligation dies;
And grateful feelings in the bosom wake,
For 'tis their offerings, not their alms, we take.
'Long may these founts of charity remain,
And never shrink, but to be fill'd again;
True! to the author they are now confined,
To him who gave the treasure of his mind,
His time, his health, and thankless found mankind:
But there is hope that from these founts may flow
A sideway stream, and equal good bestow;
Good that may reach us, whom the day's distress
Keeps from the fame and perils of the press;
Whom study beckons from the ills of life,
And they from study; melancholy strife!
Who then can say, but bounty now so free,
And so diffused, may find its way to me?
'Yes! I may see my decent table yet
Cheer'd with the meal that adds not to my debt;
May talk of those to whom so much we owe,
And guess their names whom yet we may not know;
Bless'd we shall say are those who thus can give,
And next who thus upon the bounty live;
Then shall I close with thanks my humble meal,
And feel so well—Oh! God! how I shall feel!'

10. CLUBS AND SOCIAL MEETINGS

You say you envy in your calm retreat
Our social meetings;—'tis with joy we meet:
In these our parties you are pleased to find
Good sense and wit, with intercourse of mind;
Composed of men, who read, reflect, and write,
Who, when they meet, must yield and share delight:
To you our Book-club has peculiar charm,
For which you sicken in your quiet farm;
Here you suppose us at our leisure placed,
Enjoying freedom, and displaying taste;
With wisdom cheerful, temperately gay,
Pleased to enjoy, and willing to display.
  If thus your envy gives your ease its gloom,
Give wings to fancy, and among us come.
We're now assembled; you may soon attend—
I'll introduce you—'Gentlemen, my friend.'
  'Now are you happy? you have pass'd a night
In gay discourse, and rational delight.'
  'Alas! not so: for how can mortals think,
Or thoughts exchange, if thus they eat and drink?
No! I confess, when we had fairly dined,
That was no time for intercourse of mind;
There was each dish prepared with skill t'invite,
And to detain the struggling appetite;
On such occasions minds with one consent
Are to the comforts of the body lent;
There was no pause—the wine went quickly round,
Till struggling Fancy was by Bacchus bound;
Wine is to wit as water thrown on fire,
By duly sprinkling both are raised the higher;
Thus largely dealt, the vivid blaze they choke,
And all the genial flame goes off in smoke.'
  'But when no more your boards these loads contain,
When wine no more o'erwhelms the labouring brain,
But serves, a gentle stimulus; we know
How wit must sparkle, and how fancy flow.'
  It might be so, but no such club-days come;
We always find these dampers in the room:
If to converse were all that brought us here,

A few odd members would in turn appear;
Who dwelling nigh, would saunter in and out,
O'erlook the list, and toss the books about;
Or yawning read them, walking up and down,
Just as the loungers in the shops in town;
Till fancying nothing would their minds amuse,
They'd push them by, and go in search of news.
But our attractions are a stronger sort,
The earliest dainties and the oldest port;
All enter then with glee in every look,
And not a member thinks about a book.
Still let me own, there are some vacant hours,
When minds might work, and men exert their powers:
Ere wine to folly spurs the giddy guest,
But gives to wit its vigour and its zest;
Then might we reason, might in turn display
Our several talents, and be wisely gay;
We might—but who a tame discourse regards,
When whist is named, and we behold the cards?
We from that time are neither grave nor gay;
Our thought, our care, our business is to play:
Fix'd on these spots and figures, each attends
Much to his partners, nothing to his friends.
Our public cares, the long, the warm debate,
That kept our patriots from their beds so late;
War, peace, invasion, all we hope or dread,
Vanish like dreams when men forsake their bed;
And groaning nations and contending kings
Are all forgotten for these painted things;
Paper and paste, vile figures and poor spots,
Level all minds, philosophers and sots;
And give an equal spirit, pause, and force,
Join'd with peculiar diction, to discourse:
'Who deals?—you led—we're three by cards—had you
Honour in hand?'—'Upon my honour, two.'
Hour after hour, men thus contending sit,
Grave without sense, and pointed without wit.
Thus it appears these envied clubs possess
No certain means of social happiness;
Yet there's a good that flows from scenes like these—
Man meets with man at leisure and at ease;

10. Clubs and Social Meetings

We to our neighbours and our equals come,
And rub off pride that man contracts at home;
For there, admitted master, he is prone
To claim attention and to talk alone:
But here he meets with neither son nor spouse;
No humble cousin to his bidding bows;
To his raised voice his neighbours' voices rise,
To his high look as lofty look replies;
When much he speaks, he finds that ears are closed,
And certain signs inform him when he's prosed;
Here all the value of a listener know,
And claim, in turn, the favour they bestow.
  No pleasure gives the speech, when all would speak,
And all in vain a civil hearer seek.
To chance alone we owe the free discourse,
In vain you purpose what you cannot force;
'Tis when the favourite themes unbidden spring,
That fancy soars with such unwearied wing;
Then may you call in aid the moderate glass,
But let it slowly and unprompted pass;
So shall there all things for the end unite,
And give that hour of rational delight.
  Men to their clubs repair, themselves to please,
To care for nothing, and to take their ease;
In fact, for play, for wine, for news they come:
Discourse is shared with friends or found at home.

* * *

  But cards with books are incidental things;
We've nights devoted to these queens and kings:
Then if we choose the social game, we may;
Now 'tis a duty, and we're bound to play;
Nor ever meeting of the social kind
Was more engaging, yet had less of mind.
  Our eager parties, when the lunar light
Throws its full radiance on the festive night,
Of either sex, with punctual hurry come,
And fill, with one accord, an ample room;
Pleased, the fresh packs on cloth of green they see,
And seizing, handle with preluding glee;
They draw, they sit, they shuffle, cut and deal;
Like friends assembled, but like foes to feel:

But yet not all,—a happier few have joys
Of mere amusement, and their cards are toys;
No skill nor art, nor fretful hopes have they,
But while their friends are gaming, laugh and play.
  Others there are, the veterans of the game,
Who owe their pleasure to their envied fame;
Through many a year, with hard-contested strife,
Have they attain'd this glory of their life:
Such is that ancient burgess, whom in vain
Would gout and fever on his couch detain;
And that large lady, who resolves to come,
Though a first fit has warn'd her of her doom!
These are as oracles: in every cause
They settle doubts, and their decrees are laws;
But all are troubled, when, with dubious look,
Diana questions what Apollo spoke.
  Here avarice first, the keen desire of gain,
Rules in each heart, and works in every brain;
Alike the veteran-dames and virgins feel,
Nor care what gray-boards or what striplings deal;
Sex, age, and station, vanish from their view,
And gold, their sov'reign good, the mingled crowd
    pursue.
  Hence they are jealous, and as rivals, keep
A watchful eye on the beloved heap;
Meantime discretion bids the tongue be still,
And mild good-humour strives with strong ill-will;
Till prudence fails; when, all impatient grown,
They make their grief, by their suspicions, known.
  'Sir, I protest, were Job himself at play,
He'd rave to see you throw your cards away;
Not that I care a button—not a pin
For what I lose; but we had cards to win:
A saint in heaven would grieve to see such hand
Cut up by one who will not understand.'
  'Complain of me! and so you might indeed,
If I had ventured on that foolish lead,
That fatal heart—but I forgot your play—
Some folk have ever thrown their hearts away.'
  'Yes, and their diamonds; I have heard of one
Who made a beggar of an only son.'

'Better a beggar, than to see him tied
To art and spite, to insolence and pride.'
'Sir, were I you, I'd strive to be polite,
Against my nature, for a single night.'
'So did you strive, and, madam! with success;
I knew no being we could censure less!'
Is this too much? alas! my peaceful muse
Cannot with half their virulence abuse.
And hark! at other tables discord reigns,
With feign'd contempt for losses and for gains;
Passions awhile are bridled; then they rage,
In waspish youth, and in resentful age;
With scraps of insult—'Sir, when next you play,
Reflect whose money 'tis you throw away.
No one on earth can less such things regard,
But when one's partner doesn't know a card—'
'I scorn suspicion, ma'am, but while you stand
Behind that lady, pray keep down your hand.'
'Good heav'n, revoke! remember, if the set
Be lost, in honour you should pay the debt.'
'There, there's your money; but, while I have life,
I'll never more sit down with man and wife;
They snap and snarl indeed, but in the heat
Of all their spleen, their understandings meet;
They are Freemasons, and have many a sign,
That we, poor devils! never can divine:
May it be told, do ye divide th'amount,
Or goes it all to family account?'

* * *

Next is the club, where to their friends in town
Our country neighbours once a month come down;
We term it Free-and-easy, and yet we
Find it no easy matter to be free:
Ev'n in our small assembly, friends among,
Are minds perverse, there's something will be wrong;
Men are not equal; some will claim a right
To be the kings and heroes of the night;
Will their own favourite themes and notions start,
And you must hear, offend them, or depart.
There comes Sir Thomas from his village-seat,
Happy, he tells us, all his friends to meet;

He brings the ruin'd brother of his wife,
Whom he supports, and makes him sick of life;
A ready witness whom he can produce
Of all his deeds—a butt for his abuse;
Soon as he enters, has the guests espied,
Drawn to the fire, and to the glass applied—
'Well, what's the subject?—what are you about?
The news, I take it—come, I'll help you out;'—
And then, without one answer, he bestows
Freely upon us all he hears and knows;
Gives us opinions, tells us how he votes,
Recites the speeches, adds to them his notes,
And gives old ill-told tales for new-born anecdotes;
Yet cares he nothing what we judge or think,
Our only duty's to attend and drink:
At length, admonish'd by his gout, he ends
The various speech, and leaves at peace his friends;
But now, alas! we've lost the pleasant hour,
And wisdom flies from wine's superior power.
Wine, like the rising sun, possession gains,
And drives the mist of dulness from the brains;
The gloomy vapour from the spirit flies,
And views of gaiety and gladness rise:
Still it proceeds; till from the glowing heat,
The prudent calmly to their shades retreat;—
Then is the mind o'ercast—in wordy rage
And loud contention angry men engage;
Then spleen and pique, like fire-works thrown in spite,
To mischief turn the pleasures of the night;
Anger abuses, Malice loudly rails,
Revenge awakes, and Anarchy prevails:
Till wine, that raised the tempest, makes it cease,
And maudlin Love insists on instant peace;
He noisy mirth and roaring song commands,
Gives idle toasts, and joins unfriendly hands;
Till fuddled Friendship vows esteem and weeps,
And jovial Folly drinks and sings and sleeps.

* * *

A club there is of Smokers—Dare you come
To that close, clouded, hot, narcotic room?
When, midnight past, the very candles seem

Dying for air, and give a ghastly gleam;
When curling fumes in lazy wreaths arise,
And prosing topers rub their winking eyes;
When the long tale, renew'd when last they met,
Is spliced anew, and is unfinish'd yet;
When but a few are left the house to tire,
And they half-sleeping by the sleepy fire;
Ev'n the poor ventilating vane, that flew
Of late so fast, is now grown drowsy too;
When sweet, cold, clammy punch its aid bestows,
Then thus the midnight conversation flows:—
'Then, as I said, and—mind me—as I say,
At our last meeting—you remember'—'Ay;'
'Well, very well—then freely as I drink
I spoke my thought—you take me—what I think:
And sir, said I, if I a freeman be,
It is my bounden duty to be free.'
'Ay, there you posed him: I respect the chair,
But man is man, although the man's a mayor:
If Muggins live—no, no!—if Muggins die,
He'll quit his office—neighbour, shall I try?'
'I'll speak my mind, for here are none but friends:
They're all contending for their private ends;
No public spirit—once a vote would bring,
I say a vote—was then a pretty thing;
It made a man to serve his country and his king:
But for that place, that Muggins must resign,
You've my advice—'tis no affair of mine.'

*   *   *

The poor man has his club; he comes and spends
His hoarded pittance with his chosen friends;
Nor this alone,—a monthly dole he pays,
To be assisted when his health decays;
Some part his prudence, from the day's supply,
For cares and troubles in his age, lays by;
The printed rules he guards with painted frame,
And shows his children where to read his name:
Those simple words his honest nature move,
That bond of union tied by laws of love;
This is his pride, it gives to his employ
New value, to his home another joy;

While a religious hope its balm applies
For all his fate inflicts and all his state denies.
  Much would it please you, sometimes to explore
The peaceful dwellings of our borough poor;
To view a sailor just return'd from sea,
His wife beside; a child on either knee,
And others crowding near, that none may lose
The smallest portion of the welcome news;
What dangers pass'd, 'when seas ran mountains high,
When tempests raved, and horrors veil'd the sky;
When prudence fail'd, when courage grew dismay'd,
When the strong fainted, and the wicked pray'd,—
Then in the yawning gulf far down we drove,
And gazed upon the billowy mount above;
Till up that mountain, swinging with the gale,
We view'd the horrors of the watery vale.'
  The trembling children look with stedfast eyes,
And panting, sob involuntary sighs:
Soft sleep awhile his torpid touch delays,
And all is joy and piety and praise.

* * *

  Masons are ours, Freemasons—but, alas!
To their own bards I leave the mystic class;
In vain shall one, and not a gifted man,
Attempt to sing of this enlighten'd clan:
I know no word, boast no directing sign,
And not one token of the race is mine;
Whether with Hiram, that wise widow's son,
They came from Tyre to royal Solomon,
Two pillars raising by their skill profound,
Boaz and Jachin through the East renown'd:
Whether the sacred books their rise express,
Or books profane, 'tis vain for me to guess;
It may be, lost in date remote and high,
They know not what their own antiquity:
It may be too, derived from cause so low,
They have no wish their origin to show:
If, as crusaders, they combined to wrest
From heathen lords the land they long possess'd;
Or were at first some harmless club, who made
Their idle meetings solemn by parade;

Is but conjecture—for the task unfit,
Awe-struck and mute, the puzzling theme I quit:
Yet, if such blessings from their order flow,
We should be glad their moral code to know;
Trowels of silver are but simple things,
And aprons worthless as their apron-strings;
But if indeed you have the skill to teach
A social spirit, now beyond our reach;
If man's warm passions you can guide and bind,
And plant the virtues in the wayward mind;
If you can wake to christian-love the heart,—
In mercy, something of your powers impart.
But as it seems, we Masons must become
To know the secret, and must then be dumb;
And as we venture for uncertain gains,
Perhaps the profit is not worth the pains.
When Bruce, that dauntless traveller, thought he stood
On Nile's first rise! the fountain of the flood,
And drank exulting in the sacred spring,
The critics told him it was no such thing;
That springs unnumber'd round the country ran,
But none could show him where they first began:
So might we feel, should we our time bestow,
To gain these secrets and these signs to know;
Might question still if all the truth we found,
And firmly stood upon the certain ground;
We might our title to the mystery dread,
And fear we drank not at the river-head.

* * *

Griggs and Gregorians here their meetings hold,
Convivial sects, and Bucks alert and bold;
A kind of Masons, but without their sign;
The bonds of union—pleasure, song, and wine:
Man, a gregarious creature, loves to fly
Where he the trackings of the herd can spy;
Still to be one with many he desires,
Although it leads him through the thorns and briers.
A few! but few there are, who in the mind
Perpetual source of consolation find;
The weaker many to the world will come,
For comforts seldom to be found from home.

When the faint hands no more a brimmer hold,
When flannel-wreaths the useless limbs infold,
The breath impeded, and the bosom cold;
When half the pillow'd man the palsy chains,
And the blood falters in the bloated veins,—
Then, as our friends no further aid supply
Than hope's cold phrase and courtesy's soft sigh,
We should that comfort for ourselves ensure,
Which friends could not, if we could friends, procure.
Early in life, when we can laugh aloud,
There's something pleasant in a social crowd,
Who laugh with us—but will such joy remain,
When we lie struggling on the bed of pain?
When our physician tells us with a sigh,
No more on hope and science to rely,
Life's staff is useless then; with labouring breath
We pray for hope divine—the staff of death—
This is a scene which few companions grace,
And where the heart's first favourites yield their place.
Here all the aid of man to man must end,
Here mounts the soul to her eternal Friend;
The tenderest love must here its tie resign,
And give th'aspiring heart to love divine.
Men feel their weakness, and to numbers run,
Themselves to strengthen, or themselves to shun;
But though to this our weakness may be prone,
Let's learn to live, for we must die, alone.

11. INNS

Much do I need, and therefore will I ask,
A Muse to aid me in my present task;
For then with special cause we beg for aid,
When of our subject we are most afraid:
Inns are this subject—'tis an ill-drawn lot,
So, thou who gravely triflest, fail me not.
Fail not, but haste, and to my memory bring
Scenes yet unsung, which few would choose to sing:
Thou mad'st a Shilling splendid; thou hast thrown
On humble themes the graces all thine own;
By thee the Mistress of a village school

Became a queen, enthroned upon her stool;
And far beyond the rest thou gav'st to shine
Belinda's Lock—that deathless work was thine.
  Come, lend thy cheerful light, and give to please,
These seats of revelry, these scenes of ease;
Who sings of Inns much danger has to dread,
And needs assistance from the fountain-head.
  High in the street, o'erlooking all the place,
The rampant Lion shows his kingly face;
His ample jaws extend from side to side,
His eyes are glaring, and his nostrils wide;
In silver shag the sovereign form is dress'd,
A mane horrific sweeps his ample chest;
Elate with pride, he seems t'assert his reign,
And stands the glory of his wide domain.
  Yet nothing dreadful to his friends the sight,
But sign and pledge of welcome and delight:
To him the noblest guest the town detains
Flies for repast, and in his court remains;
Him too the crowd with longing looks admire,
Sigh for his joys, and modestly retire;
Here not a comfort shall to them be lost
Who never ask or never feel the cost.
  The ample yards on either side contain
Buildings where order and distinction reign;—
The splendid carriage of the wealthier guest,
The ready chaise and driver smartly dress'd;
Whiskeys and gigs and curricles are there,
And high-fed prancers many a raw-boned pair.
On all without a lordly host sustains
The care of empire, and observant reigns;
The parting guest beholds him at his side,
With pomp obsequious, bending in his pride;
Round all the place his eyes all objects meet,
Attentive, silent, civil, and discreet.
O'er all within the lady-hostess rules,
Her bar she governs, and her kitchen schools;
To every guest th'appropriate speech is made,
And every duty with distinction paid;
Respectful, easy, pleasant, or polite—
'Your honour's servant—Mister Smith, good night.'

Next, but not near, yet honour'd through the town,
There swing, incongruous pair! the Bear and Crown;
That Crown suspended gems and ribands deck,
A golden chain hangs o'er that furry neck:
Unlike the nobler beast, the Bear is bound,
And with the Crown so near him, scowls uncrown'd;
Less his dominion, but alert are all
Without, within, and ready for the call;
Smart lads and light run nimbly here and there,
Nor for neglected duties mourns the Bear.
To his retreats, on the election-day,
The losing party found their silent way;
There they partook of each consoling good,
Like him uncrown'd, like him in sullen mood—
Threat'ning, but bound.—Here meet a social kind,
Our various clubs for various cause combined;
Nor has he pride, but thankful takes as gain
The dew-drops shaken from the Lion's mane:
A thriving couple here their skill display,
And share the profits of no vulgar sway.
Third in our Borough's list appears the sign
Of a fair queen—the gracious Caroline;
But in decay—each feature in the face
Has stain of Time, and token of disgrace.
The storm of winter, and the summer-sun,
Have on that form their equal mischief done;
The features now are all disfigured seen,
And not one charm adorns th'insulted queen:
To this poor face was never paint applied,
Th'unseemly work of cruel Time to hide;
Here we may rightly such neglect upbraid,
Paint on such faces is by prudence laid.
Large the domain, but all within combine
To correspond with the dishonour'd sign;
And all around dilapidates; you call—
But none replies—they're inattentive all:
At length a ruin'd stable holds your steed,
While you through large and dirty rooms proceed,
Spacious and cold; a proof they once had been
In honour—now magnificently mean;
Till in some small half-furnish'd room you rest,

Whose dying fire denotes it had a guest.
In those you pass'd where former splendour reign'd,
You saw the carpets torn, the paper stain'd;
Squares of discordant glass in windows fix'd,
And paper oil'd in many a space betwixt;
A soil'd and broken sconce, a mirror crack'd,
With table underpropp'd, and chairs new-back'd;
A marble side-slab with ten thousand stains,
And all an ancient tavern's poor remains.
With much entreaty, they your food prepare,
And acid wine afford, with meagre fare;
Heartless you sup; and when a dozen times
You've read the fractured window's senseless rhymes;
Have been assured that Phœbe Green was fair,
And Peter Jackson took his supper there;
You reach a chilling chamber, where you dread
Damps, hot or cold, from a tremendous bed;
Late comes your sleep, and you are waken'd soon
By rustling tatters of the old festoon.
O'er this large building, thus by time defaced,
A servile couple has its owner placed,
Who not unmindful that its style is large,
To lost magnificence adapt their charge:
Thus an old beauty, who has long declined,
Keeps former dues and dignity in mind;
And wills that all attention should be paid
For graces vanish'd and for charms decay'd.
Few years have pass'd, since brightly 'cross the way,
Lights from each window shot the lengthen'd ray,
And busy looks in every face were seen,
Through the warm precincts of the reigning Queen:
There fires inviting blazed, and all around
Was heard the tinkling bells' seducing sound;
The nimble waiters to that sound from far
Sprang to the call, then hasten'd to the bar;
Where a glad priestess of the temple sway'd,
The most obedient, and the most obey'd;
Rosy and round, adorn'd in crimson vest,
And flaming ribands at her ample breast:—
She, skill'd like Circe, tried her guests to move,
With looks of welcome and with words of love;

And such her potent charms, that men unwise
Were soon transform'd and fitted for the sties.
  Her port in bottles stood, a well-stain'd row,
Drawn for the evening from the pipe below;
Three powerful spirits fill'd a parted case,
Some cordial bottles stood in secret place;
Fair acid fruits in nets above were seen,
Her plate was splendid, and her glasses clean;
Basins and bowls were ready on the stand,
And measures clatter'd in her powerful hand.
  Inferior houses now our notice claim,
But who shall deal them their appropriate fame?
Who shall the nice, yet known distinction, tell,
Between the peal complete and single bell?
  Determine, ye, who on your shining nags
Wear oil-skin beavers, and bear seal-skin bags;
Or ye, grave topers, who with coy delight
Snugly enjoy the sweetness of the night;
Ye travellers all, superior inns denied
By moderate purse, the low by decent pride;
Come and determine,—will ye take your place
At the *full* orb, or *half* the lunar face?
With the Black-Boy or Angel will ye dine?
Will ye approve the Fountain or the Vine?
Horses the *white* or *black* will ye prefer?
The Silver-Swan, or swan opposed to her—
Rare bird! whose form the raven-plumage decks,
And graceful curve her three alluring necks?
  All these a decent entertainment give,
And by their comforts comfortably live.
  Shall I pass by the Boar?—there are who cry,
'Beware the Boar,' and pass determined by:
Those dreadful tusks, those little peering eyes
And churning chaps, are tokens to the wise.
There dwells a kind old aunt, and there you see
Some kind young nieces in her company;
Poor village nieces, whom the tender dame
Invites to town, and gives their beauty fame;
The grateful sisters feel th'important aid,
And the good aunt is flatter'd and repaid.
  What though it may some cool observers strike,

That such fair sisters should be so unlike;
That still another and another comes,
And at the matron's table smiles and blooms;
That all appear as if they meant to stay
Time undefined, nor name a parting day;
And yet, though all are valued, all are dear,
Causeless, they go, and seldom more appear:
  Yet let Suspicion hide her odious head,
And Scandal vengeance from a burgess dread:
A pious friend, who with the ancient dame
At sober cribbage takes an evening game;
His cup beside him, through their play he quaffs,
And oft renews, and innocently laughs;
Or growing serious, to the text resorts,
And from the Sunday-sermon makes reports;
While all, with grateful glee, his wish attend,
A grave protector and a powerful friend:
But Slander says, who indistinctly sees,
Once he was caught with Silvia on his knees;—
A cautious burgess with a careful wife
To be so caught!—'tis false, upon my life.
  Next are a lower kind, yet not so low
But they, among them, their distinctions know;
And when a thriving landlord aims so high
As to exchange the Chequer for the Pye,
Or from Duke William to the Dog repairs,
He takes a finer coat and fiercer airs.
  Pleased with his power, the poor man loves to say
What favourite inn shall share his evening's pay;
Where he shall sit the social hour, and lose
His past day's labours and his next day's views.
Our seamen too have choice: one takes a trip
In the warm cabin of his favourite ship:
And on the morrow in the humbler boat
He rows, till fancy feels herself afloat;
Can he the sign—Three Jolly Sailors pass,
Who hears a fiddle and who sees a lass?
The Anchor too affords the seaman joys,
In small smoked room, all clamour, crowd and noise;
Where a curved settle half surrounds the fire,
Where fifty voices purl and punch require:

They come for pleasure in their leisure hour,
And they enjoy it to their utmost power;
Standing they drink, they swearing smoke, while all
Call or make ready for a second call:
There is no time for trifling—'Do ye see?
We drink and drub the French extempore.'
  See! round the room, on every beam and balk,
Are mingled scrolls of hieroglyphic chalk;
Yet nothing heeded—would one stroke suffice
To blot out all, here honour is too nice,—
'Let knavish landsmen think such dirty things,
We're British tars, and British tars are kings.'
  But the Green-Man shall I pass by unsung,
Which mine own James upon his sign-post hung?
His sign, his image,—for he once was seen
A squire's attendant, clad in keeper's green;
Ere yet with wages more, and honour less,
He stood behind me in a graver dress.
  James in an evil hour went forth to woo
Young Juliet Hart, and was her Romeo:
They'd seen the play, and thought it vastly sweet
For two young lovers by the moon to meet;
The nymph was gentle, of her favours free,
Ev'n at a word—no Rosalind was she;
Nor, like that other Juliet, tried his truth
With—'Be thy purpose marriage, gentle youth?'
But him received, and heard his tender tale
When sang the lark, and when the nightingale:
So in a few months the generous lass was seen
I' the way that all the Capulets had been.
  Then first repentance seized the amorous man,
And—shame on love—he reason'd and he ran;
The thoughtful Romeo trembled for his purse,
And the sad sounds, 'for better and for worse.'
  Yet could the lover not so far withdraw,
But he was haunted both by love and law:
Now law dismay'd him as he view'd its fangs,
Now pity seized him for his Juliet's pangs;
Then thoughts of justice and some dread of jail,
Where all would blame him and where none
    might bail;

These drew him back, till Juliet's hut appear'd,
Where love had drawn him when he should have fear'd.
   There sat the father in his wicker throne,
Uttering his curses in tremendous tone;
With foulest names his daughter he reviled,
And look'd a very Herod at the child:
Nor was she patient, but with equal scorn,
Bade him remember when his Joe was born:
Then rose the mother, eager to begin
Her plea for frailty, when the swain came in.
   To him she turn'd, and other theme began,
Show'd him his boy, and bade him be a man;
'An honest man, who, when he breaks the laws,
Will make a woman honest if there's cause.'
With lengthen'd speech she proved what came to pass
Was no reflection on a loving lass:
'If she your love as wife and mother claim,
What can it matter which was first the name?
But 'tis most base, 'tis perjury and theft,
When a lost girl is like a widow left;
The rogue who ruins'—here the father found
His spouse was treading on forbidden ground.
   'That's not the point,' quoth he,—'I don't suppose
My good friend Fletcher to be one of those;
What's done amiss he'll mend in proper time—
I hate to hear of villainy and crime:
'Twas my misfortune, in the days of youth,
To find two lasses pleading for my truth;
The case was hard, I would with all my soul
Have wedded both, but law is our control;
So one I took, and when we gain'd a home,
Her friend agreed—what could she more?—to come;
And when she found that I'd a widow'd bed,
Me she desired—what could I less?—to wed.
An easier case is yours: you've not the smart
That two fond pleaders cause in one man's heart;
You've not to wait from year to year distress'd,
Before your conscience can be laid at rest;
There smiles your bride, there sprawls your
      new-born son,
—A ring, a licence, and the thing is done.'

'My loving James,'—the lass began her plea,
'I'll make thy reason take a part with me:
Had I been froward, skittish, or unkind,
Or to thy person or thy passion blind;
Had I refused, when 'twas thy part to pray,
Or put thee off with promise and delay;
Thou might'st in justice and in conscience fly,
Denying her who taught thee to deny:
But, James, with me thou hadst an easier task,
Bonds and conditions I forbore to ask;
I laid no traps for thee, no plots or plans,
Nor marriage named by licence or by banns;
Nor would I now the parson's aid employ,
But for this cause,'—and up she held her boy.
Motives like these could heart of flesh resist?
James took the infant and in triumph kiss'd;
Then to his mother's arms the child restored,
Made his proud speech, and pledged his worthy word.
'Three times at church our banns shall publish'd be,
Thy health be drank in bumpers three times three;
And thou shalt grace (bedeck'd in garments gay)
The christening dinner on the wedding day.'
James at my door then made his parting bow,
Took the Green-Man, and is a master now.

13. THE ALMS-HOUSE AND TRUSTEES

Leave now our streets, and in yon plain behold
Those pleasant seats for the reduced and old;
A merchant's gift, whose wife and children died,
When he to saving all his powers applied;
He wore his coat till bare was every thread,
And with the meanest fare his body fed.
He had a female cousin, who with care
Walk'd in his steps and learn'd of him to spare;
With emulation and success they strove,
Improving still, still seeking to improve,
As if that useful knowledge they would gain—
How little food would human life sustain:
No pauper came their table's crums to crave;
Scraping they lived, but not a scrap they gave:

When beggars saw the frugal merchant pass,
It moved their pity, and they said, 'Alas!
Hard is thy fate, my brother,' and they felt
A beggar's pride as they that pity dealt:
The dogs, who learn of man to scorn the poor,
Bark'd him away from ev'ry decent door;
While they who saw him bare, but thought him rich,
To show respect or scorn, they knew not which.
But while our merchant seem'd so base and mean,
He had his wanderings, sometimes, 'not unseen;'
To give in secret was a favourite act,
Yet more than once they took him in the fact:
To scenes of various wo he nightly went,
And serious sums in healing misery spent;
Oft has he cheer'd the wretched, at a rate
For which he daily might have dined on plate;
He has been seen—his hair all silver-white,
Shaking and shining—as he stole by night,
To feed unenvied on his still delight.
A two-fold taste he had; to give and spare,
Both were his duties, and had equal care;
It was his joy, to sit alone and fast,
Then send a widow and her boys repast:
Tears in his eyes would, spite of him, appear,
But he from other eyes has kept the tear:
All in a wint'ry night from far he came,
To soothe the sorrows of a suff'ring dame;
Whose husband robb'd him, and to whom he meant
A ling'ring, but reforming punishment:
Home then he walk'd, and found his anger rise,
When fire and rush-light met his troubled eyes;
But these extinguish'd, and his prayer address'd
To Heaven in hope, he calmly sank to rest.
His seventieth year was pass'd, and then was seen
A building rising on the northern green;
There was no blinding all his neighbours' eyes,
Or surely no one would have seen it rise:
Twelve rooms contiguous stood, and six were near,
There men were placed, and sober matrons here;
There were behind small useful gardens made,
Benches before, and trees to give them shade;

In the first room were seen, above, below,
Some marks of taste, a few attempts at show;
The founder's picture and his arms were there,
(Not till he left us,) and an elbow chair;
There, 'mid these signs of his superior place,
Sat the mild ruler of this humble race.
Within the row are men who strove in vain,
Through years of trouble, wealth and ease to gain;
Less must they have than an appointed sum,
And freemen been, or hither must not come;
They should be decent and command respect
(Though needing fortune,) whom these doors protect,
And should for thirty dismal years have tried
For peace unfelt and competence denied.
Strange! that o'er men thus train'd in sorrow's school,
Power must be held, and they must live by rule;
Infirm, corrected by misfortunes, old,
Their habits settled and their passions cold;
Of health, wealth, power, and worldly cares, bereft,
Still must they not at liberty be left;
There must be one to rule them, to restrain
And guide the movements of his erring train.
If then control imperious, check severe,
Be needed where such reverend men appear;
To what would youth, without such checks, aspire,
Free the wild wish, uncurb'd the strong desire?
And where (in college or in camp) they found
The heart ungovern'd and the hand unbound?
His house endow'd, the generous man resign'd
All power to rule, nay power of choice declined;
He and the female saint survived to view
Their work complete, and bade the world adieu!
Six are the guardians of this happy seat,
And one presides when they on business meet;
As each expires, the five a brother choose;
Nor would Sir Denys Brand the charge refuse;
True, 'twas beneath him, 'but to do men good
Was motive never by his heart withstood;'
He too is gone, and they again must strive
To find a man in whom his gifts survive.
Now, in the various records of the dead,

Thy worth, Sir Denys, shall be weigh'd and read;
There we the glory of thy house shall trace,
With each alliance of thy noble race.
   Yes! here we have him!—'Came in William's reign,
The Norman-Brand; the blood without a stain;
From the fierce Dane and ruder Saxon clear,
Pict, Irish, Scot, or Cambrian mountaineer;
But the pure Norman was the sacred spring,
And he, Sir Denys, was in heart a king:
Erect in person and so firm in soul,
Fortune he seem'd to govern and control;
Generous as he who gives his all away,
Prudent as one who toils for weekly pay;
In him all merits were decreed to meet,
Sincere though cautious, frank and yet discreet,
Just all his dealings, faithful every word,
His passions' master, and his temper's lord.'
   Yet more, kind dealers in decaying fame?
His magnanimity you next proclaim;
You give him learning, join'd with sound good sense,
And match his wealth with his benevolence;
What hides the multitude of sins, you add,
Yet seem to doubt if sins he ever had.
   Poor honest Truth! thou writ'st of living men,
And art a railer and detractor then;
They die, again to be described, and now
A foe to merit and mankind art thou!
   Why banish truth? it injures not the dead,
It aids not them with flattery to be fed;
And when mankind such perfect pictures view,
They copy less, the more they think them true.
Let us a mortal as he was behold,
And see the dross adhering to the gold;
When we the errors of the virtuous state,
Then erring men their worth may emulate.
   View then this picture of a noble mind,
Let him be wise, magnanimous, and kind;
What was the wisdom? Was it not the frown
That keeps all question, all inquiry down?
His words were powerful and decisive all,
But his slow reasons came for no man's call.

''Tis thus,' he cried, no doubt with kind intent,
To give results and spare all argument:—
'Let it be spared—all men at least agree
Sir Denys Brand had magnanimity:
His were no vulgar charities; none saw
Him like the merchant to the hut withdraw;
He left to meaner minds the simple deed,
By which the houseless rest, the hungry feed;
His was a public bounty vast and grand,
'Twas not in him to work with viewless hand;
He raised the room that towers above the street,
A public room where grateful parties meet;
He first the life-boat plann'd; to him the place
Is deep in debt—'twas he revived the race;
To every public act this hearty friend
Would give with freedom or with frankness lend;
His money built the jail, nor prisoner yet
Sits at his ease, but he must feel the debt;
To these let candour add his vast display,
Around his mansion all is grand and gay,
And this is bounty with the name of pay.'
I grant the whole, nor from one deed retract,
But wish recorded too the private act;
All these were great, but still our hearts approve
Those simpler tokens of the christian love;
'Twould give me joy some gracious deed to meet,
That has not call'd for glory, through the street:
Who felt for many, could not always shun,
In some soft moment, to be kind to one;
And yet they tell us, when Sir Denys died,
That not a widow in the Borough sigh'd;
Great were his gifts, his mighty heart I own,
But why describe what all the world has known?
The rest is petty pride, the useless art
Of a vain mind to hide a swelling heart:
Small was his private room; men found him there
By a plain table, on a paltry chair;
A wretched floor-cloth, and some prints around,
The easy purchase of a single pound:
These humble trifles and that study small
Make a strong contrast with the servants' hall;

There barely comfort, here a proud excess,
The pompous seat of pamper'd idleness,
Where the sleek rogues with one consent declare,
They would not live upon his honour's fare;
He daily took but one half-hour to dine,
On one poor dish and some three sips of wine;
Then he'd abuse them for their sumptuous feasts,
And say, 'My friends! you make yourselves like beasts;
One dish suffices any man to dine,
But you are greedy as a herd of swine;
Learn to be temperate.'—Had they dared t'obey,
He would have praised and turn'd them all away.
  Friends met Sir Denys riding in his ground,
And there the meekness of his spirit found:
For that grey coat, not new for many a year,
Hides all that would like decent dress appear;
An old brown pony 'twas his will to ride,
Who shuffled onward, and from side to side;
A five-pound purchase, but so fat and sleek,
His very plenty made the creature weak.
  'Sir Denys Brand! and on so poor a steed!'
'Poor! it may be—such things I never heed:'
And who that youth behind, of pleasant mien,
Equipp'd as one who wishes to be seen,
Upon a horse, twice victor for a plate,
A noble hunter, bought at dearest rate?—
Him the lad fearing, yet resolved to guide,
He curbs his spirit, while he strokes his pride.
  'A handsome youth, Sir Denys; and a horse
Of finer figure never trod the course,—
Yours without question?'—'Yes! I think a groom
Bought me the beast; I cannot say the sum:
I ride him not, it is a foolish pride
Men have in cattle—but my people ride;
The boy is—hark ye, sirrah! what's your name?
Ay, Jacob, yes! I recollect—the same;
As I bethink me now, a tenant's son—
I think a tenant—is your father one?'
  There was an idle boy who ran about,
And found his master's humble spirit out;
  He would at awful distance snatch a look,

Then run away and hide him in some nook;
'For oh!' quoth he, 'I dare not fix my sight
On him, his grandeur puts me in a fright;
Oh! Mister Jacob, when you wait on him,
Do you not quake and tremble every limb?'
  The steward soon had orders—'Summers, see
That Sam be clothed, and let him wait on me.'
  Sir Denys died, bequeathing all affairs
In trust to Laughton's long experienced cares;
Before a guardian, and Sir Denys dead,
All rule and power devolved upon his head:
Numbers are call'd to govern, but in fact
Only the powerful and assuming act.
  Laughton, too wise to be a dupe to fame,
Cared not a whit of what descent he came,
Till he was rich; he then conceived the thought
To fish for pedigree, but never caught:
All his desire, when he was young and poor,
Was to advance; he never cared for more:
'Let me buy, sell, be factor, take a wife,
Take any road to get along in life.'
  Was he a miser then? a robber? foe
To those who trusted? a deceiver?—No!
He was ambitious; all his powers of mind
Were to one end controll'd, improved, combined;
Wit, learning, judgment, were, by his account,
Steps for the ladder he design'd to mount:
Such step was money: wealth was but his slave,
For power he gain'd it, and for power he gave;
Full well the Borough knows that he'd the art
Of bringing money to the surest mart;
Friends too were aids, they led to certain ends,
Increase of power and claim on other friends.
A favourite step was marriage: then he gain'd
Seat in our hall, and o'er his party reign'd;
Houses and lands he bought, and long'd to buy,
But never drew the springs of purchase dry,
And thus at last they answer'd every call,
The failing found him ready for their fall:
He walks along the street, the mart, the quay,
And looks and mutters, 'This belongs to me.'

His passions all partook the general bent;
Interest inform'd him when he should resent,
How long resist, and on what terms relent:
In points where he determined to succeed,
In vain might reason or compassion plead;
But gain'd his point, he was the best of men,
'Twas loss of time to be vexatious then:
Hence he was mild to all men whom he led,
Of all who dared resist the scourge and dread.
Falsehood in him was not the useless lie
Of boasting pride or laughing vanity;
It was the gainful, the persuading art,
That made its way, and won the doubting heart,
Which argued, soften'd, humbled, and prevail'd;
Nor was it tried till ev'ry truth had fail'd;
No sage on earth could more than he despise
Degrading, poor, unprofitable lies.
Though fond of gain, and grieved by wanton waste,
To social parties he had no distaste;
With one presiding purpose in his view,
He sometimes could descend to trifle too!
Yet, in these moments, he had still the art
To ope the looks and close the guarded heart;
And, like the public host, has sometimes made
A grand repast, for which the guests have paid.
At length, with power endued and wealthy grown,
Frailties and passions, long suppress'd, were shown;
Then to provoke him was a dangerous thing,
His pride would punish, and his temper sting;
His powerful hatred sought th'avenging hour,
And his proud vengeance struck with all his power,
Save when th' offender took a prudent way
The rising storm of fury to allay:
This might he do, and so in safety sleep,
By largely casting to the angry deep;
Or, better yet (its swelling force t'assuage,)
By pouring oil of flattery on its rage.
And now, of all the heart approved, possess'd,
Fear'd, favour'd, follow'd, dreaded, and caress'd,
He gently yields to one mellifluous joy,
The only sweet that is not found to cloy,

Bland adulation! other pleasures pall
On the sick taste, and transient are they all;
But this one sweet has such enchanting power,
The more we take, the faster we devour;
Nauseous to those who must the dose apply,
And most disgusting to the standers-by;
Yet in all companies will Laughton feed,
Nor care how grossly men perform the deed.
As gapes the nursling, or, what comes more near,
Some Friendly-island chief, for hourly cheer;
When wives and slaves, attending round his seat,
Prepare by turns the masticated meat:
So for this master, husband, parent, friend,
His ready slaves their various efforts blend,
And, to their lord still eagerly inclined,
Pour the crude trash of a dependent mind.
But let the muse assign the man his due:
Worth he possess'd, nor were his virtues few;—
He sometimes help'd the injured in their cause;
His power and purse have back'd the failing laws
He for religion has a due respect,
And all his serious notions are correct;
Although he pray'd and languish'd for a son,
He grew resign'd when Heaven denied him one;
He never to this quiet mansion sends
Subject unfit, in compliment to friends:
Not so Sir Denys, who would yet protest
He always chose the worthiest and the best;
Not men in trade by various loss brought down,
But those whose glory once amazed the town,
Who their last guinea in their pleasures spent,
Yet never fell so low as to repent;
To these his pity he could largely deal,
Wealth they had known, and therefore want could feel.
Three seats were vacant while Sir Denys reign'd,
And three such favourites their admission gain'd;
These let us view, still more to understand
The moral feelings of Sir Denys Brand.

14. INHABITANTS OF THE ALMS-HOUSE

BLANEY

Observe that tall pale veteran! what a look
Of shame and guilt! who cannot read that book?
Misery and mirth are blended in his face,
Much innate vileness and some outward grace;
There wishes strong and stronger griefs are seen,
Looks ever changed, and never one serene:
Show not that manner, and these features all,
The serpent's cunning and the sinner's fall?
  Hark to that laughter!—'tis the way he takes
To force applause for each vile jest he makes;
Such is yon man, by partial favour sent
To these calm seats to ponder and repent.
  Blaney, a wealthy heir at twenty-one,
At twenty-five was ruin'd and undone:
These years with grievous crimes we need not load,
He found his ruin in the common road;—
Gamed without skill, without inquiry bought,
Lent without love, and borrow'd without thought.
But, gay and handsome, he had soon the dower
Of a kind wealthy widow in his power:
Then he aspired to loftier flights of vice,
To singing harlots of enormous price:
He took a jockey in his gig to buy
A horse so valued, that a duke was shy:
To gain the plaudits of the knowing few,
Gamblers and grooms, what would not Blaney do?
His dearest friend, at that improving age,
Was Hounslow Dick, who drove the western stage.
  Cruel he was not—If he left his wife,
He left her to her own pursuits in life;
Deaf to reports, to all expenses blind,
Profuse, not just, and careless, but not kind.
  Yet thus assisted, ten long winters pass'd
In wasting guineas ere he saw his last;
Then he began to reason, and to feel
He could not dig, nor had he learn'd to steal;
And should he beg as long as he might live,

He justly fear'd that nobody would give:
But he could charge a pistol, and at will,
All that was mortal, by a bullet kill:
And he was taught, by those whom he would call
Man's surest guides—that he was mortal all.
  While thus he thought, still waiting for the day,
When he should dare to blow his brains away,
A place for him a kind relation found,
Where England's monarch ruled, but far from English
    ground;
He gave employ that might for bread suffice,
Correct his habits and restrain his vice.
  Here Blaney tried (what such man's miseries teach)
To find what pleasures were within his reach;
These he enjoy'd, though not in just the style
He once possess'd them in his native isle;
Congenial souls he found in every place,
Vice in all soils, and charms in every race:
His lady took the same amusing way,
And laugh'd at Time till he had turn'd them grey:
At length for England once again they steer'd,
By ancient views and new designs endear'd;
His kindred died, and Blaney now became
An heir to one who never heard his name.
  What could he now?—The man had tried before
The joys of youth, and they were joys no more;
To vicious pleasures he was still inclined,
But vice must now be season'd and refined;
Then as a swine he would on pleasure seize,
Now common pleasures had no power to please:
Beauty alone has for the vulgar charms,
He wanted beauty trembling with alarms:
His was no more a youthful dream of joy,
The wretch desired to ruin and destroy;
He bought indulgence with a boundless price,
Most pleased when decency bow'd down to vice,
When a fair dame her husband's honour sold,
And a frail countess play'd for Blaney's gold.
  'But did not conscience in her anger rise?'
Yes! and he learn'd her terrors to despise;
When stung by thought, to soothing books he fled,

And grew composed and harden'd as he read;
Tales of Voltaire, and essays gay and slight,
Pleased him and shone with their phosphoric light;
Which, though it rose from objects vile and base,
Where'er it came threw splendour on the place,
And was that light which the deluded youth,
And this grey sinner, deem'd the light of truth.
He different works for different cause admired,
Some fix'd his judgment, some his passions fired;
To cheer the mind and raise a dormant flame,
He had the books, decreed to lasting shame,
Which those who read are careful not to name:
These won to vicious act the yielding heart,
And then the cooler reasoners soothed the smart.
He heard of Blount, and Mandeville, and Chubb,
How they the doctors of their day would drub;
How Hume had dwelt on miracles so well,
That none would now believe a miracle;
And though he cared not works so grave to read,
He caught their faith and sign'd the sinner's creed.
Thus was he pleased to join the laughing side,
Nor ceased the laughter when his lady died;
Yet was he kind and careful of her fame,
And on her tomb inscribed a virtuous name;
'A tender wife, respected, and so forth,'—
The marble still bears witness to the worth.
He has some children, but he knows not where;
Something they cost, but neither love nor care;
A father's feelings he has never known,
His joys, his sorrows, have been all his own.
He now would build—and lofty seat he built,
And sought, in various ways, relief from guilt.
Restless, for ever anxious to obtain
Ease for the heart by ramblings of the brain,
He would have pictures, and of course a taste,
And found a thousand means his wealth to waste.
Newmarket steeds he bought at mighty cost;
They sometimes won, but Blaney always lost.
Quick came his ruin, came when he had still
For life a relish, and in pleasure skill:
By his own idle reckoning he supposed

His wealth would last him till his life was closed;
But no! he found his final hoard was spent,
While he had years to suffer and repent.
Yet at the last, his noble mind to show,
And in his misery how he bore the blow,
He view'd his only guinea, then suppress'd,
For a short time, the tumults in his breast,
And, moved by pride, by habit and despair,
Gave it an opera-bird to hum an air.
  Come ye! who live for pleasure, come, behold
A man of pleasure when he's poor and old;
When he looks back through life, and cannot find
A single action to relieve his mind;
When he looks forward, striving still to keep
A steady prospect of eternal sleep;
When not one friend is left, of all the train
Whom 'twas his pride and boast to entertain,—
Friends now employ'd from house to house to run
And say, 'Alas! poor Blaney is undone!'—
Those whom he shook with ardour by the hand,
By whom he stood as long as he could stand,
Who seem'd to him from all deception clear,
And who, more strange! might think themselves sincere.
  Lo! now the hero shuffling through the town,
To hunt a dinner and to beg a crown;
To tell an idle tale, that boys may smile;
To bear a strumpet's billet-doux a mile;
To cull a wanton for a youth of wealth,
(With reverent view to both his taste and health);
To be a useful, needy thing between
Fear and desire—the pander and the screen;
To flatter pictures, houses, horses, dress,
The wildest fashion or the worst excess;
To be the grey seducer, and entice
Unbearded folly into acts of vice;
And then, to level every fence which law
And virtue fix to keep the mind in awe,
He first inveigles youth to walk astray,
Next prompts and soothes them in their fatal way,
Then vindicates the deed, and makes the mind his prey.
  Unhappy man! what pains he takes to state—

(Proof of his fear!) that all below is fate;
That all proceed in one appointed track,
Where none can stop, or take their journey back:
Then what is vice or virtue?—Yet he'll rail
At priests till memory and quotation fail;
He reads, to learn the various ills they've done,
And calls them vipers, every mother's son.
He is the harlot's aid, who wheedling tries
To move her friend for vanity's supplies;
To weak indulgence he allures the mind,
Loth to be duped, but willing to be kind;
And if successful—what the labour pays?
He gets the friend's contempt and Chloe's praise,
Who, in her triumph, condescends to say,
'What a good creature Blaney was to-day!'
Hear the poor dæmon when the young attend,
And willing ear to vile experience lend;
When he relates (with laughing, leering eye)
The tale licentious, mix'd with blasphemy:
No genuine gladness his narrations cause,
The frailest heart denies sincere applause;
And many a youth has turn'd him half aside,
And laugh'd aloud, the sign of shame to hide.
Blaney, no aid in his vile cause to lose,
Buys pictures, prints, and a licentious muse;
He borrows every help from every art,
To stir the passions and mislead the heart:
But from the subject let us soon escape,
Nor give this feature all its ugly shape:
Some to their crimes escape from satire owe;
Who shall describe what Blaney dares to show?
While thus the man, to vice and passion slave,
Was, with his follies, moving to the grave,
The ancient ruler of this mansion died,
And Blaney boldly for the seat applied;
Sir Denys Brand, then guardian, join'd his suit;
''Tis true,' said he, 'the fellow's quite a brute—
A very beast; but yet, with all his sin,
He has a manner—let the devil in.'
They half complied, they gave the wish'd retreat,
But raised a worthier to the vacant seat.

Thus forced on ways unlike each former way,
Thus led to prayer without a heart to pray,
He quits the gay and rich, the young and free,
Among the badge-men with a badge to be:
He sees an humble tradesman raised to rule
The grey-beard pupils of his moral school;
Where he himself, an old licentious boy,
Will nothing learn, and nothing can enjoy;
In temp'rate measures he must eat and drink,
And, pain of pains! must live alone and think.
In vain, by fortune's smiles, thrice affluent made,
Still has he debts of ancient date unpaid;
Thrice into penury by error thrown,
Not one right maxim has he made his own;
The old men shun him,—some his vices hate,
And all abhor his principles and prate;
Nor love nor care for him will mortal show,
Save a frail sister in the female row.

16. INHABITANTS OF THE ALMS-HOUSE

BENBOW

See! yonder badgeman, with that glowing face,
A meteor shining in this sober place;
Vast sums were paid, and many years were past,
Ere gems so rich around their radiance cast!
Such was the fiery front that Bardolph wore,
Guiding his master to the tavern-door;
There first that meteor rose, and there alone,
In its due place, the rich effulgence shone:
But this strange fire the seat of peace invades,
And shines portentous in these solemn shades.
Benbow, a boon companion, long approved
By jovial sets, and (as he thought) beloved,
Was judged as one to joy and friendship prone,
And deem'd injurious to himself alone;
Gen'rous and free, he paid but small regard
To trade, and fail'd; and some declared ''twas hard:'
These were his friends—his foes conceived the case
Of common kind; he sought and found disgrace:

The reasoning few, who neither scorn'd nor loved,
His feelings pitied and his faults reproved.
  Benbow, the father, left possessions fair,
A worthy name and business to his heir;
Benbow, the son, those fair possessions sold,
And lost his credit, while he spent the gold:
He was a jovial trader: men enjoy'd
The night with him; his day was unemploy'd;
So when his credit and his cash were spent,
Here, by mistaken pity, he was sent;
Of late he came, with passions unsubdued,
And shared and cursed the hated solitude,
Where gloomy thoughts arise, where grievous
    cares intrude.
  Known but in drink—he found an easy friend,
Well pleased his worth and honour to commend;
And thus inform'd, the guardian of the trust
Heard the applause and said the claim was just;
A worthy soul! unfitted for the strife,
Care and contention of a busy life;—
Worthy, and why?—that o'er the midnight bowl
He made his friend the partner of his soul,
And any man his friend:—then thus in glee,
'I speak my mind, I love the truth,' quoth he;
Till 'twas his fate that useful truth to find,
'Tis sometimes prudent not to speak the mind.
  With wine inflated, man is all upblown,
And feels a power which he believes his own;
With fancy soaring to the skies, he thinks
His all the virtues all the while he drinks;
But when the gas from the balloon is gone,
When sober thoughts and serious cares come on,
Where then the worth that in himself he found?—
Vanish'd—and he sank grov'ling on the ground.
  Still some conceit will Benbow's mind inflate,
Poor as he is,—'tis pleasant to relate
The joys he once possess'd—it soothes his present state.
  Seated with some grey beadsman, he regrets
His former feasting, though it swell'd his debts;
Topers once famed, his friends in earlier days,
Well he describes, and thinks description praise:

Each hero's worth with much delight he paints;
Martyrs they were, and he would make them saints.
'Alas! alas!' Old England now may say,
'My glory withers; it has had its day:
We're fallen on evil times; men read and think;
Our bold forefathers loved to fight and drink.
'Then lived the good 'Squire Asgill—what a change
Has death and fashion shown us at the Grange!
He bravely thought it best became his rank,
That all his tenants and his tradesmen drank;
He was delighted from his favourite room
To see them 'cross the park go daily home,
Praising aloud the liquor and the host,
And striving who should venerate him most.
'No pride had he, and there was difference small
Between the master's and the servants' hall;
And here or there the guests were welcome all.
Of Heaven's free gifts he took no special care,
He never quarrel'd for a simple hare;
But sought, by giving sport, a sportsman's name,
Himself a poacher though at other game:
He never planted nor inclosed—his trees
Grew like himself, untroubled and at ease:
Bounds of all kinds he hated, and had felt
Choked and imprison'd in a modern belt,
Which some rare genius now has twined about
The good old house, to keep old neighbours out:
Along his valleys, in the evening-hours,
The borough-damsels stray'd to gather flowers,
Or by the brakes and brushwood of the park,
To take their pleasant rambles in the dark.
'Some prudes, of rigid kind, forbore to call
On the kind females—favourites at the hall;
But better natures saw, with much delight,
The different orders of mankind unite;
'Twas schooling pride to see the footman wait,
Smile on his sister and receive her plate.
'His worship ever was a churchman true,
He held in scorn the methodistic crew;
May God defend the Church, and save the King,
He'd pray devoutly and divinely sing.

Admit that he the holy day would spend
As priests approved not, still he was a friend:
Much then I blame the preacher, as too nice,
To call such trifles by the name of vice;
Hinting, though gently and with cautious speech,
Of good example—'tis their trade to preach:
But still 'twas pity, when the worthy 'squire
Stuck to the church; what more could they require?
'Twas almost joining that fanatic crew,
To throw such morals at his honour's pew;
A weaker man, had he been so reviled,
Had left the place—he only swore and smiled.
'But think, ye rectors and ye curates, think,
Who are your friends, and at their frailties wink;
Conceive not—mounted on your Sunday-throne,
Your fire-brands fall upon your foes alone;
They strike your patrons—and, should all withdraw,
In whom your wisdoms may discern a flaw,
You would the flower of all your audience lose,
And spend your crackers on their empty pews.
'The father dead, the son has found a wife,
And lives a formal, proud, unsocial life;—
The lands are now enclosed; the tenants all,
Save at a rent-day, never see the hall:
No lass is suffer'd o'er the walks to come,
And if there's love, they have it all at home.
'Oh! could the ghost of our good 'squire arise,
And see such change; would it believe its eyes?
Would it not glide about from place to place,
And mourn the manners of a feebler race?
At that long table, where the servants found
Mirth and abundance while the year went round;
Where a huge pollard on the winter-fire,
At a huge distance made them all retire;
Where not a measure in the room was kept,
And but one rule—they tippled till they slept,—
There would it see a pale old hag preside,
A thing made up of stinginess and pride;
Who carves the meat, as if the flesh could feel,
Careless whose flesh must miss the plenteous meal:
Here would the ghost a small coal-fire behold,

Not fit to keep one body from the cold;
Then would it flit to higher rooms, and stay
To view a dull, dress'd company at play;
All the old comfort, all the genial fare
For ever gone! how sternly would it stare:
And though it might not to their view appear,
'Twould cause among them lassitude and fear;
Then wait to see—where he delight has seen—
The dire effect of fretfulness and spleen.
'Such were the worthies of these better days;
We had their blessings—they shall have our praise.
'Of Captain Dowling would you hear me speak?
I'd sit and sing his praises for a week:
He was a man, and man-like all his joy,—
I'm led to question was he ever boy?
Beef was his breakfast;—if from sea and salt,
It relish'd better with his wine of malt;
Then, till he dined, if walking in or out,
Whether the gravel teased him or the gout,
Though short in wind and flannel'd every limb,
He drank with all who had concerns with him:
Whatever trader, agent, merchant, came,
They found him ready, every hour the same;
Whatever liquors might between them pass,
He took them all, and never balk'd his glass:
Nay, with the seamen working in the ship,
At their request he'd share the grog and flip:
But in the club-room was his chief delight,
And punch the favourite liquor of the night;
Man after man they from the trial shrank,
And Dowling ever was the last who drank:
Arrived at home, he, ere he sought his bed,
With pipe and brandy would compose his head;
Then half an hour was o'er the news beguiled,
When he retired as harmless as a child.
Set but aside the gravel and the gout,
And breathing short—his sand ran fairly out.
'At fifty-five we lost him—after that
Life grows insipid and its pleasures flat;
He had indulged in all that man can have,
He did not drop a dotard to his grave;

Still to the last, his feet upon the chair,
With rattling lungs now gone beyond repair;
When on each feature death had fix'd his stamp,
And not a doctor could the body vamp;
Still at the last, to his beloved bowl
He clung, and cheer'd the sadness of his soul;
For though a man may not have much to fear,
Yet death looks ugly, when the view is near:
—"I go," he said, "but still my friends shall say,
'Twas as a man—I did not sneak away;
An honest life with worthy souls I've spent,—
Come, fill my glass;"—he took it and he went.
'Poor Dolly Murrey!—I might live to see
My hundredth year, but no such lass as she.
Easy by nature, in her humour gay,
She chose her comforts, ratafia and play:
She loved the social game, the decent glass;
And was a jovial, friendly, laughing lass;
We sat not then at Whist demure and still,
But pass'd the pleasant hours at gay Quadrille:
Lame in her side, we placed her in her seat,
Her hands were free, she cared not for her feet;
As the game ended, came the glass around,
(So was the loser cheer'd, the winner crown'd.)
Mistress of secrets, both the young and old
In her confided—not a tale she told;
Love never made impression on her mind,
She held him weak, and all his captives blind;
She suffer'd no man her free soul to vex,
Free from the weakness of her gentle sex;
One with whom ours unmoved conversing sate,
In cool discussion or in free debate.
'Once in her chair we'd placed the good old lass,
Where first she took her preparation-glass;
By lucky thought she'd been that day at prayers,
And long before had fix'd her small affairs;
So all was easy—on her cards she cast
A smiling look; I saw the thought that pass'd:
"A king," she call'd—though conscious of her skill,
"Do more," I answer'd—"More," she said, "I will;"
And more she did—cards answer'd to her call,

She saw the mighty to her mightier fall:
"A vole! a vole!" she cried, "'tis fairly won,
My game is ended and my work is done;"—
This said, she gently, with a single sigh,
Died as one taught and practised how to die.
'Such were the dead-departed; I survive,
To breathe in pain among the dead-alive.'
The bell then call'd these ancient men to pray,
'Again!' said Benbow,—'tolls it every day?
Where is the life I led?'—He sigh'd and walk'd his way.

22. THE POOR OF THE BOROUGH

PETER GRIMES

Old Peter Grimes made fishing his employ,
His wife he cabin'd with him and his boy,
And seem'd that life laborious to enjoy:
To town came quiet Peter with his fish,
And had of all a civil word and wish.
He left his trade upon the sabbath-day,
And took young Peter in his hand to pray:
But soon the stubborn boy from care broke loose,
At first refused, then added his abuse:
His father's love he scorn'd, his power defied,
But being drunk, wept sorely when he died.
Yes! then he wept, and to his mind there came
Much of his conduct, and he felt the shame,—
How he had oft the good old man reviled,
And never paid the duty of a child;
How, when the father in his Bible read,
He in contempt and anger left the shed:
'It is the word of life,' the parent cried;
—'This is the life itself,' the boy replied;
And while old Peter in amazement stood,
Gave the hot spirit to his boiling blood:—
How he, with oath and furious speech, began
To prove his freedom and assert the man;
And when the parent check'd his impious rage,
How he had cursed the tyranny of age,—
Nay, once had dealt the sacrilegious blow

On his bare head, and laid his parent low;
The father groan'd—'If thou art old,' said he,
'And hast a son—thou wilt remember me:
Thy mother left me in a happy time,
Thou kill'dst not her—Heav'n spares the double crime.'
   On an inn-settle, in his maudlin grief,
This he revolved, and drank for his relief.
   Now lived the youth in freedom, but debarr'd
From constant pleasure, and he thought it hard;
Hard that he could not every wish obey,
But must awhile relinquish ale and play;
Hard! that he could not to his cards attend,
But must acquire the money he would spend.
   With greedy eye he look'd on all he saw,
He knew not justice, and he laugh'd at law;
On all he mark'd he stretch'd his ready hand;
He fish'd by water, and he filch'd by land:
Oft in the night has Peter dropp'd his oar,
Fled from his boat and sought for prey on shore;
Oft up the hedge-row glided, on his back
Bearing the orchard's produce in a sack,
Or farm-yard load, tugg'd fiercely from the stack;
And as these wrongs to greater numbers rose,
The more he look'd on all men as his foes.
   He built a mud-wall'd hovel, where he kept
His various wealth, and there he oft-times slept;
But no success could please his cruel soul,
He wish'd for one to trouble and control;
He wanted some obedient boy to stand
And bear the blow of his outrageous hand;
And hoped to find in some propitious hour
A feeling creature subject to his power.
   Peter had heard there were in London then,—
Still have they being!—workhouse-clearing men,
Who, undisturb'd by feelings just or kind,
Would parish-boys to needy tradesmen bind:
They in their want a trifling sum would take,
And toiling slaves of piteous orphans make.
   Such Peter sought, and when a lad was found,
The sum was dealt him, and the slave was bound.
Some few in town observed in Peter's trap

A boy, with jacket blue and woollen cap;
But none inquired how Peter used the rope,
Or what the bruise, that made the stripling stoop;
None could the ridges on his back behold,
None sought him shiv'ring in the winter's cold;
None put the question,—'Peter, dost thou give
The boy his food?—What, man! the lad must live:
Consider, Peter, let the child have bread,
He'll serve thee better if he's stroked and fed.'
None reason'd thus—and some, on hearing cries,
Said calmly, 'Grimes is at his exercise.'
   Pinn'd, beaten, cold, pinch'd, threaten'd, and abused—
His efforts punish'd and his food refused,—
Awake tormented,—soon aroused from sleep,—
Struck if he wept, and yet compell'd to weep,
The trembling boy dropp'd down and strove to pray,
Received a blow, and trembling turn'd away,
Or sobb'd and hid his piteous face;—while he,
The savage master, grinn'd in horrid glee:
He'd now the power he ever loved to show,
A feeling being subject to his blow.
   Thus lived the lad, in hunger, peril, pain,
His tears despised, his supplications vain:
Compell'd by fear to lie, by need to steal,
His bed uneasy and unbless'd his meal,
For three sad years the boy his tortures bore,
And then his pains and trials were no more.
   'How died he, Peter?' when the people said,
He growl'd—'I found him lifeless in his bed;'
Then tried for softer tone, and sigh'd, 'Poor Sam is dead.'
Yet murmurs were there, and some questions ask'd,—
How he was fed, how punish'd, and how task'd?
Much they suspected, but they little proved,
And Peter pass'd untroubled and unmoved.
   Another boy with equal ease was found,
The money granted, and the victim bound;
And what his fate?—One night it chanced he fell
From the boat's mast and perish'd in her well,
Where fish were living kept, and where the boy
(So reason'd men) could not himself destroy:—
   'Yes! so it was,' said Peter, 'in his play,

(For he was idle both by night and day,)
He climb'd the main-mast and then fell below;'—
Then show'd his corpse and pointed to the blow:
What said the jury?—they were long in doubt,
But sturdy Peter faced the matter out:
So they dismiss'd him, saying at the time,
'Keep fast your hatchway when you've boys who climb.'
This hit the conscience, and he colour'd more
Than for the closest questions put before.
  Thus all his fears the verdict set aside,
And at the slave-shop Peter still applied.
  Then came a boy, of manners soft and mild,—
Our seamen's wives with grief beheld the child;
All thought (the poor themselves) that he was one
Of gentle blood, some noble sinner's son,
Who had, belike, deceived some humble maid,
Whom he had first seduced and then betray'd:—
However this, he seem'd a gracious lad,
In grief submissive and with patience sad.
  Passive he labour'd, till his slender frame
Bent with his loads, and he at length was lame:
Strange that a frame so weak could bear so long
The grossest insult and the foulest wrong;
But there were causes—in the town they gave
Fire, food, and comfort, to the gentle slave;
And though stern Peter, with a cruel hand,
And knotted rope, enforced the rude command,
Yet he consider'd what he'd lately felt,
And his vile blows with selfish pity dealt.
  One day such draughts the cruel fisher made,
He could not vend them in his borough-trade,
But sail'd for London-mart: the boy was ill,
But ever humbled to his master's will;
And on the river, where they smoothly sail'd,
He strove with terror and awhile prevail'd;
But new to danger on the angry sea,
He clung affrighten'd to his master's knee:
The boat grew leaky and the wind was strong,
Rough was the passage and the time was long;
His liquor fail'd, and Peter's wrath arose,—
No more is known—the rest we must suppose,

Or learn of Peter;—Peter says, he 'spied
The stripling's danger and for harbour tried;
Meantime the fish, and then th'apprentice died.'
  The pitying women raised a clamour round,
And weeping said, 'Thou hast thy 'prentice drown'd.'
  Now the stern man was summon'd to the hall,
To tell his tale before the burghers all:
He gave th'account; profess'd the lad he loved,
And kept his brazen features all unmoved.
  The mayor himself with tone severe replied,—
'Henceforth with thee shall never boy abide;
Hire thee a freeman, whom thou durst not beat,
But who, in thy despite, will sleep and eat:
Free thou art now!—again shouldst thou appear,
Thou'lt find thy sentence, like thy soul, severe.'
  Alas! for Peter, not a helping hand,
So was he hated, could he now command;
Alone he row'd his boat, alone he cast
His nets beside, or made his anchor fast;
To hold a rope or hear a curse was none,—
He toil'd and rail'd; he groan'd and swore alone.
  Thus by himself compell'd to live each day,
To wait for certain hours the tide's delay;
At the same times the same dull views to see,
The bounding marsh-bank and the blighted tree;
The water only, when the tides were high,
When low, the mud half-cover'd and half-dry;
The sun-burnt tar that blisters on the planks,
And bank-side stakes in their uneven ranks;
Heaps of entangled weeds that slowly float,
As the tide rolls by the impeded boat.
  When tides were neap, and, in the sultry day,
Through the tall bounding mud-banks made their way,
Which on each side rose swelling, and below
The dark warm flood ran silently and slow;
There anchoring, Peter chose from man to hide,
There hang his head, and view the lazy tide
In its hot slimy channel slowly glide;
Where the small eels that left the deeper way
For the warm shore, within the shallows play;
Where gaping muscles, left upon the mud,

Slope their slow passage to the fallen flood;—
Here dull and hopeless he'd lie down and trace
How sidelong crabs had scrawl'd their crooked race;
Or sadly listen to the tuneless cry
Of fishing gull or clanging golden-eye;
What time the sea-birds to the marsh would come,
And the loud bittern, from the bull-rush home,
Gave from the salt-ditch side the bellowing boom:
He nursed the feelings these dull scenes produce,
And loved to stop beside the opening sluice;
Where the small stream, confined in narrow bound,
Ran with a dull, unvaried, sadd'ning sound;
Where all, presented to the eye or ear,
Oppress'd the soul with misery, grief, and fear.
  Besides these objects, there were places three,
Which Peter seem'd with certain dread to see;
When he drew near them he would turn from each,
And loudly whistle till he pass'd the reach.
  A change of scene to him brought no relief;
In town, 'twas plain, men took him for a thief:
The sailors' wives would stop him in the street,
And say, 'Now, Peter, thou'st no boy to beat:'
Infants at play, when they perceived him, ran,
Warning each other—'That's the wicked man:'
He growl'd an oath, and in an angry tone
Cursed the whole place and wish'd to be alone.
  Alone he was, the same dull scenes in view,
And still more gloomy in his sight they grew:
Though man he hated, yet employ'd alone
At bootless labour, he would swear and groan,
Cursing the shoals that glided by the spot,
And gulls that caught them when his arts could not.
  Cold nervous tremblings shook his sturdy frame,
And strange disease—he couldn't say the name;
Wild were his dreams, and oft he rose in fright,
Waked by his view of horrors in the night,—
Horrors that would the sternest minds amaze,
Horrors that demons might be proud to raise:
And though he felt forsaken, grieved at heart,
To think he lived from all mankind apart;
Yet, if a man approach'd, in terrors he would start.

A winter pass'd since Peter saw the town,
And summer-lodgers were again come down;
These, idly curious, with their glasses spied
The ships in bay as anchor'd for the tide,—
The river's craft,—the bustle of the quay,—
And sea-port views, which landmen love to see.
One, up the river, had a man and boat
Seen day by day, now anchor'd, now afloat;
Fisher he seem'd, yet used no net nor hook;
Of sea-fowl swimming by no heed he took,
But on the gliding waves still fix'd his lazy look:
At certain stations he would view the stream,
As if he stood bewilder'd in a dream,
Or that some power had chain'd him for a time,
To feel a curse or meditate on crime.
This known, some curious, some in pity went,
And others question'd—'Wretch, dost thou repent?'
He heard, he trembled, and in fear resign'd
His boat: new terror fill'd his restless mind;
Furious he grew, and up the country ran,
And there they seized him—a distemper'd man:—
Him we received, and to a parish-bed,
Follow'd and cursed, the groaning man was led.
Here, when they saw him, whom they used to shun,
A lost, lone man, so harass'd and undone;
Our gentle females, ever prompt to feel,
Perceived compassion on their anger steal;
His crimes they could not from their memories blot,
But they were grieved, and trembled at his lot.
A priest too came, to whom his words are told;
And all the signs they shudder'd to behold.
'Look! look!' they cried; 'his limbs with horror shake,
And as he grinds his teeth, what noise they make!
How glare his angry eyes, and yet he's not awake:
See! what cold drops upon his forehead stand,
And how he clenches that broad bony hand.'
The priest attending, found he spoke at times
As one alluding to his fears and crimes:
'It was the fall,' he mutter'd, 'I can show
The manner how—I never struck a blow:'—
And then aloud—'Unhand me, free my chain;

On oath, he fell—it struck him to the brain:—
Why ask my father?—that old man will swear
Against my life; besides, he wasn't there:—
What, all agreed?—Am I to die to-day?—
My Lord, in mercy, give me time to pray.'
  Then, as they watch'd him, calmer he became,
And grew so weak he couldn't move his frame,
But murmuring spake,—while they could see and hear
The start of terror and the groan of fear;
See the large dew-beads on his forehead rise,
And the cold death-drop glaze his sunken eyes;
Nor yet he died, but with unwonted force
Seem'd with some fancied being to discourse:
He knew not us, or with accustom'd art
He hid the knowledge, yet exposed his heart;
'Twas part confession and the rest defence,
A madman's tale, with gleams of waking sense.
  'I'll tell you all,' he said, 'the very day
When the old man first placed them in my way:
My father's spirit—he who always tried
To give me trouble, when he lived and died—
When he was gone, he could not be content
To see my days in painful labour spent,
But would appoint his meetings, and he made
Me watch at these, and so neglect my trade.
  ''Twas one hot noon, all silent, still, serene,
No living being had I lately seen;
I paddled up and down and dipp'd my net,
But (such his pleasure) I could nothing get,—
A father's pleasure, when his toil was done,
To plague and torture thus an only son!
And so I sat and look'd upon the stream,
How it ran on, and felt as in a dream:
But dream it was not; no!—I fix'd my eyes
On the mid stream and saw the spirits rise;
I saw my father on the water stand,
And hold a thin pale boy in either hand;
And there they glided ghastly on the top
Of the salt flood, and never touch'd a drop:
I would have struck them, but they knew th'intent,
And smiled upon the oar, and down they went.

'Now, from that day, whenever I began
To dip my net, there stood the hard old man—
He and those boys: I humbled me and pray'd
They would be gone;—they heeded not, but stay'd:
Nor could I turn, nor would the boat go by,
But gazing on the spirits, there was I:
They bade me leap to death, but I was loth to die:
And every day, as sure as day arose,
Would these three spirits meet me ere the close;
To hear and mark them daily was my doom,
And "Come," they said, with weak, sad voices, "come."
To row away with all my strength I try'd,
But there were they, hard by me in the tide,
The three unbodied forms—and "Come," still "come,"
they cried.

'Fathers should pity—but this old man shook
His hoary locks, and froze me by a look:
Thrice, when I struck them, through the water came
A hollow groan, that weaken'd all my frame:
"Father!" said I, "have mercy:"—He replied,
I know not what—the angry spirit lied,—
"Didst thou not draw thy knife?" said he:—'Twas true,
But I had pity and my arm withdrew:
He cried for mercy which I kindly gave,
But he has no compassion in his grave.

'There were three places, where they ever rose,—
The whole long river has not such as those,—
Places accursed, where, if a man remain,
He'll see the things which strike him to the brain;
And there they made me on my paddle lean,
And look at them for hours;—accursed scene!
When they would glide to that smooth eddy-space,
Then bid me leap and join them in the place;
And at my groans each little villain sprite
Enjoy'd my pains and vanish'd in delight.

'In one fierce summer-day, when my poor brain
Was burning hot and cruel was my pain,
Then came this father-foe, and there he stood
With his two boys again upon the flood;
There was more mischief in their eyes, more glee
In their pale faces when they glared at me:

Still did they force me on the oar to rest,
And when they saw me fainting and oppress'd,
He, with his hand, the old man, scoop'd the flood,
And there came flame about him mix'd with blood;
He bade me stoop and look upon the place,
Then flung the hot-red liquor in my face;
Burning it blazed, and then I roar'd for pain,
I thought the demons would have turn'd my brain.
'Still there they stood, and forced me to behold
A place of horrors—they cannot be told—
Where the flood open'd, there I heard the shriek
Of tortured guilt—no earthly tongue can speak:
"All days alike! for ever!" did they say,
"And unremitted torments every day"—
Yes, so they said:'—But here he ceased and gazed
On all around, affrighten'd and amazed;
And still he tried to speak, and look'd in dread
Of frighten'd females gathering round his bed;
Then dropp'd exhausted and appear'd at rest,
Till the strong foe the vital powers possess'd;
Then with an inward, broken voice he cried,
'Again they come,' and mutter'd as he died.

23. PRISONS

'Tis well—that man to all the varying states
Of good and ill his mind accommodates;
He not alone progressive grief sustains,
But soon submits to unexperienced pains:
Change after change, all climes his body bears;
His mind repeated shocks of changing cares:
Faith and fair virtue arm the nobler breast;
Hope and mere want of feeling aid the rest.
Or who could bear to lose the balmy air
Of summer's breath, from all things fresh and fair,
With all that man admires or loves below;
All earth and water, wood and vale bestow,
Where rosy pleasures smile, whence real blessings flow;
With sight and sound of every kind that lives,
And crowning all with joy that freedom gives?
Who could from these, in some unhappy day,

Bear to be drawn by ruthless arms away,
To the vile nuisance of a noisome room,
Where only insolence and misery come?
(Save that the curious will by chance appear,
Or some in pity drop a fruitless tear;)
To a damp prison, where the very sight
Of the warm sun is favour and not right;
Where all we hear or see the feelings shock,
The oath and groan, the fetter and the lock?
  Who could bear this and live?—Oh! many a year
All this is borne, and miseries more severe;
And some there are, familiar with the scene,
Who live in mirth, though few become serene.
  Far as I might the inward man perceive,
There was a constant effort—not to grieve;
Not to despair, for better days would come,
And the freed debtor smile again at home:
Subdued his habits, he may peace regain,
And bless the woes that were not sent in vain.
  Thus might we class the debtors here confined,
The more deceived, the more deceitful kind;
Here are the guilty race, who mean to live
On credit, that credulity will give;
Who purchase, conscious they can never pay;
Who know their fate, and traffic to betray;
On whom no pity, fear, remorse, prevail,
Their aim a statute, their resource a jail;—
These as the public spoilers we regard,
No dun so harsh, no creditor so hard.
  A second kind are they, who truly strive
To keep their sinking credit long alive;
Success, nay prudence, they may want, but yet
They would be solvent, and deplore a debt;
All means they use, to all expedients run,
And are by slow, sad steps, at last undone:
Justly, perhaps, you blame their want of skill,
But mourn their feelings and absolve their will.
  There is a debtor, who his trifling *all*
Spreads in a shop; it would not fill a stall:
There at one window his temptation lays,
And in new modes disposes and displays:

Above the door you shall his name behold,
And what he vends in ample letters told,
The words *repository, warehouse,* all
He uses to enlarge concerns so small:
He to his goods assigns some beauty's name,
Then in her reign, and hopes they'll share her fame;
And talks of credit, commerce, traffic, trade,
As one important by their profit made;
But who can paint the vacancy, the gloom,
And spare dimensions of one backward room?
Wherein he dines, if so 'tis fit to speak,
Of one day's herring and the morrow's steak;
An anchorite in diet, all his care
Is to display his stock and vend his ware.
  Long waiting hopeless, then he tries to meet
A kinder fortune in a distant street;
There he again displays, increasing yet
Corroding sorrow and consuming debt:
Alas! he wants the requisites to rise—
The true connexions, the availing ties;
They who proceed on certainties advance,
These are not times when men prevail by chance:
But still he tries, till, after years of pain,
He finds, with anguish, he has tried in vain.
Debtors are these on whom 'tis hard to press,
'Tis base, impolitic, and merciless.
  To these we add a miscellaneous kind,
By pleasure, pride, and indolence confined;
Those whom no calls, no warnings could divert,
The unexperienced and the inexpert;
The builder, idler, schemer, gamester, sot,—
The follies different, but the same their lot;
Victims of horses, lasses, drinking, dice,
Of every passion, humour, whim, and vice.
  See! that sad merchant, who but yesterday
Had a vast household in command and pay;
He now entreats permission to employ
A boy he needs, and then entreats the boy.
  And there sits one, improvident but kind,
Bound for a friend, whom honour could not bind;
Sighing, he speaks to any who appear,

'A treach'rous friend—'twas that which sent me here:
I was too kind,—I thought I could depend
On his bare word—he was a treach'rous friend.'
A female too!—it is to her a home,
She came before—and she again will come:
Her friends have pity; when their anger drops,
They take her home;—she's tried her schools and shops—
Plan after plan;—but fortune would not mend,
She to herself was still the treach'rous friend;
And wheresoe'er began, all here was sure to end:
And there she sits as thoughtless and as gay,
As if she'd means, or not a debt to pay—
Or knew to-morrow she'd be call'd away—
Or felt a shilling and could dine to-day.
While thus observing, I began to trace
The sober'd features of a well-known face—
Looks once familiar, manners form'd to please,
And all illuminated by a heart at ease:
But fraud and flattery ever claim'd a part
(Still unresisted) of that easy heart;
But he at length beholds me—'Ah! my friend!
And have thy pleasures this unlucky end?'
'Too sure,' he said, and smiling as he sigh'd;
'I went astray, though prudence seem'd my guide;
All she proposed I in my heart approved,
And she was honour'd, but my pleasure loved—
Pleasure, the mistress to whose arms I fled,
From wife-like lectures angry prudence read.
'Why speak the madness of a life like mine,
The powers of beauty, novelty, and wine?
Why paint the wanton smile, the venal vow,
Or friends whose worth I can appreciate now?
'Oft I perceived my fate, and then would say,
I'll think to-morrow, I must live to-day:
So am I here—I own the laws are just—
And here, where thought is painful, think I must:
But speech is pleasant, this discourse with thee
Brings to my mind the sweets of liberty,
Breaks on the sameness of the place, and gives
The doubtful heart conviction that it lives.

'Let me describe my anguish in the hour
When law detain'd me and I felt its power.
'When in that shipwreck, this I found my shore,
And join'd the wretched, who were wreck'd before;
When I perceived each feature in the face,
Pinch'd through neglect or turbid by disgrace;
When in these wasting forms affliction stood
In my afflicted view, it chill'd my blood;—
And forth I rush'd, a quick retreat to make,
Till a loud laugh proclaim'd the dire mistake:
But when the groan had settled to a sigh,
When gloom became familiar to the eye,
When I perceive how others seem to rest,
With every evil rankling in my breast,—
Led by example, I put on the man,
Sing off my sighs, and trifle as I can.
'Homer! nay Pope! (for never will I seek
Applause for learning—nought have I with Greek)
Gives us the secrets of his pagan hell,
Where ghost with ghost in sad communion dwell;
Where shade meets shade, and round the gloomy
meads
They glide and speak of old heroic deeds,—
What fields they conquer'd, and what foes they slew
And sent to join the melancholy crew.
'When a new spirit in that world was found,
A thousand shadowy forms came flitting round;
Those who had known him, fond inquiries made,—
"Of all we left, inform us, gentle shade,
Now as we lead thee in our realms to dwell,
Our twilight groves, and meads of asphodel."
'What paints the poet, is our station here,
Where we like ghosts and flitting shades appear:
This is the hell he sings, and here we meet,
And former deeds to new-made friends repeat;
Heroic deeds, which here obtain us fame,
And are in fact the causes why we came:
Yes! this dim region is old Homer's hell,
Abate but groves and meads of asphodel.
'Here, when a stranger from your world we spy,
We gather round him and for news apply;

He hears unheeding, nor can speech endure,
But shivering gazes on the vast obscure:
We smiling pity, and by kindness show
We felt his feelings and his terrors know;
Then speak of comfort—time will give him sight,
Where now 'tis dark; where now 'tis wo—delight.
 '"Have hope," we say, "and soon the place to thee
Shall not a prison but a castle be;
When to the wretch whom care and guilt confound,
The world's a prison, with a wider bound;
Go where he may, he feels himself confined,
And wears the fetters of an abject mind."
 'But now adieu! those giant keys appear,
Thou art not worthy to be inmate here:
Go to thy world, and to the young declare
What we, our spirits and employments, are;
Tell them how we the ills of life endure,
Our empire stable, and our state secure;
Our dress, our diet, for their use describe,
And bid them haste to join the gen'rous tribe:
Go to thy world, and leave us here to dwell,
Who to its joys and comforts bid farewell.'
 Farewell to these; but other scenes I view,
And other griefs, and guilt of deeper hue;
Where conscience gives to outward ills her pain,
Gloom to the night, and pressure to the chain:
Here separate cells awhile in misery keep
Two doom'd to suffer: there they strive for sleep;
By day indulged, in larger space they range,
Their bondage certain, but their bounds have change.
 One was a female, who had grievous ill
Wrought in revenge, and she enjoy'd it still:
With death before her, and her fate in view,
Unsated vengeance in her bosom grew:
Sullen she was and threat'ning; in her eye
Glared the stern triumph that she dared to die:
But first a being in the world must leave—
'Twas once reproach; 'twas now a short reprieve.
 She was a pauper bound, who early gave
Her mind to vice, and doubly was a slave;
Upbraided, beaten, held by rough control,

Revenge sustain'd, inspired, and fill'd her soul:
She fired a full-stored barn, confess'd the fact,
And laugh'd at law and justified the act:
Our gentle vicar tried his powers in vain,
She answer'd not, or answer'd with disdain;
Th' approaching fate she heard without a sigh,
And neither cared to live nor fear'd to die.
Not so he felt, who with her was to pay
The forfeit, life—with dread he view'd the day,
And that short space which yet for him remain'd,
Till with his limbs his faculties were chain'd:
He paced his narrow bounds some ease to find,
But found it not,—no comfort reach'd his mind:
Each sense was palsied; when he tasted food,
He sigh'd and said, 'Enough—'tis very good.'
Since his dread sentence, nothing seem'd to be
As once it was—he seeing could not see,
Nor hearing, hear aright;—when first I came
Within his view, I fancied there was shame,
I judged resentment; I mistook the air,—
These fainter passions live not with despair;
Or but exist and die:—Hope, fear, and love,
Joy, doubt, and hate, may other spirits move,
But touch not his, who every waking hour
Has one fix'd dread, and always feels its power.
'But will not mercy?'—No! she cannot plead
For such an outrage;—'twas a cruel deed:
He stopp'd a timid traveller;—to his breast,
With oaths and curses, was the danger press'd:—
No! he must suffer; pity we may find
For one man's pangs, but must not wrong mankind.
Still I behold him, every thought employ'd
On one dire view!—all others are destroy'd;
This makes his features ghastly, gives the tone
Of his few words resemblance to a groan:
He takes his tasteless food, and when 'tis done,
Counts up his meals, now lessen'd by that one;
For expectation is on time intent,
Whether he brings us joy or punishment.
Yes! e'en in sleep the impressions all remain,
He hears the sentence and he feels the chain;

He sees the judge and jury, when he shakes,
And loudly cries, 'Not guilty,' and awakes:
Then chilling tremblings o'er his body creep,
Till worn-out nature is compell'd to sleep.
  Now comes the dream again; it shows each scene,
With each small circumstance that comes between—
The call to suffering and the very deed—
There crowds go with him, follow, and precede;
Some heartless shout, some pity, all condemn,
While he in fancied envy looks at them:
He seems the place for that sad act to see,
And dreams the very thirst which then will be:
A priest attends—it seems, the one he knew
In his best days, beneath whose care he grew.
  At this his terrors take a sudden flight,
He sees his native village with delight;
The house, the chamber, where he once array'd
His youthful person; where he knelt and pray'd:
Then too the comforts he enjoy'd at home,
The days of joy; the joys themselves are come;—
The hours of innocence;—the timid look
Of his loved maid, when first her hand he took
And told his hope; her trembling joy appears,
Her forced reserve and his retreating fears.
  All now is present;—'tis a moment's gleam
Of former sunshine—stay, delightful dream!
Let him within his pleasant garden walk,
Give him her arm, of blessings let them talk.
  Yes! all are with him now, and all the while
Life's early prospects and his Fanny's smile:
Then come his sister and his village-friend,
And he will now the sweetest moments spend
Life has to yield;—No! never will he find
Again on earth such pleasure in his mind:
He goes through shrubby walks these friends among,
Love in their looks and honour on the tongue:
Nay, there's a charm beyond what nature shows,
The bloom is softer and more sweetly glows;—
Pierced by no crime, and urged by no desire
For more than true and honest hearts require,
They feel the calm delight, and thus proceed

Through the green lane,—then linger in the mead,—
Stray o'er the heath in all its purple bloom,—
And pluck the blossom where the wild bees hum;
Then through the broomy bound with ease they pass,
And press the sandy sheep-walk's slender grass,
Where dwarfish flowers among the gorse are spread,
And the lamb browses by the linnet's bed;
Then 'cross the bounding brook they make their way
O'er its rough bridge—and there behold the bay!—
The ocean smiling to the fervid sun—
The waves that faintly fall and slowly run—
The ships at distance and the boats at hand;
And now they walk upon the sea-side sand,
Counting the number and what kind they be,
Ships softly sinking in the sleepy sea:
Now arm in arm, now parted, they behold
The glitt'ring waters on the shingles roll'd:
The timid girls, half dreading their design,
Dip the small foot in the retarded brine,
And search for crimson weeds, which spreading flow,
Or lie like pictures on the sand below;
With all those bright red pebbles that the sun
Through the small waves so softly shines upon;
And those live lucid jellies which the eye
Delights to trace as they swim glitt'ring by:
Pearl-shells and rubied star-fish they admire,
And will arrange above the parlour-fire,—
Tokens of bliss!—'Oh! horrible! a wave
Roars as it rises—save me, Edward! save!'
She cries:—Alas! the watchman on his way
Calls and lets in—truth, terror, and the day!

TALES, 1812

1. THE DUMB ORATORS

OR

THE BENEFIT OF SOCIETY

With fair round belly with good capon lined,
With eyes severe——
Full of wise saws and modern instances.
As you Like it, Act II, Scene 7

Deep shame hath struck me dumb.
King John, Act IV, Scene 2

He gives the bastinado with his tongue,
Our ears are cudgell'd. *King John*, Act II, Scene 1

Let's kill all the lawyers;
Now show yourselves men: 'tis for liberty:
We will not leave one lord or gentleman.
2 Henry VI, Act IV, Scene 2

And thus the whirligig of time brings in his revenges.
Twelfth Night, Act V, Scene last

That all men would be cowards if they dare,
Some men we know have courage to declare;
And this the life of many an hero shows,
That like the tide, man's courage ebbs and flows:
With friends and gay companions round them, then
Men boldly speak and have the hearts of men;
Who, with opponents seated, miss the aid
Of kind applauding looks, and grow afraid;
Like timid trav'llers in the night, they fear
Th' assault of foes, when not a friend is near.
In contest mighty and of conquest proud
Was Justice Bolt, impetuous, warm, and loud;
His fame, his prowess all the country knew,
And disputants, with one so fierce, were few:
He was a younger son, for law design'd,
With dauntless look and persevering mind;
While yet a clerk, for disputation famed,
No efforts tired him, and no conflicts tamed.

Scarcely he bade his master's desk adieu,
When both his brothers from the world withdrew.
An ample fortune he from them possess'd,
And was with saving care and prudence bless'd.
Now would he go and to the country give
Example how an English 'squire should live;
How bounteous, yet how frugal man may be,
By a well-order'd hospitality;
He would the rights of all so well maintain,
That none should idle be, and none complain.
All this and more he purposed—and what man
Could do, he did to realize his plan:
But time convinced him that we cannot keep
A breed of reasoners like a flock of sheep;
For they, so far from following as we lead,
Make that a cause why they will not proceed.
Man will not follow where a rule is shown,
But loves to take a method of his own;
Explain the way with all your care and skill,
This will he quit, if but to prove he will.—
Yet had our Justice honour—and the crowd,
Awed by his presence, their respect avow'd.
In later years he found his heart incline,
More than in youth, to gen'rous food and wine;
But no indulgence check'd the powerful love
He felt to teach, to argue, and reprove.
Meetings, or public calls, he never miss'd—
To dictate often, always to assist.
Oft he the clergy join'd, and not a cause
Pertain'd to them but he could quote the laws;
He upon tithes and residence display'd
A fund of knowledge for the hearer's aid;
And could on glebe and farming, wool and grain,
A long discourse, without a pause, maintain.
To his experience and his native sense
He join'd a bold imperious eloquence;
The grave, stern look of man inform'd and wise,
A full command of feature, heart, and eyes,
An awe-compelling frown, and fear-inspiring size.
When at the table, not a guest was seen
With appetite so ling'ring, or so keen;

But when the outer man no more required,
The inner waked, and he was man inspired.
His subjects then were those, a subject true
Presents in fairest form to public view;
Of Church and State, of Law, with mighty strength
Of words he spoke, in speech of mighty length:
And now, into the vale of years declined,
He hides too little of the monarch-mind:
He kindles anger by untimely jokes,
And opposition by contempt provokes;
Mirth he suppresses by his awful frown,
And humble spirits, by disdain, keeps down;
Blamed by the mild, approved by the severe,
The prudent fly him, and the valiant fear.
  For overbearing is his proud discourse,
And overwhelming of his voice the force;
And overpowering is he when he shows
What floats upon a mind that always overflows.
  This ready man at every meeting rose,
Something to hint, determine, or propose;
And grew so fond of teaching, that he taught
Those who instruction needed not or sought:
Happy our hero, when he could excite
Some thoughtless talker to the wordy fight:
Let him a subject at his pleasure choose,
Physic or Law, Religion or the Muse;
On all such themes he was prepared to shine,
Physician, poet, lawyer, and divine.
Hemm'd in by some tough argument, borne down
By press of language and the awful frown,
In vain for mercy shall the culprit plead;
His crime is past, and sentence must proceed:
Ah! suffering man, have patience, bear thy woes—
For lo! the clock—at ten the Justice goes.
  This powerful man, on business or to please
A curious taste, or weary grown of ease,
On a long journey travell'd many a mile
Westward, and halted midway in our isle;
Content to view a city large and fair,
Though none had notice—what a man was there!
  Silent two days, he then began to long

Again to try a voice so loud and strong;
To give his favourite topics some new grace,
And gain some glory in such distant place;
To reap some present pleasure, and to sow
Seeds of fair fame, in after-time to grow:
Here will men say, 'We heard, at such an hour,
The best of speakers—wonderful his power.'
  Inquiry made, he found that day would meet
A learned club, and in the very street:
Knowledge to gain and give, was the design;
To speak, to hearken, to debate, and dine:
This pleased our traveller, for he felt his force
In either way, to eat or to discourse.
  Nothing more easy than to gain access
To men like these, with his polite address:
So he succeeded, and first look'd around,
To view his objects and to take his ground;
And therefore silent chose awhile to sit,
Then enter boldly by some lucky hit;
Some observation keen or stroke severe,
To cause some wonder or excite some fear.
  Now, dinner past, no longer he suppress'd
His strong dislike to be a silent guest;
Subjects and words were now at his command—
When disappointment frown'd on all he plann'd;
For, hark!—he heard amazed, on every side,
His church insulted and her priests belied;
The laws reviled, the ruling power abused,
The land derided, and its foes excused:—
He heard and ponder'd.—What, to men so vile,
Should be his language? For his threat'ning style
They were too many;—if his speech were meek,
They would despise such poor attempts to speak:
At other times with every word at will,
He now sat lost, perplex'd, astonish'd, still.
  Here were Socinians, Deists, and indeed
All who, as foes to England's church, agreed;
But still with creeds unlike, and some without a creed:
Here, too, fierce friends of liberty he saw,
Who own'd no prince and who obey no law;
There were Reformers of each different sort,

Foes to the laws, the priesthood, and the court;
Some on their favourite plans alone intent,
Some purely angry and malevolent:
The rash were proud to blame their country's laws;
The vain, to seem supporters of a cause;
One call'd for change that he would dread to see;
Another sigh'd for Gallic liberty!
And numbers joining with the forward crew,
For no one reason—but that numbers do.
  'How,' said the Justice, 'can this trouble rise,
This shame and pain, from creatures I despise?'
And conscience answer'd—'The prevailing cause
Is thy delight in listening to applause;
Here, thou art seated with a tribe, who spurn
Thy favourite themes, and into laughter turn
Thy fears and wishes; silent and obscure,
Thyself, shalt thou the long harangue endure;
And learn, by feeling, what it is to force
On thy unwilling friends the long discourse:
What though thy thoughts be just, and these, it seems,
Are traitors' projects, idiots' empty schemes;
Yet minds like bodies cramm'd, reject their food,
Nor will be forced and tortured for their good!'
  At length, a sharp, shrewd, sallow man arose,
And begg'd he briefly might his mind disclose;
'It was his duty, in these worst of times,
T' inform the govern'd of their rulers' crimes:'
This pleasant subject to attend, they each
Prepared to listen, and forbore to teach.
  Then voluble and fierce the wordy man
Through a long chain of favourite horrors ran:—
First, of the church, from whose enslaving power
He was deliver'd, and he bless'd the hour;
'Bishops and deans, and prebendaries all,'
He said, 'were cattle fatt'ning in the stall;
Slothful and pursy, insolent and mean,
Were every bishop, prebendary, dean,
And wealthy rector: curates, poorly paid,
Were only dull;—he would not them upbraid.'
  From priests he turn'd to canons, creeds, and prayers,
Rubrics and rules, and all our church affairs;

Churches themselves, desk, pulpit, altar, all
The Justice reverenced—and pronounced their fall.
  Then from religion Hammond turn'd his view,
To give our rulers the correction due;
Not one wise action had these triflers plann'd;
There was, it seem'd, no wisdom in the land;
Save in this patriot tribe, who meet at times
To show the statesman's errors and his crimes.
  Now here was Justice Bolt compell'd to sit,
To hear the deist's scorn, the rebel's wit;
The fact mis-stated, the envenom'd lie,
And staring, spell-bound, made not one reply.
  Then were our laws abused—and with the laws,
All who prepare, defend, or judge a cause:
'We have no lawyer whom a man can trust,'
Proceeded Hammond—'if the laws were just;
But they are evil; 'tis the savage state
Is only good, and ours sophisticate!
See! the free creatures in their woods and plains,
Where without laws each happy monarch reigns,
King of himself—while we a number dread,
By slaves commanded and by dunces led;
Oh, let the name with either state agree—
Savage our own we'll name, and civil theirs shall be.'
  The silent Justice still astonish'd sate,
And wonder'd much whom he was gazing at;
Twice he essay'd to speak—but in a cough
The faint, indignant, dying speech went off:
'But who is this?' thought he—'a dæmon vile,
With wicked meaning and a vulgar style:
Hammond they call him; they can give the name
Of man to devils.—Why am I so tame?
Why crush I not the viper?'—Fear replied,
'Watch him awhile, and let his strength be tried;
He will be foil'd, if man; but if his aid
Be from beneath, 'tis well to be afraid.'
'We are call'd free!' said Hammond—'doleful times
When rulers add their insult to their crimes;
For should our scorn expose each powerful vice,
It would be libel, and we pay the price.'
  Thus with licentious words the man went on,

Proving that liberty of speech was gone;
That all were slaves—nor had we better chance
For better times than as allies to France.
Loud groan'd the stranger—Why, he must relate;
And own'd, 'In sorrow for his country's fate;'
'Nay, she were safe,' the ready man replied,
'Might patriots rule her, and could reasoners guide;
When all to vote, to speak, to teach, are free,
Whate'er their creeds or their opinions be;
When books of statutes are consumed in flames,
And courts and copyholds are empty names;
Then will be times of joy—but ere they come,
Havock, and war, and blood must be our doom.'
The man here paused—then loudly for reform
He call'd, and hail'd the prospect of the storm;
The wholesome blast, the fertilizing flood—
Peace gain'd by tumult, plenty bought with blood:
Sharp means, he own'd; but when the land's disease
Asks cure complete, no med'cines are like these.
Our Justice now, more led by fear than rage,
Saw it in vain with madness to engage;
With imps of darkness no man seeks to fight,
Knaves to instruct, or set deceivers right:
Then as the daring speech denounced these woes,
Sick at the soul, the grieving guest arose;
Quick on the board his ready cash he threw,
And from the dæmons to his closet flew:
There when secured, he pray'd with earnest zeal,
That all they wish'd these patriot-souls might feel;
'Let them to France, their darling country, haste,
And all the comforts of a Frenchman taste;
Let them his safety, freedom, pleasure know,
Feel all their rulers on the land bestow;
And be at length dismiss'd by one unerring blow;
Not hack'd and hew'd by one afraid to strike,
But shorn by that which shears all men alike;
Nor, as in Britain, let them curse delay
Of law, but borne without a form away—
Suspected, tried, condemn'd, and carted in a day;
Oh! let them taste what they so much approve,
These strong fierce freedoms of the land they love.'

Home came our hero, to forget no more
The fear he felt and ever must deplore:
For though he quickly join'd his friends again,
And could with decent force his themes maintain,
Still it occurr'd that, in a luckless time,
He fail'd to fight with heresy and crime;
It was observed his words were not so strong,
His tones so powerful, his harangues so long,
As in old times—for he would often drop
The lofty look, and of a sudden stop;
When conscience whisper'd, that he once was still,
And let the wicked triumph at their will;
And therefore now, when not a foe was near,
He had no right so valiant to appear.

Some years had pass'd, and he perceived his fears
Yield to the spirit of his earlier years—
When at a meeting, with his friends beside,
He saw an object that awaked his pride;
His shame, wrath, vengeance, indignation—all
Man's harsher feelings did that sight recall.

For lo! beneath him fix'd, our man of law
That lawless man the foe of order saw;
Once fear'd, now scorn'd; once dreaded, now abhorr'd;
A wordy man, and evil every word:
Again he gazed—'It is,' said he, 'the same;
Caught and secure: his master owes him shame:'
So thought our hero, who each instant found
His courage rising, from the numbers round.

As when a felon has escaped and fled,
So long, that law conceives the culprit dead;
And back recall'd her myrmidons, intent
On some new game, and with a stronger scent;
Till she beholds him in a place, where none
Could have conceived the culprit would have gone;
There he sits upright in his seat, secure,
As one whose conscience is correct and pure;
This rouses anger for the old offence,
And scorn for all such seeming and pretence;
So on this Hammond look'd our hero bold,
Rememb'ring well that vile offence of old;
And now he saw the rebel dared t'intrude

Among the pure, the loyal, and the good;
The crime provoked his wrath, the folly stirr'd his blood:
Nor wonder was it if so strange a sight
Caused joy with vengeance, terror with delight;
Terror like this a tiger might create,
A joy like that to see his captive state,
At once to know his force and then decree his fate.
 Hammond, much praised by numerous friends, was come
To read his lectures, so admired at home;
Historic lectures, where he loved to mix
His free plain hints on modern politics:
Here, he had heard, that numbers had design,
Their business finish'd, to sit down and dine;
This gave him pleasure, for he judged it right
To show by day, that he could speak at night.
Rash the design—for he perceived, too late,
Not one approving friend beside him sate;
The greater number, whom he traced around,
Were men in black, and he conceived they frown'd.
'I will not speak,' he thought; 'no pearls of mine
Shall be presented to this herd of swine;'
Not this avail'd him, when he cast his eye
On Justice Bolt; he could not fight, nor fly:
He saw a man to whom he gave the pain,
Which now he felt must be return'd again;
His conscience told him with what keen delight
He, at that time, enjoy'd a stranger's fright;
That stranger now befriended—he alone,
For all his insult, friendless, to atone;
Now he could feel it cruel that a heart
Should be distress'd, and none to take its part;
'Though one by one,' said Pride, 'I would defy
Much greater men, yet meeting every eye,
I do confess a fear—but he will pass me by.'
 Vain hope! the Justice saw the foe's distress,
With exultation he could not suppress;
He felt the fish was hook'd—and so forbore,
In playful spite, to draw it to the shore.
Hammond look'd round again; but none were near,
With friendly smile, to still his growing fear;

But all above him seem'd a solemn row
Of priests and deacons, so they seem'd below;
He wonder'd who his right-hand man might be—
Vicar of Holt cum Uppingham was he;
And who the man of that dark frown possess'd—
Rector of Bradley and of Barton-west;
'A pluralist,' he growl'd—but check'd the word,
That warfare might not, by his zeal, be stirr'd.
  But now began the man above to show
Fierce looks and threat'nings to the man below;
Who had some thoughts his peace by flight to seek—
But how then lecture, if he dared not speak!—
  Now as the Justice for the war prepared,
He seem'd just then to question if he dared;
'He may resist, although his power be small,
And growing desperate may defy us all;
One dog attack, and he prepares for flight—
Resist another, and he strives to bite;
Nor can I say, if this rebellious cur
Will fly for safety, or will scorn to stir.'
Alarm'd by this, he lash'd his soul to rage,
Burn'd with strong shame, and hurried to engage.
  As a male turkey straggling on the green,
When by fierce harriers, terriers, mongrels seen,
He feels the insult of the noisy train,
And skulks aside, though moved by much disdain;
But when that turkey, at his own barn-door,
Sees one poor straying puppy and no more,
(A foolish puppy who had left the pack,
Thoughtless what foe was threat'ning at his back,)
He moves about, as ship prepared to sail,
He hoists his proud rotundity of tail,
The half-seal'd eyes and changeful neck he shows,
Where, in its quick'ning colours, vengeance glows;
From red to blue the pendant wattles turn,
Blue mix'd with red, as matches when they burn;
And thus th' intruding snarler to oppose,
Urged by enkindling wrath, he gobbling goes.
  So look'd our hero in his wrath, his cheeks
Flush'd with fresh fires and glow'd in tingling streaks;
His breath by passion's force awhile restrain'd,

Like a stopp'd current, greater force regain'd;
So spoke, so look'd he, every eye and ear
Were fix'd to view him, or were turn'd to hear.
'My friends, you know me, you can witness all,
How, urged by passion, I restrain my gall;
And every motive to revenge withstand—
Save when I hear abused my native land.
'Is it not known, agreed, confirm'd, confess'd,
That of all people, we are govern'd best?
We have the force of monarchies; are free,
As the most proud republicans can be;
And have those prudent counsels that arise
In grave and cautious aristocracies;
And live there those, in such all-glorious state,
Traitors protected in the land they hate?
Rebels, still warring with the laws that give
To them subsistence?—Yes, such wretches live.
'Ours is a church reform'd, and now no more
Is aught for man to mend or to restore;
'Tis pure in doctrines, 'tis correct in creeds,
Has nought redundant, and it nothing needs;
No evil is therein—no wrinkle, spot,
Stain, blame, or blemish:—I affirm there's not.
'All this you know—now mark what once befell,
With grief I bore it, and with shame I tell;
I was entrapp'd—yes, so it came to pass,
'Mid heathen rebels, a tumultuous class;
Each to his country bore a hellish mind,
Each like his neighbour was of cursed kind;
The land that nursed them they blasphemed; the laws,
Their sovereign's glory, and their country's cause;
And who their mouth, their master-fiend, and who
Rebellion's oracle?——You, caitiff, you!'
He spoke, and standing stretch'd his mighty arm,
And fix'd the man of words, as by a charm.
'How raved that railer! Sure some hellish power
Restrain'd my tongue in that delirious hour,
Or I had hurl'd the shame and vengeance due
On him, the guide of that infuriate crew;
But to mine eyes such dreadful looks appear'd,

Such mingled yell of lying words I heard,
That I conceived around were dæmons all,
And till I fled the house, I fear'd its fall.
'Oh! could our country from our coasts expel
Such foes! to nourish those who wish her well:
This her mild laws forbid, but we may still
From us eject them by our sovereign will;
This let us do.'—He said, and then began
A gentler feeling for the silent man;
Ev'n in our hero's mighty soul arose
A touch of pity for experienced woes;
But this was transient, and with angry eye
He sternly look'd, and paused for a reply.
'Twas then the man of many words would speak—
But, in his trial, had them all to seek:
To find a friend he look'd the circle round,
But joy or scorn in every feature found;
He sipp'd his wine, but in those times of dread
Wine only adds confusion to the head;
In doubt he reason'd with himself—'And how
Harangue at night, if I be silent now?'
From pride and praise received, he sought to draw
Courage to speak, but still remain'd the awe;
One moment rose he with a forced disdain,
And then abash'd, sunk sadly down again;
While in our hero's glance he seem'd to read,
'Slave and insurgent! what hast thou to plead?'—
By desperation urged, he now began:
'I seek no favour—I—the Rights of Man!
Claim; and I—nay!—but give me leave—and I
Insist—a man—that is—and in reply,
I speak.'——Alas! each new attempt was vain:
Confused he stood, he sate, he rose again;
At length he growl'd defiance, sought the door,
Cursed the whole synod, and was seen no more.
'Laud we,' said Justice Bolt, 'the Powers above;
Thus could our speech the sturdiest foe remove.'
Exulting now he gain'd new strength of fame,
And lost all feelings of defeat and shame.
'He dared not strive, you witness'd—dared not lift
His voice, nor drive at his accursed drift:

So all shall tremble, wretches who oppose
Our church or state—thus be it to our foes.'
He spoke, and, seated with his former air,
Look'd his full self, and fill'd his ample chair;
Took one full bumper to each favourite cause,
And dwelt all night on politics and laws,
With high applauding voice, that gain'd him high applause.

2. THE PARTING HOUR

I did not take my leave of him, but had
Most pretty things to say: ere I could tell him
How I would think of him, at certain hours,
Such thoughts and such;—or ere I could
Give him that parting kiss, which I had set
Betwixt two charming words—comes in my father—
Cymbeline, Act I, Scene 3

Grief hath changed me since you saw me last,
And careful hours with Time's deformed hand
Have written strange defeatures o'er my face.
Comedy of Errors, Act V, Scene 1

Oh! if thou be the same Egean, speak,
And speak unto the same Emilia.
Comedy of Errors, Act V, Scene 1

I ran it through, ev'n from my boyish days
To the very moment that she bad me tell it,
Wherein I spake of most disastrous chances,
Of moving accidents, by flood, and field;
Of being taken by th' insolent foe
And sold to slavery. *Othello*, Act I, Scene 3

An old man, broken with the storms of fate,
Is come to lay his weary bones among you;
Give him a little earth for charity.
Henry VIII, Act IV, Scene 2

Minutely trace man's life; year after year,
Through all his days let all his deeds appear,
And then, though some may in that life be strange,
Yet there appears no vast nor sudden change:
The links that bind those various deeds are seen,
And no mysterious void is left between.
But let these binding links be all destroy'd,
All that through years he suffer'd or enjoy'd;

Let that vast gap be made, and then behold—
This was the youth, and he is thus when old;
Then we at once the work of Time survey,
And in an instant see a life's decay;
Pain mix'd with pity in our bosoms rise,
And sorrow takes new sadness from surprise.
Beneath yon tree, observe an ancient pair—
A sleeping man; a woman in her chair,
Watching his looks with kind and pensive air;
No wife, nor sister she, nor is the name
Nor kindred of this friendly pair the same;
Yet so allied are they, that few can feel
Her constant, warm, unwearied, anxious zeal;
Their years and woes, although they long have loved,
Keep their good name and conduct unreproved;
Thus life's small comforts they together share,
And while life lingers for the grave prepare.
No other subjects on their spirits press,
Nor gain such int'rest as the past distress;
Grievous events that from the mem'ry drive
Life's common cares, and those alone survive,
Mix with each thought, in every action share,
Darken each dream, and blend with every prayer.
To David Booth, his fourth and last-born boy,
Allen his name, was more than common joy;
And as the child grew up, there seem'd in him
A more than common life in every limb;
A strong and handsome stripling he became,
And the gay spirit answer'd to the frame;
A lighter, happier lad was never seen,
For ever easy, cheerful, or serene;
His early love he fix'd upon a fair
And gentle maid—they were a handsome pair.
They at an infant-school together play'd,
Where the foundation of their love was laid;
The boyish champion would his choice attend
In every sport, in every fray defend.
As prospects open'd and as life advanced,
They walk'd together, they together danced;
On all occasions, from their early years,
They mix'd their joys and sorrows, hopes and fears;

Each heart was anxious, till it could impart
Its daily feelings to its kindred heart;
As years increased, unnumber'd petty wars
Broke out between them; jealousies and jars;
Causeless indeed, and follow'd by a peace,
That gave to love—growth, vigour, and increase.
Whilst yet a boy, when other minds are void,
Domestic thoughts young Allen's hours employ'd;
Judith in gaining hearts had no concern,
Rather intent the matron's part to learn;
Thus early prudent and sedate they grew,
While lovers, thoughtful—and though children, true.
To either parents not a day appear'd,
When with this love they might have interfered:
Childish at first, they cared not to restrain;
And strong at last, they saw restriction vain;
Nor knew they when that passion to reprove—
Now idle fondness, now resistless love.
  So while the waters rise, the children tread
On the broad estuary's sandy bed;
But soon the channel fills, from side to side
Comes danger rolling with the deep'ning tide;
Yet none who saw the rapid current flow
Could the first instant of that danger know.
  The lovers waited till the time should come
When they together could possess a home:
In either house were men and maids unwed,
Hopes to be soothed, and tempers to be led.
Then Allen's mother of his favourite maid
Spoke from the feelings of a mind afraid:
'Dress and amusements were her sole employ,'
She said—'entangling her deluded boy;'
And yet, in truth, a mother's jealous love
Had much imagined and could little prove;
Judith had beauty—and if vain, was kind,
Discreet, and mild, and had a serious mind.
  Dull was their prospect—when the lovers met,
They said, we must not—dare not venture yet:
'Oh! could I labour for thee,' Allen cried,
'Why should our friends be thus dissatisfied?
On my own arm I could depend, but they

Still urge obedience—must I yet obey?'
Poor Judith felt the grief, but grieving begg'd delay.
  At length a prospect came that seem'd to smile,
And faintly woo them, from a Western Isle;
A kinsman there a widow's hand had gain'd,
'Was old, was rich, and childless yet remain'd;
Would some young Booth to his affairs attend,
And wait awhile, he might expect a friend.'
The elder brothers, who were not in love,
Fear'd the false seas, unwilling to remove;
But the young Allen, an enamour'd boy,
Eager an independence to enjoy,
Would through all perils seek it,—by the sea,—
Through labour, danger, pain, or slavery.
The faithful Judith his design approved,
For both were sanguine, they were young and loved.
The mother's slow consent was then obtain'd;
The time arrived, to part alone remain'd:
All things prepared, on the expected day
Was seen the vessel anchor'd in the bay.
From her would seamen in the evening come,
To take th' advent'rous Allen from his home;
With his own friends the final day he pass'd,
And every painful hour, except the last.
The grieving father urged the cheerful glass,
To make the moments with less sorrow pass;
Intent the mother look'd upon her son,
And wish'd th' assent withdrawn, the deed undone;
The younger sister, as he took his way,
Hung on his coat, and begg'd for more delay:
But his own Judith call'd him to the shore,
Whom he must meet, for they might meet no more;—
And there he found her—faithful, mournful, true,
Weeping and waiting for a last adieu!
The ebbing tide had left the sand, and there
Moved with slow steps the melancholy pair:
Sweet were the painful moments—but how sweet,
And without pain, when they again should meet!
Now either spoke, as hope and fear impress'd
Each their alternate triumph in the breast.
  Distance alarm'd the maid—she cried, ''Tis far!'

And danger too—'it is a time of war:
Then in those countries are diseases strange,
And women gay, and men are prone to change;
What then may happen in a year, when things
Of vast importance every moment brings!
But hark! an oar!' she cried, yet none appear'd—
'Twas love's mistake, who fancied what it fear'd;
And she continued—'Do, my Allen, keep
Thy heart from evil, let thy passions sleep;
Believe it good, nay glorious, to prevail,
And stand in safety where so many fail;
And do not, Allen, or for shame, or pride,
Thy faith abjure, or thy profession hide;
Can I believe *his* love will lasting prove,
Who has no rev'rence for the God I love?
I know thee well! how good thou art and kind;
But strong the passions that invade thy mind.—
Now, what to me hath Allen to commend?'—
'Upon my mother,' said the youth, 'attend;
Forget her spleen, and in my place appear;
Her love to me will make my Judith dear:
Oft I shall think, (such comfort lovers seek),
Who speaks of me, and fancy what they speak;
Then write on all occasions, always dwell
On hope's fair prospects, and be kind and well,
And ever choose the fondest, tenderest style.'
She answer'd, 'No,' but answer'd with a smile.
'And now, my Judith, at so sad a time,
Forgive my fear, and call it not my crime;
When with our youthful neighbours 'tis thy chance
To meet in walks, the visit or the dance,
When every lad would on my lass attend,
Choose not a smooth designer for a friend;
That fawning Philip!—nay, be not severe,
A rival's hope must cause a lover's fear.'
  Displeased she felt, and might in her reply
Have mix'd some anger, but the boat was nigh,
Now truly heard!—it soon was full in sight;—
Now the sad farewell, and the long good-night;
For, see!—his friends come hast'ning to the beach,
And now the gunwale is within the reach;

'Adieu!—farewell!—remember!'—and what more
Affection taught, was utter'd from the shore!
But Judith left them with a heavy heart,
Took a last view, and went to weep apart!
And now his friends went slowly from the place,
Where she stood still, the dashing oar to trace,
Till all were silent!—for the youth she pray'd,
And softly then return'd the weeping maid.
They parted, thus by hope and fortune led,
And Judith's hours in pensive pleasure fled;
But when return'd the youth?—the youth no more
Return'd exulting to his native shore;
But forty years were past, and then there came
A worn-out man with wither'd limbs and lame,
His mind oppress'd with woes, and bent with age his frame:
Yes! old and grieved, and trembling with decay,
Was Allen landing in his native bay,
Willing his breathless form should blend with kindred
clay.
In an autumnal eve he left the beach,
In such an eve he chanced the port to reach:
He was alone; he press'd the very place
Of the sad parting, of the last embrace:
There stood his parents, there retired the maid,
So fond, so tender, and so much afraid;
And on that spot, through many a year, his mind
Turn'd mournful back, half sinking, half resign'd.
No one was present; of its crew bereft,
A single boat was in the billows left;
Sent from some anchor'd vessel in the bay,
At the returning tide to sail away:
O'er the black stern the moonlight softly play'd,
The loosen'd foresail flapping in the shade;
All silent else on shore; but from the town
A drowsy peal of distant bells came down:
From the tall houses here and there, a light
Served some confused remembrance to excite:
'There,' he observed, and new emotions felt,
'Was my first home—and yonder Judith dwelt;
Dead! dead are all! I long—I fear to know,'
He said, and walk'd impatient, and yet slow.

Sudden there broke upon his grief a noise
Of merry tumult and of vulgar joys:
Seamen returning to their ship, were come,
With idle numbers straying from their home;
Allen among them mix'd, and in the old
Strove some familiar features to behold;
While fancy aided memory:—'Man! what cheer?'
A sailor cried; 'Art thou at anchor here?'
Faintly he answer'd, and then tried to trace
Some youthful features in some aged face:
A swarthy matron he beheld, and thought
She might unfold the very truths he sought:
Confused and trembling, he the dame address'd:
'The Booths! yet live they?' pausing and oppress'd;
Then spake again:—'Is there no ancient man,
David his name?—assist me, if you can.—
Flemmings there were—and Judith, doth she live?'
The woman gazed, nor could an answer give;
Yet wond'ring stood, and all were silent by,
Feeling a strange and solemn sympathy.
The woman musing said—'She knew full well
Where the old people came at last to dwell;
They had a married daughter and a son,
But they were dead, and now remain'd not one.'
'Yes,' said an elder, who had paused intent
On days long past, 'there was a sad event;—
One of these Booths—it was my mother's tale—
Here left his lass, I know not where to sail:
She saw their parting, and observed the pain;
But never came th' unhappy man again.'
'The ship was captured'—Allen meekly said
'And what became of the forsaken maid?'
The woman answer'd: 'I remember now,
She used to tell the lasses of her vow,
And of her lover's loss, and I have seen
The gayest hearts grow sad where she has been;
Yet in her grief she married, and was made
Slave to a wretch, whom meekly she obey'd
And early buried—but I know no more.
And hark! our friends are hast'ning to the shore.'
Allen soon found a lodging in the town,

And walk'd a man unnoticed up and down.
This house, and this, he knew, and thought a face
He sometimes could among a number trace:
Of names remember'd there remain'd a few,
But of no favourites, and the rest were new;
A merchant's wealth, when Allen went to sea,
Was reckon'd boundless.—Could he living be?
Or lived his son? for one he had, the heir
To a vast business, and a fortune fair.
No! but that heir's poor widow, from her shed,
With crutches went to take her dole of bread:
There was a friend whom he had left a boy,
With hope to sail the master of a hoy;
Him, after many a stormy day, he found
With his great wish, his life's whole purpose, crown'd.
This hoy's proud captain look'd in Allen's face,—
'Yours is, my friend,' said he 'a woful case;
We cannot all succeed; I now command
The Betsy sloop, and am not much at land;
But when we meet, you shall your story tell
Of foreign parts—I bid you now farewell!'
  Allen so long had left his native shore,
He saw but few whom he had seen before;
The older people, as they met him, cast
A pitying look, oft speaking as they pass'd—
'The man is Allen Booth, and it appears
He dwelt among us in his early years;
We see the name engraved upon the stones,
Where this poor wanderer means to lay his bones.'
Thus where he lived and loved—unhappy change!—
He seems a stranger, and finds all are strange.
  But now a widow, in a village near,
Chanced of the melancholy man to hear;
Old as she was, to Judith's bosom came
Some strong emotions at the well-known name;
He was her much-loved Allen, she had stay'd
Ten troubled years, a sad afflicted maid;
Then was she wedded, of his death assured,
And much of mis'ry in her lot endured;
Her husband died; her children sought their bread
In various places, and to her were dead.

The once fond lovers met; not grief nor age,
Sickness or pain, their hearts could disengage:
Each had immediate confidence; a friend
Both now beheld, on whom they might depend:
'Now is there one to whom I can express
My nature's weakness and my soul's distress.'
Allen look'd up, and with impatient heart—
'Let me not lose thee—never let us part:
So Heaven this comfort to my sufferings give,
It is not all distress to think and live.'
Thus Allen spoke—for time had not removed
The charms attach'd to one so fondly loved;
Who with more health, the mistress of their cot,
Labours to soothe the evils of his lot.
To her, to her alone, his various fate,
At various times, 'tis comfort to relate;
And yet his sorrow—she too loves to hear
What rings her bosom, and compels the tear.
  First he related how he left the shore,
Alarm'd with fears that they should meet no more:
Then, ere the ship had reach'd her purposed course,
They met and yielded to the Spanish force;
Then 'cross th' Atlantic seas they bore their prey,
Who grieving landed from their sultry bay;
And marching many a burning league, he found
Himself a slave upon a miner's ground:
There a good priest his native language spoke,
And gave some ease to his tormenting yoke;
Kindly advanced him in his master's grace,
And he was station'd in an easier place:
There, hopeless ever to escape the land,
He to a Spanish maiden gave his hand;
In cottage shelter'd from the blaze of day
He saw his happy infants round him play;
Where summer shadows, made by lofty trees,
Waved o'er his seat, and soothed his reveries;
E'en then he thought of England, nor could sigh,
But his fond Isabel demanded, 'Why?'
Grieved by the story, she the sigh repaid,
And wept in pity for the English maid:
Thus twenty years were pass'd, and pass'd his views

Of further bliss, for he had wealth to lose:
His friend now dead, some foe had dared to paint
'His faith as tainted: he his spouse would taint;
Make all his children infidels, and found
An English heresy on Christian ground.'
'Whilst I was poor,' said Allen, 'none would care
What my poor notions of religion were;
None ask'd me whom I worshipp'd, how I pray'd,
If due obedience to the laws were paid:
My good adviser taught me to be still,
Nor to make converts had I power or will.
I preach'd no foreign doctrine to my wife,
And never mention'd Luther in my life;
I, all they said, say what they would, allow'd,
And when the fathers bade me bow, I bow'd,
Their forms I follow'd, whether well or sick,
And was a most obedient Catholic.
But I had money, and these pastors found
My notions vague, heretical, unsound:
A wicked book they seized; the very Turk
Could not have read a more pernicious work;
To me pernicious, who if it were good
Or evil question'd not nor understood:
Oh! had I little but the book possess'd,
I might have read it, and enjoy'd my rest.'
  Alas! poor Allen, through his wealth was seen
Crimes that by poverty conceal'd had been:
Faults that in dusty pictures rest unknown
Are in an instant through the varnish shown.
  He told their cruel mercy; how at last,
In Christian kindness for the merits past,
They spared his forfeit life, but bade him fly,
Or for his crime and contumacy die;
Fly from all scenes, all objects of delight:
His wife, his children, weeping in his sight,
All urging him to flee, he fled, and cursed his flight.
  He next related how he found a way,
Guideless and grieving, to Campeachy Bay:
There in the woods he wrought, and there, among
Some lab'ring seamen, heard his native tongue:
The sound, one moment, broke upon his pain

With joyful force; he long'd to hear again:
Again he heard; he seized an offer'd hand,
'And when beheld you last our native land?'
He cry'd, 'and in what county? quickly say'—
The seamen answer'd—strangers all were they;
One only at his native port had been;
He, landing once, the quay and church had seen,
For that esteem'd; but nothing more he knew.
Still more to know, would Allen join the crew,
Sail where they sail'd, and, many a peril past,
They at his kinsman's isle their anchor cast;
But him they found not, nor could one relate
Aught of his will, his wish, or his estate.
This grieved not Allen; then again he sail'd
For England's coast, again his fate prevail'd:
War raged, and he, an active man and strong,
Was soon impress'd, and served his country long.
By various shores he pass'd, on various seas,
Never so happy as when void of ease.—
And then he told how in a calm distress'd,
Day after day his soul was sick of rest;
When, as a log upon the deep they stood,
Then roved his spirit to the inland wood;
Till, while awake, he dream'd, that on the seas
Were his loved home, the hill, the stream, the trees:
He gazed, he pointed to the scenes:—'There stand
My wife, my children, 'tis my lovely land;
See! there my dwelling—oh! delicious scene
Of my best life—unhand me—are ye men?'
   And thus the frenzy ruled him, till the wind
Brushed the fond pictures from the stagnant mind.
   He told of bloody fights, and how at length
The rage of battle gave his spirits strength:
'Twas in the Indian seas his limb he lost,
And he was left half-dead upon the coast;
But living gain'd, 'mid rich aspiring men,
A fair subsistence by his ready pen.
'Thus,' he continued, 'pass'd unvaried years,
Without events producing hopes or fears.'
Augmented pay procured him decent wealth,
But years advancing undermined his health;

Then oft-times in delightful dream he flew
To England's shore, and scenes his childhood knew:
He saw his parents, saw his fav'rite maid,
No feature wrinkled, not a charm decay'd;
And thus excited, in his bosom rose
A wish so strong, it baffled his repose;
Anxious he felt on English earth to lie;
To view his native soil, and there to die.
  He then described the gloom, the dread he found,
When first he landed on the chosen ground,
Where undefined was all he hoped and fear'd,
And how confused and troubled all appear'd;
His thoughts in past and present scenes employ'd,
All views in future blighted and destroy'd.
His were a medley of bewild'ring themes,
Sad as realities, and wild as dreams.
  Here his relation closes, but his mind
Flies back again some resting-place to find;
Thus silent, musing through the day, he sees
His children sporting by those lofty trees,
Their mother singing in the shady scene,
Where the fresh springs burst o'er the lively green;—
So strong his eager fancy, he affrights
The faithful widow by its powerful flights;
For what disturbs him he aloud will tell,
And cry—' 'Tis she, my wife! my Isabel!
Where are my children?'—Judith grieves to hear
How the soul works in sorrows so severe;
Assiduous all his wishes to attend,
Deprived of much, he yet may boast a friend;
Watch'd by her care, in sleep, his spirit takes
Its flight, and watchful finds her when he wakes.
  'Tis now her office; her attention see!
While her friend sleeps beneath that shading tree,
Careful she guards him from the glowing heat,
And pensive muses at her Allen's feet.
  And where is he? Ah! doubtless in those scenes
Of his best days, amid the vivid greens,
Fresh with unnumber'd rills, where ev'ry gale
Breathes the rich fragrance of the neighb'ring vale;
Smiles not his wife, and listens as there comes

The night-bird's music from the thick'ning glooms?
And as he sits with all these treasures nigh,
Blaze not with fairy light the phosphor-fly,
When like a sparkling gem it wheels illumined by?
This is the joy that now so plainly speaks
In the warm transient flushing of his cheeks;
For he is list'ning to the fancied noise
Of his own children, eager in their joys:
All this he feels, a dream's delusive bliss
Gives the expression, and the glow like this.
And now his Judith lays her knitting by,
These strong emotions in her friend to spy;
For she can fully of their nature deem—
But see! he breaks the long-protracted theme,
And wakes and cries—'My God! 'twas but a dream.'

3. THE GENTLEMAN FARMER

Pause then,
And weigh thy value with an even hand;
If thou beest rated by thy estimation,
Thou dost deserve enough.

Merchant of Venice, Act II, Scene 7

Because I will not do them wrong to mistrust any, I will do myself the right to trust none; and the fine is (for which I may go the finer), I will live a bachelor.

Much Ado about Nothing, Act I, Scene 1

Throw physic to the dogs, I'll none of it.

Macbeth, Act V, Scene 3

His promises are, as he then was, mighty;
And his performance, as he now is, nothing.

Henry VIII, Act IV, Scene 2

Gwyn was a farmer, whom the farmers all,
Who dwelt around, the Gentleman would call;
Whether in pure humility or pride,
They only knew, and they would not decide.
Far diff'rent he from that dull plodding tribe,
Whom it was his amusement to describe;
Creatures no more enliven'd than a clod,
But treading still as their dull fathers trod;

Who lived in times when not a man had seen
Corn sown by drill, or thresh'd by a machine:
He was of those whose skill assigns the prize
For creatures fed in pens, and stalls, and sties;
And who, in places where improvers meet,
To fill the land with fatness, had a seat;
Who in large mansions live like petty kings,
And speak of farms but as amusing things;
Who plans encourage, and who journals keep,
And talk with lords about a breed of sheep.
  Two are the species in this genus known;
One, who is rich in his profession grown,
Who yearly finds his ample stores increase,
From fortune's favours and a favouring lease;
Who rides his hunter, who his house adorns;
Who drinks his wine, and his disbursements scorns;
Who freely lives, and loves to show he can—
This is the farmer made the gentleman.
  The second species from the world is sent,
Tired with its strife, or with his wealth content;
In books and men beyond the former read,
To farming solely by a passion led,
Or by a fashion; curious in his land;
Now planning much, now changing what he plann'd;
Pleased by each trial, not by failures vex'd,
And ever certain to succeed the next;
Quick to resolve, and easy to persuade—
This is the gentleman, a farmer made.
  Gwyn was of these; he from the world withdrew
Early in life, his reasons known to few;
Some disappointment said, some pure good sense,
The love of land, the press of indolence;
His fortune known, and coming to retire,
If not a farmer, men had call'd him 'squire.
  Forty and five his years, no child or wife
Cross'd the still tenour of his chosen life;
Much land he purchased, planted far around,
And let some portions of superfluous ground
To farmers near him, not displeased to say,
'My tenants,' nor 'our worthy landlord,' they.
  Fix'd in his farm, he soon display'd his skill

In small-boned lambs, the horse-hoe, and the drill;
From these he rose to themes of nobler kind,
And show'd the riches of a fertile mind;
To all around their visits he repaid,
And thus his mansion and himself display'd.
His rooms were stately, rather fine than neat,
And guests politely call'd his house a seat;
At much expense was each apartment graced,
His taste was gorgeous, but it still was taste;
In full festoons the crimson curtains fell,
The sofas rose in bold elastic swell;
Mirrors in gilded frames display'd the tints
Of glowing carpets and of colour'd prints;
The weary eye saw every object shine,
And all was costly, fanciful, and fine.
  As with his friends he pass'd the social hours,
His generous spirit scorn'd to hide its powers;
Powers unexpected, for his eye and air
Gave no sure signs that eloquence was there;
Oft he began with sudden fire and force,
As loth to lose occasion for discourse;
Some, 'tis observed, who feel a wish to speak,
Will a due place for introduction seek;
On to their purpose step by step they steal,
And all their way, by certain signals, feel;
Others plunge in at once, and never heed
Whose turn they take, whose purpose they impede;
Resolved to shine, they hasten to begin,
Of ending thoughtless—and of these was Gwyn.
And thus he spake——
                ——'It grieves me to the soul
To see how man submits to man's control;
How overpower'd and shackled minds are led
In vulgar tracks, and to submission bred;
The coward never on himself relies,
But to an equal for assistance flies;
Man yields to custom as he bows to fate,
In all things ruled—mind, body, and estate;
In pain, in sickness, we for cure apply
To them we know not, and we know not why;
But that the creature has some jargon read,

And got some Scotchman's system in his head;
Some grave impostor, who will health insure,
Long as your patience or your wealth endure;
But mark them well, the pale and sickly crew,
They have not health, and can they give it you?
These solemn cheats their various methods choose;
A system fires them, as a bard his muse:
Hence wordy wars arise; the learn'd divide,
And groaning patients curse each erring guide.
'Next, our affairs are govern'd, buy or sell,
Upon the deed the law must fix its spell;
Whether we hire or let, we must have still
The dubious aid of an attorney's skill;
They take a part in every man's affairs,
And in all business some concern is theirs;
Because mankind in ways prescribed are found,
Like flocks that follow on a beaten ground,
Each abject nature in the way proceeds,
That now to shearing, now to slaughter leads.
'Should you offend, though meaning no offence,
You have no safety in your innocence;
The statute broken then is placed in view,
And men must pay for crimes they never knew:
Who would by law regain his plunder'd store,
Would pick up fallen merc'ry from the floor;
If he pursue it, here and there it slides;
He would collect it, but it more divides;
This part and this he stops, but still in vain,
It slips aside, and breaks in parts again;
Till, after time and pains, and care and cost,
He finds his labour and his object lost.
'But most it grieves me, (friends alone are round),
To see a man in priestly fetters bound;
Guides to the soul, these friends of Heaven contrive,
Long as man lives, to keep his fears alive;
Soon as an infant breathes, their rites begin;
Who knows not sinning, must be freed from sin;
Who needs no bond, must yet engage in vows;
Who has no judgment, must a creed espouse:
Advanced in life, our boys are bound by rules,
Are catechised in churches, cloisters, schools,

And train'd in thraldom to be fit for tools:
The youth grown up, he now a partner needs,
And lo! a priest, as soon as he succeeds.
What man of sense can marriage-rites approve?
What man of spirit can be bound to love?
Forced to be kind! compell'd to be sincere!
Do chains and fetters make companions dear?
Pris'ners indeed we bind; but though the bond
May keep them safe, it does not make them fond:
The ring, the vow, the witness, licence, prayers,
All parties known! made public all affairs!
Such forms men suffer, and from these they date
A deed of love begun with all they hate:
Absurd! that none the beaten road should shun,
But love to do what other dupes have done.
  'Well, now your priest has made you one of twain,
Look you for rest? Alas! you look in vain.
If sick, he comes; you cannot die in peace,
Till he attends to witness your release;
To vex your soul, and urge you to confess
The sins you feel, remember, or can guess:
Nay, when departed, to your grave he goes,
But there indeed he hurts not your repose.
  'Such are our burthens; part we must sustain,
But need not link new grievance to the chain:
Yet men like idiots will their frames surround
With these vile shackles, nor confess they're bound:
In all that most confines them they confide,
Their slavery boast, and make their bonds their pride;
E'en as the pressure galls them, they declare,
(Good souls!) how happy and how free they are!
As madmen, pointing round their wretched cells,
Cry, "Lo! the palace where our honour dwells."
  'Such is our state: but I resolve to live
By rules my reason and my feelings give;
No legal guards shall keep enthrall'd my mind,
No slaves command me, and no teachers blind.
  'Tempted by sins, let me their strength defy,
But have no second in a surplice by;
No bottle-holder, with officious aid,
To comfort conscience, weaken'd and afraid:

Then if I yield, my frailty is not known;
And, if I stand, the glory is my own.
  'When Truth and Reason are our friends, we seem
Alive! awake!—the superstitious dream.
  'Oh! then, fair Truth, for thee alone I seek,
Friend to the wise, supporter of the weak;
From thee we learn whate'er is right and just;
Forms to despise, professions to distrust;
Creeds to reject, pretensions to deride,
And, following thee, to follow none beside.'
  Such was the speech; it struck upon the ear
Like sudden thunder, none expect to hear.
He saw men's wonder with a manly pride,
And gravely smiled at guest electrified;
'A farmer this!' they said, 'Oh! let him seek
That place where he may for his country speak;
On some great question to harangue for hours,
While speakers hearing, envy nobler powers!'
  Wisdom like this, as all things rich and rare,
Must be acquired with pains, and kept with care;
In books he sought it, which his friends might view,
When their kind host the guarding curtain drew.
There were historic works for graver hours,
And lighter verse, to spur the languid powers;
There metaphysics, logic there had place;
But of devotion not a single trace—
Save what is taught in Gibbon's florid page,
And other guides of this inquiring age;
There Hume appear'd, and near, a splendid book
Composed by Gay's good Lord of Bolingbroke:
With these were mix'd the light, the free, the vain,
And from a corner peep'd the sage Tom Paine:
Here four neat volumes Chesterfield were named,
For manners much and easy morals famed;
With chaste Memoirs of Females, to be read
When deeper studies had confused the head.
  Such his resources, treasures where he sought
For daily knowledge till his mind was fraught:
Then when his friends were present, for their use
He would the riches he had stored produce;
He found his lamp burn clearer, when each day

He drew for all he purposed to display:
For these occasions, forth his knowledge sprung,
As mustard quickens on a bed of dung;
All was prepared, and guests allow'd the praise,
For what they saw he could so quickly raise.
  Such this new friend; and when the year came round,
The same impressive, reasoning sage was found:
Then, too, was seen the pleasant mansion graced
With a fair damsel—his no vulgar taste;
The neat Rebecca—sly, observant, still;
Watching his eye, and waiting on his will;
Simple yet smart her dress, her manners meek,
Her smiles spoke for her, she would seldom speak:
But watch'd each look, each meaning to detect,
And (pleased with notice) felt for all neglect.
  With her lived Gwyn a sweet harmonious life,
Who, forms excepted, was a charming wife:
The wives indeed, so made by vulgar law,
Affected scorn, and censured what they saw;
And what they saw not, fancied; said 'twas sin,
And took no notice of the wife of Gwyn:
But he despised their rudeness, and would prove
Theirs was compulsion and distrust, not love;
'Fools as they were! could they conceive that rings
And parsons' blessings were substantial things?'
They answer'd 'Yes;' while he contemptuous spoke
Of the low notions held by simple folk;
Yet, strange that anger in a man so wise
Should from the notions of these fools arise;
Can they so vex us, whom we so despise?
  Brave as he was, our hero felt a dread
Lest those who saw him kind should think him led;
If to his bosom fear a visit paid,
It was, lest he should be supposed afraid:
Hence sprang his orders; not that he desired
The things when done: obedience he required;
And thus, to prove his absolute command,
Ruled every heart, and moved each subject hand,
Assent he ask'd for every word and whim,
To prove that *he alone was king of him.*
  The still Rebecca, who her station knew,

With ease resign'd the honours not her due;
Well pleased, she saw that men her board would grace,
And wish'd not there to see a female face;
When by her lover she his spouse was styled,
Polite she thought it, and demurely smiled;
But when he wanted wives and maidens round
So to regard her, she grew grave, and frown'd;
And sometimes whisper'd—'Why should you respect
These people's notions, yet their forms reject?'
  Gwyn, though from marriage bond and fetter free,
Still felt abridgment in his liberty;
Something of hesitation he betray'd,
And in her presence thought of what he said.
Thus fair Rebecca, though she walk'd astray,
His creed rejecting, judged it right to pray;
To be at church, to sit with serious looks,
To read her Bible and her Sunday-books:
She hated all those new and daring themes,
And call'd his free conjectures, 'devil's dreams:'
She honour'd still the priesthood in her fall,
And claim'd respect and reverence for them all;
Call'd them 'of sin's destructive power the foes,
And not such blockheads as he might suppose.'
Gwyn to his friends would smile, and sometimes say,
''Tis a kind fool, why vex her in her way?'
Her way she took, and still had more in view,
For she contrived that he should take it too.
The daring freedom of his soul, 'twas plain,
In part was lost in a divided reign
A king and queen, who yet in prudence sway'd
Their peaceful state, and were in turn obey'd.
  Yet such our fate, that when we plan the best,
Something arises to disturb our rest:
For though in spirits high, in body strong,
Gwyn something felt—he knew not what—was wrong;
He wish'd to know, for he believed the thing,
If unremoved, would other evil bring:
'She must perceive, of late he could not eat,
And when he walk'd, he trembled on his feet:
He had forebodings, and he seem'd as one
Stopp'd on the road, or threaten'd by a dun;

He could not live, and yet, should he apply
To those physicians—he must sooner die.'
  The mild Rebecca heard with some disdain,
And some distress, her friend and lord complain:
His death she fear'd not, but had painful doubt
What his distemper'd nerves might bring about;
With power like hers she dreaded an ally,
And yet there was a person in her eye;—
She thought, debated, fix'd—'Alas!' she said,
A case like yours must be no more delay'd:
You hate these doctors: well! but were a friend
And doctor one, your fears would have an end:
My cousin Mollet—Scotland holds him now—
Is above all men skilful, all allow;
Of late a doctor, and within a while
He means to settle in this favour'd isle;
Should he attend you, with his skill profound,
You must be safe, and shortly would be sound.'
  When men in health against physicians rail,
They should consider that their nerves may fail;
Who calls a lawyer rogue, may find, too late,
On one of these depends his whole estate:
Nay, when the world can nothing more produce,
The priest, th' insulted priest, may have his use;
Ease, health, and comfort, lift a man so high,
These powers are dwarfs that he can scarcely spy;
Pain, sickness, languor, keep a man so low,
That these neglected dwarfs to giants grow.
Happy is he who through the medium sees
Of clear good sense—but Gwyn was not of these.
  He heard and he rejoiced: 'Ah! let him come,
And till he fixes, make my house his home.'
Home came the doctor—he was much admired;
He told the patient what his case required;
His hours for sleep, his time to eat and drink;
When he should ride, read, rest, compose, or think.
Thus join'd peculiar skill and art profound,
To make the fancy-sick no more than fancy-sound.
  With such attention, who could long be ill?
Returning health proclaim'd the doctor's skill.
Presents and praises from a grateful heart

Were freely offer'd on the patient's part;
In high repute the doctor seem'd to stand,
But still had got no footing in the land;
And, as he saw the seat was rich and fair,
He felt disposed to fix his station there:
To gain his purpose he perform'd the part
Of a good actor, and prepared to start;
Not like a traveller in a day serene,
When the sun shone and when the roads were clean:
Not like the pilgrim, when the morning gray,
The ruddy eve succeeding, sends his way;
But in a season when the sharp east wind
Had all its influence on a nervous mind;
When past the parlour's front it fiercely blew,
And Gwyn sat pitying every bird that flew,
This strange physician said—'Adieu! adieu!
Farewell!—Heaven bless you!—if you should—but no,
You need not fear—farewell! 'tis time to go.'
  The doctor spoke; and as the patient heard,
His old disorders (dreadful train!) appear'd;
'He felt the tingling tremor, and the stress
Upon his nerves that he could not express;
Should his good friend forsake him, he perhaps
Might meet his death, and surely a relapse.'
  So, as the doctor seem'd intent to part,
He cried in terror—'Oh! be where thou art:
Come, thou art young, and unengaged; oh! come,
Make me thy friend, give comfort to mine home;
I have now symptoms that require thine aid,
Do, doctor, stay'—th' obliging doctor stay'd.
  Thus Gwyn was happy; he had now a friend,
And a meek spouse on whom he could depend:
But now possess'd of male and female guide,
Divided power he thus must subdivide:
In earlier days he rode, or sat at ease
Reclined, and having but himself to please;
Now if he would a fav'rite nag bestride
He sought permission—'Doctor, may I ride?'
(Rebecca's eye her sovereign pleasure told)—
'I think you may, but guarded from the cold,
Ride forty minutes.'—Free and happy soul!

He scorn'd submission, and a man's control;
But where such friends in every care unite
All for his good, obedience is delight.
Now Gwyn a sultan bade affairs adieu,
Led and assisted by the faithful two;
The favourite fair, Rebecca, near him sat,
And whisper'd whom to love, assist, or hate;
While the chief vizier eased his lord of cares,
And bore himself the burden of affairs:
No dangers could from such alliance flow,
But from that law, that changes all below.
When wint'ry winds with leaves bestrew'd the ground,
And men were coughing all the village round;
When public papers of invasion told,
Diseases, famines, perils new and old;
When philosophic writers fail'd to clear
The mind of gloom, and lighter works to cheer;
Then came fresh terrors on our hero's mind—
Fears unforeseen, and feelings undefined.
'In outward ills,' he cried, 'I rest assured
Of my friend's aid; they will in time be cured:
But can his art subdue, resist, control
These inward griefs and troubles of the soul?
Oh! my Rebecca! my disorder'd mind,
No help in study, none in thought can find:
What must I do, Rebecca?' She proposed
The parish-guide; but what could be disclosed
To a proud priest?—'No! him I have defied,
Insulted, slighted—shall he be my guide?
But one there is, and if report be just,
A wise good man, whom I may safely trust;
Who goes from house to house, from ear to ear,
To make his truths, his Gospel truths, appear;
True if indeed they be, 'tis time that I should hear:
Send for that man; and if report be just,
I, like Cornelius, will the teacher trust;
But if deceiver, I the vile deceit
Shall soon discover, and discharge the cheat.'
To Doctor Mollet was the grief confess'd,
While Gwyn the freedom of his mind express'd;

Yet own'd it was to ills and errors prone,
And he for guilt and frailty must atone.
'My books, perhaps,' the wav'ring mortal cried,
'Like men deceive—I would be satisfied;
And to my soul the pious man may bring
Comfort and light—do let me try the thing.'
  The cousins met, what pass'd with Gwyn was told:
'Alas!' the doctor said, 'how hard to hold
These easy minds, where all impressions made
At first sink deeply, and then quickly fade;
For while so strong these new-born fancies reign,
We must divert them, to oppose is vain:
You see him valiant now, he scorns to heed
The bigot's threat'nings or the zealot's creed:
Shook by a dream, he next for truth receives
What frenzy teaches, and what fear believes;
And this will place him in the power of one
Whom we must seek, because we cannot shun.'
  Wisp had been ostler at a busy inn,
Where he beheld and grew in dread of sin;
Then to a Baptists' meeting found his way,
Became a convert, and was taught to pray;
Then preach'd; and being earnest and sincere,
Brought other sinners to religious fear:
Together grew his influence and his fame,
Till our dejected hero heard his name:
His little failings were a grain of pride,
Raised by the numbers he presumed to guide:
A love of presents, and of lofty praise
For his meek spirit and his humble ways;
But though this spirit would on flattery feed,
No praise could blind him and no arts mislead:—
To him the doctor made the wishes known
Of his good patron, but conceal'd his own;
He of all teachers had distrust and doubt,
And was reserved in what he came about;
Though on a plain and simple message sent,
He had a secret and a bold intent:
Their minds at first were deeply veil'd; disguise
Form'd the slow speech, and op'd the eager eyes;
Till by degrees sufficient light was thrown

On every view, and all the business shown.
Wisp, as a skilful guide who led the blind,
Had powers to rule and awe the vapourish mind;
But not the changeful will, the wavering fear to bind:
And should his conscience give him leave to dwell
With Gwyn, and every rival power expel
(A dubious point), yet he, with every care,
Might soon the lot of the rejected share;
And other Wisps be found like him to reign,
And then be thrown upon the world again:
He thought it prudent then, and felt it just,
The present guides of his new friend to trust;
True, he conceived, to touch the harder heart
Of the cool doctor, was beyond his art;
But mild Rebecca he could surely sway,
While Gwyn would follow where she led the way:
So to do good, (and why a duty shun,
Because rewarded for the good when done?)
He with his friends would join in all they plann'd,
Save when his faith or feelings should withstand;
There he must rest, sole judge of his affairs,
While they might rule exclusively in theirs.
    When Gwyn his message to the teacher sent,
He fear'd his friends would show their discontent;
And prudent seem'd it to th' attendant pair,
Not all at once to show an aspect fair:
On Wisp they seem'd to look with jealous eye,
And fair Rebecca was demure and shy;
But by degrees the teacher's worth they knew,
And were so kind, they seem'd converted too.
    Wisp took occasion to the nymph to say,
'You must be married: will you name the day?'
She smiled,—' 'Tis well; but should he not comply,
Is it quite safe th' experiment to try?'—
'My child,' the teacher said, 'who feels remorse,
(And feels not he?) must wish relief of course;
And can he find it, while he fears the crime?—
You must be married; will you name the time?'
    Glad was the patron as a man could be,
Yet marvell'd too, to find his guides agree;
'But what the cause?' he cried; ' 'tis genuine love for me.'

Each found his part, and let one act describe
The powers and honours of th' accordant tribe:—
A man for favour to the mansion speeds,
And cons his threefold task as he proceeds;
To teacher Wisp he bows with humble air,
And begs his interest for a barn's repair:
Then for the doctor he inquires, who loves
To hear applause for what his skill improves,
And gives for praise, assent,—and to the fair
He brings of pullets a delicious pair;
Thus sees a peasant with discernment nice,
A love of power, conceit, and avarice.
Lo! now the change complete: the convert Gwyn
Has sold his books, and has renounced his sin;
Mollet his body orders, Wisp his soul,
And o'er his purse the lady takes control;
No friends beside he needs, and none attend—
Soul, body, and estate, has each a friend;
And fair Rebecca leads a virtuous life—
She rules a mistress, and she reigns a wife.

4. PROCRASTINATION

Heaven witness
I have been to you ever true and humble.
Henry VIII, Act II, Scene 4

Gentle lady,
When first I did impart my love to you,
I freely told you all the wealth I had.
Merchant of Venice, Act III, Scene 2

The fatal time
Casts off all ceremonies and vows of love,
And ample interchange of sweet discourse,
Which so long sunder'd friends should dwell upon.
Richard III, Act V, Scene 3

I know thee not, old man; fall to thy prayers.
2 Henry IV, Act V, Scene 5

Farewell,
Thou pure impiety, thou impious purity,
For thee I'll lock up all the gates of love.
Much Ado About Nothing, Act IV, Scene 1

Love will expire, the gay, the happy dream
Will turn to scorn, indiff'rence, or esteem:
Some favour'd pairs, in this exchange, are bless'd,
Nor sigh for raptures in a state of rest;
Others, ill match'd, with minds unpair'd, repent
At once the deed, and know no more content;
From joy to anguish they, in haste, decline,
And with their fondness, their esteem resign:
More luckless still their fate, who are the prey
Of long-protracted hope and dull delay;
'Mid plans of bliss the heavy hours pass on,
Till love is wither'd, and till joy is gone.
This gentle flame two youthful hearts possess'd,
The sweet disturber of unenvied rest:
The prudent Dinah was the maid beloved,
And the kind Rupert was the swain approved:
A wealthy aunt her gentle niece sustain'd,
He, with a father, at his desk, remain'd;
The youthful couple, to their vows sincere,
Thus loved expectant; year succeeding year,
With pleasant views and hopes, but not a prospect near.
Rupert some comfort in his station saw,
But the poor virgin lived in dread and awe;
Upon her anxious looks the widow smiled,
And bade her wait, 'for she was yet a child.'
She for her neighbour had a due respect,
Nor would his son encourage or reject;
And thus the pair, with expectations vain,
Beheld the seasons change and change again:
Meantime the nymph her tender tales perused,
Where cruel aunts impatient girls refused;
While hers, though teasing, boasted to be kind,
And she, resenting, to be all resign'd.
The dame was sick, and when the youth applied
For her consent, she groan'd, and cough'd, and cried:
Talk'd of departing, and again her breath
Drew hard, and cough'd, and talk'd again of death:
'Here you may live, my Dinah! here the boy
And you together my estate enjoy;'
Thus to the lovers was her mind express'd,
Till they forbore to urge the fond request.

4. *Procrastination*

Servant, and nurse, and comforter, and friend,
Dinah had still some duty to attend;
But yet their walk, when Rupert's evening call
Obtain'd an hour, made sweet amends for all;
So long they now each other's thoughts had known,
That nothing seem'd exclusively their own;
But with the common wish, the mutual fear,
They now had travell'd to their thirtieth year.
At length a prospect open'd—but, alas!
Long time must yet, before the union, pass;
Rupert was call'd in other clime, t'increase
Another's wealth, and toil for future peace;
Loth were the lovers; but the aunt declared
'Twas fortune's call, and they must be prepared;
'You now are young, and for this brief delay,
And Dinah's care, what I bequeath will pay;
All will be yours; nay, love, suppress that sigh;
The kind must suffer, and the best must die.'
Then came the cough, and strong the signs it gave
Of holding long contention with the grave.
The lovers parted with a gloomy view,
And little comfort but that both were true;
He for uncertain duties doom'd to steer,
While hers remain'd too certain and severe.
Letters arrived, and Rupert fairly told
'His cares were many, and his hopes were cold;
The view more clouded, that was never fair,
And love alone preserved him from despair:'
In other letters brighter hopes he drew,
'His friends were kind, and he believed them true.'
When the sage widow Dinah's grief descried,
She wonder'd much why one so happy sigh'd:
Then bade her see how her poor aunt sustain'd
The ills of life, nor murmur'd nor complain'd.
To vary pleasures, from the lady's chest
Were drawn the pearly string and tabby vest;
Beads, jewels, laces, all their value shown,
With the kind notice—'They will be your own.'
This hope, these comforts cherish'd day by day,
To Dinah's bosom made a gradual way;
Till love of treasure had as large a part,

As love of Rupert, in the virgin's heart.
Whether it be that tender passions fail,
From their own nature, while the strong prevail;
Or whether av'rice, like the poison-tree,
Kills all beside it, and alone will be;
Whatever cause prevail'd, the pleasure grew
In Dinah's soul,—she loved the hoards to view;
With lively joy those comforts she survey'd,
And love grew languid in the careful maid.
Now the grave niece partook the widow's cares,
Look'd to the great and ruled the small affairs;
Saw clean'd the plate, arranged the china show,
And felt her passion for a shilling grow:
Th' indulgent aunt increased the maid's delight,
By placing tokens of her wealth in sight;
She loved the value of her bonds to tell,
And spake of stocks, and how they rose and fell.
This passion grew, and gain'd at length such sway,
That other passions shrank to make it way;
Romantic notions now the heart forsook,
She read but seldom, and she changed her book;
And for the verses she was wont to send,
Short was her prose, and she was Rupert's friend.
Seldom she wrote, and then the widow's cough,
And constant call, excused her breaking off;
Who, now oppress'd, no longer took the air,
But sate and dozed upon an easy chair.
The cautious doctor saw the case was clear,
But judged it best to have companions near;
They came, they reason'd, they prescribed—at last,
Like honest men, they said their hopes were past;
Then came a priest—'tis comfort to reflect,
When all is over, there was no neglect;
And all was over—by her husband's bones,
The widow rests beneath the sculptured stones,
That yet record their fondness and their fame,
While all they left the virgin's care became;
Stock, bonds, and buildings;—it disturb'd her rest,
To think what load of troubles she possess'd:
Yet, if a trouble, she resolved to take
Th' important duty, for the donor's sake;

She too was heiress to the widow's taste,
Her love of hoarding, and her dread of waste.
  Sometimes the past would on her mind intrude,
And then a conflict full of care ensued;
The thoughts of Rupert on her mind would press,
His worth she knew, but doubted his success;
Of old she saw him heedless; what the boy
Forbore to save, the man would not enjoy;
Oft had he lost the chance that care would seize,
Willing to live, but more to live at ease:
Yet could she not a broken vow defend,
And Heav'n, perhaps, might yet enrich her friend.
  Month after month was pass'd, and all were spent
In quiet comfort and in rich content:
Miseries there were, and woes the world around,
But these had not her pleasant dwelling found;
She knew that mothers grieved, and widows wept,
And she was sorry, said her prayers, and slept:
Thus pass'd the seasons, and to Dinah's board
Gave what the seasons to the rich afford;
For she indulged, nor was her heart so small,
That one strong passion should engross it all.
  A love of splendour now with av'rice strove,
And oft appear'd to be the stronger love:
A secret pleasure fill'd the widow's breast,
When she reflected on the hoards possess'd;
But livelier joy inspired th' ambitious maid,
When she the purchase of those hoards display'd:
In small but splendid room she loved to see
That all was placed in view and harmony;
There, as with eager glance she look'd around,
She much delight in every object found;
While books devout were near her—to destroy,
Should it arise, an overflow of joy.
  Within that fair apartment, guests might see
The comforts cull'd for wealth by vanity:
Around the room an Indian paper blazed,
With lively tint and figures boldly raised;
Silky and soft upon the floor below,
Th' elastic carpet rose with crimson glow;
All things around implied both cost and care,

What met the eye was elegant or rare:
Some curious trifles round the room were laid,
By hope presented to the wealthy maid:
Within a costly case of varnish'd wood,
In level rows, her polish'd volumes stood;
Shown as a favour to a chosen few,
To prove what beauty for a book could do:
A silver urn with curious work was fraught;
A silver lamp from Grecian pattern wrought:
Above her head, all gorgeous to behold,
A time-piece stood on feet of burnish'd gold;
A stag's-head crest adorn'd the pictured case,
Through the pure crystal shone th' enamell'd face;
And while on brilliants moved the hands of steel,
It click'd from pray'r to pray'r, from meal to meal.
  Here as the lady sate, a friendly pair
Stept in t' admire the view, and took their chair:
They then related how the young and gay
Were thoughtless wandering in the broad highway;
How tender damsels sail'd in tilted boats,
And laugh'd with wicked men in scarlet coats;
And how we live in such degen'rate times,
That men conceal their wants, and show their crimes;
While vicious deeds are screen'd by fashion's name,
And what was once our pride is now our shame.
  Dinah was musing, as her friends discoursed,
When these last words a sudden entrance forced
Upon her mind, and what was once her pride
And now her shame, some painful views supplied;
Thoughts of the past within her bosom press'd,
And there a change was felt, and was confess'd:
While thus the virgin strove with secret pain,
Her mind was wandering o'er the troubled main;
Still she was silent, nothing seem'd to see,
But sate and sigh'd in pensive reverie.
  The friends prepared new subjects to begin,
When tall Susannah, maiden starch, stalk'd in;
Not in her ancient mode, sedate and slow,
As when she came, the mind she knew, to know;
Nor as, when list'ning half an hour before,
She twice or thrice tapp'd gently at the door;

But, all decorum cast in wrath aside,
'I think the devil's in the man!' she cried;
'A huge sailor, with his tawny cheek,
And pitted face, will with my lady speak;
He grinn'd an ugly smile, and said he knew,
Please you, my lady, 'twould be joy to you;
What must I answer?'—Trembling and distress'd
Sank the pale Dinah by her fears oppress'd;
When thus alarm'd, and brooking no delay,
Swift to her room the stranger made his way.
　'Revive, my love!' said he, 'I've done thee harm,
Give me thy pardon,' and he look'd alarm:
Meantime the prudent Dinah had contrived
Her soul to question, and she then revived.
　'See! my good friend,' and then she raised her head,
'The bloom of life, the strength of youth is fled;
Living we die; to us the world is dead;
We parted bless'd with health, and I am now
Age-struck and feeble, so I find art thou;
Thine eye is sunken, furrow'd is thy face,
And downward look'st thou—so we run our race;
And happier they, whose race is nearly run,
Their troubles over, and their duties done.'
　'True, lady, true, we are not girl and boy;
But time has left us something to enjoy.'
　'What! thou hast learn'd my fortune?—yes, I live
To feel how poor the comforts wealth can give;
Thou too perhaps art wealthy; but our fate
Still mocks our wishes, wealth is come too late.'
　'To me nor late nor early; I am come
Poor as I left thee to my native home:
Nor yet,' said Rupert, 'will I grieve; 'tis mine
To share thy comforts, and the glory thine;
For thou wilt gladly take that generous part
That both exalts and gratifies the heart;
While mine rejoices.'—'Heavens!' return'd the maid,
'This talk to one so wither'd and decay'd?
No! all my care is now to fit my mind
For other spousal, and to die resign'd:
As friend and neighbour, I shall hope to see
These noble views, this pious love in thee;

That we together may the change await,
Guides and spectators in each other's fate;
When fellow-pilgrims, we shall daily crave
The mutual prayer that arms us for the grave.'
  Half angry, half in doubt, the lover gazed
On the meek maiden, by her speech amazed;
'Dinah,' said he, 'dost thou respect thy vows?
What spousal mean'st thou?—thou art Rupert's spouse;
The chance is mine to take, and thine to give;
But, trifling this, if we together live:
Can I believe, that, after all the past,
Our vows, our loves, thou wilt be false at last?
Something thou hast—I know not what—in view;
I find thee pious—let me find thee true.'
  'Ah! cruel this; but do, my friend, depart;
And to its feelings leave my wounded heart.'
  'Nay, speak at once; and Dinah, let me know,
Mean'st thou to take me, now I'm wreck'd, in tow?
Be fair; nor longer keep me in the dark;
Am I forsaken for a trimmer spark?
Heav'n's spouse thou art not; nor can I believe
That God accepts her who will man deceive:
True I am shatter'd, I have service seen,
And service done, and have in trouble been;
My cheek (it shames me not) has lost its red,
And the brown buff is o'er my features spread;
Perchance my speech is rude; for I among
Th' untamed have been, in temper and in tongue;
Have been trepann'd, have lived in toil and care,
And wrought for wealth I was not doom'd to share;
It touch'd me deeply, for I felt a pride
In gaining riches for my destined bride:
Speak then my fate; for these my sorrows past,
Time lost, youth fled, hope wearied, and at last
This doubt of thee—a childish thing to tell,
But certain truth—my very throat they swell;
They stop the breath, and but for shame could I
Give way to weakness, and with passion cry;
These are unmanly struggles, but I feel
This hour must end them, and perhaps will heal.'—
  Here Dinah sigh'd as if afraid to speak—

And then repeated—'They were frail and weak;
His soul she loved, and hoped he had the grace
To fix his thoughts upon a better place.'
She ceased;—with steady glance, as if to see
The very root of this hypocrisy,—
He her small fingers moulded in his hard
And bronzed broad hand; then told her his regard,
His best respect were gone, but love had still
Hold in his heart, and govern'd yet the will—
Or he would curse her:—saying this, he threw
The hand in scorn away, and bade adieu
To every lingering hope, with every care in view.
Proud and indignant, suffering, sick, and poor,
He grieved unseen; and spoke of love no more—
Till all he felt in indignation died,
As hers had sunk in avarice and pride.
In health declining, as in mind distress'd,
To some in power his troubles he confess'd,
And shares a parish-gift;—at prayers he sees
The pious Dinah dropp'd upon her knees;
Thence as she walks the street with stately air,
As chance directs, oft meet the parted pair:
When he, with thickset coat of badge-man's blue,
Moves near her shaded silk of changeful hue;
When his thin locks of grey approach her braid,
A costly purchase made in beauty's aid;
When his frank air, and his unstudied pace,
Are seen with her soft manner, air, and grace,
And his plain artless look with her sharp meaning face;
It might some wonder in a stranger move,
How these together could have talk'd of love.
Behold them now!—see there a tradesman stands,
And humbly hearkens to some fresh commands;
He moves to speak, she interrupts him—'Stay,'
Her air expresses—'Hark! to what I say:'
Ten paces off, poor Rupert on a seat
Has taken refuge from the noon-day heat,
His eyes on her intent, as if to find
What were the movements of that subtle mind:
How still!—how earnest is he!—it appears
His thoughts are wand'ring through his earlier years;

Through years of fruitless labour, to the day
When all his earthly prospects died away:
'Had I,' he thinks, 'been wealthier of the two,
Would she have found me so unkind, untrue?
Or knows not man when poor, what man when rich will do?
Yes, yes! I feel that I had faithful proved,
And should have soothed and raised her, bless'd and loved.'
But Dinah moves—she had observed before
The pensive Rupert at an humble door:
Some thoughts of pity raised by his distress,
Some feeling touch of ancient tenderness;
Religion, duty urged the maid to speak
In terms of kindness to a man so weak:
But pride forbad, and to return would prove
She felt the shame of his neglected love;
Nor wrapp'd in silence could she pass, afraid
Each eye should see her, and each heart upbraid;
One way remain'd—the way the Levite took,
Who without mercy could on misery look;
(A way perceived by craft, approved by pride),
She cross'd, and pass'd him on the other side.

5. THE PATRON

It were all one,
That I should love a bright peculiar star,
And think to wed it; she is so much above me:
In her bright radiance and collateral heat
Must I be comforted, not in her sphere.
All's Well that Ends Well, Act I, Scene 1

Poor wretches, that depend
On greatness' favours, dream as I have done,—
Wake and find nothing.
Cymbeline, Act v, Scene 4

And since—
Th' affliction of my mind amends, with which
I fear a madness held me. *The Tempest*, Act v

A borough-bailiff, who to law was train'd,
A wife and sons in decent state maintain'd;
He had his way in life's rough ocean steer'd,

And many a rock and coast of danger clear'd;
He saw where others fail'd, and care had he
Others in him should not such failings see;
His sons in various busy states were placed,
And all began the sweets of gain to taste,
Save John, the younger; who, of sprightly parts,
Felt not a love for money-making arts:
In childhood feeble, he, for country air,
Had long resided with a rustic pair;
All round whose room were doleful ballads, songs,
Of lovers' sufferings and of ladies' wrongs;
Of peevish ghosts who came at dark midnight,
For breach of promise, guilty men to fight;
Love, marriage, murder, were the themes, with these,
All that on idle, ardent spirits seize;
Robbers at land and pirates on the main,
Enchanters foil'd, spells broken, giants slain;
Legends of love, with tales of halls and bowers,
Choice of rare songs, and garlands of choice flowers,
And all the hungry mind without a choice devours.
  From village-children kept apart by pride,
With such enjoyments, and without a guide,
Inspired by feelings all such words infused,
John snatch'd a pen, and wrote as he perused:
With the like fancy he could make his knight
Slay half an host and put the rest to flight;
With the like knowledge, he could make him ride
From isle to isle at Parthenissa's side;
And with a heart yet free, no busy brain
Form'd wilder notions of delight and pain,
The raptures smiles create, the anguish of disdain.
  Such were the fruits of John's poetic toil,
Weeds, but still proofs of vigour in the soil:
He nothing purposed but with vast delight,
Let Fancy loose, and wonder'd at her flight:
His notions of poetic worth were high,
And of his own still-hoarded poetry;—
These to his father's house he bore with pride,
A miser's treasure, in his room to hide;
Till spurr'd by glory, to a reading friend
He kindly show'd the sonnets he had penn'd:

With erring judgment, though with heart sincere,
That friend exclaim'd, 'These beauties must appear.'
In Magazines they claim'd their share of fame,
Though undistinguish'd by their author's name;
And with delight the young enthusiast found
The muse of Marcus with applauses crown'd.
This heard the father, and with some alarm:
'The boy,' said he, 'will neither trade nor farm;
He for both law and physic is unfit;
Wit he may have, but cannot live on wit:
Let him his talents then to learning give,
Where verse is honour'd, and where poets live.'
  John kept his terms at college unreproved,
Took his degree, and left the life he loved;
Not yet ordain'd, his leisure he employ'd
In the light labours he so much enjoy'd;
His favourite notions and his daring views
Were cherish'd still, and he adored the Muse.
  'A little time, and he should burst to light,
And admiration of the world excite;
And every friend, now cool and apt to blame
His fond pursuit, would wonder at his fame.'
When led by fancy, and from view retired,
He call'd before him all his heart desired;
'Fame shall be mine, then wealth shall I possess,
And beauty next an ardent lover bless;
For me the maid shall leave her nobler state,
Happy to raise and share her poet's fate.'
He saw each day his father's frugal board,
With simple fare by cautious prudence stored;
Where each indulgence was foreweigh'd with care,
And the grand maxims were to save and spare:
Yet in his walks, his closet, and his bed,
All frugal cares and prudent counsels fled;
And bounteous Fancy, for his glowing mind,
Wrought various scenes, and all of glorious kind;
Slaves of the *ring* and *lamp*! what need of you,
When Fancy's self such magic deeds can do?
  Though rapt in visions of no vulgar kind,
To common subjects stoop'd our poet's mind;
And oft, when wearied with more ardent flight,

He felt a spur satiric song to write;
A rival burgess his bold muse attack'd,
And whipp'd severely for a well-known fact;
For while he seem'd to all demure and shy,
Our poet gazed at what was passing by;
And ev'n his father smiled when playful wit,
From his young bard, some haughty object hit.
From ancient times the borough where they dwelt
Had mighty contest at elections felt:
Sir Godfrey Ball, 'tis true, had held in pay
Electors many for the trying day;
But in such golden chains to bind them all
Required too much for e'en Sir Godfrey Ball.
A member died, and to supply his place,
Two heroes enter'd for th' important race;
Sir Godfrey's friend and Earl Fitzdonnel's son,
Lord Frederick Damer, both prepared to run;
And partial numbers saw with vast delight
Their good young lord oppose the proud old knight.
Our poet's father, at a first request,
Gave the young lord his vote and interest;
And what he could our poet, for he stung
The foe by verse satiric, said and sung.
Lord Frederick heard of all this youthful zeal,
And felt as lords upon a canvass feel;
He read the satire, and he saw the use
That such cool insult, and such keen abuse,
Might on the wavering minds of voting men produce;
Then too his praises were in contrast seen,
'A lord as noble as the knight was mean.'
'I much rejoice,' he cried, 'such worth to find;
To this the world must be no longer blind:
His glory will descend from sire to son,
The Burns of English race, the happier Chatterton.'
Our poet's mind, now hurried and elate,
Alarm'd the anxious parent for his fate;
Who saw with sorrow, should their friend succeed,
That much discretion would the poet need.
Their friend succeeded, and repaid the zeal
The poet felt, and made opposers feel,
By praise (from lords how soothing and how sweet!)

And invitation to his noble seat.
The father ponder'd, doubtful if the brain
Of his proud boy such honour could sustain;
Pleased with the favours offer'd to a son,
But seeing dangers few so ardent shun.
  Thus, when they parted, to the youthful breast
The father's fears were by his love impress'd:
'There will you find, my son, the courteous ease
That must subdue the soul it means to please;
That soft attention which ev'n beauty pays
To wake our passions, or provoke our praise;
There all the eye beholds will give delight,
Where every sense is flatter'd like the sight:
This is your peril; can you from such scene
Of splendour part, and feel your mind serene,
And in the father's humble state resume
The frugal diet and the narrow room?'
To this the youth with cheerful heart replied,
Pleased with the trial, but as yet untried;
And while professing patience, should he fail,
He suffer'd hope o'er reason to prevail.
  Impatient, by the morning mail convey'd,
The happy guest his promised visit paid;
And now arriving at the hall, he tried
For air composed, serene and satisfied;
As he had practised in his room alone,
And there acquired a free and easy tone:
There he had said, 'Whatever the degree
A man obtains, what more than man is he?'
And when arrived—'This room is but a room;
Can aught we see the steady soul o'ercome?
Let me in all a manly firmness show,
Upheld by talents, and their value know.'
  This reason urged; but it surpass'd his skill
To be in act as manly as in will:
When he his lordship and the lady saw,
Brave as he was, he felt oppress'd with awe;
And spite of verse, that so much praise had won,
The poet found he was the bailiff's son.
  But dinner came, and the succeeding hours
Fix'd his weak nerves, and raised his failing powers;

Praised and assured, he ventured once or twice
On some remark, and bravely broke the ice;
So that at night, reflecting on his words,
He found, in time, he might converse with lords.
  Now was the sister of his patron seen—
A lovely creature, with majestic mien;
Who, softly smiling while she look'd so fair,
Praised the young poet with such friendly air:
Such winning frankness in her looks express'd,
And such attention to her brother's guest,
That so much beauty, join'd with speech so kind,
Raised strong emotions in the poet's mind;
Till reason fail'd his bosom to defend
From the sweet power of this enchanting friend.—
Rash boy! what hope thy frantic mind invades?
What love confuses, and what pride persuades?
Awake to truth! shouldst thou deluded feed
On hopes so groundless, thou art mad indeed.
  What say'st thou, wise-one? 'that all-powerful love
Can fortune's strong impediments remove;
Nor is it strange that worth should wed to worth,
The pride of genius with the pride of birth.'
While thou art dreaming thus, the beauty spies
Love in thy tremor, passion in thine eyes;
And with th' amusement pleased, of conquest vain,
She seeks her pleasure, careless of thy pain;
She gives thee praise to humble and confound,
Smiles to ensnare, and flatters thee to wound.
  Why has she said that in the lowest state
The noble mind insures a noble fate?
And why thy daring mind to glory call?
That thou may'st dare and suffer, soar and fall.
Beauties are tyrants, and if they can reign,
They have no feeling for their subject's pain;
Their victim's anguish gives their charms applause,
And their chief glory is the woe they cause:
Something of this was felt, in spite of love,
Which hope, in spite of reason, would remove.
  Thus lived our youth, with conversation, books,
And Lady Emma's soul-subduing looks;
Lost in delight, astonish'd at his lot,

All prudence banish'd, all advice forgot—
Hopes, fears, and every thought, were fix'd upon the spot.
'Twas autumn yet, and many a day must frown
On Brandon-Hall, ere went my lord to town;
Meantime the father, who had heard his boy
Lived in a round of luxury and joy,
And justly thinking that the youth was one
Who, meeting danger, was unskill'd to shun;
Knowing his temper, virtue, spirit, zeal,
How prone to hope and trust, believe and feel;
These on the parent's soul their weight impress'd,
And thus he wrote the counsels of his breast.
'John, thou'rt a genius; thou hast some pretence,
I think, to wit, but hast thou sterling sense?
That which, like gold, may through the world go forth,
And always pass for what 'tis truly worth?
Whereas this genius, like a bill, must take
Only the value our opinions make.
'Men famed for wit, of dangerous talents vain,
Treat those of common parts with proud disdain;
The powers that wisdom would, improving, hide,
They blaze abroad with inconsid'rate pride;
While yet but mere probationers for fame,
They seize the honour they should then disclaim:
Honour so hurried to the light must fade,
The lasting laurels flourish in the shade.
'Genius is jealous; I have heard of some
Who, if unnoticed, grew perversely dumb:
Nay, different talents would their envy raise;
Poets have sicken'd at a dancer's praise;
And one, the happiest writer of his time,
Grew pale at hearing Reynolds was sublime;
That Rutland's duchess wore a heavenly smile—
And I, said he, neglected all the while!
'A waspish tribe are these, on gilded wings,
Humming their lays, and brandishing their stings;
And thus they move their friends and foes among,
Prepared for soothing or satiric song.
'Hear me, my boy; thou hast a virtuous mind—
But be thy virtues of the sober kind;
Be not a Quixote, ever up in arms

To give the guilty and the great alarms:
If never heeded, thy attack is vain;
And if they heed thee, they'll attack again;
Then too in striking at that heedless rate,
Thou in an instant may'st decide thy fate.
'Leave admonition—let the vicar give
Rules how the nobles of his flock should live;
Nor take that simple fancy to thy brain,
That thou canst cure the wicked and the vain.
'Our Pope, they say, once entertain'd the whim,
Who fear'd not God should be afraid of him;
But grant they fear'd him, was it further said,
That he reform'd the hearts he made afraid?
Did Chartres mend? Ward, Waters, and a score
Of flagrant felons, with his floggings sore?
Was Cibber silenced? No; with vigour bless'd,
And brazen front, half earnest, half in jest,
He dared the bard to battle, and was seen
In all his glory match'd with Pope and spleen;
Himself he stripp'd, the harder blow to hit,
Then boldly match'd his ribaldry with wit;
The poet's conquest Truth and Time proclaim,
But yet the battle hurt his peace and fame.
'Strive not too much for favour; seem at ease,
And rather pleased thyself, than bent to please:
Upon thy lord with decent care attend,
But not too near; thou canst not be a friend;
And favourite be not, 'tis a dangerous post—
Is gain'd by labour, and by fortune lost:
Talents like thine may make a man approved,
But other talents trusted and beloved.
Look round, my son, and thou wilt early see
The kind of man thou art not form'd to be.
'The real favourites of the great are they
Who to their views and wants attention pay,
And pay it ever; who, with all their skill,
Dive to the heart, and learn the secret will;
If that be vicious, soon can they provide
The favourite ill, and o'er the soul preside;
For vice is weakness, and the artful know
Their power increases as the passions grow;

If indolent the pupil, hard their task;
Such minds will ever for amusement ask;
And great the labour! for a man to choose
Objects for one whom nothing can amuse;
For ere those objects can the soul delight,
They must to joy the soul herself excite;
Therefore it is, this patient, watchful kind
With gentle friction stir the drowsy mind:
Fix'd on their end, with caution they proceed,
And sometimes give, and sometimes take the lead;
Will now a hint convey, and then retire,
And let the spark awake the lingering fire;
Or seek new joys and livelier pleasures bring,
To give the jaded sense a quick'ning spring.
'These arts, indeed, my son must not pursue;
Nor must he quarrel with the tribe that do:
It is not safe another's crimes to know,
Nor is it wise our proper worth to show:—
"My lord," you say, "engaged me for that worth;"—
True, and preserve it ready to come forth:
If question'd, fairly answer—and that done,
Shrink back, be silent, and thy father's son;
For they who doubt thy talents scorn thy boast,
But they who grant them will dislike thee most:
Observe the prudent; they in silence sit,
Display no learning, and affect no wit;
They hazard nothing, nothing they assume,
But know the useful art of *acting dumb.*
Yet to their eyes each varying look appears,
And every word finds entrance at their ears.
'Thou are religion's advocate—take heed,
Hurt not the cause, thy pleasure 'tis to plead;
With wine before thee, and with wits beside,
Do not in strength of reas'ning powers confide;
What seems to thee convincing, certain, plain,
They will deny, and dare thee to maintain;
And thus will triumph o'er thy eager youth,
While thou wilt grieve for so disgracing truth.
'With pain I've seen, these wrangling wits among,
Faith's weak defenders, passionate and young;
Weak thou art not, yet not enough on guard,

Where wit and humour keep their watch and ward:
Men gay and noisy will o'erwhelm thy sense,
Then loudly laugh at Truth's and thy expense;
While the kind ladies will do all they can
To check their mirth, and cry, "*The good young man!*"
 'Prudence, my boy, forbids thee to commend
The cause or party of thy noble friend;
What are his praises worth, who must be known
To take a patron's maxims for his own?
When ladies sing, or in thy presence play,
Do not, dear John, in rapture melt away;
'Tis not thy part, there will be list'ners round,
To cry *divine*! and dote upon the sound;
Remember too, that though the poor have ears,
They take not in the music of the spheres;
They must not feel the warble and the thrill,
Or be dissolved in ecstacy at will;
Beside, 'tis freedom in a youth like thee
To drop his awe, and deal in ecstacy!
 'In silent ease, at least in silence, dine,
Nor one opinion start of food or wine:
Thou know'st that all the science thou canst boast
Is of thy father's simple boil'd and roast;
Nor always these; he sometimes saved his cash,
By interlinear days of frugal hash:
Wine hadst thou seldom; wilt thou be so vain
As to decide on claret or champagne?
Dost thou from me derive this taste sublime,
Who order port the dozen at a time?
When (every glass held precious in our eyes)
We judged the value by the bottle's size:
Then never merit for thy praise assume,
Its worth well knows each servant in the room.
 'Hard, boy, thy task, to steer thy way among
That servile, supple, shrewd, insidious throng;
Who look upon thee as of doubtful race,
An interloper, one who wants a place:
Freedom with these let thy free soul condemn,
Nor with thy heart's concerns associate them.
 'Of all be cautious—but be most afraid
Of the pale charms that grace my lady's maid;

Of those sweet dimples, of that fraudful eye,
The frequent glance design'd for thee to spy;
The soft bewitching look, the fond bewailing sigh:
Let others frown and envy; she the while
(Insidious syren!) will demurely smile;
And for her gentle purpose, every day
Inquire thy wants, and meet thee in thy way;
She has her blandishments, and though so weak,
Her person pleases, and her actions speak:
At first her folly may her aim defeat;
But kindness shown at length will kindness meet:
Have some offended? them will she disdain,
And, for thy sake, contempt and pity feign;
She hates the vulgar, she admires to look
On woods and groves, and dotes upon a book;
Let her once see thee on her features dwell,
And hear one sigh, then liberty farewell.
  'But, John, remember, we cannot maintain
A poor, proud girl, extravagant and vain.
  'Doubt much of friendship: shouldst thou find a friend
Pleased to advise thee, anxious to commend;
Should he the praises he has heard report,
And confidence (in thee confiding) court;
Much of neglectful patrons should he say,
And then exclaim—"How long must merit stay!"
Then show how high thy modest hopes may stretch,
And point to stations far beyond thy reach;
Let such designer, by thy conduct, see
(Civil and cool) he makes no dupe of thee;
And he will quit thee, as a man too wise
For him to ruin first, and then despise.
  'Such are thy dangers;—yet, if thou canst steer
Past all the perils, all the quicksands clear,
Then may'st thou profit; but if storms prevail,
If foes beset thee, if thy spirits fail,—
No more of winds or waters be the sport,
But in thy father's mansion find a port.'
  Our poet read.—'It is in truth,' said he,
'Correct in part, but what is *this* to me?
I love a foolish Abigail! in base
And sordid office! fear not such disgrace:

Am I so blind?' 'Or thou wouldst surely see
That lady's fall, if she should stoop to thee!'
'The cases differ.' 'True! for what surprise
Could from thy marriage with the maid arise?
But through the island would the shame be spread,
Should the fair mistress deign with thee to wed.'
  John saw not this; and many a week had pass'd,
While the vain beauty held her victim fast;
The noble friend still condescension show'd,
And, as before, with praises overflow'd;
But his grave lady took a silent view
Of all that pass'd, and smiling, pitied too.
  Cold grew the foggy morn, the day was brief,
Loose on the cherry hung the crimson leaf;
The dew dwelt ever on the herb; the woods
Roar'd with strong blasts, with mighty showers the floods:
All green was vanish'd, save of pine and yew,
That still display'd their melancholy hue;
Save the green holly with its berries red,
And the green moss that o'er the gravel spread.
  To public views my lord must soon attend;
And soon the ladies—would they leave their friend?
The time was fix'd—approach'd—was near—was come;
The trying time that fill'd his soul with gloom:
Thoughtful our poet in the morning rose,
And cried, 'One hour my fortune will disclose;
Terrific hour! from thee have I to date
Life's loftier views, or my degraded state;
For now to be what I have been before
Is so to fall, that I can rise no more.'
  The morning meal was past, and all around
The mansion rang with each discordant sound;
Haste was in every foot, and every look
The trav'ller's joy for London-journey spoke:
Not so our youth; whose feelings, at the noise
Of preparation, had no touch of joys;
He pensive stood, and saw each carriage drawn,
With lackeys mounted, ready on the lawn:
The ladies came; and John in terror threw
One painful glance, and then his eyes withdrew;
Not with such speed, but he in other eyes

With anguish read—'I pity but despise—
Unhappy boy! presumptious scribbler!—you
To dream such dreams!—be sober, and adieu!'
Then came the noble friend—'And will my lord
Vouchsafe no comfort? drop no soothing word?
Yes, he must speak:' he speaks, 'My good young friend,
You know my views; upon my care depend;
My hearty thanks to your good father pay,
And be a student.—Harry, drive away.'
Stillness reign'd all around; of late so full
The busy scene, deserted now and dull:
Stern is his nature who forbears to feel
Gloom o'er his spirits on such trials steal;
Most keenly felt our poet as he went
From room to room without a fix'd intent;
'And here,' he thought, 'I was caress'd; admired
Were here my songs; she smiled, and I aspired:
The change how grievous!' As he mused, a dame
Busy and peevish to her duties came;
Aside the tables and the chairs she drew,
And sang and mutter'd in the poet's view:—
'This was her fortune; here they leave the poor;
Enjoy themselves, and think of us no more;
I had a promise—' here his pride and shame
Urged him to fly from this familiar dame;
He gave one farewell look, and by a coach
Reach'd his own mansion at the night's approach.
His father met him with an anxious air,
Heard his sad tale, and check'd what seem'd despair;
Hope was in him corrected, but alive;
My lord would something for a friend contrive;
His word was pledged; our hero's feverish mind
Admitted this, and half his grief resign'd:
But when three months had fled, and every day
Drew from the sickening hopes their strength away,
The youth became abstracted, pensive, dull;
He utter'd nothing, though his heart was full;
Teased by inquiring words and anxious looks,
And all forgetful of his muse and books;
Awake he mourn'd, but in his sleep perceived
A lovely vision that his pain relieved:

His soul transported, hail'd the happy seat,
Where once his pleasure was so pure and sweet;
Where joys departed came in blissful view,
Till reason waked, and not a joy he knew.
Questions now vex'd his spirit, most from those
Who are called friends, because they are not foes:
'John!' they would say; he, starting, turn'd around;
'John!' there was something shocking in the sound;
Ill brook'd he then the pert familiar phrase,
The untaught freedom, and th' inquiring gaze:
Much was his temper touch'd, his spleen provoked,
When ask'd how ladies talk'd, or walk'd, or look'd?
'What said my lord of politics? how spent
He there his time? and was he glad he went?'
At length a letter came, both cool and brief,
But still it gave the burthen'd heart relief:
Though not inspired by lofty hopes, the youth
Placed much reliance on Lord Frederick's truth;
Summon'd to town, he thought the visit one
Where something fair and friendly would be done;
Although he judged not, as before his fall,
When all was love and promise at the hall.
Arrived in town, he early sought to know
The fate such dubious friendship would bestow;
At a tall building trembling he appear'd,
And his low rap was indistinctly heard;
A well-known servant came—'A while,' said he,
'Be pleased to wait; my lord has company.'
Alone our hero sate; the news in hand,
Which though he read, he could not understand:
Cold was the day; in days so cold as these
There needs a fire, where minds and bodies freeze;
The vast and echoing room, the polish'd grate,
The crimson chairs, the sideboard with its plate;
The splendid sofa, which, though made for rest,
He then had thought it freedom to have press'd;
The shining tables, curiously inlaid,
Were all in comfortless proud style display'd;
And to the troubled feelings terror gave,
That made the once-dear friend, the sick'ning slave.
'Was he forgotten?' Thrice upon his ear

Struck the loud clock, yet no relief was near;
Each rattling carriage, and each thundering stroke
On the loud door, the dream of fancy broke;
Oft as a servant chanced the way to come,
'Brings he a message?' no! he pass'd the room:
At length 'tis certain; 'Sir, you will attend
At twelve on Thursday!' Thus the day had end.
  Vex'd by these tedious hours of needless pain,
John left the noble mansion with disdain;
For there was something in that still, cold place,
That seem'd to threaten and portend disgrace.
  Punctual again the modest rap declared
The youth attended; then was all prepared:
For the same servant, by his lord's command,
A paper offer'd to his trembling hand:
'No more!' he cried; 'disdains he to afford
One kind expression, one consoling word?'
  With troubled spirit he began to read
That 'In the church my lord could not succeed;'
Who had 'to peers of either kind applied,
And was with dignity and grace denied;
While his own livings were by men possess'd,
Not likely in their chancels yet to rest;
And therefore, all things weigh'd (as he, my lord,
Had done maturely, and he pledged his word),
Wisdom it seem'd for John to turn his view
To busier scenes, and bid the church adieu!'
  Here grieved the youth; he felt his father's pride
Must with his own be shock'd and mortified;
But when he found his future comforts placed
Where he, alas! conceived himself disgraced—
In some appointment on the London quays,
He bade farewell to honour and to ease;
His spirit fell, and, from that hour assured
How vain his dreams, he suffer'd and was cured.
  Our poet hurried on, with wish to fly
From all mankind, to be conceal'd, and die.
Alas! what hopes, what high romantic views
Did that one visit to the soul infuse,
Which cherish'd with such love, 'twas worse than death
    to lose!

Still he would strive, though painful was the strife,
To walk in this appointed road of life;
On these low duties duteous he would wait,
And patient bear the anguish of his fate.
Thanks to the patron, but of coldest kind,
Express'd the sadness of the poet's mind;
Whose heavy hours were pass'd with busy men,
In the dull practice of th' official pen;
Who to superiors must in time impart
(The custom this) his progress in their art:
But so had grief on his perception wrought,
That all unheeded were the duties taught;
No answers gave he when his trial came,
Silent he stood, but suffering without shame;
And they observed that words severe or kind
Made no impression on his wounded mind;
For all perceived from whence his failure rose,
Some grief whose cause he deign'd not to disclose.
A soul averse from scenes and works so new,
Fear ever shrinking from the vulgar crew;
Distaste for each mechanic law and rule,
Thoughts of past honour and a patron cool;
A grieving parent, and a feeling mind,
Timid and ardent, tender and refined:
These all with mighty force the youth assail'd,
Till his soul fainted, and his reason fail'd:
When this was known, and some debate arose
How they who saw it should the fact disclose,
He found their purpose, and in terror fled
From unseen kindness, with mistaken dread.
  Meantime the parent was distress'd to find
His son no longer for a priest design'd;
But still he gain'd some comfort by the news
Of John's promotion, though with humbler views:
For he conceived that in no distant time
The boy would learn to scramble and to climb;
He little thought a son, his hope and pride,
His favour'd boy, was now a home denied:
Yes! while the parent was intent to trace
How men in office climb from place to place,
By day, by night, o'er moor and heath and hill,

Roved the sad youth, with ever-changing will,
Of every aid bereft, exposed to every ill.
  Thus as he sate, absorb'd in all the care
And all the hope that anxious fathers share,
A friend abruptly to his presence brought,
With trembling hand, the subject of his thought;
Whom he had found afflicted and subdued
By hunger, sorrow, cold, and solitude.
  Silent he enter'd the forgotten room,
As ghostly forms may be conceived to come;
With sorrow-shrunken face and hair upright,
He look'd dismay, neglect, despair, affright;
But, dead to comfort, and on misery thrown,
His parent's loss he felt not, nor his own.
  The good man, struck with horror, cried aloud,
And drew around him an astonish'd crowd;
The sons and servants to the father ran,
To share the feelings of the grieved old man.
  'Our brother, speak!' they all exclaim'd; 'explain
Thy grief, thy suffering:'—but they ask'd in vain:
The friend told all he knew; and all was known,
Save the sad causes whence the ills had grown:
But, if obscure the cause, they all agreed
From rest and kindness must the cure proceed:
And he was cured; for quiet, love, and care,
Strove with the gloom, and broke on the despair;
Yet slow their progress, and, as vapours move
Dense and reluctant from the wintry grove;
All is confusion till the morning light
Gives the dim scene obscurely to the sight;
More and yet more defined the trunks appear,
Till the wild prospect stands distinct and clear;—
So the dark mind of our young poet grew
Clear and sedate; the dreadful mist withdrew;
And he resembled that bleak wintry scene,
Sad, though unclouded; dismal, though serene.
  At times he utter'd, 'What a dream was mine!
And what a prospect! glorious and divine!
Oh! in that room, and on that night, to see
These looks, that sweetness beaming all on me;
That syren-flattery—and to send me then,

Hope-raised and soften'd, to those heartless men;
That dark-brow'd stern director, pleased to show
Knowledge of subjects, I disdain'd to know;
Cold and controlling—but 'tis gone, 'tis past;
I had my trial, and have peace at last.'
  Now grew the youth resign'd; he bade adieu
To all that hope, to all that fancy drew;
His frame was languid, and the hectic heat
Flush'd on his pallid face, and countless beat
The quick'ning pulse, and faint the limbs that bore
The slender form that soon would breathe no more.
  Then hope of holy kind the soul sustain'd,
And not a lingering thought of earth remain'd;
Now Heaven had all, and he could smile at love,
And the wild sallies of his youth reprove;
Then could he dwell upon the tempting days,
The proud aspiring thought, the partial praise;
Victorious now, his worldly views were closed,
And on the bed of death the youth reposed.
  The father grieved—but as the poet's heart
Was all unfitted for his earthly part;
As, he conceived, some other haughty fair
Would, had he lived, have led him to despair;
As, with this fear, the silent grave shut out
All feverish hope, and all tormenting doubt;
While the strong faith the pious youth possess'd,
His hope enlivening, gave his sorrows rest;
Soothed by these thoughts, he felt a mournful joy
For his aspiring and devoted boy.
  Meantime the news through various channels spread,
The youth, once favour'd with such praise, was dead:
'Emma,' the lady cried, 'my words attend,
Your syren-smiles have kill'd your humble friend;
The hope you raised can now delude no more,
Nor charms, that once inspired, can now restore.'
  Faint was the flush of anger and of shame,
That o'er the cheek of conscious beauty came:
'You censure not,' said she, 'the sun's bright rays,
When fools imprudent dare the dangerous gaze;
And should a stripling look till he were blind,

You would not justly call the light unkind:
But is he dead? and am I to suppose
The power of poison in such looks as those?'
She spoke, and, pointing to the mirror, cast
A pleased gay glance, and curtsied as she pass'd.
  My lord, to whom the poet's fate was told,
Was much affected, for a man so cold:
'Dead!' said his lordship, 'run distracted, mad!
Upon my soul I'm sorry for the lad;
And now, no doubt, th' obliging world will say
That my harsh usage help'd him on his way:
What! I suppose, I should have nursed his muse,
And with champagne have brighten'd up his views;
Then had he made me famed my whole life long,
And stunn'd my ears with gratitude and song.
Still should the father hear that I regret
Our joint misfortune—Yes! I'll not forget.'—
  Thus they:—The father to his grave convey'd
The son he loved, and his last duties paid.
  'There lies my boy,' he cried, 'of care bereft,
And, Heav'n be praised, I've not a genius left:
No one among ye, sons! is doom'd to live
On high-raised hopes of what the great may give;
None, with exalted views and fortunes mean,
To die in anguish, or to live in spleen:
Your pious brother soon escaped the strife
Of such contention, but it cost his life;
You then, my sons, upon yourselves depend,
And in your own exertions find the friend.'

6. THE FRANK COURTSHIP

Yes, faith, it is my cousin's duty to make a curtsy, and say, 'Father, as it please you;' but for all that, cousin, let him be a handsome fellow, or else make another curtsy, and say, 'Father, as it pleases me.'

Much Ado about Nothing, Act II, Scene 1

He cannot flatter, he!
An honest mind and plain—he must speak truth.

King Lear, Act II, Scene 2

6. *The Frank Courtship*

God hath given you one face, and you make yourselves another; you jig, you amble, you nick-name God's creatures, and make your wantonness your ignorance. *Hamlet*, Act III, Scene 1

What fire is in mine ears? Can this be true?
Am I contemn'd for pride and scorn so much?
Much Ado about Nothing, Act III, Scene 1

Grave Jonas Kindred, Sybil Kindred's sire,
Was six feet high, and look'd six inches higher;
Erect, morose, determined, solemn, slow,
Who knew the man, could never cease to know;
His faithful spouse, when Jonas was not by,
Had a firm presence and a steady eye;
But with her husband dropp'd her look and tone,
And Jonas ruled unquestion'd and alone.
  He read, and oft would quote the sacred words,
How pious husbands of their wives were lords;
Sarah called Abraham lord! and who could be,
So Jonas thought, a greater man than he?
Himself he view'd with undisguised respect,
And never pardon'd freedom or neglect.
  They had one daughter, and this favourite child
Had oft the father of his spleen beguiled;
Soothed by attention from her early years,
She gain'd all wishes by her smiles or tears:
But Sybil then was in that playful time,
When contradiction is not held a crime;
When parents yield their children idle praise
For faults corrected in their after days.
  Peace in the sober house of Jonas dwelt,
Where each his duty and his station felt:
Yet not that peace some favour'd mortals find,
In equal views and harmony of mind;
Not the soft peace that blesses those who love,
Where all with one consent in union move;
But it was that which one superior will
Commands, by making all inferiors still;
Who bids all murmurs, all objections cease,
And with imperious voice announces—Peace!
  They were, to wit, a remnant of that crew,
Who, as their foes maintain, their sovereign slew;

An independent race, precise, correct,
Who ever married in the kindred sect:
No son or daughter of their order wed
A friend to England's king who lost his head;
Cromwell was still their saint, and when they met,
They mourn'd that Saints* were not our rulers yet.
Fix'd were their habits; they arose betimes,
Then pray'd their hour, and sang their party-rhymes:
Their meals were plenteous, regular, and plain;
The trade of Jonas brought him constant gain;
Vender of hops and malt, of coals and corn—
And, like his father, he was merchant born:
Neat was their house; each table, chair, and stool,
Stood in its place, or moving moved by rule;
No lively print or picture graced the room;
A plain brown paper lent its decent gloom;
But here the eye, in glancing round, survey'd
A small recess that seem'd for china made;
Such pleasing pictures seem'd this pencill'd ware,
That few would search for nobler objects there—
Yet, turn'd by chosen friends, and there appear'd
His stern, strong features, whom they all revered;
For there in lofty air was seen to stand
The bold protector of the conquer'd land;
Drawn in that look with which he wept and swore,
Turn'd out the members, and made fast the door,
Ridding the house of every knave and drone,
Forced, though it grieved his soul, to rule alone.
The stern still smile each friend approving gave,
Then turn'd the view, and all again were grave.
There stood a clock, though small the owner's need,
For habit told when all things should proceed;
Few their amusements, but when friends appear'd,
They with the world's distress their spirits cheer'd;
The nation's guilt, that would not long endure
The reign of men so modest and so pure:
Their town was large, and seldom pass'd a day
But some had fail'd, and others gone astray;

* This appellation is here used not ironically, nor with malignity; but it is taken merely to designate a morosely devout people, with peculiar austerity of manners.

Clerks had absconded, wives eloped, girls flown
To Gretna-Green, or sons rebellious grown;
Quarrels and fires arose;—and it was plain
The times were bad; the saints had ceased to reign!
A few yet lived to languish and to mourn
For good old manners never to return.
  Jonas had sisters, and of these was one
Who lost a husband and an only son:
Twelve months her sables she in sorrow wore,
And mourn'd so long that she could mourn no more.
Distant from Jonas, and from all her race,
She now resided in a lively place;
There, by the sect unseen, at whist she play'd,
Nor was of churchmen or their church afraid:
If much of this the graver brother heard,
He something censured, but he little fear'd;
He knew her rich and frugal; for the rest,
He felt no care, or, if he felt, suppress'd:
Nor for companion when she ask'd her niece,
Had he suspicions that disturb'd his peace;
Frugal and rich, these virtues as a charm
Preserved the thoughtful man from all alarm;
An infant yet, she soon would home return,
Nor stay the manners of the world to learn;
Meantime his boys would all his care engross,
And be his comforts if he felt the loss.
  The sprightly Sybil, pleased and unconfined,
Felt the pure pleasure of the op'ning mind:
All here was gay and cheerful—all at home
Unvaried quiet and unruffled gloom:
There were no changes, and amusements few;
Here, all was varied, wonderful, and new;
There were plain meals, plain dresses, and grave looks—
Here, gay companions and amusing books;
And the young beauty soon began to taste
The light vocations of the scene she graced.
  A man of business feels it as a crime
On calls domestic to consume his time;
Yet this grave man had not so cold a heart,
But with his daughter he was grieved to part:
And he demanded that in every year

The aunt and niece should at his house appear.
'Yes! we must go, my child, and by our dress
A grave conformity of mind express;
Must sing at meeting, and from cards refrain,
The more t'enjoy when we return again.'
Thus spake the aunt, and the discerning child
Was pleased to learn how fathers are beguiled.
Her artful part the young dissembler took,
And from the matron caught th' approving look:
When thrice the friends had met, excuse was sent
For more delay, and Jonas was content;
Till a tall maiden by her sire was seen,
In all the bloom and beauty of sixteen;
He gazed admiring;—she, with visage prim,
Glanced an arch look of gravity on him;
For she was gay at heart, but wore disguise,
And stood a vestal in her father's eyes:
Pure, pensive, simple, sad; the damsel's heart,
When Jonas praised, reproved her for the part;
For Sybil, fond of pleasure, gay and light,
Had still a secret bias to the right;
Vain as she was—and flattery made her vain—
Her simulation gave her bosom pain.
Again return'd, the matron and the niece
Found the late quiet gave their joy increase;
The aunt infirm, no more her visits paid,
But still with her sojourn'd the favourite maid.
Letters were sent when franks could be procured,
And when they could not, silence was endured;
All were in health, and if they older grew,
It seem'd a fact that none among them knew;
The aunt and niece still led a pleasant life,
And quiet days had Jonas and his wife.
Near him a widow dwelt of worthy fame,
Like his her manners, and her creed the same;
The wealth her husband left, her care retain'd
For one tall youth, and widow she remain'd;
His love respectful all her care repaid,
Her wishes watch'd, and her commands obey'd.
Sober he was and grave from early youth,
Mindful of forms, but more intent on truth;

In a light drab he uniformly dress'd,
And look serene th' unruffled mind express'd;
A hat with ample verge his brows o'erspread,
And his brown locks curl'd graceful on his head;
Yet might observers in his speaking eye
Some observation, some acuteness spy;
The friendly thought it keen, the treacherous deem'd it
sly;
Yet not a crime could foe or friend detect,
His actions all were, like his speech, correct;
And they who jested on a mind so sound,
Upon his virtues must their laughter found;
Chaste, sober, solemn, and devout they named
Him who was thus, and not of *this* ashamed.
Such were the virtues Jonas found in one
In whom he warmly wish'd to find a son:
Three years had pass'd since he had Sybil seen;
But she was doubtless what she once had been,
Lovely and mild, obedient and discreet;
The pair must love whenever they should meet;
Then ere the widow or her son should choose
Some happier maid, he would explain his views;
Now she, like him, was politic and shrewd,
With strong desire of lawful gain embued;
To all he said, she bow'd with much respect,
Pleased to comply, yet seeming to reject;
Cool and yet eager, each admired the strength
Of the opponent, and agreed at length:
As a drawn battle shows to each a force,
Powerful as his, he honours it of course;
So in these neighbours, each the power discern'd,
And gave the praise that was to each return'd.
Jonas now ask'd his daughter—and the aunt,
Though loth to lose her, was obliged to grant:—
But would not Sybil to the matron cling,
And fear to leave the shelter of her wing?
No! in the young there lives a love of change,
And to the easy they prefer the strange!
Then too the joys she once pursued with zeal,
From whist and visits sprung, she ceased to feel;
When with the matrons Sybil first sat down,

To cut for partners and to stake her crown,
This to the youthful maid preferment seem'd,
Who thought that woman she was then esteem'd;
But in few years, when she perceived, indeed,
The real woman to the girl succeed,
No longer tricks and honours fill'd her mind,
But other feelings, not so well defined;
She then reluctant grew, and thought it hard,
To sit and ponder o'er an ugly card;
Rather the nut-tree shade the nymph preferr'd,
Pleased with the pensive gloom and evening bird;
Thither, from company retired, she took
The silent walk, or read the fav'rite book.
  The father's letter, sudden, short, and kind,
Awaked her wonder, and disturb'd her mind;
She found new dreams upon her fancy seize,
Wild roving thoughts and endless reveries:
The parting came;—and when the aunt perceived
The tears of Sybil, and how much she grieved—
To love for her that tender grief she laid,
That various, soft, contending passions made.
  When Sybil rested in her father's arms,
His pride exulted in a daughter's charms;
A maid accomplish'd he was pleased to find,
Nor seem'd the form more lovely than the mind:
But when the fit of pride and fondness fled,
He saw his judgment by his hopes misled;
High were the lady's spirits, far more free
Her mode of speaking than a maid's should be;
Too much, as Jonas thought, she seem'd to know,
And all her knowledge was disposed to show;
'Too gay her dress, like theirs who idly dote
On a young coxcomb, or a coxcomb's coat;
In foolish spirits when our friends appear,
And vainly grave when not a man is near.'
  Thus Jonas, adding to his sorrow blame,
And terms disdainful to his sister's name:—
'The sinful wretch has by her arts defiled
The ductile spirit of my darling child.'
  'The maid is virtuous,' said the dame—Quoth he,
'Let her give proof, by acting virtuously:

Is it in gaping when the elders pray?
In reading nonsense half a summer's day?
In those mock forms that she delights to trace,
Or her loud laughs in Hezekiah's face?
She—O Susannah!—to the world belongs;
She loves the follies of its idle throngs,
And reads soft tales of love, and sings love's soft'ning songs.
But, as our friend is yet delay'd in town,
We must prepare her till the youth comes down;
You shall advise the maiden; I will threat;
Her fears and hopes may yield us comfort yet.'
Now the grave father took the lass aside,
Demanding sternly, 'Wilt thou be a bride?'
She answer'd, calling up an air sedate,
'I have not vow'd against the holy state.'
'No folly, Sybil,' said the parent; 'know
What to their parents virtuous maidens owe:
A worthy, wealthy youth, whom I approve,
Must thou prepare to honour and to love.
Formal to thee his air and dress may seem,
But the good youth is worthy of esteem;
Shouldst thou with rudeness treat him; of disdain
Should he with justice or of slight complain,
Or of one taunting speech give certain proof,
Girl! I reject thee from my sober roof.'
'My aunt,' said Sybil, 'will with pride protect
One whom a father can for this reject;
Nor shall a formal, rigid, soul-less boy
My manners alter, or my views destroy!'
Jonas then lifted up his hands on high,
And utt'ring something 'twixt a groan and sigh,
Left the determined maid, her doubtful mother by.
'Hear me,' she said, 'incline thy heart, my child,
And fix thy fancy on a man so mild:
Thy father, Sybil, never could be moved
By one who loved him, or by one he loved.
Union like ours is but a bargain made
By slave and tyrant—he will be obey'd;
Then calls the quiet, comfort—but thy youth
Is mild by nature, and as frank as truth.'

'But will he love?' said Sybil; 'I am told
That these mild creatures are by nature cold.'
'Alas!' the matron answer'd, 'much I dread
That dangerous love by which the young are led!
That love is earthy; you the creature prize,
And trust your feelings and believe your eyes:
Can eyes and feelings inward worth descry?
No! my fair daughter, on our choice rely!
Your love, like that display'd upon the stage,
Indulged is folly, and opposed is rage;—
More prudent love our sober couples show,
All that to mortal beings, mortals owe;
All flesh is grass—before you give a heart,
Remember, Sybil, that in death you part;
And should your husband die before your love,
What needless anguish must a widow prove!
No! my fair child, let all such visions cease;
Yield but esteem, and only try for peace.'
'I must be loved,' said Sybil; 'I must see
The man in terrors who aspires to me;
At my forbidding frown, his heart must ache,
His tongue must falter, and his frame must shake:
And if I grant him at my feet to kneel,
What trembling, fearful pleasure must he feel;
Nay, such the raptures that my smiles inspire,
That reason's self must for a time retire.'
'Alas! for good Josiah,' said the dame,
'These wicked thoughts would fill his soul with shame;
He kneel and tremble at a thing of dust!
He cannot, child:'—the child replied, 'He must.'
They ceased: the matron left her with a frown;
So Jonas met her when the youth came down:
'Behold,' said he, 'thy future spouse attends;
Receive him, daughter, as the best of friends;
Observe, respect him—humble be each word,
That welcomes home thy husband and thy lord.'
Forewarn'd, thought Sybil, with a bitter smile,
I shall prepare my manner and my style.
Ere yet Josiah enter'd on his task,
The father met him—'Deign to wear a mask
A few dull days, Josiah—but a few—

It is our duty, and the sex's due;
I wore it once, and every grateful wife
Repays it with obedience through her life:
Have no regard to Sybil's dress, have none
To her pert language, to her flippant tone:
Henceforward thou shalt rule unquestion'd and alone;
And she thy pleasure in thy looks, shall seek—
How she shall dress, and whether she may speak.'
  A sober smile return'd the youth, and said,
'Can I cause fear, who am myself afraid?'
  Sybil, meantime, sat thoughtful in her room,
And often wonder'd—'Will the creature come?
Nothing shall tempt, shall force me to bestow
My hand upon him—yet I wish to know.'
  The door unclosed, and she beheld her sire
Lead in the youth, then hasten to retire;
'Daughter, my friend—my daughter, friend'—he cried,
And gave a meaning look, and stepp'd aside;
That look contain'd a mingled threat and prayer,
'Do take him, child—offend him, if you dare.'
  The couple gazed—were silent, and the maid
Look'd in his face, to make the man afraid;
The man, unmoved, upon the maiden cast
A steady view—so salutation pass'd:
But in this instant Sybil's eye had seen
The tall fair person, and the still staid mien;
The glow that temp'rance o'er the cheek had spread,
Where the soft down half veil'd the purest red;
And the serene deportment that proclaim'd
A heart unspotted, and a life unblamed:
But then with these she saw attire too plain,
The pale brown coat, though worn without a stain;
The formal air, and something of the pride
That indicates the wealth it seems to hide;
And looks that were not, she conceived, exempt
From a proud pity, or a sly contempt.
  Josiah's eyes had their employment too,
Engaged and soften'd by so bright a view;
A fair and meaning face, an eye of fire,
That check'd the bold, and made the free retire:
But then with these he mark'd the studied dress

And lofty air, that scorn or pride express;
With that insidious look, that seem'd to hide
In an affected smile the scorn and pride;
And if his mind the virgin's meaning caught,
He saw a foe with treacherous purpose fraught—
Captive the heart to take, and to reject it caught.
  Silent they sate—thought Sybil, that he seeks
Something, no doubt; I wonder if he speaks:
Scarcely she wonder'd, when these accents fell
Slow in her ear—'Fair maiden, art thou well?'
'Art thou physician?' she replied; 'my hand,
My pulse, at least, shall be at thy command.'
  She said—and saw, surprised, Josiah kneel,
And gave his lips the offer'd pulse to feel;
The rosy colour rising in her cheek,
Seem'd that surprise unmix'd with wrath to speak;
Then sternness she assumed, and—'Doctor, tell,
Thy words cannot alarm me—am I well?'
  'Thou art,' said he; 'and yet thy dress so light,
I do conceive, some danger must excite:'
'In whom?' said Sybil, with a look demure:
'In more,' said he, 'than I expect to cure.
I, in thy light luxuriant robe, behold
Want and excess, abounding and yet cold;
Here needed, there display'd, in many a wanton fold:
Both health and beauty, learned authors show,
From a just medium in our clothing flow.'
  'Proceed, good doctor; if so great my need,
What is thy fee? Good doctor! pray proceed.'
  'Large is my fee, fair lady, but I take
None till some progress in my cure I make:
Thou hast disease, fair maiden; thou art vain;
Within that face sit insult and disdain;
Thou art enamour'd of thyself; my art
Can see the naughty malice of thy heart:
With a strong pleasure would thy bosom move,
Were I to own thy power, and ask thy love;
And such thy beauty, damsel, that I might,
But for thy pride, feel danger in thy sight,
And lose my present peace in dreams of vain delight.'
  'And can thy patients,' said the nymph, 'endure

Physic like this? and will it work a cure?'
'Such is my hope, fair damsel; thou, I find,
Has the true tokens of a noble mind;
But the world wins thee, Sybil, and thy joys
Are placed in trifles, fashions, follies, toys;
Thou hast sought pleasure in the world around,
That in thine own pure bosom should be found:
Did all that world admire thee, praise and love,
Could it the least of nature's pains remove?
Could it for errors, follies, sins atone,
Or give thee comfort, thoughtful and alone?
It has, believe me, maid, no power to charm
Thy soul from sorrow, or thy flesh from harm:
Turn then, fair creature, from a world of sin,
And seek the jewel happiness within.'
'Speak'st thou at meeting?' said the nymph; 'thy speech
Is that of mortal very prone to teach;
But wouldst thou, doctor, from the patient learn
Thine own disease?—The cure is thy concern.'
'Yea, with good will.'—'Then know, 'tis thy complaint,
That, for a sinner, thou 'rt too much a saint;
Hast too much show of the sedate and pure,
And without cause art formal and demure:
This makes a man unsocial, unpolite;
Odious when wrong, and insolent if right.
Thou may'st be good, but why should goodness be
Wrapt in a garb of such formality?
Thy person well might please a damsel's eye,
In decent habit with a scarlet dye;
But, jest apart—what virtue canst thou trace
In that broad brim that hides thy sober face?
Does that long-skirted drab, that over-nice
And formal clothing, prove a scorn of vice?
Then for thine accent—what in sound can be
So void of grace as dull monotony?
Love has a thousand varied notes to move
The human heart;—thou may'st not speak of love
Till thou hast cast thy formal ways aside,
And those becoming youth and nature tried:
Not till exterior freedom, spirit, ease,
Prove it thy study and delight to please;

Not till these follies meet thy just disdain,
While yet thy virtues and thy worth remain.'
'This is severe!—Oh! maiden, wilt not thou
Something for habits, manners, modes, allow?'—
'Yes! but allowing much, I much require,
In my behalf, for manners, modes, attire!'
'True, lovely Sybil; and, this point agreed,
Let me to those of greater weight proceed:
Thy father!'—'Nay,' she quickly interposed,
'Good doctor, here our conference is closed!'
Then left the youth, who, lost in his retreat,
Pass'd the good matron on her garden-seat;
His looks were troubled, and his air, once mild
And calm, was hurried:—'My audacious child!'
Exclaim'd the dame, 'I read what she has done
In thy displeasure—Ah! the thoughtless one;
But yet, Josiah, to my stern good man
Speak of the maid as mildly as you can:
Can you not seem to woo a little while
The daughter's will, the father to beguile?
So that his wrath in time may wear away;
Will you preserve our peace, Josiah? say.'
'Yes! my good neighbour,' said the gentle youth,
'Rely securely on my care and truth;
And should thy comfort with my efforts cease,
And only then—perpetual is thy peace.'
The dame had doubts: she well his virtues knew,
His deeds were friendly, and his words were true;
'But to address this vixen is a task
He is ashamed to take, and I to ask.'
Soon as the father from Josiah learn'd
What pass'd with Sybil, he the truth discern'd.
'He loves,' the man exclaim'd, 'he loves, 'tis plain,
The thoughtless girl, and shall he love in vain?
She may be stubborn, but she shall be tried,
Born as she is of wilfulness and pride.'
With anger fraught, but willing to persuade,
The wrathful father met the smiling maid:
'Sybil,' said he, 'I long, and yet I dread
To know thy conduct—hath Josiah fled?
And, grieved and fretted by thy scornful air,

For his lost peace betaken him to prayer?
Couldst thou his pure and modest mind distress,
By vile remarks upon his speech, address,
Attire, and voice?'—'All this I must confess.'—
'Unhappy child! what labour will it cost
To win him back!'—'I do not think him lost.'
'Courts he then, trifler! insult and disdain?'—
'No: but from these he courts me to refrain.'
'Then hear me, Sybil—should Josiah leave
Thy father's house?'—'My father's child would grieve:'
'That is of grace, and if he come again
To speak of love?'—'I might from grief refrain.'—
'Then wilt thou, daughter, our design embrace?'—
'Can I resist it, if it be of grace?'
'Dear child! in three plain words thy mind express—
Wilt thou have this good youth?' 'Dear father! yes.'

7. THE WIDOW'S TALE

Ah me! for aught that I could ever read,
Or ever hear by tale or history,
The course of true love never did run smooth;
But either it was different in blood,
Or else misgrafted in respect of years,
Or else it stood upon the choice of friends;
Or if there were a sympathy in choice,
War, death, or sickness did lay siege to it.
Midsummer Night's Dream, Act I, Scene 1

Oh! thou didst then ne'er love so heartily,
If thou rememberest not the slightest folly
That ever love did make thee run into.
As You Like It, Act II, Scene 4

Cry the man mercy; love him, take his offer.
As You Like It, Act III, Scene 5

To farmer Moss, in Langar Vale, came down
His only daughter, from her school in town;
A tender, timid maid! who knew not how
To pass a pig-sty, or to face a cow:
Smiling she came, with petty talents graced,
A fair complexion, and a slender waist.
Used to spare meals, disposed in manner pure,

Her father's kitchen she could ill endure;
Where by the steaming beef he hungry sat,
And laid at once a pound upon his plate;
Hot from the field, her eager brother seized
An equal part, and hunger's rage appeased;
The air, surcharged with moisture, flagg'd around,
And the offended damsel sigh'd and frown'd;
The swelling fat in lumps conglomerate laid,
And fancy's sickness seized the loathing maid:
But when the men beside their station took,
The maidens with them, and with these the cook;
When one huge wooden bowl before them stood,
Fill'd with huge balls of farinaceous food;
With bacon, mass saline, where never lean
Beneath the brown and bristly rind was seen;
When from a single horn the party drew
Their copious draughts of heavy ale and new;
When the coarse cloth she saw, with many a stain,
Soil'd by rude hinds who cut and came again—
She could not breathe; but, with a heavy sigh,
Rein'd the fair neck, and shut th'offended eye;
She minced the sanguine flesh in frustums fine,
And wonder'd much to see the creatures dine:
When she resolved her father's heart to move,
If hearts of farmers were alive to love.
    She now entreated by herself to sit
In the small parlour, if papa thought fit,
And there to dine, to read, to work alone:—
'No!' said the farmer, in an angry tone;
'These are your school-taught airs; your mother's pride
Would send you there; but I am now your guide.—
Arise betimes, our early meal prepare,
And this despatch'd, let business be your care;
Look to the lasses, let there not be one
Who lacks attention, till her tasks be done;
In every household work your portion take,
And what you make not, see that others make:
At leisure times attend the wheel, and see
The whit'ning web be sprinkled on the Lea;
When thus employ'd, should our young neighbour view
An useful lass, you may have more to do.'

Dreadful were these commands; but worse than these
The parting hint—a farmer could not please:
'Tis true she had without abhorrence seen
Young Harry Carr, when he was smart and clean;
But to be married—be a farmer's wife—
A slave! a drudge!—she could not, for her life.
With swimming eyes the fretful nymph withdrew,
And, deeply sighing, to her chamber flew;
There on her knees, to Heav'n she grieving pray'd
For change of prospect to a tortured maid.
Harry, a youth whose late-departed sire
Had left him all industrious men require,
Saw the pale beauty—and her shape and air
Engaged him much, and yet he must forbear:
'For my small farm what can the damsel do?'
He said—then stopp'd to take another view:
'Pity so sweet a lass will nothing learn
Of household cares—for what can beauty earn
By those small arts which they at school attain,
That keep them useless, and yet make them vain?'
This luckless damsel look'd the village round,
To find a friend, and one was quickly found;
A pensive widow—whose mild air and dress
Pleased the sad nymph, who wish'd her soul's distress
To one so seeming kind, confiding, to confess.—
'What lady that?' the anxious lass inquired,
Who then beheld the one she most admired:
'Here,' said the brother, 'are no ladies seen—
That is a widow dwelling on the green;
A dainty dame, who can but barely live
On her poor pittance, yet contrives to give;
She happier days has known, but seems at ease,
And you may call her lady, if you please:
But if you wish, good sister, to improve,
You shall see twenty better worth your love.'
These Nancy met; but, spite of all they taught,
This useless widow was the one she sought:
The father growl'd; but said he knew no harm
In such connexion that could give alarm;
'And if we thwart the trifler in her course,
'Tis odds against us she will take a worse.'

Then met the friends; the widow heard the sigh
That ask'd at once compassion and reply:—
'Would you, my child, converse with one so poor,
Yours were the kindness—yonder is my door;
And, save the time that we in public pray,
From that poor cottage, I but rarely stray.'
There went the nymph, and made her strong
complaints,
Painting her wo as injured feeling paints.
'Oh, dearest friend! do think how one must feel,
Shock'd all day long, and sicken'd every meal;
Could you behold our kitchen (and to you
A scene so shocking must indeed be new),
A mind like yours, with true refinement graced,
Would let no vulgar scenes pollute your taste;
And yet, in truth, from such a polish'd mind
All base ideas must resistance find,
And sordid pictures from the fancy pass,
As the breath startles from the polish'd glass.
'Here you enjoy a sweet romantic scene,
Without so pleasant, and within so clean;
These twining jess'mines, what delicious gloom
And soothing fragrance yield they to the room!
What lovely garden! there you oft retire,
And tales of wo and tenderness admire:
In that neat case your books, in order placed,
Soothe the full soul, and charm the cultured taste;
And thus, while all about you wears a charm,
How must you scorn the farmer and the farm!'
The widow smiled, and 'Know you not,' said she,
'How much these farmers scorn or pity me;
Who see what you admire, and laugh at all they see?
True, their opinion alters not my fate,
By falsely judging of an humble state:
This garden, you with such delight behold,
Tempts not a feeble dame who dreads the cold;
These plants, which please so well your livelier sense,
To mine but little of their sweets dispense;
Books soon are painful to my failing sight,
And oftener read from duty than delight;
(Yet let me own, that I can sometimes find

Both joy and duty in the act combined;)
But view me rightly, you will see no more
Than a poor female, willing to be poor;
Happy indeed, but not in books nor flowers,
Not in fair dreams, indulged in earlier hours,
Of never-tasted joys;—such visions shun,
My youthful friend, nor scorn the farmer's son.'
  'Nay,' said the damsel, nothing pleased to see
A friend's advice could like a father's be,
'Bless'd in your cottage, you must surely smile
At those who live in our detested style:
To my Lucinda's sympathizing heart
Could I my prospects and my griefs impart,
She would console me; but I dare not show
Ills that would wound her tender soul to know:
And I confess, it shocks my pride to tell
The secrets of the prison where I dwell;
For that dear maiden would be shock'd to feel
The secrets I should shudder to reveal;
When told her friend was by a parent ask'd,
Fed you the swine?—Good heav'n! how I am task'd!
What! can you smile? Ah! smile not at the grief
That woos your pity and demands relief.'
  'Trifles, my love; you take a false alarm;
Think, I beseech you, better of the farm:
Duties in every state demand your care,
And light are those that will require it there:
Fix on the youth a favouring eye, and these,
To him pertaining, or as his, will please.'
  'What words,' the lass replied, 'offend my ear!
Try you my patience? Can you be sincere?
And am I, told a willing hand to give
To a rude farmer, and with rustic live?
Far other fate was yours:—some gentle youth
Admired your beauty, and avow'd his truth;
The power of love prevail'd, and freely both
Gave the fond heart, and pledged the binding oath;
And then the rivals' plot, the parent's power,
And jealous fears, drew on the happy hour:
Ah! let not memory lose the blissful view,
But fairly show what love has done for you.'

'Agreed, my daughter; what my heart has known
Of love's strange power shall be with frankness shown:
But let me warn you, that experience finds
Few of the scenes that lively hope designs.'—
'Mysterious all,' said Nancy; 'you, I know,
Have suffer'd much; now deign the grief to show;—
I am your friend, and so prepare my heart
In all your sorrows to receive a part.'
The widow answer'd: 'I had once, like you,
Such thoughts of love; no dream is more untrue:
You judge it fated and decreed to dwell
In youthful hearts, which nothing can expel,
A passion doom'd to reign, and irresistible.
The struggling mind, when once subdued, in vain
Rejects the fury or defies the pain;
The strongest reason fails the flame t'allay,
And resolution droops and faints away:
Hence, when the destined lovers meet, they prove
At once the force of this all-powerful love;
Each from that period feels the mutual smart,
Nor seeks to cure it—heart is changed for heart;
Nor is there peace till they delighted stand,
And, at the altar—hand is join'd to hand.
'Alas! my child, there are who, dreaming so,
Waste their fresh youth, and waking feel the wo;
There is no spirit sent the heart to move
With such prevailing and alarming love;
Passion to reason will submit—or why
Should wealthy maids the poorest swains deny?
Or how could classes and degrees create
The slightest bar to such resistless fate?
Yet high and low, you see, forbear to mix;
No beggars' eyes the heart of kings transfix;
And who but am'rous peers or nobles sigh
When titled beauties pass triumphant by?
For reason wakes, proud wishes to reprove;
You cannot hope, and therefore dare not love:
All would be safe, did we at first inquire—
"Does reason sanction what our hearts desire?"
But quitting precept, let example show
What joys from love uncheck'd by prudence flow.

'A youth my father in his office placed,
Of humble fortune, but with sense and taste;
But he was thin and pale, had downcast looks;
He studied much, and pored upon his books:
Confused he was when seen, and, when he saw
Me or my sisters, would in haste withdraw;
And had this youth departed with the year,
His loss had cost us neither sigh nor tear.
'But with my father still the youth remain'd,
And more reward and kinder notice gain'd:
He often, reading, to the garden stray'd,
Where I by books or musing was delay'd;
This to discourse in summer evenings led,
Of these same evenings, or of what we read:
On such occasions we were much alone;
But, save the look, the manner, and the tone,
(These might have meaning), all that we discuss'd
We could with pleasure to a parent trust.
'At length 'twas friendship—and my friend and I
Said we were happy, and began to sigh:
My sisters first, and then my father, found
That we were wandering o'er enchanted ground;
But he had troubles in his own affairs,
And would not bear addition to his cares:
With pity moved, yet angry, "Child," said he,
"Will you embrace contempt and beggary?
Can you endure to see each other cursed
By want, of every human wo the worst?
Warring for ever with distress, in dread
Either of begging or of wanting bread;
While poverty, with unrelenting force,
Will your own offspring from your love divorce;
They, through your folly, must be doom'd to pine,
And you deplore your passion, or resign;
For, if it die, what good will then remain?
And if it live, it doubles every pain."'
'But you were true,' exclaim'd the lass, 'and fled
The tyrant's power who fill'd your soul with dread?'
'But,' said the smiling friend, 'he fill'd my mouth
with bread:
And in what other place that bread to gain

We long consider'd, and we sought in vain;
This was my twentieth year—at thirty-five
Our hope was fainter, yet our love alive;
So many years in anxious doubt had pass'd.'
'Then,' said the damsel, 'you were bless'd at last?'
A smile again adorn'd the widow's face,
But soon a starting tear usurp'd its place.
'Slow pass'd the heavy years, and each had more
Pains and vexations than the years before.
My father fail'd; his family was rent,
And to new states his grieving daughters sent;
Each to more thriving kindred found a way,
Guests without welcome—servants without pay;
Our parting hour was grievous; still I feel
The sad, sweet converse at our final meal;
Our father then reveal'd his former fears,
Cause of his sternness, and then join'd our tears;
Kindly he strove our feelings to repress,
But died, and left us heirs to his distress.
The rich, as humble friends, my sisters chose,
I with a wealthy widow sought repose;
Who with a chilling frown her friend received,
Bade me rejoice, and wonder'd that I grieved:
In vain my anxious lover tried his skill
To rise in life, he was dependent still;
We met in grief, nor can I paint the fears
Of these unhappy, troubled, trying years;
Our dying hopes and stronger fears between,
We felt no season peaceful or serene;
Our fleeting joys, like meteors in the night,
Shone on our gloom with inauspicious light;
And then domestic sorrows, till the mind,
Worn with distresses, to despair inclined;
Add too the ill that from the passion flows,
When its contemptuous frown the world bestows,
The peevish spirit caused by long delay,
When being gloomy we contemn the gay,
When, being wretched, we incline to hate
And censure others in a happier state;
Yet loving still, and still compell'd to move
In the sad labyrinth of ling'ring love:

While you, exempt from want, despair, alarm,
May wed—oh! take the farmer and the farm.'
'Nay,' said the nymph, 'joy smiled on you at last?'
'Smiled for a moment,' she replied, 'and pass'd:
My lover still the same dull means pursued,
Assistant call'd, but kept in servitude;
His spirits wearied in the prime of life,
By fears and wishes in eternal strife;
At length he urged impatient—"Now consent;
With thee united, fortune may relent."
I paused, consenting; but a friend arose,
Pleased a fair view, though distant, to disclose;
From the rough ocean we beheld a gleam
Of joy, as transient as the joys we dream;
By lying hopes deceived, my friend retired,
And sail'd—was wounded—reach'd us—and expired!
You shall behold his grave, and when I die,
There—but 'tis folly—I request to lie.'
'Thus,' said the lass, 'to joy you bade adieu!
But how a widow?—that cannot be true:
Or was it force, in some unhappy hour,
That placed you, grieving, in a tyrant's power?'
'Force, my young friend, when forty years are fled,
Is what a woman seldom has to dread;
She needs no brazen locks nor guarding walls,
And seldom comes a lover though she calls:
Yet moved by fancy, one approved my face,
Though time and tears had wrought it much disgrace.
'The man I married was sedate and meek,
And spoke of love as men in earnest speak;
Poor as I was, he ceaseless sought, for years,
A heart in sorrow, and a face in tears;
That heart I gave not; and 'twas long before
I gave attention, and then nothing more;
But in my breast some grateful feeling rose
For one whose love so sad a subject chose;
Till long delaying, fearing to repent,
But grateful still, I gave a cold assent.
'Thus we were wed; no fault had I to find,
And he but one; my heart could not be kind:
Alas! of every early hope bereft,

There was no fondness in my bosom left;
So had I told him, but had told in vain,
He lived but to indulge me and complain:
His was this cottage, he inclosed this ground,
And planted all these blooming shrubs around;
He to my room these curious trifles brought,
And with assiduous love my pleasure sought;
He lived to please me, and I ofttimes strove
Smiling, to thank his unrequited love:
"Teach me," he cried, "that pensive mind to ease,
For all my pleasure is the hope to please."
  'Serene, though heavy, were the days we spent,
Yet kind each word, and gen'rous each intent;
But his dejection lessen'd every day,
And to a placid kindness died away:
In tranquil ease we pass'd our latter years,
By griefs untroubled, unassail'd by fears.
  'Let not romantic views your bosom sway,
Yield to your duties, and their call obey:
Fly not a youth, frank, honest, and sincere;
Observe his merits, and his passion hear!
'Tis true, no hero, but a farmer sues—
Slow in his speech, but worthy in his views;
With him you cannot that affliction prove,
That rends the bosom of the poor in love:
Health, comfort, competence, and cheerful days,
Your friends' approval, and your father's praise,
Will crown the deed, and you escape *their* fate
Who plan so wildly, and are wise too late.'
  The damsel heard; at first th' advice was strange,
Yet wrought a happy, nay, a speedy change:
'I have no care,' she said, when next they met,
'But one may wonder he is silent yet;
He looks around him with his usual stare,
And utters nothing—not that I shall care.'
  This pettish humour pleased th'experienced friend—
None need despair, whose silence can offend;
'Should I,' resumed the thoughtful lass, 'consent
To hear the man, the man may now repent:
Think you my sighs shall call him from the plough,
Or give one hint that "You may woo me now?"'

'Persist, my love,' replied the friend, 'and gain
A parent's praise, *that* cannot be in vain.'
The father saw the change, but not the cause,
And gave the alter'd maid his fond applause:
The coarser manners she in part removed,
In part endured, improving and improved;
She spoke of household works, she rose betimes,
And said neglect and indolence were crimes;
The various duties of their life she weigh'd,
And strict attention to her dairy paid;
The names of servants now familiar grew,
And fair Lucinda's from her mind withdrew:
As prudent travellers for their ease assume
Their modes and language to whose lands they come:
So to the farmer this fair lass inclined,
Gave to the business of the farm her mind;
To useful arts she turn'd her hand and eye;
And by her manners told him—'You may try.'
Th' observing lover more attention paid,
With growing pleasure, to the alter'd maid;
He fear'd to lose her, and began to see
That a slim beauty might a helpmate be:
'Twixt hope and fear he now the lass address'd,
And in his Sunday robe his love express'd:
She felt no chilling dread, no thrilling joy,
Nor was too quickly kind, too slowly coy;
But still she lent an unreluctant ear
To all the rural business of the year;
Till love's strong hopes endured no more delay,
And Harry ask'd, and Nancy named the day.
'A happy change! my boy,' the father cried:
'How lost your sister all her school-day pride?'
The youth replied, 'It is the widow's deed:
The cure is perfect, and was wrought with speed.'—
'And comes there, boy, this benefit of books,
Of that smart dress, and of those dainty looks?
We must be kind—some offerings from the farm
To the white cot will speak our feelings warm;
Will show that people, when they know the fact,
Where they have judged severely, can retract.
Oft have I smiled, when I beheld her pass

With cautious step, as if she hurt the grass;
Where if a snail's retreat she chanced to storm,
She look'd as begging pardon of the worm;
And what, said I, still laughing at the view,
Have these weak creatures in the world to do?
But some are made for action, some to speak;
And, while she looks so pitiful and meek,
Her words are weighty, though her nerves are weak.'
   Soon told the village-bells the rite was done,
That join'd the school-bred miss and farmer's son;
Her former habits some slight scandal raised,
But real worth was soon perceived and praised;
She, her neat taste imparted to the farm,
And he, th'improving skill and vigorous arm.

8. THE MOTHER

What though you have beauty,
Must you be therefore proud and pitiless?
As You Like It, Act III, Scene 5

I would not marry her, though she were endow'd with all that Adam had left him before he transgress'd.
Much Ado About Nothing, Act II, Scene 1

Wilt thou love such a woman? What! to make thee an instrument, and play false strains upon thee!—Not to be endured.
As You Like It, Act IV, Scene 3

Your son,
As mad in folly, lack'd the sense to know
Her estimation hence.
All's Well that Ends Well, Act V, Scene 3

Be this sweet Helen's knell;
He left a wife whose words all ears took captive,
Whose dear perfection, hearts that scorn'd to serve
Humbly call'd mistress.
All's Well that Ends Well, Act V, Scene 3

There was a worthy, but a simple pair,
Who nursed a daughter, fairest of the fair:
Sons they had lost, and she alone remain'd,
Heir to the kindness they had all obtain'd;
Heir to the fortune they design'd for all,

Nor had th'allotted portion then been small;
But now, by fate enrich'd with beauty rare,
They watch'd their treasure with peculiar care:
The fairest features they could early trace,
And, blind with love, saw merit in her face—
Saw virtue, wisdom, dignity, and grace;
And Dorothea, from her infant years,
Gain'd all her wishes from their pride or fears:
She wrote a billet, and a novel read,
And with her fame her vanity was fed;
Each word, each look, each action was a cause
For flattering wonder, and for fond applause;
She rode or danced, and ever glanced around,
Seeking for praise, and smiling when she found.
The yielding pair to her petitions gave
An humble friend to be a civil slave;
Who for a poor support herself resign'd
To the base toil of a dependent mind:
By nature cold, our heiress stoop'd to art,
To gain the credit of a tender heart.
Hence at her door must suppliant paupers stand,
To bless the bounty of her bounteous hand:
And now, her education all complete,
She talk'd of virtuous love and union sweet;
She was indeed by no soft passion moved,
But wish'd, with all her soul, to be beloved.
Here on the favour'd beauty fortune smiled;
Her chosen husband was a man so mild,
So humbly temper'd, so intent to please,
It quite distress'd her to remain at ease,
Without a cause to sigh, without pretence to tease:
She tried his patience in a thousand modes,
And tired it not upon the roughest roads.
Pleasure she sought, and, disappointed, sigh'd
For joys, she said, 'to her alone denied;'
And she was 'sure her parents, if alive,
Would many comforts for their child contrive:'
The gentle husband bade her name him one;
'No—that,' she answer'd, 'should for her be done;
'How could she say what pleasures were around?
But she was certain many might be found.'—

'Would she some sea-port, Weymouth, Scarborough, grace?'—
'He knew she hated every watering-place:'—
'The town?'—'What! now 'twas empty, joyless, dull?'
—'In winter?'—'No; she liked it worse when full.'
She talk'd of building—'Would she plan a room?'—
'No! she could live, as he desired, in gloom;'
'Call then our friends and neighbours:'—'He might call,
And they might come and fill his ugly hall;
A noisy vulgar set, he knew she scorn'd them all:'—
'Then might their two dear girls the time employ,
And their improvement yield a solid joy:'—
'Solid indeed! and heavy—oh! the bliss
Of teaching letters to a lisping Miss!'—
'My dear, my gentle Dorothea, say,
Can I oblige you?'—'You may go away.'
  Twelve heavy years this patient soul sustain'd
This wasp's attacks, and then her praise obtain'd,
Graved on a marble tomb, where he at peace remain'd.
  Two daughters wept their loss; the one a child
With a plain face, strong sense, and temper mild,
Who keenly felt the mother's angry taunt,
'Thou art the image of thy pious aunt:'
Long time had Lucy wept her slighted face,
And ten began to smile at her disgrace.
Her father's sister, who the world had seen
Near sixty years when Lucy saw sixteen,
Begg'd the plain girl: the gracious mother smiled,
And freely gave her grieved but passive child;
And with her elder-born, the beauty-bless'd,
This parent rested, if such minds can rest:
No miss her waxen babe could so admire,
Nurse with such care, or with such pride attire;
They were companions meet, with equal mind,
Bless'd with one love, and to one point inclined;
Beauty to keep, adorn, increase, and guard,
Was their sole care, and had its full reward:
In rising splendor with the one it reign'd,
And in the other was by care sustain'd,
The daughter's charms increased, the parent's yet remain'd.

8. The Mother

Leave we these ladies to their daily care,
To see how meekness and discretion fare:—
A village maid, unvex'd by want or love,
Could not with more delight than Lucy move;
The village-lark, high mounted in the spring,
Could not with purer joy than Lucy sing;
Her cares all light, her pleasures all sincere,
Her duty joy, and her companion dear;
In tender friendship and in true respect
Lived aunt and niece, no flattery, no neglect—
They read, walk'd, visited—together pray'd,
Together slept the matron and the maid:
There was such goodness, such pure nature seen
In Lucy's looks, a manner so serene;
Such harmony in motion, speech, and air,
That without fairness she was more than fair:
Had more than beauty in each speaking grace,
That lent their cloudless glory to the face;
Where mild good sense in placid looks were shown,
And felt in every bosom but her own.
The one presiding feature in her mind,
Was the pure meekness of a will resign'd;
A tender spirit, freed from all pretence
Of wit, and pleased in mild benevolence;
Bless'd in protecting fondness she reposed,
With every wish indulged though undisclosed;
But love, like zephyr on the limpid lake,
Was now the bosom of the maid to shake,
And in that gentle mind a gentle strife to make.
  Among their chosen friends, a favour'd few,
The aunt and niece a youthful rector knew;
Who, though a younger brother, might address
A younger sister, fearless of success:
His friends, a lofty race, their native pride
At first display'd, and their assent denied;
But, pleased such virtues and such love to trace,
They own'd she would adorn the loftiest race.
The aunt, a mother's caution to supply,
Had watch'd the youthful priest with jealous eye;
And, anxious for her charge, had view'd unseen
The cautious life that keeps the conscience clean:

In all she found him all she wish'd to find,
With slight exception of a lofty mind:
A certain manner that express'd desire,
To be received as brother to the 'squire.
Lucy's meek eye had beam'd with many a tear,
Lucy's soft heart had beat with many a fear,
Before he told (although his looks, she thought,
Had oft confess'd) that he her favour sought:
But when he kneel'd, (she wish'd him not to kneel)
And spoke the fears and hopes that lovers feel;
When too the prudent aunt herself confess'd,
Her wishes on the gentle youth would rest;
The maiden's eye with tender passion beam'd,
She dwelt with fondness on the life she schemed;
The household cares, the soft and lasting ties
Of love, with all his binding charities;
Their village taught, consoled, assisted, fed,
Till the young zealot tears of pleasure shed.
  But would her mother? Ah! she fear'd it wrong
To have indulged these forward hopes so long;
Her mother loved, but was not used to grant
Favours so freely as her gentle aunt.—
Her gentle aunt, with smiles that angels wear,
Dispell'd her Lucy's apprehensive tear:
Her prudent foresight the request had made
To one whom none could govern, few persuade;
She doubted much if one in earnest woo'd
A girl with not a single charm endued;
The sister's nobler views she then declared,
And what small sum for Lucy could be spared;
'If more than this the foolish priest requires,
Tell him,' she wrote, 'to check his vain desires.'
At length, with many a cold expression mix'd,
With many a sneer on girls so fondly fix'd,
There came a promise—should they not repent,
But take with grateful minds the portion meant,
And wait the sister's day—the mother might consent.
  And here, might pitying hope o'er truth prevail,
Or love o'er fortune, we would end our tale:
For who more bless'd than youthful pair removed
From fear of want—by mutual friends approved—

Short time to wait, and in that time to live
With all the pleasures hope and fancy give;
Their equal passion raised on just esteem,
When reason sanctions all that love can dream?
Yes! reason sanctions what stern fate denies:
The early prospect in the glory dies,
As the soft smiles on dying infants play
In their mild features, and then pass away.
The beauty died, ere she could yield her hand
In the high marriage by the mother plann'd:
Who grieved indeed, but found a vast relief
In a cold heart, that ever warr'd with grief.
Lucy was present when her sister died,
Heiress to duties that she ill supplied:
There were no mutual feelings, sister arts,
No kindred taste, nor intercourse of hearts;
When in the mirror play'd the matron's smile,
The maiden's thoughts were trav'lling all the while;
And when desired to speak, she sigh'd to find
Her pause offended; 'Envy made her blind:
Tasteless she was, nor had a claim in life
Above the station of a rector's wife;
Yet as an heiress, she must shun disgrace,
Although no heiress to her mother's face:
It is your duty,' said th' imperious dame,
'(Advanced your fortune) to advance your name,
And with superior rank, superior offers claim:
Your sister's lover, when his sorrows die,
May look upon you, and for favour sigh;
Nor can you offer a reluctant hand;
His birth is noble, and his seat is grand.'
Alarm'd was Lucy, was in tears—'A fool!
Was she a child in love?—a miss at school?
Doubts any mortal, if a change of state
Dissolves all claims and ties of earlier date?'
The rector doubted, for he came to mourn
A sister dead, and with a wife return:
Lucy with heart unchanged received the youth,
True in herself, confiding in his truth;
But own'd her mother's change: the haughty dame
Pour'd strong contempt upon the youthful flame;

She firmly vow'd her purpose to pursue,
Judged her own cause, and bade the youth adieu!
The lover begg'd, insisted, urged his pain,
His brother wrote to threaten and complain,
Her sister reasoning proved the promise made,
Lucy appealing to a parent pray'd;
But all opposed th' event that she design'd,
And all in vain—she never changed her mind;
But coldly answer'd in her wonted way,
That she 'would rule, and Lucy must obey.'
  With peevish fear, she saw her health decline,
And cried, 'Oh! monstrous, for a man to pine;
But if your foolish heart must yield to love,
Let him possess it whom I now approve;
This is my pleasure:'—Still the rector came
With larger offers and with bolder claim;
But the stern lady would attend no more—
She frown'd, and rudely pointed to the door;
Whate'er he wrote, he saw unread return'd,
And he, indignant, the dishonour spurn'd;
Nay, fix'd suspicion where he might confide,
And sacrificed his passion to his pride.
  Lucy, meantime, though threaten'd and distress'd,
Against her marriage made a strong protest:
All was domestic war: the aunt rebell'd
Against the sovereign will, and was expell'd;
And every power was tried and every art,
To bend to falsehood one determined heart;
Assail'd, in patience it received the shock,
Soft as the wave, unshaken as the rock:
But while th' unconquered soul endures the storm
Of angry fate, it preys upon the form;
With conscious virtue she resisted still,
And conscious love gave vigour to her will:
But Lucy's trial was at hand; with joy
The mother cried—'Behold your constant boy—
Thursday—was married:—take the paper, sweet,
And read the conduct of your reverend cheat;
See with what pomp of coaches, in what crowd
The creature married—of his falsehood proud!
False, did I say?—at least no whining fool;

And thus will hopeless passions ever cool:
But shall his bride your single state reproach?
No! give him crowd for crowd, and coach for coach.
Oh! you retire; reflect then, gentle miss,
And gain some spirit in a cause like this.'
  Some spirit Lucy gain'd; a steady soul,
Defying all persuasions, all control:
In vain reproach, derision, threats were tried;
The constant mind all outward force defied,
By vengeance vainly urged, in vain assail'd by pride:
Fix'd in her purpose, perfect in her part,
She felt the courage of a wounded heart;
The world receded from her rising view,
When Heaven approach'd as earthly things withdrew;
Not strange before, for in the days of love,
Joy, hope, and pleasure, she had thoughts above;
Pious when most of worldly prospects fond,
When they best pleased her she could look beyond;
Had the young priest a faithful lover died,
Something had been her bosom to divide;
Now Heaven had all, for in her holiest views
She saw the matron whom she fear'd to lose;
While from her parent, the dejected maid
Forced the unpleasant thought, or thinking pray'd.
  Surprised, the mother saw the languid frame,
And felt indignant, yet forbore to blame:
Once with a frown she cried, 'And do you mean
To die of love—the folly of fifteen?'
But as her anger met with no reply,
She let the gentle girl in quiet die;
And to her sister wrote, impell'd by pain,
'Come quickly, Martha, or you come in vain.'
Lucy meantime profess'd with joy sincere,
That nothing held, employ'd, engaged her here.
  'I am an humble actor, doom'd to play
A part obscure, and then to glide away;
Incurious how the great or happy shine,
Or who have parts obscure and sad as mine;
In its best prospect I but wish'd, for life,
To be th' assiduous, gentle, useful wife;
That lost, with wearied mind, and spirit poor,

I drop my efforts, and can act no more;
With growing joy I feel my spirits tend
To that last scene where all my duties end.'
  Hope, ease, delight, the thoughts of dying gave,
Till Lucy spoke with fondness of the grave;
She smiled with wasted form, but spirit firm,
And said, 'She left but little for the worm;'
As toll'd the bell, 'There's one,' she said, 'hath press'd
Awhile before me to the bed of rest;'
And she beside her with attention spread
The decorations of the maiden dead.
  While quickly thus the mortal part declined,
The happiest visions fill'd the active mind;
A soft, religious melancholy gain'd
Entire possession, and for ever reign'd:
On holy writ her mind reposing dwelt,
She saw the wonders, she the mercies felt;
Till in a bless'd and glorious reverie,
She seem'd the Saviour as on earth to see,
And, fill'd with love divine, th' attending friend to be;
Or she who trembling, yet confiding, stole
Near to the garment, touch'd it, and was whole;
When, such th' intenseness of the working thought,
On her it seem'd the very deed was wrought;
She the glad patient's fear and rapture found,
The holy transport, and the healing wound;
This was so fix'd, so grafted in the heart,
That she adopted, nay became the part:
But one chief scene was present to her sight,
Her Saviour resting in the tomb by night;
Her fever rose, and still her wedded mind
Was to that scene, that hallow'd cave, confined—
Where in the shade of death the body laid,
There watch'd the spirit of the wandering maid;
Her looks were fix'd, entranced, illumed, serene,
In the still glory of the midnight scene:
There at her Saviour's feet, in visions bless'd,
Th' enraptured maid a sacred joy possess'd;
In patience waiting for the first-born ray
Of that all-glorious and triumphant day:
To this idea all her soul she gave,

Her mind reposing by the sacred grave;
Then sleep would seal the eye, the vision close,
And steep the solemn thoughts in brief repose.
Then grew the soul serene, and all its powers
Again restored illumed the dying hours;
But reason dwelt where fancy stray'd before,
And the mind wander'd from its views no more;
Till death approach'd, when every look express'd
A sense of bliss, till every sense had rest.
The mother lives, and has enough to buy
Th' attentive ear and the submissive eye
Of abject natures—these are daily told,
How triumph'd beauty in the days of old;
How, by her window seated, crowds have cast
Admiring glances, wondering as they pass'd;
How from her carriage as she stepp'd to pray,
Divided ranks would humbly make her way;
And how each voice in the astonish'd throng
Pronounced her peerless as she moved along.
Her picture then the greedy dame displays;
Touch'd by no shame, she now demands its praise;
In her tall mirror then she shows a face,
Still coldly fair with unaffecting grace;
These she compares, 'It has the form,' she cries,
'But wants the air, the spirit, and the eyes;
This, as a likeness, is correct and true
But there alone the living grace we view.'
This said, th' applauding voice the dame required,
And, gazing, slowly from the glass retired.

9. ARABELLA

Thrice blessed they that master so their blood—
But earthly happier is the rose distill'd,
Than that which, withering on the virgin thorn,
Grows, lives, and dies in single blessedness.
Midsummer Night's Dream, Act I, Scene 1

I sometimes do excuse the thing I hate,
For his advantage whom I dearly love.
Measure for Measure, Act II, Scene 4

Contempt, farewell! and maiden pride, adieu!
Much Ado about Nothing, Act III, Scene 1

Of a fair town where Doctor Rack was guide,
His only daughter was the boast and pride;
Wise Arabella, yet not wise alone,
She like a bright and polish'd brilliant shone;
Her father own'd her for his prop and stay,
Able to guide, yet willing to obey;
Pleased with her learning while discourse could please,
And with her love in languor and disease:
To every mother were her virtues known,
And to their daughters as a pattern shown;
Who in her youth had all that age requires,
And with her prudence, all that youth admires:
These odious praises made the damsels try
Not to obtain such merits, but deny;
For, whatsoever wise mammas might say,
To guide a daughter, this was not the way;
From such applause disdain and anger rise,
And envy lives where emulation dies.
In all his strength, contends the noble horse,
With one who just precedes him on the course;
But when the rival flies too far before,
His spirit fails, and he attempts no more.
  This reasoning maid, above her sex's dread,
Had dared to read, and dared to say she read;
Not the last novel, not the new-born play;
Not the mere trash and scandal of the day;
But (though her young companions felt the shock)
She studied Berkeley, Bacon, Hobbes, and Locke:
Her mind within the maze of history dwelt,
And of the moral muse the beauty felt;
The merits of the Roman page she knew,
And could converse with Moore and Montagu:
Thus she became the wonder of the town,
From that she reap'd, to that she gave renown,
And strangers coming, all were taught t'admire
The learned lady, and the lofty spire.
  Thus fame in public fix'd the maid, where all
Might throw their darts, and see the idol fall;
A hundred arrows came with vengeance keen,
From tongues envenom'd, and from arms unseen;
A thousand eyes were fix'd upon the place,

That, if she fell, she might not fly disgrace:
But malice vainly throws the poison'd dart,
Unless our frailty shows the peccant part;
And Arabella still preserved her name
Untouch'd, and shone with undisputed fame;
Her very notice some respect would cause,
And her esteem was honour and applause.
  Men she avoided; not in childish fear,
As if she thought some savage foe was near;
Not as a prude, who hides that man should seek,
Or who by silence hints that they should speak;
But with discretion all the sex she view'd,
Ere yet engaged, pursuing, or pursued;
Ere love had made her to his vices blind,
Or hid the favourite's failings from her mind.
  Thus was the picture of the man portray'd,
By merit destined for so rare a maid;
At whose request she might exchange her state,
Or still be happy in a virgin's fate.
  He must be one with manners like her own,
His life unquestion'd, his opinions known;
His stainless virtue must all tests endure,
His honour spotless, and his bosom pure;
She no allowance made for sex or times,
Of lax opinion—crimes were ever crimes;
No wretch forsaken must his frailty curse,
No spurious offspring drain his private purse:
He at all times his passions must command,
And yet possess—or be refused her hand.
  All this without reserve the maiden told,
And some began to weigh the rector's gold;
To ask what sum a prudent man might gain,
Who had such store of virtues to maintain?
  A Doctor Campbell, north of Tweed, came forth,
Declared his passion, and proclaim'd his worth;
Not unapproved, for he had much to say
On every cause, and in a pleasant way;
Not all his trust was in a pliant tongue,
His form was good, and ruddy he, and young:
But though the Doctor was a man of parts,
He read not deeply male or female hearts;

But judged that all whom he esteem'd as wise
Must think alike, though some assumed disguise;
That every reasoning Bramin, Christian, Jew,
Of all religions took their liberal view;
And of her own, no doubt, this learned maid
Denied the substance, and the forms obey'd;
And thus persuaded, he his thoughts express'd
Of her opinions, and his own profess'd:
'All states demand this aid, the vulgar need
Their priests and pray'rs, their sermons and their creed;
And those of stronger minds should never speak
(In his opinion) what might hurt the weak:
A man may smile, but still he should attend
His hour at church, and be the church's friend,
What there he thinks conceal, and what he hears commend.'
Frank was the speech, but heard with high disdain,
Nor had the Doctor leave to speak again;
A man who own'd, nay gloried in deceit,
'He might despise her, but he should not cheat.'
Then Vicar Holmes appear'd; he heard it said
That ancient men best pleased the prudent maid;
And true it was her ancient friends she loved,
Servants when old she favour'd and approved;
Age in her pious parents she revered,
And neighbours were by length of days endear'd;
But, if her husband too must ancient be,
The good old Vicar found it was not he.
On Captain Bligh her mind in balance hung—
Though valiant, modest; and reserved, though young:
Against these merits must defects be set—
Though poor, imprudent; and though proud, in debt:
In vain the Captain close attention paid;
She found him wanting, whom she fairly weigh'd.
Then came a youth, and all their friends agreed,
That Edward Huntley was the man indeed;
Respectful duty he had paid awhile,
Then ask'd her hand, and had a gracious smile:
A lover now declared, he led the fair
To woods and fields, to visits and to pray'r;

Then whisper'd softly—'Will you name the day?'
She softly whisper'd—'If you love me, stay:'
'Oh! try me not beyond my strength,' he cried:
'Oh! be not weak,' the prudent maid replied;
'But by some trial your affection prove—
Respect and not impatience argues love:
And love no more is by impatience known,
Than Ocean's depth is by its tempests shown:
He whom a weak and fond impatience sways,
But for himself with all his fervour prays,
And not the maid he woos, but his own will obeys;
And will she love the being who prefers,
With so much ardour, his desire to hers?'
  Young Edward grieved, but let not grief be seen;
He knew obedience pleased his fancy's queen:
Awhile he waited, and then cried—'Behold!
The year advancing, be no longer cold!'
For she had promised—'Let the flowers appear,
And I will pass with thee the smiling year:'
Then pressing grew the youth; the more he press'd,
The less inclined the maid to his request:
'Let June arrive.'—Alas! when April came,
It brought a stranger, and the stranger, shame;
Nor could the lover from his house persuade
A stubborn lass whom he had mournful made;
Angry and weak, by thoughtless vengeance moved,
She told her story to the fair beloved;
In strongest words th' unwelcome truth was shown,
To blight his prospects, careless of her own.
  Our heroine grieved, but had too firm a heart
For him to soften, when she swore to part;
In vain his seeming penitence and pray'r,
His vows, his tears; she left him in despair:
His mother fondly laid her grief aside,
And to the reason of the nymph applied—
  'It well becomes thee, lady, to appear,
But not to be, in very truth, severe;
Although the crime be odious in thy sight,
That daring sex is taught such things to slight:
His heart is thine, although it once was frail;
Think of his grief, and let his love prevail!—'

'Plead thou no more,' the lofty lass return'd;
'Forgiving woman is deceived and spurn'd:
Say that the crime is common—shall I take
A common man my wedded lord to make?
See! a weak woman by his arts betray'd,
An infant born his father to upbraid;
Shall I forgive his vileness, take his name,
Sanction his error, and partake his shame?
No! this assent would kindred frailty prove,
A love for him would be a vicious love:
Can a chaste maiden secret counsel hold
With one whose crime by every mouth is told?
Forbid it spirit, prudence, virtuous pride;
He must despise me, were he not denied:
The way from vice the erring mind to win
Is with presuming sinners to begin,
And show, by scorning them, a just contempt for sin.'
The youth repulsed, to one more mild convey'd
His heart, and smiled on the remorseless maid;
The maid, remorseless in her pride, the while
Despised the insult, and return'd the smile.
First to admire, to praise her, and defend,
Was (now in years advanced) a virgin friend:
Much she preferr'd, she cried, a single state,
'It was her choice'—it surely was her fate;
And much it pleased her in the train to view
A maiden vot'ress, wise and lovely too.
Time to the yielding mind his change imparts,
He varies notions, and he alters hearts;
'Tis right, 'tis just to feel contempt for vice,
But he that shows it may be over-nice:
There are who feel, when young, the false sublime,
And proudly love to show disdain for crime;
To whom the future will new thoughts supply,
The pride will soften, and the scorn will die;
Nay, where they still the vice itself condemn,
They bear the vicious, and consort with them:
Young Captain Grove, when one had changed his side,
Despised the venal turn-coat, and defied;
Old Colonel Grove now shakes him by the hand,

Though he who bribes may still his vote command:
Why would not Ellen to Belinda speak,
When she had flown to London for a week;
And then return'd, to every friend's surprise,
With twice the spirit, and with half the size?
She spoke not then—but after years had flown,
A better friend had Ellen never known:
Was it the lady her mistake had seen?
Or had she also such a journey been?
No: 'twas the gradual change in human hearts,
That time, in commerce with the world, imparts;
That on the roughest temper throws disguise,
And steals from virtue her asperities.
The young and ardent, who with glowing zeal
Felt wrath for trifles, and were proud to feel,
Now find those trifles all the mind engage,
To soothe dull hours, and cheat the cares of age;
As young Zelinda, in her quaker-dress,
Disdain'd each varying fashion's vile excess,
And now her friends on old Zelinda gaze,
Pleased in rich silks and orient gems to blaze:
Changes like these 'tis folly to condemn,
So virtue yields not, nor is changed with them.
  Let us proceed:—Twelve brilliant years were past,
Yet each with less of glory than the last;
Whether these years to this fair virgin gave
A softer mind—effect they often have;
Whether the virgin-state was not so bless'd
As that good maiden in her zeal profess'd;
Or whether lovers falling from her train,
Gave greater price to those she could retain,
Is all unknown;—but Arabella now
Was kindly listening to a merchant's vow;
Who offer'd terms so fair, against his love
To strive was folly, so she never strove.—
Man in his earlier days we often find
With a too easy and unguarded mind;
But by increasing years and prudence taught,
He grows reserved, and locks up every thought:
Not thus the maiden, for in blooming youth
She hides her thought, and guards the tender truth:

This, when no longer young, no more she hides,
But frankly in the favour'd swain confides:
Man, stubborn man, is like the growing tree,
That longer standing, still will harder be;
And like its fruit, the virgin, first austere,
Then kindly softening with the ripening year.
  Now was the lover urgent, and the kind
And yielding lady to his suit inclined:
'A little time, my friend, is just, is right;
We must be decent in our neighbours' sight:'
Still she allow'd him of his hopes to speak,
And in compassion took off week by week;
Till few remain'd, when, wearied with delay,
She kindly meant to take off day by day.
  That female friend who gave our virgin praise
For flying man and all his treacherous ways,
Now heard with mingled anger, shame and fear,
Of one accepted, and a wedding near;
But she resolved again with friendly zeal
To make the maid her scorn of wedlock feel;
For she was grieved to find her work undone,
And like a sister mourn'd the failing nun.
  Why are these gentle maidens prone to make
Their sister-doves the tempting world forsake?
Why all their triumph when a maid disdains
The tyrant-sex, and scorns to wear its chains?
Is it pure joy to see a sister flown
From the false pleasures they themselves have known?
Or do they, as the call-birds in the cage,
Try, in pure envy, others to engage;
And therefore paint their native woods and groves,
As scenes of dangerous joys and naughty loves?
  Strong was the maiden's hope; her friend was proud,
And had her notions to the world avow'd;
And, could she find the Merchant weak and frail,
With power to prove it, then she must prevail;
For she aloud would publish his disgrace,
And save his victim from a man so base.
  When all inquiries had been duly made,
Came the kind friend her burthen to unlade—

'Alas! my dear! not all our care and art
Can tread the maze of man's deceitful heart:
Look not surprise—nor let resentment swell
Those lovely features, all will yet be well;
And thou, from love's and man's deceptions free,
Wilt dwell in virgin-state, and walk to heav'n with me.'
  The maiden frown'd, and then conceived 'that wives
Could walk as well, and lead as holy lives
As angry prudes who scorn'd the marriage-chain,
Or luckless maids who sought it still in vain.'
  The friend was vex'd—she paused, at length she cried:
'Know your own danger, then your lot decide;
That traitor Beswell, while he seeks your hand,
Has, I affirm, a wanton at command;
A slave, a creature from a foreign place,
The nurse and mother of a spurious race;
Brown, ugly bastards—(Heaven the word forgive,
And the deed punish!)—in his cottage live;
To town if business calls him, there he stays
In sinful pleasures wasting countless days;
Nor doubt the facts, for I can witness call
For every crime, and prove them one and all.'
  Here ceased th' informer; Arabella's look
Was like a school-boy's puzzled by his book;
Intent she cast her eyes upon the floor,
Paused—then replied—
                    'I wish to know no more:
I question not your motive, zeal, or love,
But must decline such dubious points to prove—
All is not true, I judge, for who can guess
Those deeds of darkness men with care suppress?
He brought a slave perhaps to England's coast,
And made her free; it is our country's boast!
And she perchance too grateful—good and ill
Were sown at first, and grow together still;
The colour'd infants on the village-green,
What are they more than we have often seen?
Children half-clothed who round their village stray,
In sun or rain, now starved, now beaten, they
Will the dark colour of their fate betray:

Let us in Christian love for all account,
And then behold to what such tales amount.'
'His heart is evil,' said th' impatient friend:
'My duty bids me try that heart to mend,'
Replied the virgin—'We may be too nice,
And lose a soul in our contempt of vice;
If false the charge, I then shall show regard
For a good man, and be his just reward:
And what for virtue can I better do
Than to reclaim him, if the charge be true?'
She spoke, nor more her holy work delay'd;
'Twas time to land an erring mortal aid:
'The noblest way,' she judged, 'a soul to win,
Was with an act of kindness to begin,
To make the sinner sure, and then t' attack the sin.'*

10. THE LOVER'S JOURNEY

The sun is in the heavens, and the proud day,
Attended with the pleasures of the world,
Is all too wanton. *King John*, Act III, Scene 3

The lunatic, the lover, and the poet,
Are of imagination all compact.
Midsummer Night's Dream, Act v, Scene 2

Oh! how the spring of love resembleth
Th' uncertain glory of an April day,
Which now shows all her beauty to the sun,
And by and by a cloud bears all away.

And happily I have arrived at last
Unto the wished haven of my bliss.
Taming of the Shrew, Act v, Scene 1

It is the soul that sees; the outward eyes
Present the object, but the mind descries;
And thence delight, disgust, or cool indiff'rence rise:
When minds are joyful, then we look around,

* As the author's purpose in this Tale may be mistaken, he wishes to observe, that conduct like that of the lady's here described must be meritorious or censurable just as the motives to it are pure or selfish; that these motives may in a great measure be concealed from the mind of the agent; and that we often take credit to our virtue for actions which spring originally from our tempers, inclinations, or our indifference. It cannot therefore be improper, much less immoral, to give an instance of such self-deception.

And what is seen is all on fairy ground;
Again they sicken, and on every view
Cast their own dull and melancholy hue;
Or, if absorb'd by their peculiar cares,
The vacant eye on viewless matter glares,
Our feelings still upon our views attend,
And their own natures to the objects lend;
Sorrow and joy are in their influence sure,
Long as the passion reigns th' effects endure;
But love in minds his various changes makes,
And clothes each object with the change he takes;
His light and shade on every view he throws,
And on each object, what he feels, bestows.
  Fair was the morning, and the month was June,
When rose a lover; love awakens soon;
Brief his repose, yet much he dreamt the while
Of that day's meeting, and his Laura's smile;
Fancy and love that name assign'd to her,
Call'd Susan in the parish-register;
And he no more was John—his Laura gave
The name Orlando to her faithful slave.
  Bright shone the glory of the rising day,
When the fond traveller took his favourite way;
He mounted gaily, felt his bosom light,
And all he saw was pleasing in his sight.
  'Ye hours of expectation, quickly fly,
And bring on hours of blest reality;
When I shall Laura see, beside her stand,
Hear her sweet voice, and press her yielded hand.'
  First o'er a barren heath beside the coast
Orlando rode, and joy began to boast.
  'This neat low gorse,' said he, 'with golden bloom,
Delights each sense, is beauty, is perfume;
And this gay ling, with all its purple flowers,
A man at leisure might admire for hours;
This green-fringed cup-moss has a scarlet tip,
That yields to nothing but my Laura's lip;
And then how fine this herbage! men may say
A heath is barren; nothing is so gay:
Barren or bare to call such charming scene
Argues a mind possess'd by care and spleen.'

Onward he went, and fiercer grew the heat,
Dust rose in clouds before the horse's feet;
For now he pass'd through lanes of burning sand,
Bounds to thin crops or yet uncultured land;
Where the dark poppy flourish'd on the dry
And sterile soil, and mock'd the thin-set rye.
'How lovely this!' the rapt Orlando said;
With what delight is labouring man repaid!
The very lane has sweets that all admire,
The rambling suckling and the vigorous brier;
See! wholesome wormwood grows beside the way,
Where dew-press'd yet the dog-rose bends the spray;
Fresh herbs the fields, fair shrubs the banks adorn,
And snow-white bloom falls flaky from the thorn;
No fostering hand they need, no sheltering wall,
They spring uncultured and they bloom for all.'
The lover rode as hasty lovers ride,
And reach'd a common pasture wild and wide;
Small black-legg'd sheep devour with hunger keen
The meagre herbage, fleshless, lank, and lean;
Such o'er thy level turf, Newmarket! stray,
And there, with other *black-legs* find their prey:
He saw some scatter'd hovels; turf was piled
In square brown stacks; a prospect bleak and wild!
A mill, indeed, was in the centre found,
With short sear herbage withering all around;
A smith's black shed opposed a wright's long shop,
And join'd an inn where humble travellers stop.
'Ay, this is Nature,' said the gentle 'squire;
'This ease, peace, pleasure—who would not admire?
With what delight these sturdy children play,
And joyful rustics at the close of day;
Sport follows labour, on this even space
Will soon commence the wrestling and the race;
Then will the village-maidens leave their home,
And to the dance with buoyant spirits come;
No affectation in their looks is seen,
Nor know they what disguise or flattery mean;
Nor aught to move an envious pang they see,
Easy their service, and their love is free;
Hence early springs that love, it long endures,

And life's first comfort, while they live, ensures:
They the low roof and rustic comforts prize,
Nor cast on prouder mansions envying eyes:
Sometimes the news at yonder town they hear,
And learn what busier mortals feel and fear;
Secure themselves, although by tales amazed,
Of towns bombarded and of cities razed;
As if they doubted, in their still retreat,
The very news that makes their quiet sweet,
And their days happy—happier only knows
He on whom Laura her regard bestows.'
  On rode Orlando, counting all the while
The miles he pass'd and every coming mile;
Like all attracted things, he quicker flies,
The place approaching where th' attraction lies;
When next appear'd a *dam*—so call the place—
Where lies a road confined in narrow space;
A work of labour, for on either side
Is level fen, a prospect wild and wide,
With dikes on either hand by ocean's self supplied:
Far on the right the distant sea is seen,
And salt the springs that feed the marsh between;
Beneath an ancient bridge, the straiten'd flood
Rolls through its sloping banks of slimy mud;
Near it a sunken boat resists the tide,
That frets and hurries to th' opposing side;
The rushes sharp, that on the borders grow,
Bend their brown flow'rets to the stream below,
Impure in all its course, in all its progress slow:
Here a grave *Flora scarcely deigns to bloom,

* The ditches of a fen so near the ocean are lined with irregular patches of a coarse and stained lava; a muddy sediment rests on the horse-tail and other perennial herbs, which in part conceal the shallowness of the stream; a fat-leaved pale-flowering scurvy-grass appears early in the year, and the razor-edged bull-rush in the summer and autumn. The fen itself has a dark and saline herbage; there are rushes and *arrow-head*, and in a few patches the flakes of the cotton-grass are seen, but more commonly the *sea-aster*, the dullest of that numerous and hardy genus; a *thrift*, blue in flower, but withering and remaining withered till the winter scatters it; the *saltwort*, both simple and shrubby; a few kinds of grass changed by their soil and atmosphere, and low plants of two or three denominations undistinguished in a general view of the scenery;—such is the vegetation of the fen when it is at a small distance from the ocean; and in this case there arise from it effluvia strong and peculiar, half-saline, half-putrid, which would be considered by most people as offensive, and by some as dangerous; but there are others to whom singularity of taste or association of ideas has rendered it agreeable and pleasant.

Nor wears a rosy blush, nor sheds perfume;
The few dull flowers that o'er the place are spread
Partake the nature of their fenny bed;
Here on its wiry stem, in rigid bloom,
Grows the salt lavender that lacks perfume;
Here the dwarf sallows creep, the septfoil harsh,
And the soft slimy mallow of the marsh;
Low on the ear the distant billows sound,
And just in view appears their stony bound;
No hedge nor tree conceals the glowing sun,
Birds, save a wat'ry tribe, the district shun,
Nor chirp among the reeds where bitter waters run.
 'Various as beauteous, Nature, is thy face,'
Exclaim'd Orlando: 'all that grows has grace;
All are appropriate—bog, and marsh, and fen,
Are only poor to undiscerning men;
Here may the nice and curious eye explore
How Nature's hand adorns the rushy moor;
Here the rare moss in secret shade is found,
Here the sweet myrtle of the shaking ground;
Beauties are these that from the view retire,
But well repay th' attention they require;
For these my Laura will her home forsake,
And all the pleasures they afford partake.'
 Again the country was enclosed, a wide
And sandy road has banks on either side;
Where, lo! a hollow on the left appear'd,
And there a gipsy-tribe their tent had rear'd;
'Twas open spread, to catch the morning sun,
And they had now their early meal begun,
When two brown boys just left their grassy seat,
The early trav'ller with their pray'rs to greet:
While yet Orlando held his pence in his hand,
He saw their sister on her duty stand;
Some twelve years old, demure, affected, sly,
Prepared the force of early powers to try;
Sudden a look of languor he descries,
And well-feign'd apprehension in her eyes;
Train'd but yet savage, in her speaking face
He mark'd the features of her vagrant race;
When a light laugh and roguish leer express'd

The vice implanted in her youthful breast:
Forth from the tent her elder brother came,
Who seem'd offended, yet forbore to blame
The young designer, but could only trace
The looks of pity in the trav'ller's face:
Within, the father, who from fences nigh
Had brought the fuel for the fire's supply,
Watch'd now the feeble blaze, and stood dejected by:
On ragged rug, just borrow'd from the bed,
And by the hand of coarse indulgence fed,
In dirty patchwork negligently dress'd,
Reclined the wife, an infant at her breast;
In her wild face some touch of grace remain'd,
Of vigour palsied and of beauty stain'd;
Her bloodshot eyes on her unheeding mate
Were wrathful turn'd, and seem'd her wants to state,
Cursing his tardy aid—her mother there
With gipsy-state engrass'd the only chair;
Solemn and dull her look; with such she stands,
And reads the milk-maid's fortune in her hands,
Tracing the lines of life; assumed through years,
Each feature now the steady falsehood wears;
With hard and savage eye she views the food,
And grudging pinches their intruding brood;
Last in the group, the worn-out grandsire sits
Neglected, lost, and living but by fits;
Useless, despised, his worthless labours done,
And half protected by the vicious son,
Who half supports him; he with heavy glance
Views the young ruffians who around him dance;
And, by the sadness in his face, appears
To trace the progress of their future years
Through what strange course of misery, vice, deceit,
Must wildly wander each unpractised cheat!
What shame and grief, what punishment and pain,
Sport of fierce passions, must each child sustain—
Ere they like him approach their latter end,
Without a hope, a comfort, or a friend!

But this Orlando felt not; 'Rogues,' said he,
'Doubtless they are, but merry rogues they be;
They wander round the land, and be it true,

They break the laws—then let the laws pursue
The wanton idlers; for the life they live,
Acquit I cannot, but I can forgive.'
This said, a portion from his purse was thrown,
And every heart seem'd happy like his own.
  He hurried forth, for now the town was nigh—
'The happiest man of mortal men am I.'
Thou art! but change in every state is near,
(So while the wretched hope, the blest may fear);
'Say, where is Laura?'—'That her words must show,'
A lass replied; 'read this, and thou shalt know!'
  'What, gone!'—her friend insisted—forced to go:—
'Is vex'd, was teased, could not refuse her!—No?'
'But you can follow:' 'Yes:' 'The miles are few,
The way is pleasant; will you come?—Adieu!
Thy Laura!' 'No! I feel I must resign
The pleasing hope, thou hadst been here, if mine:
A lady was it?—Was no brother there?
But why should I afflict me if there were?'
'The way is pleasant:' 'What to me the way?
I cannot reach her till the close of day.
My dumb companion! is it thus we speed?
Not I from grief nor thou from toil art freed;
Still art thou doom'd to travel and to pine,
For my vexation—What a fate is mine!
  'Gone to a friend, she tells me; I commend
Her purpose; means she to a female friend?
By Heaven, I wish she suffer'd half the pain
Of hope protracted through the day in vain:
Shall I persist to see th' ungrateful maid?
Yes, I will see her, slight her, and upbraid:
What! in the very hour? She knew the time,
And doubtless chose it to increase her crime.'
  Forth rode Orlando by a river's side,
Inland and winding, smooth, and full and wide,
That roll'd majestic on, in one soft-flowing tide;
The bottom gravel, flow'ry were the banks,
Tall willows, waving in their broken ranks;
The road, now near, now distant, winding led
By lovely meadows which the waters fed;
He pass'd the way-side inn, the village spire,

Nor stopp'd to gaze, to question, or admire;
On either side the rural mansions stood,
With hedge-row trees, and hills high-crown'd with wood,
And many a devious stream that reach'd the nobler flood.
'I hate these scenes,' Orlando angry cried,
'And these proud farmers! yes, I hate their pride:
See! that sleek fellow, how he strides along,
Strong as an ox, and ignorant as strong;
Can yon close crops a single eye detain
But his who counts the profits of the grain?
And these vile beans with deleterious smell,
Where is their beauty? can a mortal tell?
These deep fat meadows I detest; it shocks
One's feelings there to see the grazing ox;—
For slaughter fatted, as a lady's smile
Rejoices man, and means his death the while.
Lo! now the sons of labour! every day
Employ'd in toil, and vex'd in every way;
Theirs is but mirth assumed, and they conceal,
In their affected joys, the ills they feel:
I hate these long green lanes; there's nothing seen
In this vile country but eternal green;
Woods! waters! meadows! Will they never end?
'Tis a vile prospect:—Gone to see a friend!'—
Still on he rode! a mansion fair and tall
Rose on his view—the pride of Loddon-Hall:
Spread o'er the park he saw the grazing steer,
The full-fed steed, the herds of bounding deer:
On a clear stream the vivid sunbeams play'd,
Through noble elms, and on the surface made
That moving picture, checker'd light and shade;
Th' attended children, there indulged to stray,
Enjoy'd and gave new beauty to the day;
Whose happy parents from their room were seen
Pleased with the sportive idlers on the green.
'Well!' said Orlando, 'and for one so bless'd,
A thousand reasoning wretches are distress'd;
Nay, these so seeming glad, are grieving like the rest:
Man is a cheat—and all but strive to hide

Their inward misery by their outward pride.
What do yon lofty gates and walls contain,
But fruitless means to soothe unconquer'd pain?
The parents read each infant daughter's smile,
Form'd to seduce, encouraged to beguile;
They view the boys unconscious of their fate,
Sure to be tempted, sure to take the bait;
These will be Lauras, sad Orlando these—
There's guilt and grief in all one hears and sees.'
  Our trav'ller, lab'ring up a hill, look'd down
Upon a lively, busy, pleasant town;
All he beheld were there alert, alive,
The busiest bees that ever stock'd a hive:
A pair were married, and the bells aloud
Proclaim'd their joy, and joyful seem'd the crowd;
And now proceeding on his way, he spied,
Bound by strong ties, the bridegroom and the bride:
Each by some friends attended, near they drew,
And spleen beheld them with prophetic view.
  'Married! nay, mad!' Orlando cried in scorn;
'Another wretch on this unlucky morn:
What are this foolish mirth, these idle joys?
Attempts to stifle doubt and fear by noise:
To me these robes, expressive of delight,
Foreshow distress, and only grief excite;
And for these cheerful friends, will they behold
Their wailing brood in sickness, want, and cold;
And his proud look, and her soft languid air
Will—but I spare you—go, unhappy pair!'
  And now approaching to the journey's end,
His anger fails, his thoughts to kindness tend,
He less offended feels, and rather fears t' offend:
Now gently rising, hope contends with doubt,
And casts a sunshine on the views without;
And still reviving joy and lingering gloom
Alternate empire o'er his soul assume;
Till, long perplex'd, he now began to find
The softer thoughts engross the settling mind:
He saw the mansion, and should quickly see
His Laura's self—and angry could he be?
No! the resentment melted all away—

'For this my grief a single smile will pay,'
Our trav'ller cried;—'And why should it offend,
That one so good should have a pressing friend?
Grieve not, my heart! to find a favourite guest
Thy pride and boast—ye selfish sorrows, rest;
She will be kind, and I again be blest.'
  While gentler passions thus his bosom sway'd,
He reach'd the mansion, and he saw the maid;
'My Laura!'—'My Orlando!—this is kind;
In truth I came persuaded, not inclined:
Our friends' amusement let us now pursue,
And I to-morrow will return with you.'
  Like man entranced, the happy lover stood—
'As Laura wills, for she is kind and good;
Ever the truest, gentlest, fairest, best—
As Laura wills, I see her and am blest.'
  Home went the lovers through that busy place,
By Loddon-Hall, the country's pride and grace;
By the rich meadows where the oxen fed,
Through the green vale that form'd the river's bed;
And by unnumber'd cottages and farms,
That have for musing minds unnumber'd charms;
And how affected by the view of these
Was then Orlando—did they pain or please?
  Nor pain nor pleasure could they yield—and why?
The mind was fill'd, was happy, and the eye
Roved o'er the fleeting views, that but appear'd to die.
  Alone Orlando on the morrow paced
The well-known road; the gypsy-tent he traced;
The dam high-raised, the reedy dikes between,
The scatter'd hovels on the barren green,
The burning sand, the fields of thin-set rye,
Mock'd by the useless Flora, blooming by;
And last the heath with all its various bloom,
And the close lanes that led the trav'ller home.
  Then could these scenes the former joys renew?
Or was there now dejection in the view?—
Nor one or other would they yield—and why?
The mind was absent, and the vacant eye
Wander'd o'er viewless scenes, that but appear'd to die.

11. EDWARD SHORE

Seem they grave or learned?
Why, so didst thou—Seem they religious?
Why, so didst thou; or are they spare in diet,
Free from gross passion, or of mirth or anger,
Constant in spirit, not swerving with the blood,
Garnish'd and deck'd in modest compliment,
Not working with the eye without the ear,
And but with purged judgment trusting neither?
Such and so finely bolted didst thou seem.

Henry V, Act II, Scene 2

Better I were distract,
So should my thoughts be sever'd from my griefs,
And woes by strong imagination lose
The knowledge of themselves.

Lear, Act IV, Scene 6

Genius! thou gift of Heav'n! thou light divine!
Amid what dangers art thou doom'd to shine!
Oft will the body's weakness check thy force,
Oft damp thy vigour, and impede thy course;
And trembling nerves compel thee to restrain
Thy nobler efforts, to contend with pain;
Or Want (sad guest!) will in thy presence come,
And breathe around her melancholy gloom;
To life's low cares will thy proud thought confine,
And make her sufferings, her impatience, thine.
Evil and strong, seducing passions prey
On soaring minds, and win them from their way;
Who then to vice the subject spirits give,
And in the service of the conqu'ror live;
Like captive Samson making sport for all,
Who fear'd their strength, and glory in their fall.
Genius, with virtue, still may lack the aid
Implored by humble minds and hearts afraid;
May leave to timid souls the shield and sword
Of the tried faith, and the resistless word;
Amid a world of dangers venturing forth,
Frail, but yet fearless, proud in conscious worth,
Till strong temptation, in some fatal time,
Assails the heart, and wins the soul to crime;

When left by honour, and by sorrow spent,
Unused to pray, unable to repent,
The nobler powers that once exalted high
Th' aspiring man, shall then degraded lie:
Reason, through anguish, shall her throne forsake,
And strength of mind but stronger madness make.
   When EDWARD SHORE had reach'd his twentieth year,
He felt his bosom light, his conscience clear;
Applause at school the youthful hero gain'd,
And trials there with manly strength sustain'd:
With prospects bright upon the world he came,
Pure love of virtue, strong desire of fame:
Men watch'd the way his lofty mind would take,
And all foretold the progress he would make.
   Boast of these friends, to older men a guide,
Proud of his parts, but gracious in his pride;
He bore a gay good-nature in his face,
And in his air were dignity and grace;
Dress that became his state and years he wore,
And sense and spirit shone in Edward Shore.
   Thus while admiring friends the youth beheld,
His own disgust their forward hopes repell'd;
For he unfix'd, unfixing, look'd around,
And no employment but in seeking found;
He gave his restless thoughts to views refined,
And shrank from worldly cares with wounded mind.
   Rejecting trade, awhile he dwelt on laws,
'But who could plead, if unapproved the cause?'
A doubting, dismal tribe physicians seem'd;
Divines o'er texts and disputations dream'd;
War and its glory he perhaps could love,
But there again he must the cause approve.
   Our hero thought no deed should gain applause,
Where timid virtue found support in laws;
He to all good would soar, would fly all sin,
By the pure prompting of the will within;
'Who needs a law that binds him not to steal,'
Ask'd the young teacher, 'can he rightly feel?
To curb the will, or arm in honour's cause,
Or aid the weak—are these enforced by laws?
Should we a foul, ungenerous action dread,

Because a law condemns th' adulterous bed?
Or fly pollution, not for fear of stain,
But that some statute tells us to refrain?
The grosser herd in ties like these we bind,
In virtue's freedom moves th' enlighten'd mind.'
'Man's heart deceives him,' said a friend: 'Of course,'
Replied the youth, 'but, has it power to force?
Unless it forces, call it as you will,
It is but wish, and proneness to the ill.'
'Art thou not tempted?' 'Do I fall?' said Shore:
'The pure have fallen.'—'Then are pure no more:
While reason guides me, I shall walk aright,
Nor need a steadier hand, or stronger light;
Nor this in dread of awful threats, design'd
For the weak spirit and the grov'ling mind;
But that, engaged by thoughts and views sublime,
I wage free war with grossness and with crime.'
Thus look'd he proudly on the vulgar crew,
Whom statutes govern, and whom fears subdue.
Faith, with his virtue, he indeed profess'd,
But doubts deprived his ardent mind of rest;
Reason, his sovereign mistress, fail'd to show
Light through the mazes of the world below;
Questions arose, and they surpass'd the skill
Of his sole aid, and would be dubious still;
These to discuss he sought no common guide,
But to the doubters in his doubts applied;
When all together might in freedom speak,
And their loved truth with mutual ardour seek.
Alas! though men who feel their eyes decay
Take more than common pains to find their way,
Yet, when for this they ask each other's aid,
Their mutual purpose is the more delay'd:
Of all their doubts, their reasoning clear'd not one,
Still the same spots were present in the sun;
Still the same scruples haunted Edward's mind,
Who found no rest, nor took the means to find.
But though with shaken faith, and slave to fame,
Vain and aspiring on the world he came;
Yet was he studious, serious, moral, grave,
No passion's victim, and no system's slave;

Vice he opposed, indulgence he disdain'd,
And o'er each sense in conscious triumph reign'd.
Who often reads, will sometimes wish to write,
And Shore would yield instructions and delight:
A serious drama he design'd, but found
'Twas tedious travelling in that gloomy ground;
A deep and solemn story he would try,
But grew ashamed of ghosts, and laid it by;
Sermons he wrote, but they who knew his creed,
Or knew it not, were ill disposed to read;
And he would lastly be the nation's guide,
But, studying, fail'd to fix upon a side;
Fame he desired, and talents he possess'd,
But loved not labour, though he could not rest,
Nor firmly fix the vacillating mind,
That, ever working, could no centre find.
'Tis thus a sanguine reader loves to trace
The Nile forth rushing on his glorious race;
Calm and secure the fancied traveller goes
Through sterile deserts and by threat'ning foes;
He thinks not then of Afric's scorching sands,
Th' Arabian sea, the Abyssinian bands;
Fasils and Michaels, and the robbers all,
Whom we politely chiefs and heroes call:
He of success alone delights to think,
He views that fount, he stands upon the brink,
And drinks a fancied draught, exulting so to drink.
In his own room, and with his books around,
His lively mind its chief employment found;
Then idly busy, quietly employ'd,
And, lost to life, his visions were enjoy'd:
Yet still he took a keen inquiring view
Of all that crowds neglect, desire, pursue;
And thus abstracted, curious, still, serene,
He, unemploy'd, beheld life's shifting scene;
Still more averse from vulgar joys and cares,
Still more unfitted for the world's affairs.
There was a house where Edward ofttimes went,
And social hours in pleasant trifling spent;
He read, conversed and reason'd, sang and play'd,
And all were happy while the idler stay'd;

Too happy one, for thence arose the pain,
Till this engaging trifler came again.
But did he love? We answer, day by day,
The loving feet would take th' accustom'd way,
The amorous eye would rove as if in quest
Of something rare, and on the mansion rest;
The same soft passion touch'd the gentle tongue,
And Anna's charms in tender notes were sung;
The ear too seem'd to feel the common flame,
Sooth'd and delighted with the fair one's name;
And thus as love each other part possess'd,
The heart, no doubt, its sovereign power confess'd.
Pleased in her sight, the youth required no more;
Not rich himself, he saw the damsel poor;
And he too wisely, nay, too kindly loved,
To pain the being whom his soul approved.
A serious friend our cautious youth possess'd,
And at his table sat a welcome guest;
Both unemploy'd, it was their chief delight
To read what free and daring authors write;
Authors who loved from common views to soar,
And seek the fountains never traced before;
Truth they profess'd, yet often left the true
And beaten prospect, for the wild and new.
His chosen friend his fiftieth year had seen,
His fortune easy, and his air serene;
Deist and atheist call'd; for few agreed
What were his notions, principles, or creed;
His mind reposed not, for he hated rest,
But all things made a query or a jest;
Perplex'd himself, he ever sought to prove
That man is doom'd in endless doubt to rove;
Himself in darkness he profess'd to be,
And would maintain that not a man could see.
The youthful friend, dissentient, reason'd still
Of the soul's prowess, and the subject will;
Of virtue's beauty, and of honour's force,
And a warm zeal gave life to his discourse:
Since from his feelings all his fire arose,
And he had interest in the themes he chose.
The friend, indulging a sarcastic smile,

Said—'Dear enthusiast! thou wilt change thy style,
When man's delusions, errors, crimes, deceit,
No more distress thee, and no longer cheat.'
  Yet lo! this cautious man, so coolly wise,
On a young beauty fix'd unguarded eyes;
And her he married: Edward at the view
Bade to his cheerful visits long adieu;
But haply err'd, for this engaging bride
No mirth suppress'd, but rather cause supplied:
And when she saw the friends, by reasoning long,
Confused if right, and positive if wrong,
With playful speech and smile, that spoke delight,
She made them careless both of wrong and right.
  This gentle damsel gave consent to wed,
With school and school-day dinners in her head:
She now was promised choice of daintiest food,
And costly dress, that made her sovereign good;
With walks on hilly heath to banish spleen,
And summer-visits when the roads were clean.
All these she loved, to these she gave consent,
And she was married to her heart's content.
  Their manner this—the friends together read,
Till books a cause for disputation bred;
Debate then follow'd, and the vapour'd child
Declared they argued till her head was wild;
And strange to her it was that mortal brain
Could seek the trial, or endure the pain.
  Then as the friend reposed, the younger pair
Sat down to cards, and play'd beside his chair;
Till he awaking, to his books applied,
Or heard the music of th' obedient bride:
If mild the evening, in the fields they stray'd,
And their own flock with partial eye survey'd;
But oft the husband, to indulgence prone,
Resumed his book, and bade them walk alone.
  'Do, my kind Edward! I must take mine ease,
Name the dear girl the planets and the trees;
Tell her what warblers pour their evening song,
What insects flutter, as you walk along;
Teach her to fix the roving thoughts, to bind
The wandering sense, and methodize the mind.'

This was obey'd; and oft when this was done,
They calmly gazed on the declining sun;
In silence saw the glowing landscape fade,
Or, sitting, sang beneath the arbour's shade:
Till rose the moon, and on each youthful face
Shed a soft beauty, and a dangerous grace.
When the young wife beheld in long debate
The friends, all careless as she seeming sate;
It soon appear'd, there was in one combined
The nobler person and the richer mind:
He wore no wig, no grisly beard was seen,
And none beheld him careless or unclean;
Or watch'd him sleeping:—we indeed have heard
Of sleeping beauty, and it has appear'd;
'Tis seen in infants—there indeed we find
The features soften'd by the slumbering mind;
But other beauties, when disposed to sleep,
Should from the eye of keen inspector keep:
The lovely nymph who would her swain surprise,
May close her mouth, but not conceal her eyes;
Sleep from the fairest face some beauty takes,
And all the homely features homelier makes;
So thought our wife, beholding with a sigh
Her sleeping spouse, and Edward smiling by.
A sick relation for the husband sent,
Without delay the friendly sceptic went;
Nor fear'd the youthful pair, for he had seen
The wife untroubled, and the friend serene:
No selfish purpose in his roving eyes,
No vile deception in her fond replies:
So judged the husband, and with judgment true,
For neither yet the guilt or danger knew.
What now remain'd? but they again should play
Th' accustom'd game, and walk th' accustom'd way;
With careless freedom should converse or read,
And the friend's absence neither fear nor heed:
But rather now they seem'd confused, constrain'd;
Within their room still restless they remain'd,
And painfully they felt, and knew each other pain'd.—
Ah! foolish men! how could ye thus depend,
One on himself, the other on his friend?

The youth with troubled eye the lady saw,
Yet felt too brave, too daring to withdraw;
While she, with tuneless hand the jarring keys
Touching, was not one moment at her ease:
Now would she walk, and call her friendly guide,
Now speak of rain, and cast her cloak aside;
Seize on a book, unconscious what she read,
And restless still, to new resources fled;
Then laugh'd aloud, then tried to look serene,
And ever changed, and every change was seen.
Painful it is to dwell on deeds of shame—
The trying day was past, another came;
The third was all remorse, confusion, dread,
And (all too late!) the fallen hero fled.
Then felt the youth, in that seducing time,
How feebly honour guards the heart from crime:
Small is his native strength; man needs the stay,
The strength imparted in the trying day;
For all that honour brings against the force
Of headlong passion, aids its rapid course;
Its slight resistance but provokes the fire,
As wood-work stops the flame, and then conveys it higher.
The husband came; a wife by guilt made bold
Had, meeting, sooth'd him, as in days of old;
But soon this fact transpired; her strong distress,
And his friend's absence, left him nought to guess.
Still cool, though grieved, thus prudence bade him write—
'I cannot pardon, and I will not fight;
Thou art too poor a culprit for the laws,
And I too faulty to support my cause:
All must be punish'd; I must sigh alone,
At home thy victim for her guilt atone;
And thou, unhappy! virtuous now no more,
Must loss of fame, peace, purity, deplore;
Sinners with praise will pierce thee to the heart,
And saints deriding, tell thee what thou art.'
Such was his fall; and Edward, from that time,
Felt in full force the censure and the crime—
Despised, ashamed; his noble views before,
And his proud thoughts, degraded him the more:

Should he repent—would that conceal his shame?
Could peace be his? It perish'd with his fame:
Himself he scorn'd, nor could his crime forgive;
He fear'd to die, yet felt ashamed to live:
Grieved, but not contrite was his heart; oppress'd,
Not broken; not converted, but distress'd;
He wanted will to bend the stubborn knee,
He wanted light the cause of ill to see,
To learn how frail is man, how humble then should be;
For faith he had not, or a faith too weak
To gain the help that humbled sinners seek;
Else had he pray'd—to an offended God
His tears had flown a penitential flood;
Though far astray, he would have heard the call
Of mercy—'Come! return, thou prodigal;'
Then, though confused, distress'd, ashamed, afraid,
Still had the trembling penitent obey'd;
Though faith had fainted, when assail'd by fear,
Hope to the soul had whisper'd, 'Persevere!'
Till in his Father's house an humbled guest,
He would have found forgiveness, comfort, rest.
   But all this joy was to our youth denied
By his fierce passions and his daring pride;
And shame and doubt impell'd him in a course,
Once so abhorr'd, with unresisted force.
Proud minds and guilty, whom their crimes oppress,
Fly to new crimes for comfort and redress;
So found our fallen youth a short relief
In wine, the opiate guilt applies to grief,—
From fleeting mirth that o'er the bottle lives,
From the false joy its inspiration gives;
And from associates pleased to find a friend,
With powers to lead them, gladden, and defend,
In all those scenes where transient ease is found,
For minds whom sins oppress, and sorrows wound.
   Wine is like anger; for it makes us strong,
Blind and impatient, and it leads us wrong;
The strength is quickly lost, we feel the error long:
Thus led, thus strengthen'd in an evil cause,
For folly pleading, sought the youth applause;
Sad for a time, then eloquently wild,

He gaily spoke as his companions smiled;
Lightly he rose, and with his former grace
Proposed some doubt, and argued on the case;
Fate and fore-knowledge were his favourite themes—
How vain man's purpose, how absurd his schemes:
'Whatever is, was ere our birth decreed;
We think our actions from ourselves proceed,
And idly we lament th' inevitable deed;
It seems our own, but there's a power above
Directs the motion, nay, that makes us move;
Nor good nor evil can you beings name,
Who are but rooks and castles in the game;
Superior natures with their puppets play,
Till, bagg'd or buried, all are swept away.'
  Such were the notions of a mind to ill
Now prone, but ardent, and determined still:
Of joy now eager, as before of fame,
And screen'd by folly when assail'd by shame,
Deeply he sank; obey'd each passion's call,
And used his reason to defend them all.
  Shall I proceed, and step by step relate
The odious progress of a sinner's fate?
No—let me rather hasten to the time
(Sure to arrive) when misery waits on crime.
  With virtue, prudence fled; what Shore possess'd
Was sold, was spent, and he was now distress'd:
And Want, unwelcome stranger, pale and wan,
Met with her haggard looks the hurried man;
His pride felt keenly what he must expect
From useless pity and from cold neglect.
  Struck by new terrors, from his friends he fled,
And wept his woes upon a restless bed;
Retiring late, at early hour to rise,
With shrunken features, and with bloodshot eyes:
If sleep one moment closed the dismal view,
Fancy her terrors built upon the true;
And night and day had their alternate woes,
That baffled pleasure, and that mock'd repose;
Till to despair and anguish was consign'd
The wreck and ruin of a noble mind.
  Now seized for debt, and lodged within a jail,

He tried his friendships, and he found them fail;
Then fail'd his spirits, and his thoughts were all
Fix'd on his sins, his sufferings, and his fall:
His ruffled mind was pictured in his face,
Once the fair seat of dignity and grace:
Great was the danger of a man so prone
To think of madness, and to think alone;
Yet pride still lived, and struggled to sustain
The drooping spirit and the roving brain;
But this too fail'd: a friend his freedom gave,
And sent him help the threat'ning world to brave;
Gave solid counsel what to seek or flee,
But still would stranger to his person be:
In vain! the truth determined to explore,
He traced the friend whom he had wrong'd before.
  This was too much; both aided and advised
By one who shunn'd him, pitied, and despised:
He bore it not; 'twas a deciding stroke,
And on his reason like a torrent broke:
In dreadful stillness he appear'd awhile,
With vacant horror and a ghastly smile;
Then rose at once into the frantic rage,
That force controll'd not, nor could love assuage.
  Friends now appear'd, but in the man was seen
The angry maniac, with vindictive mien;
Too late their pity gave to care and skill
The hurried mind and ever-wandering will;
Unnoticed pass'd all time, and not a ray
Of reason broke on his benighted way;
But now he spurn'd the straw in pure disdain,
And now laugh'd loudly at the clinking chain.
  Then as its wrath subsided, by degrees
The mind sank slowly to infantine ease;
To playful folly, and to causeless joy,
Speech without aim, and without end, employ;
He drew fantastic figures on the wall,
And gave some wild relation of them all;
With brutal shape he join'd the human face,
And idiot smiles approved the motley race.
  Harmless at length th' unhappy man was found,
The spirit settled, but the reason drown'd;

And all the dreadful tempest died away,
To the dull stillness of the misty day.
  And now his freedom he attain'd—if free,
The lost to reason, truth, and hope, can be;
His friends, or wearied with the charge, or sure
The harmless wretch was now beyond a cure,
Gave him to wander where he pleased, and find
His own resources for the eager mind;
The playful children of the place he meets,
Playful with them he rambles through the streets;
In all they need, his stronger arm he lends,
And his lost mind to these approving friends.
  That gentle maid, whom once the youth had loved,
Is now with mild religious pity moved;
Kindly she chides his boyish flights, while he
Will for a moment fix'd and pensive be;
And as she trembling speaks, his lively eyes
Explore her looks, he listens to her sighs;
Charm'd by her voice, th' harmonious sounds invade
His clouded mind, and for a time persuade:
Like a pleased infant, who has newly caught
From the maternal glance a gleam of thought;
He stands enrapt, the half-known voice to hear,
And starts, half-conscious, at the falling tear.
  Rarely from town, nor then unwatch'd, he goes,
In darker mood, as if to hide his woes;
Returning soon, he with impatience seeks
His youthful friends, and shouts, and sings, and speaks;
Speaks a wild speech with action all as wild—
The children's leader, and himself a child;
He spins their top, or, at their bidding, bends
His back, while o'er it leap his laughing friends;
Simple and weak, he acts the boy once more,
And heedless children call him Silly Shore.

12. 'SQUIRE THOMAS

OR

THE PRECIPITATE CHOICE

Such smiling rogues as these,
Like rats, oft bite the holy cords in twain,
Too intrinsicate t' unloose—
Lear, Act II, Scene 2

My other self, my counsel's consistory,
My oracle, my prophet,—
I as a child will go by thy direction.
Richard III, Act II, Scene 2

If I do not have pity upon her, I'm a villain; if I do not love her, I am a Jew. *Much Ado about Nothing*, Act II, Scene 3

Women are soft, mild, pitiable, flexible;
But thou art obdurate, flinty, rough, remorseless.
3 Henry VI, Act I, Scene 4

He must be told of it, and he shall; the office
Becomes a woman best; I'll take it upon me;
If I prove honey-mouth'd, let my tongue blister.
Winter's Tale, Act II, Scene 2

Disguise—I see thou art a wickedness.
Twelfth Night, Act II, Scene 2

'Squire Thomas flatter'd long a wealthy aunt,
Who left him all that she could give or grant:
Ten years he tried, with all his craft and skill,
To fix the sovereign lady's varying will;
Ten years enduring at her board to sit,
He meekly listen'd to her tales and wit;
He took the meanest office man can take,
And his aunt's vices for her money's sake:
By many a threat'ning hint she waked his fear,
And he was pain'd to see a rival near;
Yet all the taunts of her contemptuous pride
He bore, nor found his grov'ling spirit tried:
Nay, when she wish'd his parents to traduce,
Fawning he smiled, and justice call'd th' abuse;
'They taught you nothing; are you not, at best,'
Said the proud dame, 'a trifler, and a jest?
Confess you are a fool!'—he bow'd and he confess'd.

This vex'd him much, but could not always last:
The dame is buried, and the trial past.
There was a female, who had courted long
Her cousin's gifts, and deeply felt the wrong;
By a vain boy forbidden to attend
The private councils of her wealthy friend,
She vow'd revenge, nor should that crafty boy
In triumph undisturb'd his spoils enjoy;
He heard, he smiled, and when the will was read,
Kindly dismiss'd the kindred of the dead;
'The dear deceased,' he call'd her, and the crowd
Moved off with curses deep and threat'nings loud.
The youth retired, and, with a mind at ease,
Found he was rich, and fancied he must please:
He might have pleased, and to his comfort found
The wife he wish'd, if he had sought around;
For there were lasses of his own degree,
With no more hatred to the state than he:
But he had courted spleen and age so long,
His heart refused to woo the fair and young;
So long attended on caprice and whim,
He thought attention now was due to him;
And as his flattery pleased the wealthy dame,
Heir to the wealth he might the flattery claim;
But this the fair, with one accord, denied,
Nor waved for man's caprice the sex's pride:
There is a season when to them is due
Worship and awe, and they will claim it too:
'Fathers,' they cry, 'long hold us in their chain,
Nay, tyrant brothers claim a right to reign;
Uncles and guardians we in turn obey,
And husbands rule with ever-during sway;
Short is the time when lovers at the feet
Of beauty kneel, and own the slavery sweet;
And shall we this our triumph, this the aim
And boast of female power, forbear to claim?
No! we demand that homage, that respect,
Or the proud rebel punish and reject.'
Our hero, still too indolent, too nice
To pay for beauty the accustom'd price,
No less forbore t'address the humbler maid,

Who might have yielded with the price unpaid;
But lived, himself to humour and to please,
To count his money, and enjoy his ease.
  It pleased a neighbouring 'squire to recommend
A faithful youth, as servant to his friend;
Nay, more than servant, whom he praised for parts
Ductile yet strong, and for the best of hearts;
One who might ease him in his small affairs,
With tenants, tradesmen, taxes, and repairs;
Answer his letters, look to all his dues,
And entertain him with discourse and news.
  The 'squire believed, and found the trusted youth
A very pattern for his care and truth;
Not for his virtues to be praised alone,
But for a modest mien and humble tone;
Assenting always, but as if he meant
Only to strength of reason to assent:
For was he stubborn, and retain'd his doubt,
Till the more subtle 'squire had forced it out;
'Nay, still was right, but he perceived that strong
And powerful minds could make the right the wrong.'
  When the 'squire's thoughts on some fair damsel dwelt,
The faithful friend his apprehensions felt;
It would rejoice his faithful heart to find
A lady suited to his master's mind;
But who deserved that master? who would prove
That hers was pure, uninterested love?
Although a servant, he would scorn to take
A countess, till she suffer'd for his sake;
Some tender spirit, humble, faithful, true,
Such, my dear master! must be sought for you.
  Six months had pass'd, and not a lady seen,
With just this love, 'twixt fifty and fifteen;
All seem'd his doctrine or his pride to shun,
All would be woo'd, before they would be won;
When the chance naming of a race and fair,
Our 'squire disposed to take his pleasure there:
The friend profess'd, 'although he first began
To hint the thing, it seem'd a thoughtless plan:

The roads, he fear'd, were foul, the days were short,
The village far, and yet there might be sport.'
'What! you of roads and starless nights afraid?
You think to govern! you to be obey'd!'
Smiling he spoke, the humble friend declared
His soul's obedience, and to go prepared.
The place was distant, but with great delight
They saw a race, and hail'd the glorious sight:
The 'squire exulted, and declared the ride
Had amply paid, and he was satisfied.
They gazed, they feasted, and, in happy mood,
Homeward return'd, and hastening as they rode;
For short the day, and sudden was the change
From light to darkness, and the way was strange;
Our hero soon grew peevish, then distress'd;
He dreaded darkness, and he sigh'd for rest:
Going, they pass'd a village; but alas!,
Returning saw no village to repass;
The 'squire remember'd too a noble hall,
Large as a church, and whiter than its wall:
This he had noticed as they rode along,
And justly reason'd that their road was wrong.
George, full of awe, was modest in reply—
'The fault was his, 'twas folly to deny;
And of his master's safety were he sure,
There was no grievance he would not endure.'
This made his peace with the relenting 'squire,
Whose thoughts yet dwelt on supper and a fire;
When, as they reach'd a long and pleasant green,
Dwellings of men, and next a man, were seen.
'My friend,' said George, 'to travellers astray
Point out an inn, and guide us on the way.'
The man look'd up; 'Surprising! can it be
My master's son? as I'm alive, 'tis he.'
'How! Robin,' George replied, 'and are we near
My father's house? how strangely things appear!—
Dear sir, though wanderers, we at last are right:
Let us proceed, and glad my father's sight;
We shall at least be fairly lodged and fed,
I can ensure a supper and a bed;
Let us this night, as one of pleasure date,

And of surprise: it is an act of fate.'
'Go on,' the 'squire in happy temper cried;
'I like such blunder! I approve such guide.'
They ride, they halt, the farmer comes in haste,
Then tells his wife how much their house is graced;
They bless the chance, they praise the lucky son,
That caused the error—Nay! it was not one;
But their good fortune—Cheerful grew the 'squire,
Who found dependants, flattery, wine, and fire;
He heard the jack turn round; the busy dame
Produced her damask; and with supper came
The daughter, dress'd with care, and full of maiden-shame.
Surprised, our hero saw the air and dress,
And strove his admiration to express;
Nay! felt it too—for Harriot was, in truth,
A tall fair beauty in the bloom of youth;
And from the pleasure and surprise, a grace
Adorn'd the blooming damsel's form and face;
Then too, such high respect and duty paid
By all—such silent reverence in the maid;
Vent'ring with caution, yet with haste, a glance;
Loth to retire, yet trembling to advance,
Appear'd the nymph, and in her gentle guest
Stirr'd soft emotions till the hour of rest:
Sweet was his sleep, and in the morn again
He felt a mixture of delight and pain:
'How fair, how gentle,' said the 'squire, 'how meek,
And yet how sprightly, when disposed to speak!
Nature has bless'd her form, and Heaven her mind,
But in her favours Fortune is unkind;
Poor is the maid—nay, poor she cannot prove
Who is enrich'd with beauty, worth, and love.'
The 'squire arose, with no precise intent
To go or stay—uncertain what he meant:
He moved to part—they begg'd him first to dine;
And who could then escape from love and wine?
As came the night, more charming grew the fair,
And seem'd to watch him with a two-fold care:
On the third morn, resolving not to stay,
Though urged by love, he bravely rode away.

Arrived at home, three pensive days he gave
To feelings fond and meditations grave;
Lovely she was, and, if he did not err,
As fond of him as his fond heart of her;
Still he delay'd, unable to decide
Which was the master-passion, love or pride:
He sometimes wonder'd how his friend could make,
And then exulted in, the night's mistake;
Had she but fortune, 'doubtless then,' he cried,
'Some happier man had won the wealthy bride.'
While thus he hung in balance, now inclined
To change his state, and then to change his mind—
That careless George dropp'd idly on the ground
A letter, which his crafty master found;
The stupid youth confess'd his fault, and pray'd
The generous 'squire to spare a gentle maid;
Of whom her tender mother, full of fears,
Had written much—'She caught her oft in tears,
For ever thinking on a youth above
Her humble fortune—still she own'd not love;
Nor can define, dear girl! the cherish'd pain,
But would rejoice to see the cause again:
That neighbouring youth, whom she endured before,
She now rejects, and will behold no more:
Raised by her passion, she no longer stoops
To her own equals, but she pines and droops,
Like to a lily, on whose sweets the sun
Has withering gazed—she saw and was undone:
His wealth allured her not—nor was she moved
By his superior state, himself she loved;
So mild, so good, so gracious, so genteel—
But spare your sister, and her love conceal;
We must the fault forgive, since she the pain must feel.'
'Fault!' said the 'squire, 'there's coarseness in the mind
That thus conceives of feelings so refined;
Here end my doubts, nor blame yourself, my friend,
Fate made you careless—here my doubts have end.'
The way is plain before us—there is now
The lover's visit first, and then the vow
Mutual and fond, the marriage-rite, the bride
Brought to her home with all a husband's pride;

The 'squire receives the prize his merits won,
And the glad parents leave the patron-son.
  But in short time he saw with much surprise,
First gloom, then grief, and then resentment rise,
From proud, commanding frowns and anger-darting eyes:
'Is there in Harriot's humble mind this fire,
This fierce impatience?' ask'd the puzzled 'squire:
'Has marriage changed her? or the mask she wore
Has she thrown by, and is herself once more?'
  Hour after hour, when clouds on clouds appear,
Dark and more dark, we know the tempest near;
And thus the frowning brow, the restless form,
And threat'ning glance, forerun domestic storm:
So read the husband, and, with troubled mind,
Reveal'd his fears—'My love, I hope you find
All here is pleasant—but I must confess
You seem offended, or in some distress;
Explain the grief you feel, and leave me to redress.'
  'Leave it to you?' replied the nymph—'indeed!
What—to the cause from whence the ills proceed?
Good Heaven! to take me from a place, where I
Had every comfort underneath the sky;
And then immure me in a gloomy place,
With the grim monsters of your ugly race,
That from their canvas staring, make me dread
Through the dark chambers where they hang to tread!
No friend nor neighbour comes to give that joy,
Which all things here must banish or destroy:
Where is the promised coach? the pleasant ride?
Oh! what a fortune has a farmer's bride!
Your sordid pride has placed me just above
Your hired domestics—and what pays me? love!
A selfish fondness I endure each hour,
And share unwitness'd pomp, unenvied power;
I hear your folly, smile at your parade,
And see your favourite dishes duly made;
Then am I richly dress'd for you t'admire,
Such is my duty and my lord's desire;
Is this a life for youth, for health, for joy?
Are these my duties—this my base employ?
No! to my father's house I will repair,

And make your idle wealth support me there;
Was it your wish to have an humble bride
For bondage thankful? Curse upon your pride!
Was it a slave you wanted? You shall see,
That if not happy, I at least am free;
Well, sir, your answer:'—silent stood the 'squire,
As looks a miser at his house on fire;
Where all he deems is vanish'd in that flame,
Swept from the earth his substance and his name;
So, lost to every promised joy of life,
Our 'squire stood gaping at his angry wife;—
His fate, his ruin, where he saw it vain
To hope for peace, pray, threaten, or complain;
And thus, betwixt his wonder at the ill
And his despair—there stood he gaping still.

'Your answer, sir—shall I depart a spot
I thus detest?'—'Oh, miserable lot!'
Exclaim'd the man. 'Go, serpent! nor remain
To sharpen wo by insult and disdain:
A nest of harpies was I doom'd to meet;
What plots, what combinations of deceit!
I see it now—all plann'd, design'd, contrived;
Served by that villain; by this fury wived—
What fate is mine! What wisdom, virtue, truth,
Can stand, if dæmons set their traps for youth?
He lose his way! vile dog! he cannot lose
The way a villain through his life pursues;
And thou, deceiver! thou afraid to move,
And hiding close the serpent in the dove!
I saw—but, fated to endure disgrace—
Unheeding saw, the fury in thy face;
And call'd it spirit—Oh! I might have found
Fraud and imposture—all the kindred round!
A nest of vipers'————

————'Sir, I'll not admit
These wild effusions of your angry wit:
Have you that value, that we all should use
Such mighty arts for such important views?
Are you such prize—and is my state so fair,
That they should sell their souls to get me there?
Think you that we alone our thoughts disguise?

When in pursuit of some contended prize,
Mask we alone the heart, and soothe whom we despise!
Speak you of craft and subtle schemes, who know
That all your wealth you to deception owe;
Who play'd for ten dull years a scoundrel-part,
To worm yourself into a widow's heart?
Now, when you guarded, with superior skill,
That lady's closet, and preserved her will,
Blind in your craft, you saw not one of those
Opposed by you might you in turn oppose;
Or watch your motions, and by art obtain
Share of that wealth you gave your peace to gain?
Did conscience never'————
　　　　　————'Cease, Tormentor, cease—
Or reach me poison——let me rest in peace!'
'Agreed—but hear me—let the truth appear;'
'Then state your purpose—I'll be calm and hear.'—
'Know then, this wealth, sole object of your care,
I had some right, without your hand, to share;
My mother's claim was just—but soon she saw
Your power, compell'd, insulted, to withdraw:
'Twas then my father, in his anger, swore
You should divide the fortune, or restore;
Long we debated—and you find me now
Heroic victim to a father's vow;
Like Jephtha's daughter, but in different state,
And both decreed to mourn our early fate;
Hence was my brother servant to your pride,
Vengeance made him your slave—and me your bride:
Now all is known—a dreadful price I pay
For our revenge—but still we have our day;
All that you love you must with others share,
Or all you dread from their resentment dare!
Yet terms I offer—let contention cease:
Divide the spoil, and let us part in peace.'
Our hero trembling heard—he sat—he rose—
Nor could his motions nor his mind compose;
He paced the room—and, stalking to her side,
Gazed on the face of his undaunted bride;
And nothing there but scorn and calm aversion spied.
He would have vengeance, yet he fear'd the law:

Her friends would threaten, and their power he saw;
'Then let her go:'—but oh! a mighty sum
Would that demand, since he had let her come;
Nor from his sorrows could he find redress,
Save that which led him to a like distress,
And all his ease was in his wife to see
A wretch as anxious and distress'd as he:
Her strongest wish, the fortune to divide
And part in peace, his avarice denied;
And thus it happen'd, as in all deceit,
The cheater found the evil of the cheat;
The husband grieved—nor was the wife at rest;
Him she could vex, and he could her molest;
She could his passion into frenzy raise,
But when the fire was kindled, fear'd the blaze:
As much they studied, so in time they found
The easiest way to give the deepest wound;
But then, like fencers, they were equal still,
Both lost in danger what they gain'd in skill;
Each heart a keener kind of rancour gain'd,
And paining more, was more severely pain'd;
And thus by both were equal vengeance dealt,
And both the anguish they inflicted felt.

13. JESSE AND COLIN

Then she plots, then she ruminates, then she devises, and what they think in their hearts they may effect, they will break their hearts but they will effect. *Merry Wives of Windsor*, Act II, Scene 2

She hath spoken that she should not, I am sure of that; Heaven knows what she hath known. *Macbeth*, Act V, Scene 1

Our house is hell, and thou a merry devil.
Merchant of Venice, Act II, Scene 3

And yet, for aught I see, they are as sick that surfeit of too much, as they that starve with nothing; it is no mean happiness, therefore, to be seated in the mean. *Merchant of Venice*, Act I, Scene 2

A vicar died, and left his daughter poor—
It hurt her not, she was not rich before:
Her humble share of worldly goods she sold,
Paid every debt, and then her fortune told;

And found, with youth and beauty, hope and health,
Two hundred guineas was her worldly wealth;
It then remain'd to choose her path in life,
And first, said Jesse, 'Shall I be a wife?—
Colin is mild and civil, kind and just,
I know his love, his temper I can trust;
But small his farm, it asks perpetual care,
And we must toil as well as trouble share:
True, he was taught in all the gentle arts
That raise the soul, and soften human hearts;
And boasts a parent, who deserves to shine
In higher class, and I could wish her mine;
Nor wants he will his station to improve,
A just ambition waked by faithful love;—
Still is he poor—and here my father's friend
Deigns for his daughter, as her own, to send;
A worthy lady, who it seems has known
A world of griefs and troubles of her own:
I was an infant, when she came, a guest
Beneath my father's humble roof to rest;
Her kindred all unfeeling, vast her woes,
Such her complaint, and there she found repose;
Enrich'd by fortune, now she nobly lives,
And nobly, from the blest abundance, gives;
The grief, the want of human life, she knows,
And comfort there and here relief bestows;
But are they not dependants?—Foolish pride!
Am I not honour'd by such friend and guide?
Have I a home,' (here Jesse dropp'd a tear),
'Or friend beside?'—A faithful friend was near.

Now Colin came, at length resolved to lay
His heart before her and to urge her stay;
True, his own plough the gentle Colin drove,
An humble farmer with aspiring love;
Who, urged by passion, never dared till now,
Thus urged by fears, his trembling hopes avow:
Her father's glebe he managed; every year
The grateful vicar held the youth more dear;
He saw indeed the prize in Colin's view,
And wish'd his Jesse with a man so true;
Timid as true, he urged with anxious air

His tender hope, and made the trembling prayer;
When Jesse saw, nor could with coldness see,
Such fond respect, such tried sincerity:
Grateful for favours to her father dealt,
She more than grateful for his passion felt;
Nor could she frown on one so good and kind,
Yet fear'd to smile, and was unfix'd in mind;
But prudence placed the female friend in view—
What might not one so rich and grateful do?
So lately, too, the good old vicar died,
His faithful daughter must not cast aside
The signs of filial grief, and be a ready bride:
Thus, led by prudence, to the lady's seat
The village-beauty purposed to retreat;
But, as in hard-fought fields the victor knows
What to the vanquish'd he, in honour, owes,
So in this conquest over powerful love,
Prudence resolved a generous foe to prove;
And Jesse felt a mingled fear and pain
In her dismission of a faithful swain,
Gave her kind thanks, and when she saw his wo,
Kindly betray'd that she was loth to go;
'But would she promise, if abroad she met
A frowning world, she would remember yet
Where dwelt a friend?'—'That could she not forget.'
And thus they parted, but each faithful heart
Felt the compulsion, and refused to part.
  Now by the morning mail the timid maid
Was to that kind and wealthy dame convey'd;
Whose invitation, when her father died,
Jesse as comfort to her heart applied;
She knew the days her generous friend had seen—
As wife and widow, evil days had been;
She married early, and for half her life
Was an insulted and forsaken wife;
Widow'd and poor, her angry father gave,
Mix'd with reproach, the pittance of a slave;
Forgetful brothers pass'd her, but she knew
Her humbler friends, and to their home withdrew;
The good old vicar to her sire applied
For help, and help'd her when her sire denied;

When in few years death stalk'd through bower
and hall,
Sires, sons, and sons of sons, were buried all:
She then abounded, and had wealth to spare
For softening grief she once was doom'd to share;
Thus train'd in misery's school, and taught to feel,
She would rejoice an orphan's woes to heal:
So Jesse thought, who look'd within her breast,
And thence conceived how bounteous minds are bless'd.
From her vast mansion look'd the lady down
On humbler buildings of a busy town;
Thence came her friends of either sex, and all
With whom she lived on terms reciprocal:
They pass'd the hours with their accustom'd ease,
As guests inclined, but not compell'd to please;
But there were others in the mansion found,
For office chosen, and by duties bound;
Three female rivals, each of power possess'd,
Th' attendant-maid, poor friend, and kindred-guest.
To these came Jesse, as a seaman thrown
By the rude storm upon a coast unknown:
The view was flattering, civil seem'd the race,
But all unknown, the dangers of the place.
Few hours had pass'd, when, from attendants freed,
The lady utter'd—'This is kind indeed;
Believe me, love! that I for one like you
Have daily pray'd, a friend discreet and true;
Oh! wonder not that I on you depend,
You are mine own hereditary friend:
Hearken, my Jesse, never can I trust
Beings ungrateful, selfish, and unjust;
But you are present, and my load of care
Your love will serve to lighten and to share:
Come near me, Jesse—let not those below
Of my reliance on your friendship know;
Look as they look, be in their freedoms free—
But all they say do you convey to me.'
Here Jesse's thoughts to Colin's cottage flew,
And with such speed she scarce their absence knew.
'Jane loves her mistress, and should she depart,
I lose her service, and she breaks her heart;

My ways and wishes, looks and thoughts she knows,
And duteous care by close attention shows:
But is she faithful? in temptation strong?
Will she not wrong me? ah! I fear the wrong:
Your father loved me; now, in time of need,
Watch for my good, and to his place succeed.
'Blood doesn't bind—that girl, who every day
Eats of my bread, would wish my life away;
I am her *dear relation*, and she thinks
To make her fortune, an ambitious minx!
She only courts me for the prospect's sake,
Because she knows I have a will to make;
Yes, love! my will delay'd, I know not how—
But you are here, and I will make it now.
'That idle creature, keep her in your view,
See what she does, what she desires to do;
On her young mind may artful villains prey,
And to my plate and jewels find a way;
A pleasant humour has the girl: her smile
And cheerful manner tedious hours beguile:
But well observe her, ever near her be,
Close in your thoughts, in your professions free.
'Again, my Jesse, hear what I advise,
And watch a woman ever in disguise;
Issop, that widow, serious, subtle, sly—
But what of this?—I must have company;
She markets for me, and although she makes
Profit, no doubt, of all she undertakes,
Yet she is one I can to all produce,
And all her talents are in daily use;
Deprived of her, I may another find
As sly and selfish, with a weaker mind:
But never trust her, she is full of art,
And worms herself into the closest heart;
Seem then, I pray you, careless in her sight,
Nor let her know, my love, how we unite.
'Do, my good Jesse, cast a view around,
And let no wrong within my house be found;
That girl associates with——I know not who
Are her companions, nor what ill they do;
'Tis then the widow plans, 'tis then she tries

Her various arts and schemes for fresh supplies;
'Tis then, if ever, Jane her duty quits,
And, whom I know not, favours and admits:
Oh! watch their movements all; for me 'tis hard,
Indeed is vain, but you may keep a guard;
And I, when none your watchful glance deceive,
May make my will, and think what I shall leave.'
Jesse, with fear, disgust, alarm, surprise,
Heard of these duties for her ears and eyes;
Heard by what service she must gain her bread,
And went with scorn and sorrow to her bed.
Jane was a servant fitted for her place,
Experienced, cunning, fraudful, selfish, base;
Skill'd in those mean humiliating arts
That make their way to proud and selfish hearts;
By instinct taught, she felt an awe, a fear,
For Jesse's upright, simple character;
Whom with gross flattery she awhile assail'd,
And then beheld with hatred when it fail'd;
Yet trying still upon her mind for hold,
She all the secrets of the mansion told;
And to invite an equal trust, she drew
Of every mind a bold and rapid view;
But on the widow'd friend with deep disdain,
And rancorous envy, dwelt the treacherous Jane:—
In vain such arts; without deceit or pride,
With a just taste and feeling for her guide,
From all contagion Jesse kept apart,
Free in her manners, guarded in her heart.
Jesse one morn was thoughtful, and her sigh
The widow heard as she was passing by;
And—'Well!' she said, 'is that some distant swain,
Or aught with us, that gives your bosom pain?
Come, we are fellow-sufferers, slaves in thrall,
And tasks and griefs are common to us all;
Think not my frankness strange: they love to paint
Their state with freedom, who endure restraint;
And their is something in that speaking eye
And sober mien, that prove I may rely:
You came a stranger; to my words attend,
Accept my offer, and you find a friend;

It is a labyrinth in which you stray,
Come, hold my clue, and I will lead the way.
'Good Heav'n! that one so jealous, envious, base,
Should be the mistress of so sweet a place;
She, who so long herself was low and poor,
Now broods suspicious on her useless store;
She loves to see us abject, loves to deal
Her insult round, and then pretends to feel;
Prepare to cast all dignity aside,
For know your talents will be quickly tried;
Nor think, from favours past, a friend to gain,
'Tis but by duties we our posts maintain:
I read her novels, gossip through the town,
And daily go, for idle stories, down;
I cheapen all she buys, and bear the curse
Of honest tradesmen for my niggard-purse;
And, when for her this meanness I display,
She cries, "I heed not what I throw away;"
Of secret bargains I endure the shame,
And stake my credit for our fish and game;
Oft has she smiled to hear "her generous soul
Would gladly give, but stoops to my control:"
Nay! I have heard her, when she chanced to come
Where I contended for a petty sum,
Affirm 'twas painful to behold such care,
"But Issop's nature is to pinch and spare:"
Thus all the meanness of the house is mine,
And my reward—to scorn her, and to dine.
'See next that giddy thing with neither pride
To keep her safe, nor principle to guide:
Poor, idle, simple flirt! as sure as fate
Her maiden-fame will have an early date:
Of her beware; for all who live below
Have faults they wish not all the world to know;
And she is fond of listening, full of doubt,
And stoops to guilt to find an error out.
'And now once more observe the artful maid,
A lying, prying, jilting, thievish jade;
I think, my love, you would not condescend
To call a low, illiterate girl your friend:
But in our troubles we are apt, you know,

To lean on all who some compassion show;
And she has flexile features, acting eyes,
And seems with every look to sympathise;
No mirror can a mortal's grief express
With more precision, or can feel it less;
That proud, mean spirit, she by fawning courts,
By vulgar flattery, and by vile reports;
And, by that proof she every instant gives
To one so mean, that yet a meaner lives.—
  'Come, I have drawn the curtain, and you can see
Your fellow-actors, all our company;
Should you incline to throw reserve aside,
And in my judgment and my love confide,
I could some prospects open to your view,
That ask attention—and, till then, adieu.'
  'Farewell!' said Jesse, hastening to her room,
Where all she saw within, without, was gloom:
Confused, perplex'd, she pass'd a dreary hour,
Before her reason could exert its power;
To her all seem'd mysterious, all allied
To avarice, meanness, folly, craft, and pride;
Wearied with thought, she breathed the garden's air,
Then came the laughing lass, and join'd her there.
  'My sweetest friend has dwelt with us a week,
And does she love us? be sincere and speak;
My aunt you cannot—Lord! how I should hate
To be like her, all misery and state;
Proud, and yet envious, she disgusted sees
All who are happy, and who look at ease.
Let friendship bind us, I will quickly show
Some favourites near us, you'll be bless'd to know;
My aunt forbids it—but, can she expect
To soothe her spleen, we shall ourselves neglect?
Jane and the widow were to watch and stay
My free-born feet; I watch'd as well as they;
Lo! what is this? this simple key explores
The dark recess that holds the spinster's stores;
And led by her ill star, I chanced to see
Where Issop keeps her stock of ratafie;
Used in the hours of anger and alarm,
It makes her civil, and it keeps her warm;

Thus bless'd with secrets, both would choose to hide,
Their fears now grant me what their scorn denied.
'My freedom thus by their assent secured,
Bad as it is, the place may be endured;
And bad it is, but her estates, you know,
And her beloved hoards, she must bestow;
So we can slyly our amusements take,
And friends of dæmons, if they help us, make.'
'Strange creatures these,' thought Jesse, half inclined
To smile at one malicious and yet kind;
Frank and yet cunning, with a heart to love
And malice prompt—the serpent and the dove;
Here could she dwell? or could she yet depart?
Could she be artful? could she bear with art?—
This splendid mansion gave the cottage grace,
She thought a dungeon was a happier place;
And Colin pleading, when he pleaded best,
Wrought not such sudden change in Jesse's breast.
The wondering maiden, who had only read
Of such vile beings, saw them now with dread;
Safe in themselves—for nature has design'd
The creature's poison harmless to the kind;
But all beside who in the haunts are found
Must dread the poison, and must feel the wound.
Days full of care, slow weary weeks pass'd on,
Eager to go, still Jesse was not gone;
Her time in trifling or in tears she spent,
She never gave, she never felt content:
The lady wonder'd that her humble guest
Strove not to please, would neither lie nor jest;
She sought no news, no scandal would convey,
But walk'd for health, and was at church to pray;
All this displeased, and soon the widow cried:
'Let me be frank—I am not satisfied;
You know my wishes, I your judgment trust;
You can be useful, Jesse, and you must;
Let me be plainer, child—I want an ear,
When I am deaf, instead of mine to hear;
When mine is sleeping, let your eye awake;
When I observe not, observation take;
Alas! I rest not on my pillow laid,

Then threat'ning whispers make my soul afraid;
The tread of strangers to my ear ascends,
Fed at my cost, the minions of my friends;
While you, without a care, a wish to please,
Eat the vile bread of idleness and ease.'
  Th' indignant girl astonish'd answer'd—'Nay!
This instant, madam, let me haste away;
Thus speaks my father's, thus an orphan's friend?
This instant, lady, let your bounty end.'
  The lady frown'd indignant—'What!' she cried,
'A vicar's daughter with a princess' pride!
And pauper's lot! but pitying I forgive;
How, simple Jesse, do you think to live?
Have I not power to help you, foolish maid?
To my concerns be your attention paid;
With cheerful mind th' allotted duties take,
And recollect I have a will to make.'
  Jesse, who felt as liberal natures feel,
When thus the baser their designs reveal,
Replied—'Those duties were to her unfit,
Nor would her spirit to her tasks submit.'
  In silent scorn the lady sate awhile,
And then replied with stern contemptuous smile—
  'Think you, fair madam, that you came to share
Fortunes like mine without a thought or care?
A guest, indeed! from every trouble free,
Dress'd by my help, with not a care for me;
When I a visit to your father made,
I for the poor assistance largely paid;
To his domestics I their tasks assign'd,
I fix'd the portion for his hungry hind;
And had your father (simple man!) obey'd
My good advice, and watch'd as well as pray'd,
He might have left you something with his prayers,
And lent some colour for these lofty airs.—
  'In tears! my love! Oh, then my soften'd heart
Cannot resist—we never more will part;
I need your friendship—I will be your friend,
And thus determined, to my will attend.'
  Jesse went forth, but with determined soul
To fly such love, to break from such control;

'I hear enough,' the trembling damsel cried;
'Flight be my care, and Providence my guide:
Ere yet a prisoner, I escape will make;
Will, thus display'd, th' insidious arts forsake,
And, as the rattle sounds, will fly the fatal snake.'
  Jesse her thanks upon the morrow paid,
Prepared to go, determined though afraid.
  'Ungrateful creature,' said the lady, 'this
Could I imagine?—are you frantic, miss?
What! leave your friend, your prospects—is it true?'
This Jesse answer'd by a mild 'Adieu!'
  The dame replied, 'Then houseless may you rove,
The starving victim to a guilty love;
Branded with shame, in sickness doom'd to nurse
An ill-form'd cub, your scandal and your curse;
Spurn'd by its scoundrel father, and ill fed
By surly rustics with the parish-bread!—
Relent you not?—speak—yet I can forgive;
Still live with me'—'With you,' said Jesse, 'live?
No! I would first endure what you describe,
Rather than breathe with your detested tribe;
Who long have feign'd, till now their very hearts
Are firmly fix'd in their accursed parts;
Who all profess esteem, and feel disdain,
And all, with justice, of deceit complain;
Whom I could pity, but that, while I stay,
My terror drives all kinder thoughts away;
Grateful for this, that when I think of you,
I little fear what poverty can do.'
  The angry matron her attendant Jane
Summon'd in haste to soothe the fierce disdain:
  'A vile detested wretch!' the lady cried,
Yet shall she be, by many an effort, tried,
And, clogg'd with debt and fear, against her will abide;
And once secured, she never shall depart
Till I have proved the firmness of her heart;
Then when she dares not, would not, cannot go,
I'll make her feel what 'tis to use me so.'
  The pensive Colin in his garden stray'd,
But felt not then the beauties it display'd;
There many a pleasant object met his view,

A rising wood of oaks behind it grew;
A stream ran by it, and the village-green
And public road were from the gardens seen;
Save where the pine and larch the bound'ry made,
And on the rose-beds threw a softening shade.
The mother sat beside the garden-door,
Dress'd as in times ere she and hers were poor;
The broad-laced cap was known in ancient days,
When madam's dress compell'd the village praise;
And still she look'd as in the times of old,
Ere his last farm the erring husband sold;
While yet the mansion stood in decent state,
And paupers waited at the well-known gate.
'Alas! my son!' the mother cried, 'and why
That silent grief and oft-repeated sigh?
True we are poor, but thou hast never felt
Pangs to thy father for his error dealt;
Pangs from strong hopes of visionary gain,
For ever raised, and ever found in vain.
He rose unhappy! from his fruitless schemes,
As guilty wretches from their blissful dreams;
But thou wert then, my son, a playful child,
Wondering at grief, gay, innocent, and wild;
Listening at times to thy poor mother's sighs,
With curious looks and innocent surprise;
Thy father dying, thou, my virtuous boy,
My comfort always, waked my soul to joy;
With the poor remnant of our fortune left,
Thou hast our station of its gloom bereft:
Thy lively temper, and thy cheerful air,
Have cast a smile on sadness and despair;
Thy active hand has dealt to this poor space
The bliss of plenty and the charm of grace;
And all around us wonder when they find
Such taste and strength, such skill and power combined;
There is no mother, Colin, no not one,
But envies me so kind, so good a son;
By thee supported on this failing side,
Weakness itself awakes a parent's pride:
I bless the stroke that was my grief before,
And feel such joy that 'tis disease no more;

Shielded by thee, my want becomes my wealth—
And soothed by Colin, sickness smiles at health;
The old men love thee, they repeat thy praise,
And say, like thee were youth in earlier days;
While every village-maiden cries, "How gay,
How smart, how brave, how good is Colin Grey!"
'Yet art thou sad; alas! my son, I know
Thy heart is wounded, and the cure is slow;
Fain would I think that Jesse still may come
To share the comforts of our rustic home:
She surely loved thee; I have seen the maid,
When thou hast kindly brought the vicar aid—
When thou hast eased his bosom of its pain,
Oh! I have seen her—she will come again.'
The matron ceased; and Colin stood the while
Silent, but striving for a grateful smile;
He then replied—'Ah! sure, had Jesse stay'd,
And shared the comforts of our sylvan shade,
The tenderest duty and the fondest love
Would not have fail'd that generous heart to move;
A grateful pity would have ruled her breast,
And my distresses would have made me blest.
'But she is gone, and ever has in view
Grandeur and taste—and what will then ensue?
Surprise and then delight in scenes so fair and new;
For many a day, perhaps for many a week,
Home will have charms, and to her bosom speak;
But thoughtless ease, and affluence, and pride,
Seen day by day, will draw the heart aside:
And she at length, though gentle and sincere,
Will think no more of our enjoyments here.'
Sighing he spake—but hark! he hears th' approach
Of rattling wheels! and lo! the evening coach;
Once more the movement of the horses' feet
Makes the fond heart with strong emotion beat;
Faint were his hopes, but ever had the sight
Drawn him to gaze beside his gate at night;
And when with rapid wheels it hurried by,
He grieved his parent with a hopeless sigh;
And could the blessing have been bought—what sum
Had he not offer'd, to have Jesse come!

She came—he saw her bending from the door,
Her face, her smile, and he beheld no more;
Lost in his joy—the mother lent her aid
T' assist and to detain the willing maid;
Who thought her late, her present home to make,
Sure of a welcome for the vicar's sake:
But the good parent was so pleased, so kind,
So pressing Colin, she so much inclined,
That night advanced; and then so long detain'd,
No wishes to depart she felt, or feign'd;
Yet long in doubt she stood, and then perforce remain'd.
  Here was a lover fond, a friend sincere;
Here was content and joy, for she was here:
In the mild evening, in the scene around,
The maid, now free, peculiar beauties found;
Blended with village-tones, the evening-gale
Gave the sweet night-bird's warblings to the vale;
The youth embolden'd, yet abash'd, now told
His fondest wish, nor found the maiden cold;
The mother smiling whisper'd—'Let him go
And seek the licence!' Jesse answer'd, 'No:'
But Colin went. I know not if they live
With all the comforts wealth and plenty give;
But with pure joy to envious souls denied,
To suppliant meanness and suspicious pride;
And village-maids of happy couples say,
'They live like Jesse Bourn and Colin Grey.'

14. THE STRUGGLES OF CONSCIENCE

I am a villain; yet I lie, I am not;
Fool! of thyself speak well:—Fool! do not flatter.
My Conscience hath a thousand several tongues,
And every tongue brings in a several tale.
Richard III, Act v, Scene 3

My Conscience is but a kind of hard Conscience...The fiend gives the more friendly counsel. *Merchant of Venice*, Act II, Scene 2

Thou hast it now—and I fear
Thou playd'st most foully for it.
Macbeth, Act III, Scene 1

14. The Struggles of Conscience

Canst thou not minister to a mind diseased,
Pluck from the memory a rooted sorrow,
Rase out the written troubles of the brain,
And with some sweet oblivious antidote
Cleanse the foul bosom of that perilous stuff
Which weighs upon the heart?

Macbeth, Act v, Scene 3

Soft! I did but dream—
Oh! coward Conscience, how dost thou afflict me!

Richard III, Act v, Scene 3

A serious toyman in the city dwelt,
Who much concern for his religion felt;
Reading, he changed his tenets, read again,
And various questions could with skill maintain;
Papist and quaker if we set aside,
He had the road of every traveller tried;
There walk'd awhile, and on a sudden turn'd
Into some by-way he had just discern'd:
He had a nephew, Fulham—Fulham went
His uncle's way, with every turn content;
He saw his pious kinsman's watchful care,
And thought such anxious pains his own might spare,
And he, the truth obtain'd, without the toil, might share.
In fact, young Fulham, though he little read,
Perceived his uncle was by fancy led;
And smiled to see the constant care he took,
Collating creed with creed, and book with book.
At length the senior fix'd; I pass the sect
He call'd a church, 'twas precious and elect;
Yet the seed fell not in the richest soil,
For few disciples paid the preacher's toil;
All in an attic-room were wont to meet,
These few disciples at their pastor's feet;
With these went Fulham, who, discreet and grave,
Follow'd the light his worthy uncle gave;
Till a warm preacher found a way t'impart
Awakening feelings to his torpid heart:
Some weighty truths, and of unpleasant kind,
Sank, though resisted, in his struggling mind;
He wish'd to fly them, but compell'd to stay,

Truth to the waking Conscience found her way;
For though the youth was call'd a prudent lad,
And prudent was, yet serious faults he had;
Who now reflected—'Much am I surprised,
I find these notions cannot be despised;
No! there is something I perceive at last,
Although my uncle cannot hold it fast;
Though I the strictness of these men reject,
Yet I determine to be circumspect:
This man alarms me, and I must begin
To look more closely to the things within;
These sons of zeal have I derided long,
But now begin to think the laughers wrong;
Nay, my good uncle, by all teachers moved,
Will be preferr'd to him who none approved;
Better to love amiss than nothing to have loved.'
  Such were his thoughts, when Conscience first began
To hold close converse with th' awaken'd man:
He from that time reserved and cautious grew,
And for his duties felt obedience due;
Pious he was not, but he fear'd the pain
Of sins committed, nor would sin again.
Whene'er he stray'd, he found his Conscience rose,
Like one determined what was ill t'oppose,
What wrong t' accuse, what secret to disclose:
To drag forth every latent act to light,
And fix them fully in the actor's sight:
This gave him trouble, but he still confess'd
The labour useful, for it brought him rest.
  The uncle died, and when the nephew read
The will, and saw the substance of the dead—
Five hundred guineas, with a stock in trade—
He much rejoiced, and thought his fortune made;
Yet felt aspiring pleasure at the sight,
And for increase, increasing appetite:
Desire of profit, idle habits check'd,
(For Fulham's virtue was to be correct);
He and his Conscience had their compact made—
'Urge me with truth, and you will soon persuade;
'But not,' he cried, 'for mere ideal things
Give me to feel those terror-breeding stings.'

'Let not such thoughts,' she said, 'your mind confound;
Trifles may wake me, but they never wound;
In them indeed there is a wrong and right,
But you will find me pliant and polite;
Not like a Conscience of the dotard kind,
Awake to dreams, to dire offences blind:
Let all within be pure, in all beside
Be your own master, governor, and guide;
Alive to danger, in temptation strong,
And I shall sleep our whole existence long.'
'Sweet be thy sleep,' said Fulham; 'strong must be
The tempting ill that gains access to me:
Never will I to evil deed consent,
Or, if surprised, oh! how will I repent!
Should gain be doubtful, soon would I restore
The dangerous good, or give it to the poor;
Repose for them my growing wealth shall buy—
Or build—who knows?—an hospital like Guy?—
Yet why such means to soothe the smart within,
While firmly purposed to renounce the sin?'
Thus our young Trader and his Conscience dwelt
In mutual love, and great the joy they felt;
But yet in small concerns, in trivial things,
'She was,' he said, 'too ready with the stings;'
And he too apt, in search of growing gains,
To lose the fear of penalties and pains:
Yet these were trifling bickerings, petty jars,
Domestic strifes, preliminary wars;
He ventured little, little she express'd
Of indignation, and they both had rest.
Thus was he fix'd to walk the worthy way,
When profit urged him to a bold essay:—
A time was that when all at pleasure gamed
In lottery-chances, yet of law unblamed;
This Fulham tried, who would to him advance
A pound or crown, he gave in turn a chance
For weighty prize—and should they nothing share,
They had their crown or pound in Fulham's ware;
Thus the old stores within the shop were sold
For that which none refuses, new or old.
Was this unjust? yet Conscience could not rest,

But made a mighty struggle in the breast;
And gave th' aspiring man an early proof,
That should they war he would have work enough:
'Suppose,' said she, 'your vended numbers rise
The same with those which gain each real prize,
(Such your proposal), can you ruin shun?'
'A hundred thousand,' he replied, 'to one.'
'Still it may happen:' 'I the sum must pay.'
'You know you cannot:' 'I can run away.'
'That is dishonest:'—'Nay, but you must wink
At a chance-hit; it cannot be, I think:
Upon my conduct as a whole decide,
Such trifling errors let my virtues hide;
Fail I at meeting? am I sleepy there?
My purse refuse I with the priest to share?
Do I deny the poor a helping hand?
Or stop the wicked women in the Strand?
Or drink at club beyond a certain pitch?
Which are your charges? Conscience, tell me which?'
  ''Tis well,' said she, 'but—' 'Nay, I pray, have done:
Trust me, I will not into danger run.'
  The lottery drawn, not one demand was made;
Fulham gain'd profit and increase of trade.
'See now,' said he—for Conscience yet arose—
'How foolish 'tis such measures to oppose:
Have I not blameless thus my state advanced?'—
'Still,' mutter'd Conscience, 'still it might have chanced.'
'Might!' said our hero, 'who is so exact
As to inquire what might have been a fact?'
  Now Fulham's shop contain'd a curious view
Of costly trifles elegant and new:
The papers told where kind mammas might buy
The gayest toys to charm an infant's eye;
Where generous beaux might gentle damsels please,
And travellers call who cross the land or seas,
And find the curious art, the neat device
Of precious value and of trifling price.
  Here Conscience rested, she was pleased to find
No less an active than an honest mind;
But when he named his price, and when he swore,
His Conscience check'd him, that he ask'd no more,

When half he sought had been a large increase
On fair demand, she could not rest in peace:
(Beside th' affront to call th' adviser in,
Who would prevent, to justify the sin?)
She therefore told him, that 'he vainly tried
To soothe her anger, conscious that he lied;
If thus he grasp'd at such usurious gains,
He must deserve, and should expect her pains.'

The charge was strong; he would in part confess
Offence there was—But, who offended less?
'What! is a mere assertion call'd a lie?
And if it be, are men compell'd to buy?
'Twas strange that Conscience on such points should dwell,
While he was acting (he would call it) well;
He bought as others buy, he sold as others sell:
There was no fraud, and he demanded cause
Why he was troubled, when he kept the laws?'

'My laws?' said Conscience: 'What,' said he, 'are thine?
Oral or written, human or divine?
Show me the chapter, let me see the text;
By laws uncertain subjects are perplex'd:
Let me my finger on the statute lay,
And I shall feel it duty to obey.'

'Reflect,' said Conscience, ''twas your own desire
That I should warn you—does the compact tire?
Repent you this? then bid me not advise,
And rather hear your passions as they rise;
So you may counsel and remonstrance shun,
But then remember it is war begun;
And you may judge from some attacks, my friend,
What serious conflicts will on war attend.'

'Nay, but,' at length the thoughtful man replied,
'I say not that; I wish you for my guide;
Wish for your checks and your reproofs—but then
Be like a Conscience of my fellow-men;
Worthy I mean, and men of good report,
And not the wretches who with conscience sport:
There's Bice, my friend, who passes off his grease
Of pigs for bears', in pots a crown apiece;
His Conscience never checks him when he swears
The fat he sells is honest fat of bears;

And so it is, for he contrives to give
A drachm to each—'tis thus that tradesmen live:
Now why should you and I be over-nice;
What man is held in more repute than Bice?'
   Here ended the dispute; but yet 'twas plain
The parties both expected strife again:
Their friendship cool'd, he look'd about and saw
Numbers who seem'd unshackled by his awe;
While like a school-boy he was threaten'd still,
Now for the deed, now only for the will;
Here Conscience answer'd, 'To thy neighbour's guide
Thy neighbour leave, and in thine own confide.'
   Such were each day the charges and replies,
When a new object caught the trader's eyes;
A vestry-patriot, could he gain the name,
Would famous make him, and would pay the fame:
He knew full well the sums bequeath'd in charge
For schools, for alms-men, for the poor, were large;
Report had told, and he could feel it true,
That most unfairly dealt the trusted few;
No partners would they in their office take,
Nor clear accounts at annual meetings make;
Aloud our hero in the vestry spoke
Of hidden deeds, and vow'd to draw the cloak;
It was the poor man's cause, and he for one
Was quite determined to see justice done:
His foes affected laughter, then disdain,
They too were loud and threat'ning, but in vain;
The pauper's friend, their foe, arose and spoke again:
Fiercely he cried, 'Your garbled statements show
That you determine we shall nothing know;
But we shall bring your hidden crimes to light,
Give you to shame, and to the poor their right.'
   Virtue like this might some approval ask—
But Conscience sternly said, 'You wear a mask!'
'At least,' said Fulham, 'if I have a view
To serve myself, I serve the public too.'
   Fulham, though check'd, retain'd his former zeal,
And this the cautious rogues began to feel:
'Thus will he ever bark,' in peevish tone,
An elder cried—'the cur must have a bone.'

They then began to hint, and to begin
Was all they needed—it was felt within;
In terms less veil'd an offer then was made,
Though distant still, it fail'd not to persuade:
More plainly then was every point proposed,
Approved, accepted, and the bargain closed.
'Th' exulting paupers hail'd their friend's success,
And bade adieu to murmurs and distress.'

Alas! their friend had now superior light,
And, view'd by that, he found that all was right;
'There were no errors, the disbursements small;
This was the truth, and truth was due to all.'

And rested Conscience? No! she would not rest,
Yet was content with making a protest:
Some acts she now with less resistance bore,
Nor took alarm so quickly as before:
Like those in towns besieged, who every ball
At first with terror view, and dread them all,
But, grown familiar with the scenes, they fear
The danger less, as it approaches near;
So Conscience, more familiar with the view
Of growing evils, less attentive grew:
Yet he who felt some pain, and dreaded more,
Gave a peace-offering to the angry poor.

Thus had he quiet—but the time was brief,
From his new triumph sprang a cause of grief;
In office join'd, and acting with the rest,
He must admit the sacramental test:
Now, as a sectary, who had all his life,
As he supposed, been with the church at strife,
(No rules of hers, no laws had he perused,
Nor knew the tenets he by rote abused);
Yet Conscience here arose more fierce and strong,
Than when she told of robbery and wrong;
'Change his religion! No! he must be sure
That was a blow no conscience could endure.'

Though friend to virtue, yet she oft abides
In early notions, fix'd by erring guides;
And is more startled by a call from those,
Than when the foulest crimes her rest oppose;
By error taught, by prejudice misled,

She yields her rights, and fancy rules instead;
When Conscience all her stings and terror deals,
Not as truth dictates, but as fancy feels:
And thus within our hero's troubled breast,
Crime was less torture than the odious test.
New forms, new measures, he must now embrace,
With sad conviction that they warr'd with grace;
To his new church no former friend would come,
They scarce preferr'd her to the church of Rome:
But thinking much, and weighing guilt and gain,
Conscience and he commuted for her pain;
Then promised Fulham to retain his creed,
And their peculiar paupers still to feed;
Their attic-room (in secret) to attend,
And not forget he was the preacher's friend;
Thus he proposed, and Conscience, troubled, tried,
And wanting peace, reluctantly complied.
  Now care subdued, and apprehensions gone,
In peace our hero went aspiring on;
But short the period—soon a quarrel rose,
Fierce in the birth, and fatal in the close;
With times of truce between, which rather proved
That both were weary, than that either loved.
  Fulham ev'n now disliked the heavy thrall,
And for her death would in his anguish call,
As Rome's mistaken friend exclaim'd, *Let Carthage fall!*
So felt our hero, so his wish express'd,
Against this powerful sprite—*delenda est:*
Rome in her conquest saw not danger near,
Freed from her rival, and without a fear;
So, Conscience conquer'd, men perceive how free,
But not how fatal such a state must be.
Fatal not free our hero's; foe or friend,
Conscience on him was destined to attend:
She dozed indeed, grew dull, nor seem'd to spy
Crime following crime, and each of deeper dye;
But all were noticed, and the reckoning time
With her account came on—crime following crime.
  This, once a foe, now brother in the trust,
Whom Fulham late described as fair and just,
Was the sole guardian of a wealthy maid,

Placed in his power, and of his frown afraid:
Not quite an idiot, for her busy brain
Sought, by poor cunning, trifling points to gain;
Success in childish projects her delight,
She took no heed of each important right.
The friendly parties met—the guardian cried,
'I am too old; my sons have each a bride:
Martha, my ward, would make an easy wife;
On easy terms I'll make her yours for life;
And then the creature is so weak and mild,
She may be soothed and threaten'd as a child;'—
'Yet not obey,' said Fulham, 'for your fools,
Female and male, are obstinate as mules.'
Some points adjusted, these new friends agreed,
Proposed the day, and hurried on the deed.
''Tis a vile act,' said Conscience:—'It will prove,'
Replied the bolder man, 'an act of love;
Her wicked guardian might the girl have sold
To endless misery for a tyrant's gold;
Now may her life be happy—for I mean
To keep my temper even and serene.'
'I cannot thus compound,' the spirit cried,
'Nor have my laws thus broken and defied:
This is a fraud, a bargain for a wife;
Expect my vengeance, or amend your life.'
The wife was pretty, trifling, childish, weak;
She could not think, but would not cease to speak:
This he forbad—she took the caution ill,
And boldly rose against his sovereign will;
With idiot-cunning she would watch the hour,
When friends were present, to dispute his power:
With tyrant-craft, he then was still and calm,
But raised in private terror and alarm:
By many trials she perceived how far,
To vex and tease, without an open war;
And he discover'd that so weak a mind
No art could lead, and no compulsion bind;
The rudest force would fail such mind to tame,
And she was callous to rebuke and shame;
Proud of her wealth, the power of law she knew,
And would assist him in the spending too:

His threat'ning words with insult she defied,
To all his reasoning with a stare replied;
And when he begg'd her to attend, would say,
'Attend I will—but let me have my way.'
  Nor rest had Conscience: 'While you merit pain
From me,' she cried, 'you seek redress in vain.'
His thoughts were grievous: 'All that I possess
From this vile bargain adds to my distress;
To pass a life with one who will not mend,
Who cannot love, nor save, nor wisely spend,
Is a vile prospect, and I see no end;
For if we part, I must of course restore
Much of her money, and must wed no more.
  'Is there no way?'—here Conscience rose in power,
'Oh! fly the danger of this fatal hour;
I am thy Conscience faithful, fond, and true,
Ah, fly this thought, or evil must ensue;
Fall on thy knees, and pray with all thy soul,
Thy purpose banish, thy design control;
Let every hope of such advantage cease,
Or never more expect a moment's peace.'
  Th' affrighten'd man a due attention paid,
Felt the rebuke, and the command obey'd.
  Again the wife rebell'd, again express'd
A love for pleasure—a contempt of rest;
'She, whom she pleased, would visit, would receive
Those who pleased her, nor deign to ask for leave.'
  'One way there is,' said he; 'I might contrive
Into a trap this foolish thing to drive:
Who pleased her, said she?—I'll be certain who—'
'Take heed,' said Conscience, 'what thou means't to do:
Ensnare thy wife?'—'Why yes,' he must confess,
'It might be wrong—but there was no redress;
Beside, to think,' said he, 'is not to sin.'
'Mistaken man!' replied the power within.
No guest unnoticed to the lady came,
He judged th' event with mingled joy and shame;
Oft he withdrew, and seem'd to leave her free,
But still as watchful as a lynx was he;
Meanwhile the wife was thoughtless, cool, and gay,
And, without virtue, had no wish to stray.

14. The Struggles of Conscience

Though thus opposed, his plans were not resign'd;
'Revenge,' said he, 'will prompt that daring mind;
Refused supplies, insulted and distress'd,
Enraged with me, and near a favourite guest—
Then will her vengeance prompt the daring deed,
And I shall watch, detect her, and be freed.'
There was a youth—but let me hide the name,
With all the progress of this deed of shame;
He had his views—on him the husband cast
His net, and saw him in his trammels fast.
'Pause but a moment—think what you intend,'
Said the roused sleeper: 'I am yet a friend:
Must all our days in enmity be spent?'
'No!' and he paused—'I surely shall repent:'
Then hurried on—the evil plan was laid,
The wife was guilty, and her friend betray'd,
And Fulham gain'd his wish, and for his will was paid.
Had crimes less weighty on the spirit press'd,
This troubled Conscience might have sunk to rest;
And, like a foolish guard, been bribed to peace,
By a false promise, that offence should cease;
Past faults had seem'd familiar to the view,
Confused if many, and obscure though true;
And Conscience, troubled with the dull account,
Had dropp'd her tale, and slumber'd o'er th' amount:
But, struck by daring guilt, alert she rose,
Disturb'd, alarm'd, and could no more repose;
All hopes of friendship, and of peace, were past,
And every view with gloom was overcast.
Hence from that day, that day of shame and sin,
Arose the restless enmity within;
On no resource could Fulham now rely,
Doom'd all expedients, and in vain, to try;
For Conscience, roused, sat boldly on her throne,
Watch'd every thought, attack'd the foe alone,
And with envenom'd sting drew forth the inward groan:
Expedients fail'd that brought relief before,
In vain his alms gave comfort to the poor,
Give what he would, to him the comfort came no more:
Not prayer avail'd, and when (his crimes confess'd)
He felt some ease—she said—'are they redress'd?

You still retain the profit, and be sure,
Long as it lasts, this anguish shall endure.'
Fulham still tried to soothe her, cheat, mislead;
But Conscience laid her finger on the deed,
And read the crime with power, and all that must succeed:
He tried t'expel her, but was sure to find
Her strength increased by all that he design'd;
Nor ever was his groan more loud and deep,
Than when refresh'd she rose from momentary sleep.
Now desperate grown, weak, harass'd, and afraid,
From new allies he sought for doubtful aid;
To thought itself he strove to bid adieu,
And from devotions to diversions flew;
He took a poor domestic for a slave,
(Though Avarice grieved to see the price he gave);
Upon his board, once frugal, press'd a load
Of viands rich, the appetite to goad;
The long-protracted meal, the sparkling cup,
Fought with his gloom, and kept his courage up:
Soon as the morning came, there met his eyes
Accounts of wealth, that he might reading rise;
To profit then he gave some active hours,
Till food and wine again should renovate his powers;
Yet, spite of all defence, of every aid,
The watchful foe her close attention paid;
In every thoughtful moment, on she press'd,
And gave at once her dagger to his breast;
He waked at midnight, and the fears of sin,
As waters, through a bursten dam, broke in;
Nay, in the banquet, with his friends around,
When all their cares and half their crimes were drown'd,
Would some chance act awake the slumbering fear,
And care and crime in all their strength appear:
The news is read, a guilty victim swings,
And troubled looks proclaim the bosom-stings;
Some pair are wed; this brings the wife in view,
And some divorced: this shows the parting too;
Nor can he hear of evil word or deed,
But they to thought, and thought to sufferings lead.
Such was his life—no other changes came,
The hurrying day, the conscious night the same;

The night of horror—when he starting cried,
To the poor startled sinner at his side;
'Is it in law? am I condemn'd to die?
Let me escape!—I'll give—oh! let me fly—
How! but a dream—no judges! dungeon! chain!
Or these grim men!—I will not sleep again.—
Wilt thou, dread being! thus thy promise keep?
Day is thy time—and wilt thou murder sleep?
Sorrow and want repose, and wilt thou come,
Nor give one hour of pure untroubled gloom?
  'Oh! Conscience! Conscience! man's most faithful friend,
Him canst thou comfort, ease, relieve, defend;
But if he will thy friendly checks forego,
Thou art, oh! woe for me, his deadliest foe!'

15. ADVICE

OR

THE 'SQUIRE AND THE PRIEST

His hours fill'd up with riots, banquets, sports—
And never noted in him any study,
Any retirement, any sequestration.
Henry V, Act I, Scene 1

I will converse with iron-witted fools,
With unrespective boys; none are for me,
Who look into me with considerate eyes.
Richard III, Act IV, Scene 2

You cram these words into mine ears, against
The stomach of my sense.
Tempest, Act II, Scene 1

A wealthy lord of far-extended land
Had all that pleased him placed at his command;
Widow'd of late, but finding much relief
In the world's comforts, he dismiss'd his grief;
He was by marriage of his daughters eased,
And knew his sons could marry if they pleased;
Meantime in travel he indulged the boys,
And kept no spy nor partner of his joys.
  These joys, indeed, were of the grosser kind,
That fed the cravings of an earthly mind;

A mind that, conscious of its own excess,
Felt the reproach his neighbours would express.
Long at th' indulgent board he loved to sit,
Where joy was laughter, and profaneness wit;
And such the guest and manners of the hall,
No wedded lady on the 'squire would call:
Here reign'd a favourite, and her triumph gain'd
O'er other favourites who before had reign'd;
Reserved and modest seem'd the nymph to be,
Knowing her lord was charm'd with modesty;
For he, a sportsman keen, the more enjoy'd,
The greater value had the thing destroy'd.
 Our 'squire declared, that, from a wife released,
He would no more give trouble to a priest;
Seem'd it not, then, ungrateful and unkind,
That he should trouble from the priesthood find?
The church he honour'd, and he gave the due
And full respect to every son he knew;
But envied those who had the luck to meet
A gentle pastor, civil, and discreet;
Who never bold and hostile sermon penn'd,
To wound a sinner, or to shame a friend;
One whom no being either shunn'd or fear'd,
Such must be loved wherever they appear'd.
 Not such the stern old rector of the time,
Who soothed no culprit, and who spared no crime;
Who would his fears and his contempt express,
For irreligion and licentiousness;
Of him our village lord, his guests among,
By speech vindictive proved his feelings stung.
 'Were he a bigot,' said the 'squire, 'whose zeal
Condemn'd us all, I should disdain to feel:
But when a man of parts, in college train'd,
Prates of our conduct—who would not be pain'd?
While he declaims (where no one dares reply)
On men abandon'd, grov'ling in the sty
(Like beasts in human shape) of shameless luxury.
Yet with a patriot's zeal I stand the shock
Of vile rebuke, example to his flock:
But let this rector, thus severe and proud,
Change his wide surplice for a narrow shroud,

And I will place within his seat a youth,
Train'd by the Graces, to explain the truth;
Then shall the flock with gentle hand be led,
By wisdom won, and by compassion fed.'
  This purposed teacher was a sister's son,
Who of her children gave the priesthood one;
And she had early train'd for this employ
The pliant talents of her college-boy:
At various times her letters painted all
Her brother's views—the manners of the hall;
The rector's harshness, and the mischief made
By chiding those whom preachers should persuade:
This led the youth to views of easy life,
A friendly patron, an obliging wife;
His tithe, his glebe, the garden and the steed,
With books as many as he wish'd to read.
  All this accorded with the uncle's will;
He loved a priest compliant, easy, still;
Sums he had often to his favourite sent,
'To be,' he wrote, 'in manly freedom spent;
For well it pleased his spirit to assist
An honest lad, who scorn'd a Methodist:'
His mother too, in her maternal care,
Bade him of canting hypocrites beware;
Who from his duties would his heart seduce,
And make his talents of no earthly use.
  Soon must a trial of his worth be made—
The ancient priest is to the tomb convey'd;
And the youth summon'd from a serious friend,
His guide and host, new duties to attend.
  Three months before, the nephew and the 'squire
Saw mutual worth to praise and to admire;
And though the one too early left his wine,
The other still exclaim'd—'My boy will shine:
Yes, I perceive that he will soon improve,
And I shall form the very guide I love;
Decent abroad, he will my name defend,
And, when at home, be social and unbend.'
  The plan was specious, for the mind of James
Accorded duly with his uncle's schemes:
He then aspired not to a higher name

Than sober clerks of moderate talents claim;
Gravely to pray, and rev'rendly to preach,
Was all he saw, good youth! within his reach:
Thus may a mass of sulphur long abide,
Cold and inert, but, to the flame applied,
Kindling it blazes, and consuming turns
To smoke and poison, as it boils and burns.
 James, leaving college, to a preacher stray'd;
What call'd, he knew not—but the call obey'd:
Mild, idle, pensive, ever led by those
Who could some specious novelty propose;
Humbly he listen'd, while the preacher dwelt
On touching themes, and strong emotions felt;
And in this night was fix'd that pliant will
To one sole point, and he retains it still.
 At first his care was to himself confined;
Himself assured, he gave it to mankind:
His zeal grew active—honest, earnest zeal,
And comfort dealt to him, he long'd to deal;
He to his favourite preacher now withdrew,
Was taught to teach, instructed to subdue;
And train'd for ghostly warfare, when the call
Of his new duties reach'd him from the hall.
 Now to the 'squire, although alert and stout,
Came unexpected an attack of gout;
And the grieved patron felt such serious pain,
He never thought to see a church again:
Thrice had the youthful rector taught the crowd,
Whose growing numbers spoke his powers aloud,
Before the patron could himself rejoice
(His pain still lingering) in the general voice;
For he imputed all this early fame
To graceful manner, and the well-known name;
And to himself assumed a share of praise,
For worth and talents he was pleased to raise.
 A month had flown, and with it fled disease;
What pleased before, began again to please;
Emerging daily from his chamber's gloom,
He found his old sensations hurrying home;
Then call'd his nephew, and exclaim'd, 'My boy,
Let us again the balm of life enjoy;

The foe has left me, and I deem it right,
Should he return, to arm me for the fight.'
  Thus spoke the 'squire, the favourite nymph stood by,
And view'd the priest with insult in her eye:
She thrice had heard him when he boldly spoke
On dangerous points, and fear'd he would revoke:
For James she loved not—and her manner told,
'This warm affection will be quickly cold:'
And still she fear'd impression might be made
Upon a subject, nervous and decay'd;
She knew her danger, and had no desire
Of reformation in the gallant 'squire;
And felt an envious pleasure in her breast
To see the rector daunted and distress'd.
  Again the uncle to the youth applied—
'Cast, my dear lad, that cursed gloom aside:
There are for all things time and place; appear
Grave in your pulpit, and be merry here:
Now take your wine—for woes a sure resource,
And the best prelude to a long discourse.'
  James half obey'd, but cast an angry eye
On the fair lass, who still stood watchful by;
Resolving thus, 'I have my fears—but still
I must perform my duties, and I will;
No love, no interest, shall my mind control;
Better to lose my comforts than my soul;
Better my uncle's favour to abjure,
Than the upbraidings of my heart endure.'
  He took his glass, and then address'd the 'squire:
'I feel not well, permit me to retire.'
The 'squire conceived that the ensuing day
Gave him these terrors for the grand essay,
When he himself should this young preacher try,
And stand before him with observant eye;
This raised compassion in his manly breast,
And he would send the rector to his rest:
Yet first, in soothing voice—'A moment stay,
And these suggestions of a friend obey;
Treasure these hints, if fame or peace you prize—
The bottle emptied, I shall close my eyes.

'On every priest a two-fold care attends,
To prove his talents, and insure his friends:
First, of the first—your stores at once produce,
And bring your reading to its proper use:
On doctrines dwell, and every point enforce
By quoting much, the scholar's sure resource;
For he alone can show us on each head
What ancient schoolmen and sage fathers said:
No worth has knowledge, if you fail to show
How well you studied, and how much you know:
Is faith your subject, and you judge it right
On theme so dark to cast a ray of light;
Be it that faith the orthodox maintain,
Found in the rubrick, what the creeds explain;
Fail not to show us on this ancient faith
(And quote the passage) what some martyr saith:
Dwell not one moment on a faith that shocks
The minds of men sincere and orthodox;
That gloomy faith, that robs the wounded mind
Of all the comfort it was wont to find
From virtuous acts, and to the soul denies
Its proper due for alms and charities;
That partial faith, that, weighing sins alone,
Lets not a virtue for a fault atone;
That starving faith, that would our tables clear,
And make one dreadful Lent of all the year;
And cruel too, for this is faith that rends
Confiding beauties from protecting friends;
A faith that all embracing, what a gloom
Deep and terrific o'er the land would come!
What scenes of horror would that time disclose!
No sight but misery, and no sound but woes;
Your nobler faith, in loftier style convey'd,
Shall be with praise and admiration paid:
On points like these your hearers all admire
A preacher's depth, and nothing more require;
Shall we a studious youth to college send,
That every clown his words may comprehend?
'Tis for your glory, when your hearers own
Your learning matchless, but the sense unknown.
'Thus honour gain'd, learn now to gain a friend,

And the sure way is—never to offend;
For, James, consider—what your neighbours do
Is their own business, and concerns not you:
Shun all resemblance to that forward race
Who preach of sins before a sinner's face;
And seem as if they overlook'd a pew,
Only to drag a failing man in view:
Much should I feel, when groaning in disease,
If a rough hand upon my limb should seize;
But great my anger, if this hand were found
The very doctor's, who should make it sound:
So feel our minds, young priest, so doubly feel,
When hurt by those whose office is to heal.
'Yet of our duties you must something tell,
And must at times on sin and frailty dwell;
Here you may preach in easy, flowing style,
How errors cloud us, and how sins defile:
Here bring persuasive tropes and figures forth,
To show the poor that wealth is nothing worth;
That they, in fact, possess an ample share
Of the world's good, and feel not half its care;
Give them this comfort, and, indeed, my gout
In its full vigour causes me some doubt;
And let it always, for your zeal, suffice,
That vice you combat, in the abstract—vice:
The very captious will be quiet then;
We all confess we are offending men:
In lashing sin, of every stroke beware,
For sinners feel, and sinners you must spare;
In general satire, every man perceives
A slight attack, yet neither fears nor grieves;
But name th' offence, and you absolve the rest,
And point the dagger at a single breast.
'Yet are there sinners of a class so low,
That you with safety may the lash bestow;
Poachers, and drunkards, idle rogues, who feed
At others' cost, a mark'd correction need:
And all the better sort, who see your zeal,
Will love and reverence for their pastor feel;
Reverence for one who can inflict the smart,
And love, because he deals them not a part.

'Remember well what love and age advise;
A quiet rector is a parish prize,
Who in his learning has a decent pride;
Who to his people is a gentle guide;
Who only hints at failings that he sees;
Who loves his glebe, his patron, and his ease,
And finds the way to fame and profit is to please.'
The nephew answer'd not, except a sigh
And look of sorrow might be term'd reply;
He saw the fearful hazard of his state,
And held with truth and safety strong debate;
Nor long he reason'd, for the zealous youth
Resolved, though timid, to profess the truth;
And though his friend should like a lion roar,
Truth would he preach, and neither less nor more.
The bells had toll'd—arrived the time of prayer,
The flock assembled, and the 'squire was there:
And now can poet sing, or proseman say,
The disappointment of that trying day?
As he who long had train'd a favourite steed,
(Whose blood and bone gave promise of his speed),
Sanguine with hope, he runs with partial eye
O'er every feature, and his bets are high;
Of triumph sure, he sees the rivals start,
And waits their coming with exulting heart;
Forestalling glory, with impatient glance,
And sure to see his conquering steed advance;
The conquering steed advances—luckless day!
A rival's Herod bears the prize away.
Nor second his, nor third, but lagging last,
With hanging head he comes, by all surpass'd:
Surprise and wrath the owner's mind inflame,
Love turns to scorn, and glory ends in shame;—
Thus waited, high in hope, the partial 'squire,
Eager to hear, impatient to admire:
When the young preacher in the tones that find
A certain passage to the kindling mind,
With air and accent strange, impressive, sad,
Alarm'd the judge—he trembled for the lad;
But when the text announced the power of grace,
Amazement scowl'd upon his clouded face,

At this degenerate son of his illustrious race;
Staring he stood, till hope again arose,
That James might well define the words he chose:
For this he listen'd—but, alas! he found
The preacher always on forbidden ground.
 And now the uncle left the hated pew,
With James, and James's conduct in his view:
A long farewell to all his favourite schemes!
For now no crazed fanatic's frantic dreams
Seem'd vile as James's conduct, or as James:
All he had long derided, hated, fear'd,
This from the chosen youth the uncle heard;—
The needless pause, the fierce disorder'd air,
The groan for sin, the vehemence of prayer,
Gave birth to wrath, that, in a long discourse
Of grace, triumphant rose to four-fold force:
He found his thoughts despised, his rules transgress'd,
And while the anger kindled in his breast,
The pain must be endured that could not be express'd:
Each new idea more inflamed his ire,
As fuel thrown upon a rising fire:
A hearer yet, he sought by threatening sign
To ease his heart, and awe the young divine;
But James refused those angry looks to meet,
Till he dismiss'd his flock, and left his seat:
Exhausted then he felt his trembling frame,
But fix'd his soul—his sentiments the same;
And therefore wise it seem'd to fly from rage,
And seek for shelter in his parsonage:
There, if forsaken, yet consoled to find
Some comforts left, though not a few resign'd;
There, if he lost an erring parent's love,
An honest conscience must the cause approve;
If the nice palate were no longer fed,
The mind enjoy'd delicious thoughts instead;
And if some part of earthly good was flown,
Still was the tithe of ten good farms his own.
 Fear now, and discord, in the village reign,
The cool remonstrate, and the meek complain;
But there is war within, and wisdom pleads in vain:
Now dreads the uncle, and proclaims his dread,

Lest the boy-priest should turn each rustic head;
The certain converts cost him certain wo,
The doubtful fear lest they should join the foe:
Matrons of old, with whom he used to joke,
Now pass his Honour with a pious look;
Lasses, who met him once with lively airs,
Now cross his way, and gravely walk to prayers:
An old companion, whom he long has loved,
By coward fears confess'd his conscience moved;
As the third bottle gave its spirit forth,
And they bore witness to departed worth,
The friend arose, and he too would depart:—
'Man,' said the 'squire, 'thou wert not wont to start;
Hast thou attended to that foolish boy,
Who would abridge all comforts, or destroy?'
  Yes, he had listen'd, who had slumber'd long,
And was convinced that something must be wrong:
But, though affected, still his yielding heart,
And craving palate, took the uncle's part;
Wine now oppress'd him, who, when free from wine,
Could seldom clearly utter his design;
But though by nature and indulgence weak,
Yet, half converted, he resolved to speak;
And, speaking, own'd, 'that in his mind the youth
Had gifts and learning, and that truth was truth:
The 'squire he honour'd, and, for his poor part,
He hated nothing like a hollow heart:
But 'twas a maxim he had often tried,
That right was right, and there he would abide;
He honour'd learning, and he would confess
The preacher had his talents—more or less:
Why not agree? he thought the young divine
Had no such strictness—they might drink and dine;
For them sufficient—but he said before,—
That truth was truth, and he would drink no more.'
  This heard the 'squire with mix'd contempt and pain;
He fear'd the priest this recreant sot would gain.
The favourite nymph, though not a convert made.
Conceived the man she scorn'd her cause would aid;

And when the spirits of her lord were low,
The lass presumed the wicked cause to show:
'It was the wretched life his Honour led,
And would draw vengeance on his guilty head;
Their loves (Heav'n knew how dreadfully distress'd
The thought had made her!) were as yet unbless'd:
And till the church had sanction'd'——Here she saw
The wrath that forced her trembling to withdraw.
  Add to these outward ills, some inward light,
That show'd him all was not correct and right:
Though now he less indulged—and to the poor,
From day to day, sent alms from door to door;
Though he some ease from easy virtues found,
Yet conscience told him he could not compound;
But must himself the darling sin deny,
Change the whole heart—but here a heavy sigh
Proclaim'd, 'How vast the toil! and ah! how weak am I!'
  James too has trouble—he divided sees
A parish, once harmonious and at ease:
With him united are the simply meek,
The warm, the sad, the nervous, and the weak;
The rest his uncle's, save the few beside,
Who own no doctrine, and obey no guide;
With stragglers of each adverse camp, who lend
Their aid to both, but each in turn offend.
  Though zealous still, yet he begins to feel
The heat too fierce, that glows in vulgar zeal;
With pain he hears his simple friends relate
Their week's experience, and their woful state:
With small temptation struggling every hour,
And bravely battling with the tempting power;
His native sense is hurt by strange complaints
Of inward motions in these warring saints;
Who never cast on sinful bait a hook
But they perceive the devil at the hook:
Grieved, yet compell'd to smile, he finds it hard
Against the blunders of conceit to guard;
He sighs to hear the jests his converts cause,
He cannot give their erring zeal applause;
But finds it inconsistent to condemn
The flights and follies he has nursed in them:

These, in opposing minds, contempt produce,
Or mirth occasion, or provoke abuse;
On each momentous theme disgrace they bring,
And give to Scorn her poison and her sting.

16. THE CONFIDANT

Think'st thou I'd make a life of jealousy,
To follow still the changes of the moon,
With fresh suspicion? *Othello*, Act III, Scene 3

Why hast thou lost the fresh blood in thy cheeks,
And given my treasure and my rights in thee
To thick-eyed musing and cursed melancholy?
1 Henry IV, Act II, Scene 3

It is excellent
To have a giant's strength, but tyrannous
To use it as a giant.
Measure for Measure, Act II, Scene 2

Anna was young and lovely—in her eye
The glance of beauty, in her cheek the dye;
Her shape was slender, and her features small,
But graceful, easy, unaffected all:
The liveliest tints her youthful face disclosed;
There beauty sparkled, and there health reposed;
For the pure blood that flush'd that rosy cheek
Spoke what the heart forbad the tongue to speak;
And told the feelings of that heart as well,
Nay, with more candour than the tongue could tell:
Though this fair lass had with the wealthy dwelt,
Yet like the damsel of the cot she felt;
And, at the distant hint or dark surmise,
The blood into the mantling cheek would rise.
  Now Anna's station frequent terrors wrought
In one whose looks were with such meaning fraught;
For on a lady, as an humble friend,
It was her painful office to attend.
  Her duties here were of the usual kind—
And some the body harass'd, some the mind:
Billets she wrote, and tender stories read,
To make the lady sleepy in her bed;

She play'd at whist, but with inferior skill,
And heard the summons as a call to drill;
Music was ever pleasant till she play'd
At a request that no request convey'd;
The lady's tales with anxious looks she heard,
For she must witness what her friend averr'd;
The lady's taste she must in all approve,
Hate whom she hated, whom she loved must love;
These with the various duties of her place,
With care she studied, and perform'd with grace;
She veil'd her troubles in a mask of ease,
And show'd her pleasure was a power to please.
  Such were the damsel's duties; she was poor—
Above a servant, but with service more:
Men on her face with careless freedom gazed,
Nor thought how painful was the glow they raised;
A wealthy few to gain her favour tried,
But not the favour of a grateful bride:
They spoke their purpose with an easy air,
That shamed and frighten'd the dependent fair:
Past time she view'd, the passing time to cheat,
But nothing found to make the present sweet;
With pensive soul she read life's future page,
And saw dependent, poor, repining age.
  But who shall dare t'assert what *years* may bring,
When wonders from the passing *hour* may spring?—
There dwelt a yeoman in the place, whose mind
Was gentle, generous, cultivated, kind;
For thirty years he labour'd; fortune then
Placed the mild rustic with superior men:
A richer Stafford who had lived to save,
What he had treasured to the poorer gave;
Who with a sober mind that treasure view'd,
And the slight studies of his youth renew'd:
He not profoundly, but discreetly read,
And a fair mind with useful culture fed;
Then thought of marriage—'But the great,' said he,
'I shall not suit, nor will the meaner me:'
Anna he saw, admired her modest air;
He thought her virtuous, and he knew her fair;
Love raised his pity for her humble state,

And prompted wishes for her happier fate;
No pride in money would his feelings wound,
Nor vulgar manners hurt him and confound:
He then the lady at the hall address'd,
Sought her consent, and his regard express'd;
Yet if some cause his earnest wish denied,
He begg'd to know it, and he bow'd and sigh'd.
The lady own'd that she was loth to part,
But praised the damsel for her gentle heart,
Her pleasing person, and her blooming health;
But ended thus, 'Her virtue is her wealth.'
'Then is she rich!' he cried, with lively air;
'But whence, so please you, came a lass so fair?'
'A placeman's child was Anna, one who died
And left a widow by afflictions tried;
She to support her infant daughter strove,
But early left the object of her love;
Her youth, her beauty, and her orphan-state
Gave a kind countess interest in her fate;
With her she dwelt, and still might dwelling be,
When the earl's folly caused the lass to flee;
A second friend was she compell'd to shun,
By the rude offers of an uncheck'd son;
I found her then, and with a mother's love
Regard the gentle girl whom you approve;
Yet, e'en with me protection is not peace,
Nor man's designs, nor beauty's trial, cease;
Like sordid boys by costly fruit they feel,
They will not purchase, but they try to steal.'
Now this good lady, like a witness true,
Told but the truth, and all the truth she knew;
And 'tis our duty and our pain to show
Truth this good lady had not means to know.
Yes, there was lock'd within the damsel's breast
A fact important to be now confess'd;
Gently, my muse, th' afflicting tale relate,
And have some feeling for a sister's fate.
Where Anna dwelt, a conquering hero came,—
An Irish captain, Sedley was his name;
And he too had that same prevailing art,
That gave soft wishes to the virgin's heart:

In years they differ'd; he had thirty seen
When this young beauty counted just fifteen;
But still they were a lovely lively pair,
And trod on earth as if they trod on air.
  On love, delightful theme! the captain dwelt
With force still growing with the hopes he felt;
But with some caution and reluctance told,
He had a father crafty, harsh, and old;
Who, as possessing much, would much expect,
Or both, for ever, from his love reject:
Why then offence to one so powerful give,
Who (for their comfort) had not long to live?
  With this poor prospect the deluded maid,
In words confiding, was indeed betray'd;
And, soon as terrors in her bosom rose,
The hero fled; they hinder'd his repose.
Deprived of him she to a parent's breast
Her secret trusted, and her pains impress'd:
Let her to town (so prudence urged) repair,
To shun disgrace, at least to hide it there;
But ere she went, the luckless damsel pray'd
A chosen friend might lend her timely aid:
'Yes! my soul's sister, my Eliza, come,
Hear her last sigh, and ease thy Anna's doom:'
''Tis a fool's wish,' the angry father cried,
But, lost in troubles of his own, complied;
And dear Eliza to her friend was sent,
T' indulge that wish, and be her punishment:
The time arrived, and brought a tenfold dread;
The time was past, and all the terror fled;
The infant died; the face resumed each charm,
And reason now brought trouble and alarm:
'Should her Eliza—no! she was too just,
Too good and kind—but ah! too young to trust.'
Anna return'd, her former place resumed,
And faded beauty with new grace re-bloom'd;
And if some whispers of the past were heard,
They died innoxious, as no cause appear'd;
But other cares on Anna's bosom press'd,
She saw her father gloomy and distress'd;
He died o'erwhelm'd with debt, and soon was shed

The filial sorrow o'er a mother dead:
She sought Eliza's arms, that faithful friend was wed;
Then was compassion by the countess shown,
And all th' adventures of her life are known.
And now beyond her hopes—no longer tried
By slavish awe—she lived a yeoman's bride;
Then bless'd her lot, and with a grateful mind
Was careful, cheerful, vigilant, and kind:
The gentle husband felt supreme delight,
Bless'd by her joy, and happy in her sight;
He saw with pride in every friend and guest
High admiration and regard express'd:
With greater pride, and with superior joy,
He look'd exulting on his first-born boy;
To her fond breast the wife her infant strain'd,
Some feelings utter'd, some were not explain'd;
And she enraptured with her treasure grew,
The sight familiar, but the pleasure new.
Yet there appear'd within that tranquil state
Some threat'ning prospect of uncertain fate;
Between the married when a secret lies,
It wakes suspicion from enforced disguise:
Still thought the wife upon her absent friend,
With all that must upon her truth depend;
'There is no being in the world beside,
Who can discover what that friend will hide;
Who knew the fact, knew not my name or state,
Who these can tell cannot the fact relate;
But thou, Eliza, canst the whole impart,
And all my safety is thy generous heart.'
Mix'd with these fears—but light and transient these—
Fled years of peace, prosperity, and ease;
So tranquil all that scarce a gloomy day
For days of gloom unmix'd prepared the way;
One eve, the wife, still happy in her state,
Sang gaily, thoughtless of approaching fate;
Then came a letter, that (received in dread
Not unobserved) she in confusion read;
The substance this—'Her friend rejoiced to find

That she had riches with a grateful mind;
While poor Eliza had from place to place
Been lured by hope to labour for disgrace;
That every scheme her wandering husband tried,
Pain'd while he lived, and perish'd when he died.'
She then of want in angry style complain'd,
Her child a burthen to her life remain'd,
Her kindred shunn'd her prayers, no friend her soul sustain'd.

'Yet why neglected? Dearest Anna knew
Her worth once tried, her friendship ever true;
She hoped, she trusted, though by wants oppress'd,
To lock the treasured secret in her breast;
Yet, vex'd by trouble, must apply to one,
For kindness due to her for kindness done.'

In Anna's mind was tumult, in her face
Flushings of dread had momentary place:
'I must,' she judged, 'these cruel lines expose,
Or fears, or worse than fears, my crime disclose.'

The letter shown, he said, with sober smile—
'Anna, your friend has not a friendly style:
Say, where could you with this fair lady dwell,
Who boasts of secrets that she scorns to tell?'
'At school,' she answer'd: he 'at school!' replied;
'Nay, then I know the secrets you would hide:
Some early longings these, without dispute,
Some youthful gaspings for forbidden fruit:
Why so disorder'd, love? are such the crimes
That give us sorrow in our graver times?
Come, take a present for your friend, and rest
In perfect peace—you find you are confess'd.'

This cloud, though past, alarm'd the conscious wife,
Presaging gloom and sorrow for her life;
Who to her answer join'd a fervent prayer,
That her Eliza would a sister spare:
If she again—but was there cause?—should send,
Let her direct—and then she named a friend:
A sad expedient untried friends to trust,
And still to fear the tried may be unjust:
Such is his pain, who, by his debt oppress'd,
Seeks by new bonds a temporary rest.

Few were her peaceful days till Anna read
The words she dreaded, and had cause to dread:—
'Did she believe, did she, unkind, suppose
That thus Eliza's friendship was to close?
No! though she tried, and her desire was plain,
To break the friendly bond, she strove in vain:
Ask'd she for silence? why so loud the call,
And yet the token of her love so small?
By means like these will you attempt to bind
And check the movements of an injured mind?
Poor as I am, I shall be proud to show
What dangerous secrets I may safely know:
Secrets to men of jealous minds convey'd,
Have many a noble house in ruins laid:
Anna, I trust, although with wrongs beset,
And urged by want, I shall be faithful yet;
But what temptation may from these arise,
To take a slighted woman by surprise,
Becomes a subject for your serious care—
For who offends, must for offence prepare.'
Perplex'd, dismay'd, the wife foresaw her doom;
A day deferr'd was yet a day to come;
But still, though painful, her suspended state,
She dreaded more the crisis of her fate;
Better to die than Stafford's scorn to meet,
And her strange friend perhaps would be discreet:
Presents she sent, and made a strong appeal
To woman's feelings, begging her to feel;
With too much force she wrote of jealous men,
And her tears falling spoke beyond the pen;
Eliza's silence she again implored,
And promised all that prudence could afford.
For looks composed and careless Anna tried;
She seem'd in trouble, and unconscious sigh'd:
The faithful husband, who devoutly loved
His silent partner, with concern reproved:
'What secret sorrows on my Anna press,
That love may not partake, nor care redress?'
'None, none,' she answer'd, with a look so kind,
That the fond man determined to be blind.
A few succeeding weeks of brief repose

In Anna's cheeks revived the faded rose;
A hue like this the western sky displays,
That glows awhile, and withers as we gaze.
  Again the friend's tormenting letter came—
'The wants she suffer'd were affection's shame;
She with her child a life of terrors led,
Unhappy fruit! but of a lawful bed:
Her friend was tasting every bliss in life,
The joyful mother, and the wealthy wife;
While she was placed in doubt, in fear, in want,
To starve on trifles that the happy grant;
Poorly for all her faithful silence paid,
And tantalized by ineffectual aid:
She could not thus a beggar's lot endure;
She wanted something permanent and sure:
If they were friends, then equal be their lot,
And she was free to speak if they were not.'
  Despair and terror seized the wife, to find
The artful workings of a vulgar mind:
Money she had not, but the hint of dress
Taught her new bribes, new terrors to redress:
She with such feeling then described her woes,
That envy's self might on the view repose;
Then to a mother's pains she made appeal,
And painted grief like one compell'd to feel.
  Yes! so she felt, that in her air, her face,
In every purpose, and in every place;
In her slow motion, in her languid mien,
The grief, the sickness of her soul were seen.
  Of some mysterious ill the husband sure,
Desired to trace it, for he hoped to cure;
Something he knew obscurely, and had seen
His wife attend a cottage on the green;
Love, loth to wound, endured conjecture long,
Till fear would speak, and spoke in language strong.
  'All I must know, my Anna—truly know
Whence these emotions, terrors, troubles flow;
Give me thy grief, and I will fairly prove
Mine is no selfish, no ungenerous love.'
  Now Anna's soul the seat of strife became,
Fear with respect contended, love with shame;

But fear prevailing was the ruling guide,
Prescribing what to show and what to hide.
'It is my friend,' she said—'but why disclose
A woman's weakness struggling with her woes?
Yes, she has grieved me by her fond complaints,
The wrongs she suffers, the distress she paints:
Something we do—but she afflicts me still,
And says, with power to help, I want the will;
This plaintive style I pity and excuse,
Help when I can, and grieve when I refuse;
But here my useless sorrows I resign,
And will be happy in a love like thine.'
The husband doubted; he was kind but cool:—
''Tis a strong friendship to arise at school;
Once more then, love, once more the sufferer aid,—
I too can pity, but I must upbraid;
Of these vain feelings then thy bosom free,
Nor be o'erwhelm'd by useless sympathy.'
The wife again despatch'd the useless bribe,
Again essay'd her terrors to describe;
Again with kindest words entreated peace,
And begg'd her offerings for a time might cease.
A calm succeeded, but too like the one
That causes terror ere the storm comes on:
A secret sorrow lived in Anna's heart,
In Stafford's mind a secret fear of art;
Not long they lasted—this determined foe
Knew all her claims, and nothing would forego;
Again her letter came, where Anna read,
'My child, one cause of my distress, is dead:
Heav'n has my infant:' 'Heartless wretch!' she cried,
'Is this thy joy?' 'I am no longer tied:
Now will I, hast'ning to my friend, partake
Her cares and comforts, and no more forsake;
Now shall we both in equal station move,
Save that my friend enjoys a husband's love.'
Complaint and threats so strong the wife amazed,
Who wildly on her cottage-neighbour gazed;
Her tones, her trembling, first betray'd her grief;
When floods of tears gave anguish its relief.
She fear'd that Stafford would refuse assent,

And knew her selfish friend would not relent;
She must petition, yet delay'd the task,
Ashamed, afraid, and yet compell'd to ask;
Unknown to him some object filled her mind,
And, once suspicious, he became unkind:
They sate one evening, each absorb'd in gloom,
When, hark! a noise and rushing to the room,
The friend tripp'd lightly in, and laughing said,
'I come.'
Anna received her with an anxious mind,
And meeting whisper'd, 'Is Eliza kind?'
Reserved and cool, the husband sought to prove
The depth and force of this mysterious love.
To nought that pass'd between the stranger-friend
And his meek partner seem'd he to attend;
But, anxious, listen'd to the lightest word
That might some knowledge of his guest afford;
And learn the reason one to him so dear
Should feel such fondness, yet betray such fear.
Soon he perceived this uninvited guest,
Unwelcome too, a sovereign power possess'd;
Lofty she was and careless, while the meek
And humbled Anna was afraid to speak:
As mute she listen'd with a painful smile,
Her friend sate laughing and at ease the while,
Telling her idle tales with all the glee
Of careless and unfeeling levity.
With calm good sense he knew his wife endued,
And now with wounded pride her conduct view'd;
Her speech was low, her every look convey'd—
'I am a slave, subservient and afraid.'
All trace of comfort vanish'd if she spoke,
The noisy friend upon her purpose broke;
To her remarks with insolence replied,
And her assertions doubted or denied;
While the meek Anna like an infant shook,
Wo-struck and trembling at the serpent's look.
'There is,' said Stafford, 'yes, there is a cause—
This creature frights her, overpowers and awes.'
Six weeks had pass'd—'In truth, my love, this friend
Has liberal notions; what does she intend?

Without a hint she came, and will she stay
Till she receives the hint to go away?'
  Confused the wife replied, in spite of truth,
'I love the dear companion of my youth.'
''Tis well,' said Stafford; 'then your loves renew;
Trust me, your rivals, Anna, will be few.'
  Though playful this, she felt too much distress'd
T' admit the consolation of a jest;
Ill she reposed, and in her dreams would sigh
And murmuring forth her anguish beg to die;
With sunken eye, slow pace, and pallid cheek,
She look'd confusion, and she fear'd to speak.
  All this the friend beheld, for, quick of sight,
She knew the husband eager for her flight;
And that by force alone she could retain
The lasting comforts she had hope to gain:
She now perceived, to win her post for life,
She must infuse fresh terrors in the wife;
Must bid to friendship's feebler ties adieu,
And boldly claim the object in her view;
She saw the husband's love, and knew the power
Her friend might use in some propitious hour.
  Meantime the anxious wife, from pure distress
Assuming courage, said, 'I will confess;'
But with her children felt a parent's pride,
And sought once more the hated truth to hide.
  Offended, grieved, impatient, Stafford bore
The odious change till he could bear no more;
A friend to truth, in speech and action plain,
He held all fraud and cunning in disdain;
But fraud to find, and falsehood to detect,
For once he fled to measures indirect.
  One day the friends were seated in that room
The guest with care adorn'd, and named her home:
To please the eye, there curious prints were placed,
And some light volumes to amuse the taste;
Letters and music, on a table laid,
The favourite studies of the fair betray'd;
Beneath the window was the toilet spread,
And the fire gleam'd upon a crimson bed.
  In Anna's looks and falling tears were seen

How interesting had their subjects been:
'Oh! then,' resumed the friend, 'I plainly find
That you and Stafford know each other's mind;
I must depart, must on the world be thrown,
Like one discarded, worthless and unknown;
But shall I carry, and to please a foe,
A painful secret in my bosom? No!
Think not your friend a reptile you may tread
Beneath your feet, and say, the worm is dead;
I have some feeling, and will not be made
The scorn of her whom love cannot persuade:
Would not your word, your slightest wish, effect
All that I hope, petition, or expect?
The power you have, but you the use decline—
Proof that you feel not, or you fear not mine.
There was a time, when I, a tender maid,
Flew at a call, and your desires obey'd;
A very mother to the child became,
Consoled your sorrow, and conceal'd your shame;
But now, grown rich and happy, from the door
You thrust a bosom-friend, despised and poor;
That child alive, its mother might have known
The hard, ungrateful spirit she has shown.'
   Here paused the guest, and Anna cried at length—
'You try me, cruel friend! beyond my strength;
Would I had been beside my infant laid,
Where none would vex me, threaten, or upbraid.'
   In Anna's looks the friend beheld despair;
Her speech she soften'd, and composed her air;
Yet, while professing love, she answered still—
'You can befriend me, but you want the will.'
They parted thus, and Anna went her way,
To shed her secret sorrows, and to pray.
   Stafford, amused with books, and fond of home,
By reading oft dispell'd the evening gloom;
History or tale—all heard him with delight,
And thus was pass'd this memorable night.
   The listening friend bestow'd a flattering smile;
A sleeping boy the mother held the while;
And ere she fondly bore him to his bed,
On his fair face the tear of anguish shed.

And now his task resumed, 'My tale,' said he,
'Is short and sad, short may our sadness be!'—
'The Caliph Harun, as historians tell,
Ruled, for a tyrant, admirably well;
Where his own pleasures were not touch'd, to men
He was humane, and sometimes even then;
Harun was fond of fruits, and gardens fair,
And wo to all whom he found poaching there:
Among his pages was a lively boy,
Eager in search of every trifling joy;
His feelings vivid, and his fancy strong,
He sigh'd for pleasure while he shrank from wrong;
When by the caliph in the garden placed
He saw the treasures which he long'd to taste;
And oft alone he ventured to behold
Rich hanging fruits with rind of glowing gold;
Too long he staid forbidden bliss to view,
His virtue failing, as his longings grew;
Athirst and wearied with the noon-tide heat,
Fate to the garden led his luckless feet;
With eager eyes and open mouth he stood,
Smelt the sweet breath, and touch'd the fragrant food;
The tempting beauty sparkling in the sun
Charm'd his young sense—he ate, and was undone:
When the fond glutton paused, his eyes around
He turn'd, and eyes upon him turning found;
Pleased he beheld the spy, a brother-page,
A friend allied in office and in age;
Who promised much that secret he would be,
But high the price he fix'd on secrecy.
'"Were you suspected, my unhappy friend,"
Began the boy, "where would your sorrows end?
In all the palace there is not a page
The caliph would not torture in his rage:
I think I see thee now impaled alive,
Writhing in pangs—but come, my friend! revive;
Had some beheld you, all your purse contains
Could not have saved you from terrific pains;
I scorn such meanness; and, if not in debt,
Would not an asper on your folly set."
'The hint was strong; young Osmyn search'd his store

For bribes, and found he soon could bribe no more;
That time arrived, for Osmyn's stock was small,
And the young tyrant now possess'd it all;
The cruel youth, with his companions near,
Gave the broad hint that raised the sudden fear;
Th' ungenerous insult now was daily shown,
And Osmyn's peace and honest pride were flown;
Then came augmenting woes, and fancy strong
Drew forms of suffering, a tormenting throng;
He felt degraded, and the struggling mind
Dared not be free, and could not be resign'd;
And all his pains and fervent prayers obtain'd
Was truce from insult, while the fears remain'd.
 'One day it chanced that this degraded boy
And tyrant-friend were fix'd at their employ;
Who now had thrown restraint and form aside,
And for his bribe in plainer speech applied:
"Long have I waited, and the last supply
Was but a pittance, yet how patient I!
But give me now what thy first terrors gave,
My speech shall praise thee, and my silence save."
 'Osmyn had found, in many a dreadful day,
The tyrant fiercer when he seem'd in play:
He begg'd forbearance; "I have not to give;
Spare me awhile, although 'tis pain to live:
Oh! had that stolen fruit the power possess'd
To war with life, I now had been at rest."
 '"So fond of death," replied the boy, "'tis plain
Thou hast no certain notion of the pain;
But to the caliph were a secret shown,
Death has no pain that would be then unknown."
 'Now,' says the story, 'in a closet near,
The monarch seated, chanced the boys to hear;
There oft he came, when wearied on his throne,
To read, sleep, listen, pray, or be alone.
 'The tale proceeds, when first the caliph found
That he was robb'd, although alone, he frown'd;
And swore in wrath, that he would send the boy
Far from his notice, favour, or employ;
But gentler movements soothed his ruffled mind,
And his own failings taught him to be kind.

'Relenting thoughts then painted Osmyn young,
His passion urgent, and temptation strong;
And that he suffer'd from that villain-spy
Pains worse than death till he desired to die;
Then if his morals had received a stain,
His bitter sorrows made him pure again:
To Reason, Pity lent her generous aid,
For one so tempted, troubled, and betray'd;
And a free pardon the glad boy restored
To the kind presence of a gentle lord;
Who from his office and his country drove
That traitor-friend, whom pains nor pray'rs could move;
Who raised the fears no mortal could endure,
And then with cruel av'rice sold the cure.
'My tale is ended; but, to be applied,
I must describe the place where caliphs hide.'
Here both females look'd alarm'd, distress'd,
With hurried passions hard to be express'd.
'It was a closet by a chamber placed,
Where slept a lady of no vulgar taste;
Her friend attended in that chosen room
That she had honour'd and proclaim'd her home;
To please the eye were chosen pictures placed,
And some light volumes to amuse the taste;
Letters and music on a table laid,
For much the lady wrote, and often play'd;
Beneath the window was a toilet spread,
And a fire gleam'd upon a crimson bed.'
He paused, he rose; with troubled joy the wife
Felt the new era of her changeful life;
Frankness and love appear'd in Stafford's face,
And all her trouble to delight gave place.
Twice made the guest an effort to sustain
Her feelings, twice resumed her seat in vain,
Nor could suppress her shame, nor could support her pain:
Quick she retired, and all the dismal night.
Thought of her guilt, her folly, and her flight;
Then sought unseen her miserable home,
To think of comforts lost, and brood on wants to come.

17. RESENTMENT

She hath a tear for pity, and a hand
Open as day for melting charity;
Yet, notwithstanding, being incensed, is flint—
Her temper, therefore, must be well observ'd.

2 Henry IV, Act IV, Scene 4

...Three or four wenches where I stood cried—'Alas! good soul!' and forgave him with all their hearts: but there is no heed to be taken of them; if Caesar had stabb'd their mothers, they would have done no less.

Julius Caesar, Act I, Scene 2

How dost? Art cold?
I'm cold myself—Where is the straw, my fellow?
The art of our necessities is strange,
That can make vile things precious.

King Lear, Act III, Scene 2

Females there are of unsuspicious mind,
Easy and soft, and credulous and kind;
Who, when offended for the twentieth time,
Will hear th' offender and forgive the crime:
And there are others whom, like these to cheat,
Asks but the humblest effort of deceit;
But they, once injured, feel a strong disdain,
And, seldom pardoning, never trust again;
Urged by religion, they forgive—but yet
Guard the warm heart, and never more forget:
Those are like wax—apply them to the fire,
Melting, they take th' impressions you desire;
Easy to mould, and fashion as you please,
And again moulded with an equal ease:
Like smelted iron these the forms retain,
But once impress'd will never melt again.
A busy port a serious merchant made
His chosen place to recommence his trade;
And brought his lady, who, their children dead,
Their native seat of recent sorrow fled:
The husband duly on the quay was seen,
The wife at home became at length serene;
There in short time the social couple grew
With all acquainted, friendly with a few;

When the good lady, by disease assail'd,
In vain resisted—hope and science fail'd:
Then spake the female friends, by pity led,
'Poor merchant Paul! what think ye? will he wed?
A quiet, easy, kind, religious man,
Thus can he rest?—I wonder if he can.'
He too, as grief subsided in his mind,
Gave place to notions of congenial kind;
Grave was the man, as we have told before;
His years were forty—he might pass for more;
Composed his features were, his stature low,
His air important, and his motion slow;
His dress became him, it was neat and plain,
The colour purple, and without a stain;
His words were few, and special was his care
In simplest terms his purpose to declare;
A man more civil, sober, and discreet,
More grave and courteous, you could seldom meet:
Though frugal he, yet sumptuous was his board,
As if to prove how much he could afford;
For though reserved himself, he loved to see
His table plenteous, and his neighbours free:
Among these friends he sat in solemn style,
And rarely soften'd to a sober smile;
For this observant friends their reasons gave—
'Concerns so vast would make the idlest grave;
And for such man to be of language free,
Would seem incongruous as a singing tree:
Trees have their music, but the birds they shield
The pleasing tribute for protection yield;
Each ample tree the tuneful choir defends,
As this rich merchant cheers his happy friends!'
In the same town it was his chance to meet
A gentle lady, with a mind discreet;
Neither in life's decline, nor bloom of youth,
One fam'd for maiden modesty and truth:
By nature cool, in pious habits bred,
She look'd on lovers with a virgin's dread:
Deceivers, rakes, and libertines were they,
And harmless beauty their pursuit and prey;
As bad as giants in the ancient times

Were modern lovers, and the same their crimes:
Soon as she heard of her all-conquering charms,
At once she fled to her defensive arms;
Conn'd o'er the tales her maiden aunt had told,
And, statue-like, was motionless and cold;
From prayer of love, like that Pygmalion pray'd,
Ere the hard stone became the yielding maid—
A different change in this chaste nymph ensued,
And turn'd to stone the breathing flesh and blood:
Whatever youth described his wounded heart,
'He came to rob her, and she scorn'd his art;
And who of raptures once presumed to speak,
Told listening maids he thought them fond and weak:
But should a worthy man his hopes display
In few plain words, and beg a *yes* or *nay*,
He would deserve an answer just and plain,
Since adulation only moved disdain—
Sir, if my friends object not, come again.'
   Hence, our grand lover, though he liked the face,
Praised not a feature—dwelt not on a grace;
But in the simplest terms declared his state,
'A widow'd man, who wish'd a virtuous mate;
Who fear'd neglect, and was compell'd to trust
Dependents wasteful, idle, or unjust;
Or should they not the trusted stores destroy,
At best, they could not help him to enjoy;
But with her person and her prudence blest,
His acts would prosper, and his soul have rest:
Would she be his?'—'Why, that was much to say;
She would consider: he awhile might stay;
She liked his manners, and believed his word;
He did not flatter, flattery she abhorr'd:
It was her happy lot in peace to dwell—
Would change make better what was now so well?
But she would ponder.'—'This,' he said, 'was kind,'
And begg'd to know 'when she had fix'd her mind.'
   Romantic maidens would have scorn'd the air,
And the cool prudence of a mind so fair;
But well it pleased this wiser maid to find
Her own mild virtues in her lover's mind.
   His worldly wealth she sought, and quickly grew

Pleased with her search, and happy in the view
Of vessels freighted with abundant stores,
Of rooms whose treasures press'd the groaning floors;
And he of clerks and servants could display
A little army, on a public day:
Was this a man like needy bard to speak
Of balmy lip, bright eye, or rosy cheek?
 The sum appointed for her widow'd state,
Fix'd by her friend, excited no debate;
Then the kind lady gave her hand and heart,
And, never finding, never dealt with art:
In his engagements she had no concern;
He taught her not, nor had she wish to learn:
On him in all occasions she relied,
His word her surety, and his worth her pride.
 When ship was launch'd, and merchant Paul had share,
A bounteous feast became the lady's care;
Who then her entry to the dinner made,
In costly raiment, and with kind parade.
 Call'd by this duty on a certain day,
And robed to grace it in a rich array,
Forth from her room with measured step she came,
Proud of th' event, and stately look'd the dame:
The husband met her at his study door—
'This way, my love—one moment and no more:
A trifling business—you will understand,
The law requires that you affix your hand;
But first attend, and you shall learn the cause
Why forms like these have been prescribed by laws:'
Then from his chair a man in black arose,
And with much quickness hurried off his prose:
That 'Ellen Paul the wife, and so forth, freed
From all control, her own the act and deed,
And forasmuch'——said she, 'I've no distrust,
For he that asks it is discreet and just;
Our friends are waiting—where am I to sign?—
There!——Now be ready when we meet to dine.'
 This said, she hurried off in great delight,
The ship was launch'd, and joyful was the night.
 Now, says the reader, and in much disdain,

This serious merchant was a rogue in grain;
A treacherous wretch, an artful, sober knave,
And ten times worse for manners cool and grave;
And she devoid of sense, to set her hand
To scoundrel deeds she could not understand.
Alas! 'tis true; and I in vain had tried
To soften crime, that cannot be denied;
And might have labour'd many a tedious verse
The latent cause of mischief to rehearse:
Be it confess'd, that long, with troubled look,
This trader view'd a huge accompting book
(His former marriage for a time delay'd
The dreaded hour, the present lent its aid);
But he too clearly saw the evil day,
And put the terror, by deceit, away;
Thus by connecting with his sorrows crime,
He gain'd a portion of uneasy time.—
All this too late the injured lady saw,
What law had given, again she gave to law;
His guilt, her folly—these at once impress'd
Their lasting feelings on her guileless breast.
'Shame I can bear,' she cried, 'and want sustain,
But will not see this guilty wretch again:'
For all was lost, and he, with many a tear,
Confess'd the fault—she turning scorn'd to hear.
To legal claims he yielded all his worth,
But small the portion, and the wrong'd were wroth,
Nor to their debtor would a part allow;
And where to live he knew not—knew not how.
The wife a cottage found, and thither went
The suppliant man, but she would not relent:
Thenceforth she utter'd with indignant tone,
'I feel the misery, and will feel alone:'—
He would turn servant for her sake, would keep
The poorest school; the very streets would sweep,
To show his love—'It was already shown:
And her affliction should be all her own.
His wants and weakness might have touch'd her heart,
But from his meanness she resolved to part.'
In a small alley was she lodged, beside
Its humblest poor, and at the view she cried:

'Welcome—yes! let we welcome, if I can,
The fortune dealt me by this cruel man;
Welcome this low thatch'd roof, this shatter'd door,
These walls of clay, this miserable floor;
Welcome my envied neighbours; this, to you,
Is all familiar—all to me is new:
You have no hatred to the loathsome meal;
Your firmer nerves no trembling terrors feel,
Nor, what you must expose, desire you to conceal;
What your coarse feelings bear without offence,
Disgusts my taste, and poisons every sense:
Daily shall I your sad relations hear,
Of wanton women, and of men severe;
There will dire curses, dreadful oaths abound,
And vile expressions shock me and confound;
Noise of dull wheels, and songs with horrid words,
Will be the music that this lane affords;
Mirth that disgusts, and quarrels that degrade
The human mind, must my retreat invade:
Hard is my fate! yet easier to sustain,
Than to abide with guilt and fraud again;
A grave impostor! who expects to meet,
In such grey locks and gravity, deceit?
Where the sea rages, and the billows roar,
Men know the danger, and they quit the shore;
But, be there nothing in the way descried,
When o'er the rocks smooth runs the wicked tide—
Sinking unwarn'd, they execrate the shock,
And the dread peril of the sunken rock.'
  A frowning world had now the man to dread,
Taught in no arts, to no profession bred:
Pining in grief, beset with constant care,
Wandering he went, to rest he knew not where.
  Meantime the wife—but she abjured the name—
Endured her lot, and struggled with the shame;
When lo! an uncle on the mother's side,
In nature something, as in blood allied,
Admired her firmness, his protection gave,
And show'd a kindness she disdain'd to crave.
  Frugal and rich the man, and frugal grew
The sister-mind, without a selfish view;

And further still—the temp'rate pair agreed
With what they saved the patient poor to feed:
His whole estate, when to the grave consign'd,
Left the good kinsman to the kindred mind;
Assured that law, with spell secure and tight,
Had fix'd it as her own peculiar right.
Now to her ancient residence removed,
She lived as widow, well endow'd and loved;
Decent her table was, and to her door
Came daily welcomed the neglected poor:
The absent sick were soothed by her relief,
As her free bounty sought the haunts of grief;
A plain and homely charity had she,
And loved the objects of her alms to see;
With her own hands she dress'd the savoury meat,
With her own fingers wrote the choice receipt;
She heard all tales that injured wives relate,
And took a double interest in their fate;
But of all husbands not a wretch was known
So vile, so mean, so cruel, as her own.
This bounteous lady kept an active spy,
To search th' abodes of want, and to supply;
The gentle Susan served the liberal dame—
Unlike their notions, yet their deeds the same:
No practised villain could a victim find,
Than this stern lady more completely blind;
Nor (if detected in his fraud) could meet
One less disposed to pardon a deceit;
The wrong she treasured, and on no pretence
Received th' offender, or forgot th' offence:
But the kind servant, to the thrice-proved knave
A fourth time listen'd, and the past forgave.
First in her youth, when she was blithe and gay,
Came a smooth rogue, and stole her love away;
Then to another and another flew,
To boast the wanton mischief he could do:
Yet she forgave him, though so great her pain,
That she was never blithe or gay again.
Then came a spoiler, who, with villain-art,
Implored her hand, and agonized her heart;
He seized her purse, in idle waste to spend

With a vile wanton, whom she call'd her friend;
Five years she suffer'd—he had revell'd five—
Then came to show her he was just alive;
Alone he came, his vile companion dead;
And he, a wand'ring pauper, wanting bread;
His body wasted, wither'd life and limb,
When this kind soul became a slave to him:
Nay, she was sure that, should he now survive,
No better husband would be left alive;
For him she mourn'd, and then, alone and poor,
Sought and found comfort at her lady's door:
Ten years she served, and, mercy her employ,
Her tasks were pleasure, and her duty joy.
Thus lived the mistress and the maid, design'd
Each other's aid—one cautious, and both kind:
Oft at their window, working, they would sigh
To see the aged and the sick go by;
Like wounded bees, that at their home arrive,
Slowly and weak, but labouring for the hive.
The busy people of a mason's yard
The curious lady view'd with much regard;
With steady motion she perceived them draw
Through blocks of stone the slowly-working saw;
It gave her pleasure and surprise to see
Among these men the signs of revelry:
Cold was the season, and confined their view,
Tedious their tasks, but merry were the crew:
There she beheld an aged pauper wait,
Patient and still, to take an humble freight;
Within the panniers on an ass he laid
The ponderous grit, and for the portion paid;
This he re-sold, and, with each trifling gift,
Made shift to live, and wretched was the shift.
Now will it be by every reader told
Who was this humble trader, poor and old.—
In vain an author would a name suppress,
From the least hint a reader learns to guess;
Of children lost, our novels sometimes treat,
We never care—assured again to meet:
In vain the writer for concealment tries,
We trace his purpose under all disguise;

Nay, though he tells us they are dead and gone,
Of whom we wot—they will appear anon;
Our favourites fight, are wounded, hopeless lie,
Survive they cannot—nay, they cannot die;
Now, as these tricks and stratagems are known,
'Tis best, at once, the simple truth to own.
  This was the husband—in an humble shed
He nightly slept, and daily sought his bread:
Once for relief the weary man applied;
'Your wife is rich,' the angry vestry cried:
Alas! he dared not to his wife complain,
Feeling her wrongs, and fearing her disdain:
By various methods he had tried to live,
But not one effort would subsistence give:
He was an usher in a school, till noise
Made him less able than the weaker boys;
On messages he went, till he in vain
Strove names, or words, or meanings to retain;
Each small employment in each neighbouring town
By turn he took, to lay as quickly down:
For, such his fate, he fail'd in all he plann'd,
And nothing prosper'd in his luckless hand.
  At his old home, his motive half suppress'd,
He sought no more for riches, but for rest:
There lived the bounteous wife, and at her gate
He saw in cheerful groups the needy wait;
'Had he a right with bolder hope t' apply?'
He ask'd—was answer'd, and went groaning by:
For some remains of spirit, temper, pride,
Forbade a prayer he knew would be denied.
  Thus was the grieving man, with burthen'd ass,
Seen day by day along the street to pass:
'Who is he, Susan? who the poor old man?
He never calls—do make him, if you can.'—
The conscious damsel still delay'd to speak,
She stopp'd confused, and had her words to seek;
From Susan's fears the fact her mistress knew,
And cried—'The wretch! what scheme has he in view?
Is this his lot?—but let him, let him feel—
Who wants the courage, not the will to steal.'

A dreadful winter came, each day severe,
Misty when mild, and icy cold when clear;
And still the humble dealer took his load,
Returning slow, and shivering on the road:
The lady, still relentless, saw him come,
And said—'I wonder, has the wretch a home?'
'A hut! a hovel!'—'Then his fate appears
To suit his crime;'—'Yes, lady, not his years;—
No! nor his sufferings—nor that form decay'd.'
'Well! let the parish give its paupers aid:
You must the vileness of his acts allow;'
'And you, dear lady, that he feels it now.'
'When such dissemblers on their deeds reflect,
Can they the pity they refused expect?
He that doth evil, evil shall he dread.'—
'The snow,' quoth Susan, 'falls upon his bed—
It blows beside the thatch—it melts upon his head.'—
''Tis weakness, child, for grieving guilt to feel:'
'Yes, but he never sees a wholesome meal;
Through his bare dress appears his shrivell'd skin,
And ill he fares without, and worse within:
With that weak body, lame, diseased, and slow,
What cold, pain, peril, must the sufferer know!'
'Think on his crime.'—'Yes, sure 'twas very wrong;
But look, (God bless him!) how he gropes along.'—
'Brought me to shame.'—'Oh! yes, I know it all—
What cutting blast! and he can scarcely crawl;
He freezes as he moves—he dies! if he should fall:
With cruel fierceness drives this icy sleet—
And must a Christian perish in the street,
In sight of Christians?—There! at last, he lies;—
Nor unsupported can he ever rise:
He cannot live.'—'But is he fit to die?'—
Here Susan softly mutter'd a reply,
Look'd round the room—said something of its state,
Dives the rich, and Lazarus at his gate;
And then aloud—'In pity do behold
The man affrighten'd, weeping, trembling, cold:
Oh! how those flakes of snow their entrance win
Through the poor rags, and keep the frost within;
His very heart seems frozen as he goes,

Leading that starved companion of his woes:
He tried to pray—his lips, I saw them move,
And he so turn'd his piteous looks above;
But the fierce wind the willing heart opposed,
And, ere he spoke, the lips in misery closed:
Poor suffering object! yes, for ease you pray'd,
And God will hear—he only, I'm afraid.'
  'Peace! Susan, peace! Pain ever follows sin.'—
'Ah! then,' thought Susan, 'when will ours begin?'
'When reach'd his home, to what a cheerless fire
And chilling bed will those cold limbs retire!
Yet ragged, wretched as it is, that bed
Takes half the space of his contracted shed;
I saw the thorns beside the narrow grate,
With straw collected in a putrid state:
There will he, kneeling, strive the fire to raise,
And that will warm him, rather than the blaze;
The sullen, smoky blaze, that cannot last
One moment after this attempt is past:
And I so warmly and so purely laid,
To sink to rest—indeed, I am afraid.'—
'Know you his conduct?'—'Yes, indeed I know—
And how he wanders in the wind and snow:
Safe in our rooms the threat'ning storm we hear,
But he feels strongly what we faintly fear.'
'Wilful was rich, and he the storm defied;
Wilful is poor, and must the storm abide;'
Said the stern lady—''Tis in vain to feel;
Go and prepare the chicken for our meal.'
  Susan her task reluctantly began,
And utter'd as she went—'The poor old man!'—
But while her soft and ever-yielding heart
Made strong protest against her lady's part,
The lady's self began to think it wrong,
To feel so wrathful and resent so long.
  'No more the wretch would she receive again,
No more behold him—but she would sustain;
Great his offence, and evil was his mind—
But he had suffer'd, and she would be kind:
She spurn'd such baseness, and she found within
A fair acquittal from so foul a sin;

Yet she too err'd, and must of Heaven expect
To be rejected, him should she reject.'
 Susan was summon'd—'I'm about to do
A foolish act, in part seduced by you;
Go to the creature—say that I intend,
Foe to his sins, to be his sorrow's friend;
Take, for his present comforts, food and wine,
And mark his feelings at this act of mine:
Observe if shame be o'er his features spread,
By his own victim to be soothed and fed;
But, this inform him, that it is not love
That prompts my heart, that duties only move:
Say, that no merits in his favour plead,
But miseries only, and his abject need;
Nor bring me grov'ling thanks, nor high-flown praise;
I would his spirits, not his fancy raise:
Give him no hope that I shall ever more
A man so vile to my esteem restore;
But warn him rather, that, in time of rest,
His crimes be all remember'd and confess'd:
I know not all that form the sinner's debt,
But there is one that he must not forget.'
 The mind of Susan prompted her with speed
To act her part in every courteous deed:
All that was kind she was prepared to say,
And keep the lecture for a future day;
When he had all life's comforts by his side,
Pity might sleep, and good advice be tried.
 This done, the mistress felt disposed to look,
As self-approving, on a pious book:
Yet, to her native bias still inclined,
She felt her act too merciful and kind;
But when, long musing on the chilling scene
So lately past—the frost and sleet so keen—
The man's whole misery in a single view—
Yes! she could think some pity was his due.
 Thus fix'd, she heard not her attendant glide
With soft slow step—till, standing by her side,
The trembling servant gasp'd for breath, and shed
Relieving tears, then utter'd—'He is dead!'
 'Dead!' said the startled lady; 'Yes, he fell

Close at the door where he was wont to dwell;
There his sole friend, the ass, was standing by,
Half dead himself, to see his master die.'
'Expired he then, good Heaven! for want of food?'
'No! crusts and water in a corner stood;—
To have this plenty, and to wait so long,
And to be right too late, is doubly wrong:
Then, every day to see him totter by,
And to forbear—Oh! what a heart had I!'
'Blame me not, child; I tremble at the news.'
''Tis my own heart,' said Susan, 'I accuse:
To have this money in my purse—to know
What grief was his, and what to grief we owe;
To see him often, always to conceive
How he must pine and languish, groan and grieve;
And every day in ease and peace to dine,
And rest in comfort!—what a heart is mine!'—

18. THE WAGER

'Tis thought your deer doth hold you at a bay.
Taming of the Shrew, Act v, Scene 2

I choose her for myself:
If she and I are pleased, what's that to you?
Act ii, Scene 1

Let's send each one to his wife,
And he whose wife is most obedient...
Shall win the wager. Act v, Scene 2

Now by the world it is a lusty wench,
I love her ten times more than e'er I did.
Act ii, Scene 1

Counter and Clubb were men in trade, whose pains,
Credit, and prudence, brought them constant gains;
Partners and punctual, every friend agreed
Counter and Clubb were men who must succeed.
When they had fix'd some little time in life,
Each thought of taking to himself a wife:
As men in trade alike, as men in love
They seem'd with no according views to move;
As certain ores in outward view the same,

They show'd their difference when the magnet came.
Counter was vain: with spirit strong and high,
'Twas not in him like suppliant swain to sigh:
'His wife might o'er his men and maids preside,
And in her province be a judge and guide;
But what he thought, or did, or wish'd to do,
She must not know, or censure if she knew;
At home, abroad, by day, by night, if he
On aught determined, so it was to be:
How is a man,' he ask'd, 'for business fit,
Who to a female can his will submit?
Absent awhile, let no inquiring eye
Or plainer speech presume to question why:
But all be silent; and, when seen again,
Let all be cheerful—shall a wife complain?
Friends I invite, and who shall dare t'object,
Or look on them with coolness or neglect?
No! I must ever of my house be head,
And, thus obey'd, I condescend to wed.'
  Clubb heard the speech—'My friend is nice,' said he;
'A wife with less respect will do for me:
How is he certain such a prize to gain?
What he approves, a lass may learn to feign,
And so affect t'obey till she begins to reign;
Awhile complying, she may vary then,
And be as wives of more unwary men;
Beside, to him who plays such lordly part,
How shall a tender creature yield her heart?
Should he the promised confidence refuse,
She may another more confiding choose;
May show her anger, yet her purpose hide,
And wake his jealousy, and wound his pride.
In one so humbled, who can trace the friend?
I on an equal, not a slave, depend;
If true, my confidence is wisely placed,
And being false, she only is disgraced.'
  Clubb, with these notions, cast his eyes around,
And one so easy soon a partner found.
The lady chosen was of good repute;
Meekness she had not, and was seldom mute;
Though quick to anger, still she loved to smile;

And would be calm if men would wait awhile:
She knew her duty, and she loved her way,
More pleased in truth to govern than obey;
She heard her priest with reverence, and her spouse
As one who felt the pressure of her vows:
Useful and civil, all her friends confess'd—
Give her her way, and she would choose the best;
Though some indeed a sly remark would make—
Give it her not, and she would choose to take.
  All this, when Clubb some cheerful months had spent,
He saw, confess'd, and said he was content.
  Counter meantime selected, doubted, weigh'd,
And then brought home a young complying maid;—
A tender creature, full of fears as charms,
A beauteous nursling from its mother's arms;
A soft, sweet blossom, such as men must love,
But to preserve must keep it in the stove:
She had a mild, subdued, expiring look—
Raise but the voice, and this fair creature shook;
Leave her alone, she felt a thousand fears—
Chide, and she melted into floods of tears;
Fondly she pleaded and would gently sigh,
For very pity, or she knew not why;
One whom to govern none could be afraid—
Hold up the finger, this meek thing obey'd;
Her happy husband had the easiest task—
Say but his will, no question would she ask;
She sought no reasons, no affairs she knew,
Of business spoke not, and had nought to do.
  Oft he exclaim'd, 'How meek! how mild! how kind!
With her 'twere cruel but to seem unkind;
Though ever silent when I take my leave,
It pains my heart to think how hers will grieve;
'Tis heaven on earth with such a wife to dwell,
I am in raptures to have sped so well;
But let me not, my friend, your envy raise,
No! on my life, your patience has my praise.'
  His friend, though silent, felt the scorn implied—
'What need of patience?' to himself he cried:
'Better a woman o'er her house to rule,
Than a poor child just hurried from her school;

Who has no care, yet never lives at ease;
Unfit to rule, and indisposed to please;
What if he govern, there his boast should end,
No husband's power can make a slave his friend.'
  It was the custom of these friends to meet
With a few neighbours in a neighbouring street;
Where Counter ofttimes would occasion seize,
To move his silent friend by words like these:
'A man,' said he, 'if govern'd by his wife,
Gives up his rank and dignity in life;
Now better fate befalls my friend and me'—
He spoke, and look'd th' approving smile to see.
  The quiet partner, when he chose to speak,
Desired his friend, 'another theme to seek;
When thus they met, he judged that state-affairs
And such important subjects should be theirs:'
But still the partner, in his lighter vein,
Would cause in Clubb affliction or disdain;
It made him anxious to detect the cause
Of all that boasting—'Wants my friend applause?
This plainly proves him not at perfect ease,
For, felt he pleasure, he would wish to please.—
These triumphs here for some regrets atone—
Men who are blest let other men alone.'
Thus made suspicious, he observed and saw
His friend each night at early hour withdraw;
He sometimes mention'd Juliet's tender nerves,
And what attention such a wife deserves:
'In this,' thought Clubb, 'full sure some mystery lies—
He laughs at me, yet he with much complies,
And all his vaunts of bliss are proud apologies.'
  With such ideas treasured in his breast,
He grew composed, and let his anger rest;
Till Counter once (when wine so long went round
That friendship and discretion both were drown'd)
Began in teasing and triumphant mood
His evening banter—'Of all earthly good,
The best,' he said, 'was an obedient spouse,
Such as my friend's—that every one allows:
What if she wishes his designs to know?
It is because she would her praise bestow;

What if she wills that he remains at home?
She knows that mischief may from travel come.
I, who am free to venture where I please,
Have no such kind preventing checks as these;
But mine is double duty, first to guide
Myself aright, then rule a house beside;
While this our friend, more happy than the free,
Resigns all power, and laughs at liberty.'
'By Heaven,' said Clubb, 'excuse me if I swear,
I'll bet a hundred guineas, if he dare,
That uncontroll'd I will such freedoms take,
That he will fear to equal—there's my stake.'
'A match!' said Counter, much by wine inflamed,
'But we are friends—let smaller stake be named:
Wine for our future meeting, that will I
Take and no more—what peril shall we try?'
'Let's to Newmarket,' Clubb replied; 'or choose
Yourself the place, and what you like to lose;
And he who first returns, or fears to go,
Forfeits his cash—' Said Counter, 'Be it so.'
The friends around them saw with much delight
The social war, and hail'd the pleasant night;
Nor would they further hear the cause discuss'd,
Afraid the recreant heart of Clubb to trust.
Now sober thoughts return'd as each withdrew,
And of the subject took a serious view;
''Twas wrong,' thought Counter, 'and will grieve my love;'
''Twas wrong,' thought Clubb, 'my wife will not approve;
But friends were present; I must try the thing,
Or with my folly half the town will ring.'
He sought his lady—'Madam, I'm to blame,
But was reproach'd, and could not bear the shame;
Here in my folly—for 'tis best to say
The very truth—I've sworn to have my way:
To that Newmarket—(though I hate the place,
And have no taste or talents for a race,
Yet so it is—well, now prepare to chide—)
I laid a wager that I dared to ride;
And I must go: by Heaven, if you resist

I shall be scorn'd, and ridiculed, and hiss'd;
Let me with grace before my friends appear,
You know the truth, and must not be severe;
He too must go, but that he will of course;
Do you consent?—I never think of force.'
'You never need,' the worthy dame replied;
'The husband's honour is the woman's pride;
If I in trifles be the wilful wife,
Still for your credit I would lose my life;
Go! and when fix'd the day of your return,
Stay longer yet, and let the blockheads learn,
That though a wife may sometimes wish to rule,
She would not make th' indulgent man a fool;
I would at times advise—but idle they
Who think th' assenting husband *must* obey.'
The happy man, who thought his lady right
In other cases, was assured to-night;
Then for the day with proud delight prepared,
To show his doubting friends how much he dared.
Counter—who grieving sought his bed, his rest
Broken by pictures of his love distress'd—
With soft and winning speech the fair prepared;
'She all his councils, comforts, pleasures shared:
She was assured he loved her from his soul,
She never knew and need not fear control;
But so it happen'd—he was grieved at heart,
It happen'd so, that they awhile must part—
A little time—the distance was but short,
And business call'd him—he despised the sport;
But to Newmarket he engaged to ride,
With his friend Clubb,' and there he stopp'd and sigh'd.
Awhile the tender creature look'd dismay'd,
Then floods of tears the call of grief obey'd:—
'She an objection! No!' she sobb'd, 'not one;
Her work was finish'd, and her race was run;
For die she must, indeed she would not live
A week alone, for all the world could give;
He too must die in that same wicked place;
It always happen'd—was a common case;
Among those horrid horses, jockeys, crowds,
'Twas certain death—they might bespeak their shrouds;

He would attempt a race, be sure to fall—
And she expire with terror—that was all;
With love like hers she was indeed unfit
To bear such horrors, but she must submit.'
  'But for three days, my love! three days at most—'
'Enough for me; I then shall be a ghost—'
'My honour's pledged!'—'Oh! yes, my dearest life,
I know your honour must outweigh your wife;
But ere this absence, have you sought a friend?
I shall be dead—on whom can you depend?—
Let me one favour of your kindness crave,
Grant me the stone I mention'd for my grave.—'
  'Nay, love, attend—why, bless my soul—I say
I will return—there—weep no longer—nay!—'
'Well! I obey, and to the last am true,
But spirits fail me; I must die; adieu!'
  'What, madam! must?—'tis wrong—I'm angry—
    zounds!
Can I remain and lose a thousand pounds?'
  'Go then, my love! it is a monstrous sum,
Worth twenty wives—go, love! and I am dumb—
Nor be displeased—had I the power to live,
You might be angry, now you must forgive;
Alas! I faint—ah! cruel—there's no need
Of wounds or fevers—this had done the deed.'
  The lady fainted, and the husband sent
For every aid, for every comfort went;
Strong terror seized him; 'Oh! she loved so well,
And who th' effect of tenderness could tell?'
  She now recover'd, and again began
With accent querulous—'Ah! cruel man—'
Till the sad husband, conscience-struck, confess'd,
'Twas very wicked with his friend to jest;
For now he saw that those who were obey'd,
Could like the most subservient feel afraid;
And though a wife might not dispute the will
Of her liege lord, she could prevent it still.
  The morning came, and Clubb prepared to ride
With a smart boy, his servant and his guide;
When, ere he mounted on the ready steed,
Arrived a letter, and he stopp'd to read.

'My friend,' he read—'our journey I decline,
A heart too tender for such strife is mine;
Yours is the triumph, be you so inclined;
But you are too considerate and kind;
In tender pity to my Juliet's fears
I thus relent, o'ercome by love and tears;
She knows your kindness; I have heard her say,
A man like you 'tis pleasure to obey:
Each faithful wife, like ours, must disapprove
Such dangerous trifling with connubial love;
What has the idle world, my friend, to do
With our affairs? they envy me and you:
What if I could my gentle spouse command—
Is that a cause I should her tears withstand?
And what if you, a friend of peace, submit
To one you love—is that a theme for wit?
'Twas wrong, and I shall henceforth judge it weak
Both of submission and control to speak:
Be it agreed that all contention cease,
And no such follies vex our future peace;
Let each keep guard against domestic strife,
And find nor slave nor tyrant in his wife.'
'Agreed,' said Clubb, 'with all my soul agreed'—
And to the boy, delighted, gave his steed;
'I think my friend has well his mind express'd,
And I assent; such things are not a jest.'
'True,' said the wife, 'no longer he can hide
The truth that pains him by his wounded pride:
Your friend has found it not an easy thing,
Beneath his yoke, this yielding soul to bring;
These weeping willows, though they seem inclined
By every breeze, yet not the strongest wind
Can from their bent divert this weak but stubborn kind;
Drooping they seek your pity to excite,
But 'tis at once their nature and delight;
Such women feel not; while they sigh and weep,
'Tis but their habit—their affections sleep;
They are like ice that in the hand we hold,
So very melting, yet so very cold;
On such affection let not man rely,
The husbands suffer, and the ladies sigh:

But your friend's offer let us kindly take,
And spare his pride for his vexation's sake;
For he has found, and through his life will find,
'Tis easiest dealing with the firmest mind—
More just when it resists, and, when it yields, more kind.'

19. THE CONVERT

...A tapster is a good trade, and an old cloak makes a new jerkin; a wither'd serving-man, a fresh tapster.

Merry Wives of Windsor, Act I, Scene 3

A fellow, sir, that I have known go about with my troll-my-dames.

Winter's Tale, Act IV, Scene 3

...I myself, sometimes leaving the fear of Heaven on the left hand, and holding mine honour in my necessity, am forced to shuffle, to hedge, and to lurch. *Merry Wives of Windsor*, Act II, Scene 3

Yes, and at that very moment,
Consideration like an angel came,
And whipp'd th' offending Adam out of him.

Henry V, Act I, Scene 1

I have lived long enough: My May of life
Is fall'n into the sear, the yellow leaf;
And that which should accompany old age,
As honour, love, obedience, troops of friends,
I must not look to have. *Macbeth*, Act V, Scene 3

Some to our hero have a hero's name
Denied, because no father's he could claim;
Nor could his mother with precision state
A full fair claim to her certificate;
On her own word the marriage must depend—
A point she was not eager to defend:
But who, without a father's name, can raise
His own so high, deserves the greater praise:
The less advantage to the strife he brought,
The greater wonders has his prowess wrought;
He who depends upon his wind and limbs,
Needs neither cork or bladder when he swims;
Nor will by empty breath be puff'd along,
As not himself—but in his helpers—strong.
Suffice it then, our hero's name was clear,

For, call John Dighton, and he answer'd, 'Here!'
But who that name in early life assign'd
He never found, he never tried to find;
Whether his kindred were to John disgrace,
Or John to them, is a disputed case;
His infant-state owed nothing to their care—
His mind neglected, and his body bare;
All his success must on himself depend,
He had no money, counsel, guide, or friend;
But in a market-town an active boy
Appear'd, and sought in various ways employ;
Who soon, thus cast upon the world, began
To show the talents of a thriving man.
  With spirit high John learn'd the world to brave,
And in both senses was a ready knave;
Knave as of old, obedient, keen, and quick,
Knave as at present, skill'd to shift and trick;
Some humble part of many trades he caught,
He for the builder and the painter wrought;
For serving-maids on secret errands ran,
The waiter's helper, and the hostler's man;
And when he chanced (oft chanced he) place to lose,
His varying genius shone in blacking shoes:
A midnight fisher by the pond he stood,
Assistant poacher, he o'erlook'd the wood;
At an election John's impartial mind
Was to no cause nor candidate confined;
To all in turn he full allegiance swore,
And in his hat the various badges bore:
His liberal soul with every sect agreed,
Unheard their reasons, he received their creed;
At church he deign'd the organ-pipes to fill,
And at the meeting sang both loud and shrill;
But the full purse these different merits gain'd,
By strong demands his lively passions drain'd;
Liquors he loved of each inflaming kind,
To midnight revels flew with ardent mind;
Too warm at cards, a losing game he play'd,
To fleecing beauty his attention paid;
His boiling passions were by oaths express'd,
And lies he made his profit and his jest.

19. The Convert

Such was the boy, and such the man had been,
But fate or happier fortune changed the scene;
A fever seized him, 'He should surely die—'
He fear'd, and lo! a friend was praying by;
With terror moved, this teacher he address'd,
And all the errors of his youth confess'd;
The good man kindly clear'd the sinner's way
To lively hope, and counsell'd him to pray;
Who then resolved, should he from sickness rise,
To quit cards, liquors, poaching, oaths, and lies:
His health restored, he yet resolved, and grew
True to his masters, in their meeting true;
His old companions at his sober face
Laugh'd loud, while he, attesting it was grace,
With tears besought them all his calling to embrace:
To his new friends such convert gave applause,
Life to their zeal, and glory to their cause:
Though terror wrought the mighty change, yet strong
Was the impression, and it lasted long;
John at the lectures due attendance paid,
A convert meek, obedient, and afraid.
His manners strict, though form'd on fear alone,
Pleased the grave friends, nor less his solemn tone,
The lengthen'd face of care, the low and inward groan:
The stern good men exulted, when they saw
Those timid looks of penitence and awe;
Nor thought that one so passive, humble, meek,
Had yet a creed and principles to seek.
The faith that reason finds, confirms, avows,
The hopes, the views, the comforts she allows—
These were not his, who by his feelings found,
And by them only, that his faith was sound;
Feelings of terror these, for evil past,
Feelings of hope, to be received at last;
Now weak, now lively, changing with the day,
These were his feelings, and he felt his way.
Sprung from such sources, will this faith remain
While these supporters can their strength retain:
As heaviest weights the deepest rivers pass,
While icy chains fast bind the solid mass;
So, born of feelings, faith remains secure,

Long as their firmness and their strength endure:
But when the waters in their channel glide,
A bridge must bear us o'er the threat'ning tide;
Such bridge is reason, and there faith relies,
Whether the varying spirits fall or rise.
  His patrons, still disposed their aid to lend,
Behind a counter placed their humble friend;
Where pens and paper were on shelves display'd,
And pious pamphlets on the windows laid:
By nature active, and from vice restrain'd,
Increasing trade his bolder views sustain'd;
His friends and teachers, finding so much zeal
In that young convert whom they taught to feel,
His trade encouraged, and were pleased to find
A hand so ready, with such humble mind.
  And now, his health restored, his spirits eased,
He wish'd to marry, if the teachers pleased.
They, not unwilling, from the virgin-class
Took him a comely and a courteous lass;
Simple and civil, loving and beloved,
She long a fond and faithful partner proved;
In every year the elders and the priest
Were duly summon'd to a christening feast;
Nor came a babe, but by his growing trade,
John had provision for the coming made;
For friends and strangers all were pleased to deal
With one whose care was equal to his zeal.
  In human friendships, it compels a sigh,
To think what trifles will dissolve the tie.
John, now become a master of his trade,
Perceived how much improvement might be made;
And as this prospect open'd to his view,
A certain portion of his zeal withdrew;
His fear abated—'What had he to fear—
His profits certain, and his conscience clear?'
Above his door a board was placed by John,
And 'Dighton, stationer,' was gilt thereon;
His window next, enlarged to twice the size,
Shone with such trinkets as the simple prize;
While in the shop with pious works were seen
The last new play, review, or magazine:

In orders punctual, he observed—'The books
He never read, and could he judge their looks?
Readers and critics should their merits try,
He had no office but to sell and buy;
Like other traders, profit was his care;
Of what they print, the authors must beware.'
He held his patrons and his teachers dear,
But with his trade—they must not interfere.
 'Twas certain now that John had lost the dread
And pious thoughts that once such terrors bred;
His habits varied, and he more inclined
To the vain world, which he had half resign'd:
He had moreover in his brethren seen,
Or he imagined, craft, conceit, and spleen;
'They are but men,' said John, 'and shall I then
Fear man's control, or stand in awe of men?
'Tis their advice (their convert's rule and law),
And good it is—I will not stand in awe.'
 Moreover Dighton, though he thought of books
As one who chiefly on the title looks,
Yet sometimes ponder'd o'er a page to find,
When vex'd with cares, amusement for his mind;
And by degrees that mind had treasured much
From works his teachers were afraid to touch:
Satiric novels, poets bold and free,
And what their writers term philosophy;
All these were read, and he began to feel
Some self-approval on his bosom steal.
Wisdom creates humility, but he
Who thus collects it, will not humble be:
No longer John was fill'd with pure delight
And humble reverence in a pastor's sight;
Who, like a grateful zealot, listening stood,
To hear a man so friendly and so good;
But felt the dignity of one who made
Himself important by a thriving trade;
And growing pride in Dighton's mind was bred
By the strange food on which it coarsely fed.
 Their brother's fall the grieving brethren heard,
The pride indeed to all around appear'd;
The world his friends agreed had won the soul

From its best hopes, the man from their control:
To make him humble, and confine his views
Within their bounds, and books which they peruse;
A deputation from these friends select,
Might reason with him to some good effect;
Arm'd with authority, and led by love,
They might those follies from his mind remove;
Deciding thus, and with this kind intent,
A chosen body with its speaker went.
'John,' said the teacher, 'John, with great concern,
We see thy frailty, and thy fate discern—
Satan with toils thy simple soul beset,
And thou art careless, slumbering in the net;
Unmindful art thou of thy early vow;
Who at the morning-meeting sees thee now?
Who at the evening? where is brother John?
We ask—are answer'd, To the tavern gone:
Thee on the sabbath seldom we behold;
Thou canst not sing, thou 'rt nursing for a cold:
This from the churchmen thou hast learn'd, for they
Have colds and fevers on the sabbath-day;
When in some snug warm room they sit, and pen
Bills from their ledgers, (world-entangled men!)
'See with what pride thou hast enlarged thy shop;
To view thy tempting stores the heedless stop;
By what strange names dost thou these baubles know,
Which wantons wear, to make a sinful show?
Hast thou in view these idle volumes placed
To be the pander of a vicious taste?
What's here? a book of dances!—you advance
In goodly knowledge—John, wilt learn to dance?
How! "Go—" it says, and "to the devil go!
And "shake thyself!" I tremble—but 'tis so——
Wretch as thou art, what answer canst thou make?
Oh! without question, thou wilt go and shake.
What's here? the "School for Scandal"—pretty schools!
Well, and art thou proficient in the rules?
Art thou a pupil, is it thy design
To make our names contemptible as thine?
"Old Nick, a Novel!" oh! 'tis mighty well—
A fool has courage when he laughs at hell;

"Frolic and Fun," the humours of "Tim Grin;"
Why, John, thou grow'st facetious in thy sin;
And what? "the Archdeacon's Charge"—'tis mighty
well—
If Satan publish'd, thou wouldst doubtless sell;
Jests, novels, dances, and this precious stuff,
To crown thy folly, we have seen enough;
We find thee fitted for each evil work—
Do print the Koran, and become a Turk.
'John, thou art lost; success and worldly pride
O'er all thy thoughts and purposes preside,
Have bound thee fast, and drawn thee far aside;
Yet turn; these sin-traps from thy shop expel,
Repent and pray, and all may yet be well.
'And here thy wife, thy Dorothy, behold,
How fashion's wanton robes her form infold!
Can grace, can goodness with such trappings dwell?
John, thou hast made thy wife a Jezebel:
See! on her bosom rests the sign of sin,
The glaring proof of naughty thoughts within;
What? 'tis a cross; come hither—as a friend,
Thus from thy neck the shameful badge I rend.'
'Rend, if you dare,' said Dighton; 'you shall find
A man of spirit, though to peace inclined;
Call me ungrateful! have I not my pay
At all times ready for the expected day?—
To share my plenteous board you deign to come,
Myself your pupil, and my house your home;
And shall the persons who my meat enjoy
Talk of my faults, and treat me as a boy?
Have you not told how Rome's insulting priests
Led their meek laymen like a herd of beasts;
And by their fleecing and their forgery made
Their holy calling an accursed trade?
Can you such acts and insolence condemn,
Who to your utmost power resemble them?
'Concerns it you what books I set for sale?
The tale perchance may be a virtuous tale;
And for the rest, 'tis neither wise nor just,
In you, who read not, to condemn on trust;
Why should th' Archdeacon's Charge your spleen excite?

He, or perchance th' archbishop, may be right.
'That from your meetings I refrain, is true;
I meet with nothing pleasant—nothing new;
But the same proofs, that not one text explain,
And the same lights, where all things dark remain;
I thought you saints on earth—but I have found
Some sins among you, and the best unsound;
You have your failings, like the crowds below,
And at your pleasure hot and cold can blow:
When I at first your grave deportment saw,
(I own my folly), I was fill'd with awe;
You spoke so warmly, and it seems so well,
I should have thought it treason to rebel;
Is it a wonder, that a man like me
Should such perfection in such teachers see;
Nay, should conceive you sent from Heav'n to brave
The host of sin, and sinful souls to save?
But as our reason wakes, our prospects clear,
And failings, flaws, and blemishes appear.
'When you were mounted in your rostrum high,
We shrank beneath your tone, your frown, your eye;
Then you beheld us abject, fallen, low,
And felt your glory from our baseness grow;
Touch'd by your words, I trembled like the rest,
And my own vileness and your power confess'd:
These, I exclaim'd, are men divine, and gazed
On him who taught, delighted and amazed;
Glad when he finish'd, if by chance he cast
One look on such a sinner, as he pass'd.
'But when I view'd you in a clearer light,
And saw the frail and carnal appetite;
When, at his humble pray'r, you deign'd to eat,
Saints as you are, a civil sinner's meat;
When as you sat contented and at ease,
Nibbling at leisure on the ducks and peas,
And, pleased some comforts in such place to find,
You could descend to be a little kind;
And gave us hope, in Heaven there might be room
For a few souls beside your own to come;
While this world's good engaged your carnal view,
And like a sinner you enjoy'd it too;

All this perceiving, can you think it strange
That change in you should work an equal change?'
'Wretch that thou art,' an elder cried, 'and gone
For everlasting.'—'Go thyself,' said John;
'Depart this instant, let me hear no more;
My house my castle is, and that my door.'
The hint they took, and from the door withdrew,
And John to meeting bade a long adieu;
Attach'd to business, he in time became
A wealthy man of no inferior name.
It seem'd, alas! in John's deluded sight,
That all was wrong because not all was right;
And when he found his teachers had their stains,
Resentment and not reason broke his chains:
Thus on his feelings he again relied,
And never looked to reason for his guide:
Could he have wisely view'd the frailty shown,
And rightly weigh'd their wanderings and his own,
He might have known that men may be sincere,
Though gay and feasting on the savoury cheer;
That doctrines sound and sober they may teach,
Who love to eat with all the glee they preach;
Nay, who believe the duck, the grape, the pine,
Were not intended for the dog and swine:
But Dighton's hasty mind on every theme
Ran from the truth, and rested in th' extreme:
Flaws in his friends he found, and then withdrew
(Vain of his knowledge) from their virtues too.
Best of his books he loved the liberal kind,
That, if they improve not, still enlarge the mind;
And found himself, with such advisers, free
From a fix'd creed, as mind enlarged could be.
His humble wife at these opinions sigh'd,
But her he never heeded till she died;
He then assented to a last request,
And by the meeting-window let her rest;
And on her stone the sacred text was seen,
Which had her comfort in departing been.
Dighton with joy beheld his trade advance,
Yet seldom published, loth to trust to chance;
Then wed a doctor's sister—poor indeed,

But skill'd in works her husband could not read;
Who, if he wish'd new ways of wealth to seek,
Could make her half-crown pamphlet in a week:
This he rejected, though without disdain,
And chose the old and certain way to gain.
  Thus he proceeded; trade increased the while,
And fortune woo'd him with perpetual smile;
On early scenes he sometimes cast a thought,
When on his heart the mighty change was wrought;
And all the ease and comfort converts find
Was magnified in his reflecting mind:
Then on the teacher's priestly pride he dwelt,
That caused his freedom, but with this he felt
The danger of the free—for since that day,
No guide had shown, no brethren join'd his way;
Forsaking one, he found no second creed,
But reading doubted, doubting what to read.
  Still, though reproof had brought some present pain,
The gain he made was fair and honest gain;
He laid his wares indeed in public view,
But that all traders claim a right to do;
By means like these, he saw his wealth increase,
And felt his consequence, and dwelt in peace.
  Our hero's age was threescore years and five,
When he exclaim'd, 'Why longer should I strive?
Why more amass, who never must behold
A young John Dighton to make glad the old?'
(The sons he had to early graves were gone,
And girls were burdens to the mind of John.)
'Had I a boy, he would our name sustain,
That now to nothing must return again;
But what are all my profits, credit, trade,
And parish-honours?—folly and parade.'
  Thus Dighton thought, and in his looks appear'd
Sadness increased by much he saw and heard:
The brethren often at the shop would stay,
And make their comments ere they walk'd away:
They mark'd the window, fill'd in every pane
With lawless prints of reputations slain;
Distorted forms of men with honours graced,
And our chief rulers in derision placed:

Amazed they stood, remembering well the days,
When to be humble was their brother's praise;
When at the dwelling of their friend they stopp'd
To drop a word, or to receive it dropp'd;
Where they beheld the prints of men renown'd,
And far-famed preachers pasted all around;
(Such mouths! eyes! hair! so prim! so fierce! so sleek!
They look'd as speaking what is wo to speak):
On these the passing brethren loved to dwell—
How long they spake! how strongly! warmly! well!
What power had each to dive in mysteries deep,
To warm the cold, to make the harden'd weep;
To lure, to fright, to soothe, to awe the soul,
And list'ning flocks to lead and to control!
  But now discoursing, as they linger'd near,
They tempted John (whom they accused) to hear
Their weighty charge—'And can the lost-one feel,
As in the time of duty, love, and zeal;
When all were summon'd at the rising sun,
And he was ready with his friends to run;
When he, partaking with a chosen few,
Felt the great change, sensation rich and new?
No! all is lost, her favours Fortune shower'd
Upon the man, and he is overpower'd;
The world has won him with its tempting store
Of needless wealth, and that has made him poor:
Success undoes him; he has risen to fall,
Has gain'd a fortune, and has lost his all;
Gone back from Sion, he will find his age
Loth to commence a second pilgrimage;
He has retreated from the chosen track;
And now must ever bear the burden on his back.'
  Hurt by such censure, John began to find
Fresh revolutions working in his mind;
He sought for comfort in his books, but read
Without a plan or method in his head;
What once amused, now rather made him sad,
What should inform, increased the doubts he had;
Shame would not let him seek at church a guide,
And from his meeting he was held by pride;
His wife derided fears she never felt,

And passing brethren daily censures dealt;
Hope for a son was now for ever past,
He was the first John Dighton, and the last;
His stomach fail'd, his case the doctor knew,
But said, 'he still might hold a year or two:'
'No more!' he said, 'but why should I complain?
A life of doubt must be a life of pain:
Could I be sure—but why should I despair?
I'm sure my conduct has been just and fair;
In youth indeed I had a wicked will,
But I repented, and have sorrow still:
I had my comforts, and a growing trade
Gave greater pleasure than a fortune made;
And as I more possess'd and reason'd more,
I lost those comforts I enjoy'd before,
When reverend guides I saw my table round,
And in my guardian guest my safety found:
Now sick and sad, no appetite, no ease,
Nor pleasure have I, nor a wish to please;
Nor views, nor hopes, nor plans, nor taste have I,
Yet sick of life, have no desire to die.'
  He said, and died; his trade, his name is gone,
And all that once gave consequence to John.
  Unhappy Dighton! had he found a friend,
When conscience told him it was time to mend!
A friend, discreet, considerate, kind, sincere,
Who would have shown the grounds of hope and fear;
And proved that spirits, whether high or low,
No certain tokens of man's safety show;
Had reason ruled him in her proper place,
And virtue led him while he lean'd on grace;
Had he while zealous been discreet and pure,
His knowledge humble, and his hope secure;—
These guides had placed him on the solid rock,
Where faith had rested, nor received a shock;
But his, alas! was placed upon the sand,
Where long it stood not, and where none can stand.

20. THE BROTHERS

A brother noble,
Whose nature is so far from doing harms,
That he suspects none; on whose foolish honesty
My practice may ride easy.
King Lear, Act I, Scene 2

He lets me feed with hinds,
Bars me the place of brother.
As You Like It, Act I, Scene 1

'Twas I, but 'tis not I: I do not shame
To tell you what I was, being what I am.
As You Like It, Act IV, Scene 3

Than old George Fletcher, on the British coast,
Dwelt not a seaman who had more to boast;
Kind, simple, and sincere—he seldom spoke,
But sometimes sang and chorus'd—'*Hearts of Oak;*'
In dangers steady, with his lot content,
His days in labour and in love were spent.
He left a son so like him, that the old
With joy exclaim'd, ''Tis Fletcher we behold;'
But to his brother when the kinsmen came,
And view'd his form, they grudged the father's name.
George was a bold, intrepid, careless lad,
With just the failings that his father had;
Isaac was weak, attentive, slow, exact,
With just the virtues that his father lack'd.
George lived at sea: upon the land a guest—
He sought for recreation, not for rest—
While, far unlike, his brother's feebler form
Shrank from the cold, and shudder'd at the storm;
Still with the seaman's to connect his trade,
The boy was bound where blocks and ropes were made.
George, strong and sturdy, had a tender mind,
And was to Isaac pitiful and kind;
A very father, till his art was gain'd,
And then a friend unwearied he remain'd:
He saw his brother was of spirit low,
His temper peevish, and his motions slow;
Not fit to bustle in a world, or make

Friends to his fortune for his merit's sake:
But the kind sailor could not boast the art
Of looking deeply in the human heart;
Else had he seen that this weak brother knew
What men to court—what objects to pursue;
That he to distant gain the way discern'd,
And none so crooked but his genius learn'd.
  Isaac was poor, and this the brother felt;
He hired a house, and there the landman dwelt;
Wrought at his trade, and had an easy home,
For there would George with cash and comforts come;
And when they parted, Isaac look'd around,
Where other friends and helpers might be found.
  He wish'd for some port-place, and one might fall,
He wisely thought, if he should try for all;
He had a vote—and, were it well applied,
Might have its worth—and he had views beside;
Old Burgess Steel was able to promote
An humble man who served him with a vote;
For Isaac felt not what some tempers feel,
But bow'd and bent the neck to Burgess Steel;
And great attention to a lady gave,
His ancient friend, a maiden spare and grave:
One whom the visage long and look demure
Of Isaac pleased—he seem'd sedate and pure;
And his soft heart conceived a gentle flame
For her who waited on this virtuous dame:
Not an outrageous love, a scorching fire,
But friendly liking and chastised desire;
And thus he waited, patient in delay,
In present favour and in fortune's way.
  George then was coasting—war was yet delay'd,
And what he gain'd was to his brother paid;
Nor ask'd the seaman what he saved or spent:
But took his grog, wrought hard, and was content;
Till war awaked the land, and George began
To think what part became a useful man;
'Press'd, I must go; why, then, 'tis better far
At once to enter like a British tar,
Than a brave captain and the foe to shun,
As if I fear'd the music of a gun.'

'Go not!' said Isaac—'You shall wear disguise.'
'What!' said the seaman, 'clothe myself with lies?'—
'Oh! but there's danger.'—'Danger in the fleet?
You cannot mean, good brother, of defeat;
And other dangers I at land must share—
So now adieu! and trust a brother's care.'
Isaac awhile demurr'd—but, in his heart,
So might he share, he was disposed to part:
The better mind will sometimes feel the pain
Of benefactions—favour is a chain;
But they the feeling scorn, and what they wish, disdain;—
While beings form'd in coarser mould will hate
The helping hand they ought to venerate;
No wonder George should in this cause prevail,
With one contending who was glad to fail;
'Isaac, farewell! do wipe that doleful eye;
Crying we came, and groaning we may die.
Let us do something 'twixt the groan and cry:
And hear me, brother, whether pay or prize,
One half to thee I give and I devise;
For thou has oft occasion for the aid
Of learn'd physicians, and they will be paid:
Their wives and children men support, at sea,
And thou, my lad, art wife and child to me:
Farewell!—I go where hope and honour call,
Nor does it follow that who fights must fall.'
Isaac here made a poor attempt to speak,
And a huge tear moved slowly down his cheek;
Like Pluto's iron drop, hard sign of grace,
It slowly roll'd upon the rueful face,
Forced by the striving will alone its way to trace.
Years fled—war lasted—George at sea remain'd,
While the slow landman still his profits gain'd:
A humble place was vacant—he besought
His patron's interest, and the office caught;
For still the virgin was his faithful friend,
And one so sober could with truth commend,
Who of his own defects most humbly thought,
And their advice with zeal and reverence sought:
Whom thus the mistress praised, the maid approved,
And her he wedded whom he wisely loved.

No more he needs assistance—but, alas!
He fears the money will for liquor pass;
Or that the seaman might to flatterers lend,
Or give support to some pretended friend:
Still he must write—he wrote, and he confess'd
That, till absolved, he should be sore distress'd;
But one so friendly would, he thought, forgive
The hasty deed—Heav'n knew how he should live;
'But you,' he added, 'as a man of sense,
Have well consider'd danger and expense:
I ran, alas! into the fatal snare,
And now for trouble must my mind prepare;
And how, with children, I shall pick my way,
Through a hard world, is more than I can say:
Then change not, brother, your more happy state,
Or on the hazard long deliberate.'
George answer'd gravely, 'It is right and fit,
In all our crosses, humbly to submit:
Your apprehensions are unwise, unjust;
Forbear repining, and expel distrust.'—
He added, 'Marriage was the joy of life,'
And gave his service to his brother's wife;
Then vow'd to bear in all expense a part,
And thus concluded, 'Have a cheerful heart.'
Had the glad Isaac been his brother's guide,
In these same terms the seaman had replied;
At such reproofs the crafty landman smiled,
And softly said—'This creature is a child.'
Twice had the gallant ship a capture made—
And when in port the happy crew were paid,
Home went the sailor, with his pocket stored,
Ease to enjoy, and pleasure to afford;
His time was short, joy shone in every face,
Isaac half fainted in the fond embrace:
The wife resolved her honour'd guest to please,
The children clung upon their uncle's knees;
The grog went round, the neighbours drank his health,
And George exclaim'd—'Ah! what to this is wealth?
Better,' said he, 'to bear a loving heart,
Than roll in riches—but we now must part!'
All yet is still—but hark! the winds o'ersweep

The rising waves, and howl upon the deep;
Ships late becalm'd on mountain-billows ride—
So life is threaten'd, and so man is tried.
  Ill were the tidings that arrived from sea,
The worthy George must now a cripple be;
His leg was lopp'd; and though his heart was sound,
Though his brave captain was with glory crown'd—
Yet much it vex'd him to repose on shore,
An idle log, and be of use no more:
True, he was sure that Isaac would receive
All of his brother that the foe might leave;
To whom the seaman his design had sent,
Ere from the port the wounded hero went:
His wealth and expectations told, he 'knew
Wherein they fail'd, what Isaac's love would do;
That he the grog and cabin would supply,
Where George at anchor during life would lie.'
  The landman read—and, reading, grew distress'd:—
'Could he resolve t' admit so poor a guest?
Better at Greenwich might the sailor stay,
Unless his purse could for his comforts pay;'
So Isaac judged, and to his wife appeal'd,
But yet acknowledged it was best to yield:
'Perhaps his pension, with what sums remain
Due or unsquander'd, may the man maintain;
Refuse we must not.'—With a heavy sigh
The lady heard, and made her kind reply:—
'Nor would I wish it, Isaac, were we sure
How long this crazy building will endure;
Like an old house, that every day appears
About to fall—he may be propp'd for years;
For a few months, indeed, we might comply,
But these old batter'd fellows never die.'
  The hand of Isaac, George on entering took,
With love and resignation in his look;
Declared his comfort in the fortune past,
And joy to find his anchor safely cast;
'Call then my nephews, let the grog be brought,
And I will tell them how the ship was fought.'
  Alas! our simple seaman should have known,
That all the care, the kindness, he had shown,

Were from his brother's heart, if not his memory, flown:
All swept away to be perceived no more,
Like idle structures on the sandy shore;
The chance amusement of the playful boy,
That the rude billows in their rage destroy.
  Poor George confess'd, though loth the truth to find,
Slight was his knowledge of a brother's mind:
The vulgar pipe was to the wife offence,
The frequent grog to Isaac an expense;
Would friends like hers, she question'd, 'choose to come,
Where clouds of poison'd fume defiled a room?
This could their lady-friend, and Burgess Steel,
(Teased with his worship's asthma) bear to feel?
Could they associate or converse with him—
A loud rough sailor with a timber limb?'
  Cold as he grew, still Isaac strove to show,
By well-feign'd care, that cold he could not grow;
And when he saw his brother look distressd,
He strove some petty comforts to suggest;
On his wife solely their neglect to lay,
And then t' excuse it, is a woman's way;
He too was chidden when her rules he broke,
And then she sicken'd at the scent of smoke.
  George, though in doubt, was still consoled to find
His brother wishing to be reckon'd kind:
That Isaac seem'd concern'd by his distress,
Gave to his injured feelings some redress;
But none he found disposed to lend an ear
To stories, all were once intent to hear:
Except his nephew, seated on his knee,
He found no creature cared about the sea;
But George indeed—for George they call'd the boy,
When his good uncle was their boast and joy—
Would listen long, and would contend with sleep,
To hear the woes and wonders of the deep;
Till the fond mother cried—'That man will teach
The foolish boy his loud and boisterous speech.'
So judged the father—and the boy was taught
To shun the uncle, whom his love had sought.
  The mask of kindness now but seldom worn,
George felt each evil harder to be borne;

And cried (vexation growing day by day),
'Ah! brother Isaac!—What! I'm in the way!'
'No! on my credit, look ye, No! but I
Am fond of peace, and my repose would buy
On any terms—in short, we must comply:
My spouse had money—she must have her will—
Ah! brother—marriage is a bitter pill.'—
George tried the lady—'Sister, I offend.'
'Me?' she replied—'Oh no!—you may depend
On my regard—but watch your brother's way,
Whom I, like you, must study and obey.'
'Ah!' thought the seaman, 'what a head was mine,
That easy berth at Greenwich to resign!
I'll to the parish'——but a little pride,
And some affection, put the thought aside.
Now gross neglect and open scorn he bore
In silent sorrow—but he felt the more:
The odious pipe he to the kitchen took,
Or strove to profit by some pious book.
When the mind stoops to this degraded state,
New griefs will darken the dependent's fate;
'Brother!' said Isaac, 'you will sure excuse
The little freedom I'm compell'd to use:
My wife's relations—(curse the haughty crew)—
Affect such niceness, and such dread of you:
You speak so loud—and they have natures soft—
Brother——I wish——do go upon the loft!'
Poor George obey'd, and to the garret fled,
Where not a being saw the tears he shed:
But more was yet required, for guests were come,
Who could not dine if he disgraced the room.
It shock'd his spirit to be esteem'd unfit
With an own brother and his wife to sit;
He grew rebellious—at the vestry spoke
For weekly aid——they heard it as a joke:
'So kind a brother, and so wealthy——you
Apply to us?——No! this will never do:
Good neighbour Fletcher,' said the overseer,
We are engaged—you can have nothing here!'
George mutter'd something in despairing tone,
Then sought his loft, to think and grieve alone;

Neglected, slighted, restless on his bed,
With heart half broken, and with scraps ill fed;
Yet was he pleased, that hours for play design'd
Were given to ease his ever-troubled mind;
The child still listen'd with increasing joy,
And he was soothed by the attentive boy.
   At length he sicken'd, and this duteous child
Watch'd o'er his sickness, and his pains beguiled;
The mother bade him from the loft refrain,
But, though with caution, yet he went again;
And now his tales the sailor feebly told,
His heart was heavy, and his limbs were cold:
The tender boy came often to entreat
His good kind friend would of his presents eat;
Purloin'd or purchased, for he saw, with shame,
The food untouch'd that to his uncle came;
Who, sick in body and in mind, received
The boy's indulgence, gratified and grieved.
   'Uncle will die!' said George—the piteous wife
Exclaim'd, 'she saw no value in his life;
But sick or well, to my commands attend,
And go no more to your complaining friend.'
The boy was vex'd, he felt his heart reprove
The stern decree.—What! punish'd for his love!
No! he would go, but softly to the room,
Stealing in silence—for he knew his doom.
   Once in a week the father came to say,
'George, are you ill?'—and hurried him away;
Yet to his wife would on their duties dwell,
And often cry, 'Do use my brother well:'
And something kind, no question, Isaac meant,
Who took vast credit for the vague intent.
   But truly kind, the gentle boy essay'd
To cheer his uncle, firm, although afraid;
But now the father caught him at the door,
And, swearing—yes, the man in office swore,
And cried, 'Away! How! Brother, I'm surprised,
That one so old can be so ill advised:
Let him not dare to visit you again,
Your cursed stories will disturb his brain;
Is it not vile to court a foolish boy,

Your own absurd narrations to enjoy?
What! sullen!—ha! George Fetcher? you shall see,
Proud as you are, your bread depends on me!'
  He spoke, and, frowning, to his dinner went,
Then cool'd and felt some qualms of discontent;
And thought on times when he compell'd his son
To hear these stories, nay, to beg for one:
But the wife's wrath o'ercame the brother's pain,
And shame was felt, and conscience rose in vain.
  George yet stole up, he saw his uncle lie
Sick on the bed, and heard his heavy sigh:
So he resolved, before he went to rest,
To comfort one so dear and so distress'd;
Then watch'd his time, but with a child-like art,
Betray'd a something treasured at his heart:
Th' observant wife remark'd, 'the boy is grown
So like your brother, that he seems his own;
So close and sullen! and I still suspect
They often meet—do watch them and detect.'
  George now remark'd that all was still as night,
And hasten'd up with terror and delight;
'Uncle!' he cried, and softly tapp'd the door;
'Do let me in'—but he could add no more;
The careful father caught him in the fact,
And cried,—'You serpent! is it thus you act?
Back to your mother!'—and with hasty blow,
He sent th' indignant boy to grieve below;
Then at the door an angry speech began—
'Is this your conduct?—is it thus you plan?
Seduce my child, and make my house a scene
Of vile dispute——What is it that you mean?—
George, are you dumb? do learn to know your friends,
And think awhile on whom your bread depends:
What! not a word? be thankful I am cool—
But, sir, beware, nor longer play the fool;
Come! brother, come! what is that you seek
By this rebellion?—Speak, you villain, speak!—
Weeping! I warrant—sorrow makes you dumb:
I'll ope your mouth, impostor! if I come:
Let me approach—I'll shake you from the bed,
You stubborn dog——Oh God! my brother's dead!—'

Timid was Isaac, and in all the past
He felt a purpose to be kind at last;
Nor did he mean his brother to depart,
Till he had shown this kindness of his heart:
But day by day he put the cause aside,
Induced by av'rice, peevishness, or pride.
But now awaken'd, from this fatal time
His conscience Isaac felt, and found his crime:
He raised to George a monumental stone,
And there retired to sigh and think alone;
An ague seized him, he grew pale, and shook—
'So,' said his son, 'would my poor uncle look.'
'And so, my child, shall I like him expire.'
'No! you have physic and a cheerful fire.'
'Unhappy sinner! yes, I'm well supplied
With every comfort my cold heart denied.'
He view'd his brother now, but not as one
Who vex'd his wife by fondness for her son;
Not as with wooden limb, and seaman's tale,
The odious pipe, vile grog, or humbler ale:
He now the worth and grief alone can view
Of one so mild, so generous, and so true;
The frank, kind brother, with such open heart,
And I to break it——'twas a dæmon's part!'
So Isaac now, as led by conscience, feels,
Nor his unkindness palliates or conceals;
'This is your folly,' said his heartless wife:
'Alas! my folly cost my brother's life;
It suffer'd him to languish and decay,
My gentle brother, whom I could not pay,
And therefore left to pine, and fret his life away.'
He takes his son, and bids the boy unfold
All the good uncle of his feelings told,
All he lamented—and the ready tear
Falls as he listens, soothed, and grieved to hear.
'Did he not curse me, child?'—'He never cursed,
But could not breathe, and said his heart would burst:'
'And so will mine:'—'Then, father, you must pray;
My uncle said it took his pains away.'
Repeating thus his sorrows, Isaac shows
That he, repenting, feels the debt he owes,

And from this source alone his every comfort flows.
He takes no joy in office, honours, gain;
They make him humble, nay, they give him pain;
'These from my heart,' he cries, 'all feeling drove;
They made me cold to nature, dead to love:'
He takes no joy in home, but sighing, sees
A son in sorrow, and a wife at ease:
He takes no joy in office—see him now,
And Burgess Steel has but a passing bow;
Of one sad train of gloomy thoughts possess'd,
He takes no joy in friends, in food, in rest—
Dark are the evil days, and void of peace the best.
And thus he lives, if living be to sigh,
And from all comforts of the world to fly,
Without a hope in life—without a wish to die.

21. THE LEARNED BOY

Like one well studied in a sad ostent,
To please his grandam.
Merchant of Venice, Act II, Scene 2

And then the whining school-boy, with his satchel
And shining morning face, creeping like snail,
Unwillingly to school.
As You Like It, Act II, Scene 7

He is a better scholar than I thought he was—
He has a good sprag memory.
Merry Wives of Windsor, Act IV, Scene 1

One that feeds
On objects, arts, and imitations,
Which out of use, and stal'd by other men,
Begin his fashion.
Julius Caesar, Act IV, Scene 1

Oh! torture me no more—I will confess.
2 Henry VI, Act III, Scene 3

An honest man was Farmer Jones, and true,
He did by all as all by him should do;
Grave, cautious, careful, fond of gain was he,
Yet famed for rustic hospitality:
Left with his children in a widow'd state,

The quiet man submitted to his fate;
Though prudent matrons waited for his call,
With cool forbearance he avoided all;
Though each profess'd a pure maternal joy,
By kind attention to his feeble boy:
And though a friendly widow knew no rest,
Whilst neighbour Jones was lonely and distress'd;
Nay, though the maidens spoke in tender tone
Their hearts' concern to see him left alone—
Jones still persisted in that cheerless life,
As if 'twere sin to take a second wife.
  Oh! 'tis a precious thing, when wives are dead,
To find such numbers who will serve instead:
And in whatever state a man be thrown,
'Tis that precisely they would wish their own;
Left the departed infants—then their joy
Is to sustain each lovely girl and boy:
Whatever calling his, whatever trade,
To that their chief attention has been paid;
His happy taste in all things they approve,
His friends they honour, and his food they love;
His wish for order, prudence in affairs,
And equal temper, (thank their stars!) are theirs;
In fact, it seem'd to be a thing decreed,
And fix'd as fate, that marriage must succeed;
Yet some like Jones, with stubborn hearts and hard,
Can hear such claims, and show them no regard.
  Soon as our farmer, like a general, found
By what strong foes he was encompass'd round—
Engage he dared not, and he could not fly,
But saw his hope in gentle parley lie;
With looks of kindness then, and trembling heart,
He met the foe, and art opposed to art.
  Now spoke that foe insidious—gentle tones,
And gentle looks, assumed for Farmer Jones:
'Three girls,' the widow cried, 'a lively three
To govern well—indeed it cannot be.'
'Yes,' he replied, 'it calls for pains and care;
But I must bear it:'—'Sir, you cannot bear;
Your son is weak, and asks a mother's eye:'
'That, my kind friend, a father's may supply:'

'Such growing griefs your very soul will tease:'
'To grieve another would not give me ease—
I have a mother'—'She, poor ancient soul!
Can she the spirits of the young control?
Can she thy peace promote, partake thy care,
Procure thy comforts, and thy sorrows share?
Age is itself impatient, uncontroll'd:'
'But wives like mothers must at length be old.'
'Thou hast shrewd servants—they are evils sore:'
'Yet a shrewd mistress might afflict me more.'
'Wilt thou not be a weary wailing man?'
'Alas! and I must bear it as I can.'
Resisted thus, the widow soon withdrew,
That in his pride the hero might pursue;
And off his wonted guard, in some retreat,
Find from a foe prepared entire defeat:
But he was prudent, for he knew in flight
These Parthian warriors turn again and fight:
He but at freedom, not at glory aim'd,
And only safety by his caution claim'd.
Thus, when a great and powerful state decrees,
Upon a small one, in its love, to seize—
It vows in kindness to protect, defend,
And be the fond ally, the faithful friend;
It therefore wills that humbler state to place
Its hopes of safety in a fond embrace;
Then must that humbler state its wisdom prove,
By kind rejection of such pressing love;
Must dread such dangerous friendship to commence,
And stand collected in its own defence:—
Our farmer thus the proffer'd kindness fled,
And shunn'd the love that into bondage led.
The widow failing, fresh besiegers came,
To share the fate of this retiring dame:
And each foresaw a thousand ills attend
The man, that fled from so discreet a friend;
And pray'd, kind soul! that no event might make
The harden'd heart of Farmer Jones to ache.
But he still govern'd with resistless hand,
And where he could not guide he would command:
With steady view in course direct he steer'd,

And his fair daughters loved him, though they fear'd;
Each had her school, and as his wealth was known,
Each had in time a household of her own.
The boy indeed was, at the grandam's side,
Humour'd and train'd, her trouble and her pride:
Companions dear, with speech and spirits mild,
The childish widow and the vapourish child;
This nature prompts; minds uninform'd and weak
In such alliance ease and comfort seek;
Push'd by the levity of youth aside,
The cares of man, his humour, or his pride,
They feel, in their defenceless state, allied:
The child is pleased to meet regard from age,
The old are pleased ev'n children to engage;
And all their wisdom, scorn'd by proud mankind,
They love to pour into the ductile mind;
By its own weakness into error led,
And by fond age with prejudices fed.
The father, thankful for the good he had,
Yet saw with pain a whining timid lad;
Whom he instructing led through cultured fields,
To show what man performs, what nature yields:
But Stephen, listless, wander'd from the view,
From beasts he fled, for butterflies he flew,
And idly gazed about, in search of something new.
The lambs indeed he loved, and wish'd to play
With things so mild, so harmless, and so gay;
Best pleased the weakest of the flock to see,
With whom he felt a sickly sympathy.
Meantime, the dame was anxious, day and night,
To guide the notions of her babe aright,
And on the favourite mind to throw her glimmering light;
Her Bible-stories she impress'd betimes,
And fill'd his head with hymns and holy rhymes;
On powers unseen, the good and ill, she dwelt,
And the poor boy mysterious terrors felt;
From frightful dreams, he waking sobb'd in dread,
Till the good lady came to guard his bed.
The father wish'd such errors to correct,
But let them pass in duty and respect:
But more it grieved his worthy mind to see

That Stephen never would a farmer be;
In vain he tried the shiftless lad to guide,
And yet 'twas time that something should be tried:
He at the village-school perchance might gain
All that such mind could gather and retain;
Yet the good dame affirm'd her favourite child
Was apt and studious, though sedate and mild;
'That he on many a learned point could speak,
And that his body, not his mind, was weak.'
The father doubted—but to school was sent
The timid Stephen, weeping as he went:
There the rude lads compell'd the child to fight,
And sent him bleeding to his home at night;
At this the grandam more indulgent grew,
And bade her darling 'shun the beastly crew;
Whom Satan ruled, and who were sure to lie,
Howling in torments, when they came to die:'
This was such comfort, that in high disdain
He told their fate, and felt their blows again:
Yet if the boy had not a hero's heart,
Within the school he play'd a better part;
He wrote a clean fine hand, and at his slate,
With more success than many a hero, sate;
He thought not much indeed—but what depends
On pains and care, was at his fingers' ends.
This had his father's praise, who now espied
A spark of merit, with a blaze of pride:
And though a farmer he would never make,
He might a pen with some advantage take;
And as a clerk that instrument employ,
So well adapted to a timid boy.
A London cousin soon a place obtain'd,
Easy but humble—little could be gain'd:
The time arrived when youth and age must part,
Tears in each eye, and sorrow in each heart;
The careful father bade his son attend
To all his duties, and obey his friend;
To keep his church and there behave aright,
As one existing in his Maker's sight,
Till acts to habits led, and duty to delight:
'Then try, my boy, as quickly as you can,

T'assume the looks and spirit of a man;
I say, be honest, faithful, civil, true,
And this you may, and yet have courage too:
Heroic men, their country's boast and pride,
Have fear'd their God, and nothing fear'd beside;
While others daring, yet imbecile, fly
The power of man, and that of God defy:
Be manly then, though mild, for sure as fate,
Thou art, my Stephen, too effeminate;
Here, take my purse, and make a worthy use
('Tis fairly stock'd) of what it will produce:
And now my blessing, not as any charm
Or conjuration; but 'twill do no harm.'
   Stephen, whose thoughts were wandering up and down,
Now charm'd with promised sights in London-town,
Now loth to leave his grandam—lost the force,
The drift and tenor of this grave discourse;
But, in a general way, he understood
'Twas good advice, and meant, 'My son, be good;'
And Stephen knew that all such precepts mean,
That lads should read their Bible, and be clean.
   The good old lady, though in some distress,
Begg'd her dear Stephen would his grief suppress;
'Nay, dry those eyes, my child—and first of all,
Hold fast thy faith, whatever may befall:
Hear the best preacher, and preserve the text
For meditation, till you hear the next;
Within your Bible night and morning look—
There is your duty, read no other book;
Be not in crowds, in broils, in riots seen,
And keep your conscience and your linen clean:
Be you a Joseph, and the time may be,
When kings and rulers will be ruled by thee.'
   'Nay,' said the father——'Hush, my son,' replied
The dame——'The Scriptures must not be denied.'
   The lad, still weeping, heard the wheels approach,
And took his place within the evening coach,
With heart quite rent asunder: On one side
Was love, and grief, and fear, for scenes untried;
Wild-beasts and wax-work fill'd the happier part
Of Stephen's varying and divided heart:

This he betray'd by sighs and questions strange,
Of famous shows, the Tower, and the Exchange.
Soon at his desk was placed the curious boy,
Demure and silent at his new employ:
Yet as he could, he much attention paid
To all around him, cautious and afraid;
On older clerks his eager eyes were fix'd,
But Stephen never in their council mix'd:
Much their contempt he fear'd, for if like them,
He felt assured he should himself contemn;
'Oh! they were all so eloquent, so free,
No! he was nothing—nothing could he be:
They dress so smartly, and so boldly look,
And talk as if they read it from a book;
But I,' said Stephen, 'will forbear to speak,
And they will think me prudent and not weak.
They talk, the instant they have dropp'd the pen,
Of singing-women and of acting-men;
Of plays and places where at night they walk
Beneath the lamps, and with the ladies talk;
While other ladies for their pleasure sing,
Oh! 'tis a glorious and a happy thing;
They would despise me, did they understand
I dare not look upon a scene so grand;
Or see the plays when critics rise and roar,
And hiss and groan, and cry—Encore! encore!—
There's one among them looks a little kind;
If more encouraged, I would ope my mind.'
Alas! poor Stephen, happier had he kept
His purpose secret, while his envy slept;
Virtue, perhaps, had conquer'd, or his shame
At least preserved him simple as he came.
A year elapsed before this clerk began
To treat the rustic something like a man;
He then in trifling points the youth advised,
Talk'd of his coat, and had it modernized;
Or with the lad a Sunday-walk would take,
And kindly strive his passions to awake;
Meanwhile explaining all they heard and saw,
Till Stephen stood in wonderment and awe:
To a neat garden near the town they stray'd,

Where the lad felt delighted and afraid;
There all he saw was smart, and fine, and fair—
He could but marvel how he ventured there:
Soon he observed, with terror and alarm,
His friend enlock'd within a lady's arm,
And freely talking—'But it is,' said he,
'A near relation, and that makes him free;'
And much amazed was Stephen, when he knew
This was the first and only interview;
Nay, had that lovely arm by him been seized,
The lovely owner had been highly pleased:
'Alas!' he sigh'd, 'I never can contrive,
At such bold, blessed freedoms to arrive;
Never shall I such happy courage boast,
I dare as soon encounter with a ghost.'
  Now to a play the friendly couple went,
But the boy murmur'd at the money spent;
'He loved,' he said, 'to buy, but not to spend—
They only talk awhile, and there's an end.'
  'Come, you shall purchase books,' the friend replied;
'You are bewilder'd, and you want a guide;
To me refer the choice, and you shall find
The light break in upon your stagnant mind!'
  The cooler clerks exclaim'd, 'In vain your art
T' improve a cub without a head or heart;
Rustics though coarse, and savages though wild,
Our cares may render liberal and mild;
But what, my friend, can flow from all these pains?
There is no dealing with a lack of brains.'—
  'True I am hopeless to behold him man,
But let me make the booby what I can:
Though the rude stone no polish will display,
Yet you may strip the rugged coat away.'
  Stephen beheld his books—'I love to know
How money goes—now here is that to show:
And now,' he cried, 'I shall be pleased to get
Beyond the Bible—there I puzzle yet.'
  He spoke abash'd—'Nay, nay!' the friend replied,
'You need not lay the good old book aside;
Antique and curious, I myself indeed
Read it at times, but as a man should read;

A fine old work it is, and I protest
I hate to hear it treated as a jest;
The book has wisdom in it, if you look
Wisely upon it, as another book:
For superstition (as our priests of sin
Are pleased to tell us) makes us blind within:
Of this hereafter—we will now select
Some works to please you, others to direct:
Tales and romances shall your fancy feed,
And reasoners form your morals and your creed.'
  The books were view'd, the price was fairly paid,
And Stephen read undaunted, undismay'd:
But not till first he paper'd all the row,
And placed in order, to enjoy the show;
Next letter'd all the backs with care and speed,
Set them in ranks, and then began to read.
  The love of order,—I the thing receive
From reverend men, and I in part believe,—
Shows a clear mind and clean, and whoso needs
This love, but seldom in the world succeeds;
And yet with this some other love must be,
Ere I can fully to the fact agree:
Valour and study may by order gain,
By order sovereigns hold more steady reign;
Through all the tribes of nature order runs,
And rules around in systems and in suns:
Still has the love of order found a place,
With all that's low, degrading, mean, and base,
With all that merits scorn, and all that meets disgrace:
In the cold miser, of all change afraid,
In pompous men in public seats obey'd;
In humble placemen, heralds, solemn drones,
Fanciers of flowers, and lads like Stephen Jones;
Order to these is armour and defence,
And love of method serves in lack of sense.
  For rustic youth could I a list produce
Of Stephen's books, how great might be the use;
But evil fate was theirs—survey'd, enjoy'd
Some happy months, and then by force destroy'd:
So will'd the fates—but these, with patience read,
Had vast effect on Stephen's heart and head.

This soon appear'd—within a single week
He oped his lips, and made attempt to speak;
He fail'd indeed—but still his friend confess'd
The best have fail'd, and he had done his best:
The first of swimmers, when at first he swims,
Has little use or freedom in his limbs;
Nay, when at length he strikes with manly force,
The cramp may seize him, and impede his course.
Encouraged thus, our clerk again essay'd
The daring act, though daunted and afraid;
Succeeding now, though partial his success,
And pertness mark'd his manner and address,
Yet such improvement issued from his books,
That all discern'd it in his speech and looks;
He ventured then on every theme to speak,
And felt no feverish tingling in his cheek;
His friend approving, hail'd the happy change,
The clerks exclaim'd—' 'Tis famous, and 'tis strange.'
Two years had pass'd; the youth attended still,
(Though thus accomplish'd) with a ready quill;
He sat th' allotted hours, though hard the case,
While timid prudence ruled in virtue's place;
By promise bound, the son his letters penn'd
To his good parent, at the quarter's end.
At first he sent those lines, the state to tell
Of his own health, and hoped his friends were well;
He kept their virtuous precepts in his mind,
And needed nothing—then his name was sign'd:
But now he wrote of Sunday walks and views,
Of actor's names, choice novels, and strange news;
How coats were cut, and of his urgent need
For fresh supply, which he desired with speed.
The father doubted, when these letters came,
To what they tended, yet was loth to blame:
'Stephen was once *my duteous son*, and now
My most obedient—this can I allow?
Can I with pleasure or with patience see
A boy at once so heartless, and so free?'
But soon the kinsman heavy tidings told,
That love and prudence could no more withhold:
'Stephen, though steady at his desk, was grown

A rake and coxcomb—this he grieved to own;
His cousin left his church, and spent the day
Lounging about in quite a heathen way;
Sometimes he swore, but had indeed the grace
To show the shame imprinted on his face:
I search'd his room, and in his absence read
Books that I knew would turn a stronger head;
The works of atheists half the number made,
The rest were lives of harlots leaving trade;
Which neither man nor boy would deign to read,
If from the scandal and pollution freed:
I sometimes threaten'd, and would fairly state
My sense of things so vile and profligate;
But I'm a cit, such works are lost on me—
They're knowledge, and (good Lord!) philosophy.'
 'Oh, send him down,' the father soon replied;
'Let me behold him, and my skill be tried:
If care and kindness lose their wonted use,
Some rougher medicine will the end produce.'
 Stephen with grief and anger heard his doom—
'Go to the farmer? to the rustic's home?
Curse the base threat'ning—' 'Nay, child, never curse;
Corrupted long, your case is growing worse.'—
'I!' quoth the youth, 'I challenge all mankind
To find a fault; what fault have you to find?
Improve I not in manner, speech, and grace?
Inquire—my friends will tell it to your face;
Have I been taught to guard his kine and sheep?
A man like me has other things to keep;
This let him know.'—'It would his wrath excite:
But come, prepare, you must away to-night.'
'What! leave my studies, my improvements leave,
My faithful friends and intimates to grieve!'—
'Go to your father, Stephen, let him see
All these improvements; they are lost on me.'
 The youth, though loth, obey'd, and soon he saw
The farmer-father, with some signs of awe;
Who kind, yet silent, waited to behold
How one would act, so daring, yet so cold:
And soon he found, between the friendly pair
That secrets pass'd which he was not to share;

But he resolved those secrets to obtain,
And quash rebellion in his lawful reign.
Stephen, though vain, was with his father mute;
He fear'd a crisis, and he shunn'd dispute;
And yet he long'd with youthful pride to show
He knew such things as farmers could not know;
These to the grandam he with freedom spoke,
Saw her amazement, and enjoy'd the joke:
But on the father when he cast his eye,
Something he found that made his valour shy;
And thus there seem'd to be a hollow truce,
Still threat'ning something dismal to produce.
Ere this the father at his leisure read
The son's choice volumes, and his wonder fled;
He saw how wrought the works of either kind
On so presuming, yet so weak a mind;
These in a chosen hour he made his prey,
Condemn'd, and bore with vengeful thoughts away;
Then in a close recess the couple near,
He sat unseen to see, unheard to hear.
There soon a trial for his patience came;
Beneath were placed the youth and ancient dame,
Each on a purpose fix'd—but neither thought
How near a foe, with power and vengeance fraught.
And now the matron told, as tidings sad,
What she had heard of her beloved lad;
How he to graceless, wicked men gave heed,
And wicked books would night and morning read;
Some former lectures she again began,
And begg'd attention of her little man;
She brought, with many a pious boast, in view
His former studies, and condemn'd the new;
Once he the names of saints and patriarchs old,
Judges and kings, and chiefs and prophets, told;
Then he in winter-nights the Bible took,
To count how often in the sacred book
The sacred name appear'd, and could rehearse
Which were the middle chapter, word, and verse,
The very letter in the middle placed,
And so employ'd the hours that others waste.
'Such wert thou once; and now, my child, they say

Thy faith like water runneth fast away;
The prince of devils hath, I fear, beguiled
The ready wit of my backsliding child.'
  On this, with lofty looks, our clerk began
His grave rebuke, as he assumed the man—
  'There is no devil,' said the hopeful youth,
'Nor prince of devils; that I know for truth:
Have I not told you how my books describe
The arts of priests and all the canting tribe?
Your Bible mentions Egypt, where it seems
Was Joseph found when Pharaoh dream'd his dreams:
Now in that place, in some bewilder'd head,
(The learned write) religious dreams were bred;
Whence through the earth, with various forms
    combined,
They came to frighten and afflict mankind,
Prone (so I read) to let a priest invade
Their souls with awe, and by his craft be made
Slave to his will, and profit to his trade:
So say my books, and how the rogues agreed
To blind the victims, to defraud and lead;
When joys above to ready dupes were sold,
And hell was threaten'd to the shy and cold.
  'Why so amazed, and so prepared to pray?
As if a Being heard a word we say:
This may surprise you; I myself began
To feel disturb'd, and to my Bible ran;
I now am wiser—yet agree in this,
The book has things that are not much amiss;
It is a fine old work, and I protest
I hate to hear it treated as a jest:
The book has wisdom in it, if you look
Wisely upon it as another book.'—
  'Oh! wicked! wicked! my unhappy child,
How hast thou been by evil men beguiled!'
  'How! wicked, say thou? you can little guess
The gain of that which you call wickedness:
Why, sins you think it sinful but to name
Have gain'd both wives and widows wealth and fame;
And this because such people never dread
Those threaten'd pains; hell comes not in their head:

Love is our nature, wealth, we all desire,
And what we wish 'tis lawful to acquire;
So say my books—and what beside they show
'Tis time to let this honest farmer know.
Nay, look not grave; am I commanded down
To feed his cattle and become his clown?
Is such his purpose? then he shall be told
The vulgar insult——'
——'Hold, in mercy hold—'
'Father, oh! father! throw the whip away;
I was but jesting, on my knees I pray—
There, hold his arm—oh! leave us not alone:
In pity cease, and I will yet atone
For all my sin—' In vain; stroke after stroke,
On side and shoulder, quick as mill-wheels broke;
Quick as the patient's pulse, who trembling cried,
And still the parent with a stroke replied;
Till all the medicine he prepared was dealt,
And every bone the precious influence felt;
Till all the panting flesh was red and raw,
And every thought was turn'd to fear and awe;
Till every doubt to due respect gave place—
Such cures are done when doctors know the case.
'Oh! I shall die—my father! do receive
My dying words; indeed I do believe;
The books are lying books, I know it well,
There is a devil, oh! there is a hell;
And I'm a sinner; spare me, I am young,
My sinful words were only on my tongue;
My heart consented not; 'tis all a lie:
Oh! spare me then, I'm not prepared to die.'
'Vain, worthless, stupid wretch!' the father cried,
'Dost thou presume to teach? art thou a guide?
Driveller and dog, it gave the mind distress
To hear thy thoughts in their religious dress;
Thy pious folly moved my strong disdain,
Yet I forgave thee for thy want of brain:
But Job in patience must the man exceed
Who could endure thee in thy present creed;
Is it for thee, thou idiot, to pretend
The wicked cause a helping hand to lend?

Canst thou a judge in any question be?
Atheists themselves would scorn a friend like thee.—
'Lo! yonder blaze thy worthies; in one heap
Thy scoundrel-favourites must for ever sleep:
Each yields its poison to the flame in turn,
Where whores and infidels are doom'd to burn;
Two noble faggots made the flame you see,
Reserving only two fair twigs for thee;
That in thy view the instruments may stand,
And be in future ready for my hand:
The just mementos that, though silent, show
Whence thy correction and improvements flow;
Beholding these, thou wilt confess their power,
And feel the shame of this important hour.
'Hadst thou been humble, I had first design'd
By care from folly to have freed thy mind;
And when a clean foundation had been laid,
Our priest, more able, would have lent his aid:
But thou art weak, and force must folly guide,
And thou art vain, and pain must humble pride:
Teachers men honour, learners they allure;
But learners teaching, of contempt are sure;
Scorn is their certain meed, and smart their only cure!'

INFANCY—A FRAGMENT

Who on the new-born light can back return,
And the first efforts of the soul discern—
Waked by some sweet maternal smile, no more
To sleep so long or fondly as before?
No! Memory cannot reach, with all her power,
To that new birth, that life-awakening hour.
No! all the traces of her first employ
Are keen perceptions of the sense's joy,
And their distaste—what then could they impart?—
That figs were luscious, and that rods had smart.
But, though the Memory in that dubious way
Recalls the dawn and twilight of her day,
And thus encounters, in the doubtful view,
With imperfection and distortion too;
Can she not tell us, as she looks around,
Of good and evil, which the most abound?
Alas! and what is earthly good? 'tis lent
Evil to hide, to soften, to prevent,
By scenes and shows that cheat the wandering eye,
While the more pompous misery passes by;
Shifts and amusements that awhile succeed,
And heads are turn'd, that bosoms may not bleed:
For what is Pleasure, that we toil to gain?
'Tis but the slow or rapid flight of Pain.
Set Pleasure by, and there would yet remain,
For every nerve and sense the sting of Pain:
Set Pain aside, and fear no more the sting,
And whence your hopes and pleasures can ye bring?
No! there is not a joy beneath the skies,
That from no grief nor trouble shall arise.
Why does the Lover with such rapture fly
To his dear mistress?—He shall show us why:—
Because her absence is such cause of grief
That her sweet smile alone can yield relief.
Why, then, that smile is Pleasure:—True, yet still
'Tis but the absence of the former ill:
For, married, soon at will he comes and goes;

Then pleasures die, and pains become repose,
And he has none of these, and therefore none of
those.
Yes! looking back as early as I can,
I see the griefs that seize their subject Man,
That in the weeping Child their early reign began:
Yes! though Pain softens, and is absent since,
He still controls me like my lawful prince.
Joys I remember, like phosphoric light
Or squibs and crackers on a gala night.
Joys are like oil; if thrown upon the tide
Of flowing life, they mix not, nor subside:
Griefs are like waters on the river thrown,
They mix entirely, and become its own.
Of all the good that grew of early date,
I can but parts and incidents relate:
A guest arriving, or a borrow'd day
From school, or schoolboy triumph at some play:
And these from Pain may be deduced; for these
Removed some ill, and hence their power to please.
But it was Misery stung me in the day
Death of an infant sister made a prey;
For then first met and moved my early fears,
A father's terrors, and a mother's tears.
Though greater anguish I have since endured,—
Some heal'd in part, some never to be cured;
Yet was there something in that first-born ill,
So new, so strange, that memory feels it still!
That my first grief: but, oh! in after-years
Were other deaths, that call'd for other tears.
No! that I cannot, that I dare not, paint—
That patient sufferer, that enduring saint,
Holy and lovely—but all words are faint.
But here I dwell not—let me, while I can,
Go to the Child, and lose the suffering Man.
Sweet was the morning's breath, the inland tide.
And our boat gliding, where alone could glide
Small craft—and they oft touch'd on either side.
It was my first-born joy. I heard them say,
'Let the child go; he will enjoy the day.'
For children ever feel delighted when

They take their portion, and enjoy with men.
Give him the pastime that the old partake,
And he will quickly top and taw forsake.
The linnet chirp'd upon the furze as well,
To my young sense, as sings the nightingale.
Without was paradise—because within
Was a keen relish, without taint of sin.
  A town appear'd,—and where an infant went,
Could they determine, on themselves intent?
I lost my way, and my companions me,
And all, their comforts and tranquillity.
Mid-day it was, and, as the sun declined,
The good, found early, I no more could find:
The men drank much, to whet the appetite;
And, growing heavy, drank to make them light;
Then drank to relish joy, then further to excite.
Their cheerfulness did but a moment last;
Something fell short, or something overpast.
The lads play'd idly with the helm and oar,
And nervous women would be set on shore,
Till 'civil dudgeon' grew, and peace would smile no more.
  Now on the colder water faintly shone
The sloping light—the cheerful day was gone;
Frown'd every cloud, and from the gather'd frown
The thunder burst, and rain came pattering down.
My torpid senses now my fears obey'd,
When the fierce lightning on the eye-balls play'd.
Now, all the freshness of the morning fled,
My spirits burden'd, and my heart was dead;
The female servants show'd a child their fear,
And men, full wearied, wanted strength to cheer;
And when, at length, the dreaded storm went past,
And there was peace and quietness at last,
'Twas not the morning's quiet—it was not
Pleasure revived, but Misery forgot:
It was not Joy that now commenced her reign,
But mere relief from wretchedness and Pain.
  So many a day, in life's advance, I knew;
So they commenced, and so they ended too.
All Promise they—all Joy as they began!
But Joy grew less, and vanish'd as they ran!

Errors and evils came in many a form,—
The mind's delusion, and the passions' storm.
  The promised joy, that like this morning rose,
Broke on my view, then clouded at its close;
E'en Love himself, that promiser of bliss,
Made his best days of pleasure end like this:
He mix'd his bitters in the cup of joy
Nor gave a bliss uninjured by alloy.

THE WORLD OF DREAMS

I

And is thy soul so wrapt in sleep?
  Thy senses, thy affections, fled?
No play of fancy thine, to keep
  Oblivion from that grave, thy bed?
Then art thou but the breathing dead:
  I envy, but I pity too:
The bravest may *my* terrors dread,
  The happiest fain *my* joys pursue.

II

Soon as the real World I lose,
  Quick Fancy takes her wonted way,
Or Baxter's sprites my soul abuse—
  For how it is I cannot say,
Nor to what powers a passive prey,
  I feel such bliss, I fear such pain;
But all is gloom, or all is gay,
  Soon as th' ideal World I gain.

III

Come, then, I woo thee, sacred Sleep!
  Vain troubles of the world, farewell!
Spirits of Ill! your distance keep—
  And in your own dominions dwell,
Ye, the sad emigrants from hell!
  Watch, dear seraphic beings, round,
And these black Enemies repel;
  Safe be my soul, my slumbers sound!

IV

In vain I pray! It is my sin
  That thus admits the shadowy throng.
Oh! now they break tumultuous in—
  Angels of darkness fierce and strong.

Oh! I am borne of fate along;
  My soul, subdued, admits the foe,
Perceives and yet endures the wrong,
  Resists, and yet prepares to go.

V

Where am I now? and what to meet?
  Where I have been entrapt before:
The wicked city's vilest street,—
  I know what I must now explore.
The dark-brow'd throng more near and more,
  With murderous looks are on me thrust,
And lo! they ope the accursed door,
  And I must go—I know I must!

VI

That female fiend!—Why is she there?
  Alas! I know her.—Oh, begone!
Why is that tainted bosom bare,
  Why fix'd on me that eye of stone?
Why have they left us thus alone?
  I saw the deed—why then appear?
Thou art not form'd of blood and bone!
  Come not, dread being, come not near!

VII

So! all is quiet, calm, serene;
  I walk a noble mansion round—
From room to room, from scene to scene,
  I breathless pass, in gloom profound:
No human shape, no mortal sound—
  I feel an awe, I own a dread,
And still proceed!—not stop nor bound—
  And all is silent, all is dead.

VIII

Now I'm hurried, borne along,
  All is business! all alive!
Heavens! how mighty is the throng,
  Voices humming like a hive!

Through the swelling crowd I strive,
  Bustling forth my way to trace:
Never fated to arrive
  At the still-expected place.

IX

Ah me! how sweet the morning sun
  Deigns on yon sleepy town to shine!
How soft those far-off rivers run—
  Those trees their leafy heads decline!
Balm-breathing zephyrs, all divine,
  Their health-imparting influence give:
Now, all that earth allows is mine—
  Now, now I dream not, but I live.

X

My friend, my brother, lost in youth,
  I meet in doubtful, glad surprise,
In conscious love, in fearless truth:
  What pleasures in the meeting rise!
Ah! brief enjoyment!—Pleasure dies
  E'en in its birth, and turns to pain:
He meets me with hard glazed eyes!
  He quits me—spurns me—with disdain.

XI

I sail the sea, I walk the land;
  In all the world am I alone:
Silent I pace the sea-worn sand,
  Silent I view the princely throne;
I listen heartless for the tone
  Of winds and waters, but in vain;
Creation dies without a groan!
  And I without a hope remain!

XII

Unnumber'd riches I behold,
  Glories untasted I survey:
My heart is sick, my bosom cold,
  Friends! neighbours! kindred! where are they?

In the sad, last, long, endless day!
  When I can neither pray nor weep,
Doom'd o'er the sleeping world to stray,
  And not to die, and not to sleep.

XIII

Beside the summer sea I stand,
  Where the slow billows swelling shine:
How beautiful this pearly sand,
  That waves, and winds, and years refine:
Be this delicious quiet mine!
  The joy of youth! so sweet before,
When I could thus my frame recline,
  And watch th' entangled weeds ashore.

XIV

Yet, I remember not that sea,
  That other shore on yonder side:
Between them arrow bound must be,
  If equal rise th'opposing tide—
Lo! lo! they rise—and I abide
  The peril of the meeting flood:
Away, away, my footsteps slide—
  I pant upon the clinging mud!

XV

Oh let me now possession take
  Of this—it cannot be a dream.
Yes! now the soul must be awake—
  These pleasures are—they do not seem.
And is it true? Oh joy extreme!
  All whom I loved, and thought them dead,
Far down in Lethe's flowing stream,
  And, with them, life's best pleasures fled:

XVI

Yes, many a tear for them I shed—
  Tears that relieve the anxious breast;
And now, by heavenly favour led,
  We meet—and One, the fairest, best,

Among them—ever-welcome guest!
   Within the room, that seem'd destroy'd—
This room endear'd, and still possess'd,
   By this dear party still enjoy'd.

XVII

Speak to me! speak! that I may know
   I am thus happy!—dearest, speak!
Those smiles that haunt fond memory show!
   Joy makes us doubtful, wavering, weak;
But yet 'tis joy—And all I seek
   Is mine! What glorious day is this!
Now let me bear with spirit meek
   And hour of pure and perfect bliss.

XVIII

But do ye look indeed as friends?
   Is there no change? Are not ye cold?
Oh! I do dread that Fortune lends
   Fictitious good!—that I behold,
To lose, these treasures, which of old
   Were all my glory, all my pride:
May not these arms that form infold?
   Is all affection asks denied?

XIX

Say, what is this?—How are we tried,
   In this sad world!—I know not these—
All strangers, none to me allied—
   Those aspects blood and spirit freeze:
Dear forms, my wandering judgment spare;
   And thou, most dear, these fiends disarm,
Resume thy wonted looks and air,
   And break this melancholy charm.

XX

And are they vanish'd? Is she lost?
   Shall never day that form restore?
Oh! I am all by fears engross'd;
   Sad truth has broken in once more,

And I the brief delight deplore:
  How durst they such resemblance take?
Heavens! with what grace the mask they wore!
  Oh, from what visions I awake!

XXI

Once more, once more upon the shore!
  Now back the rolling ocean flows:
The rocky bed now far before
  On the receding water grows—
The treasures and the wealth it owes
  To human misery—all in view;
Fate all on me at once bestows,
  From thousands robb'd and murder'd too.

XXII

But, lo! whatever I can find
  Grows mean and worthless as I view:
They promise, but they cheat the mind,
  As promises are born to do:
How lovely every form and hue,
  Till seized and master'd—Then arise,
For all that admiration drew,
  All that our senses can despise!

XXIII

Within the basis of a tower,
  I saw a plant—it graced the spot;
There was within nor wind nor shower,
  And this had life that flowers have not.
I drew it forth—Ah, luckless lot!
  It was the mandrake; and the sound
Of anguish deeply smother'd shot
  Into my breast with pang profound.

XXIV

'I would I were a soaring bird,'
  Said Folly, 'and I then would fly:'
Some mocking Muse or Fairy heard—
  'You can but fall—suppose you try?

And though you may not mount the sky,
  You will not grovel in the mire.'
Hail, words of comfort! Now can I
  Spurn earth, and to the air aspire.

XXV

And this, before, might I have done
  If I had courage—that is all:
'T is easier now to soar than run;
  Up! up!—we neither tire nor fall.
Children of dust, be yours to crawl
  On the vile earth!—while, happier, I
Must listen to an inward call,
  That bids me mount, that makes me fly.

XXVI

I tumble from the loftiest tower,
  Yet evil have I never found;
Supported by some favouring power,
  I come in safety to the ground.
I rest upon the sea, the sound
  Of many waters in mine ear,
Yet have no dread of being drown'd,
  But see my way, and cease to fear.

XXVII

Awake, there is no living man
  Who may my fixed spirit shake;
But, sleeping, there is one who can,
  And oft does he the trial make:
Against his might resolves I take,
  And him oppose with high disdain;
But quickly all my powers forsake
  My mind, and I resume my chain.

XXVIII

I know not how, but I am brought
  Into a large and Gothic hall,
Seated with those I never sought—
  Kings, Caliphs, Kaisers,—silent all;
Pale as the dead; enrobed and tall,
  Majestic, frozen, solemn, still;

They wake my fears, my wits appal,
  And with both scorn and terror fill.

XXIX

Now are they seated at a board
  In that cold grandeur—I am there.
But what can mummied kings afford?
  This is their meagre ghostly fare,
And proves what fleshless things they stare!
  Yes! I am seated with the dead:
How great, and yet how mean they are!
  Yes! I can scorn them while I dread!

XXX

They're gone!—and in their room I see
  A fairy being, form and dress
Brilliant as light; nor can there be
  On earth that heavenly loveliness;
Nor words can that sweet look express,
  Or tell what living gems adorn
That wond'rous beauty: who can guess
  Where such celestial charms were born?

XXXI

Yet, as I wonder and admire,
  The grace is gone, the glory dead;
And now it is but mean attire
  Upon a shrivel'd beldame spread,
Laid loathsome on a pauper's bed,
  Where wretchedness and woe are found,
And the faint putrid odour shed
  By all that's foul and base around!

XXXII

A garden this? oh! lovely breeze!
  Oh! flowers that with such freshness bloom!—
Flowers shall I call such forms as these,
  Or this delicious air perfume?
Oh! this from better worlds must come;
  On earth such beauty who can meet?
No! this is not the native home
  Of things so pure, so bright, so sweet!

XXXIII

Where? where?—am I reduced to this—
  Thus sunk in poverty extreme?
Can I not these vile things dismiss?
  No! they are things that more than seem:
This room with that cross-parting beam
  Holds yonder squalid tribe and me—
But they were ever thus, nor dream
  Of being wealthy, favour'd, free!—

XXXIV

Shall I a coat and badge receive,
  And sit among these crippled men,
And not go forth without the leave
  Of him—and ask it humbly then—
Who reigns in this infernal den—
  Where all beside in woe repine?
Yes, yes, I must: nor tongue nor pen
  Can paint such misery as mine!

XXXV

Wretches! if ye were only poor,
  You would my sympathy engage;
Or were ye vicious, and no more,
  I might be fill'd with manly rage;
Or had ye patience, wise and sage
  We might such worthy sufferers call:
But ye are birds that suit your cage—
  Poor, vile, impatient, worthless all!

XXXVI

How came I hither? Oh, that Hag!
  'T is she the enchanting spell prepares;
By cruel witchcraft she can drag
  My struggling being in her snares:
Oh, how triumphantly she glares!
  But yet would leave me, could I make
Strong effort to subdue my cares.—
  'T IS MADE!—and I to Freedom wake!

TALES OF THE HALL

INTRODUCTORY NOTE

The plan of the work—for it has more of plan and unity than any of Mr Crabbe's former productions—is abundantly simple. Two brothers, both past middle age, meet together, for the first time since their infancy, in the Hall of their native parish, which the elder and richer has purchased as a place of retirement for his declining age; and there tell each other their own history, and then that of their guests, neighbours, and acquaintances. The senior [George] is much the richer, and a bachelor—having been a little distasted with the sex by the unlucky result of a very extravagant passion. He is, moreover, rather too reserved, and somewhat Toryish, though with an excellent heart and a powerful understanding. The younger [Richard] is very sensible also, but more open, social and talkative; a happy husband and father, with a tendency to Whiggism, and some notion of reform, and a disposition to think well both of men and women. The visit lasts two or three weeks in autumn; and the Tales are told in the after-dinner têtes-à-têtes that take place in that time between the worthy brothers over the bottle.

Edinburgh Review JEFFREY
Vol. XXXII (1819), p. 127.

4. ADVENTURES OF RICHARD

Eight days had past; the Brothers now could meet
With ease, and take the customary seat.
'These,' said the host, for he perceived where stray'd
His brother's eye, and what he now survey'd;
'These are the costly trifles that we buy,
Urged by the strong demands of vanity,
The thirst and hunger of a mind diseased,
That must with purchased flattery be appeased;
But yet, 'tis true, the things that you behold
Serve to amuse us as we're getting old:
These pictures, as I heard our artists say,
Are genuine all, and I believe they may;
They cost the genuine sums, and I should grieve
If, being willing, I could not believe.
And there is music; when the ladies come,
With their keen looks they scrutinize the room

To see what pleases, and I must expect
To yield them pleasure, or to find neglect:
For, as attractions from our person fly,
Our purses, Richard, must the want supply;
Yet would it vex me could the triflers know
That they can shut out comfort or bestow.
'But see this room: here, Richard, you will find
Books for all palates, food for every mind;
This readers term the ever-new delight,
And so it is, if minds have appetite:
Mine once was craving; great my joy, indeed,
Had I possess'd such food when I could feed;
When at the call of every new-born wish
I could have keenly relish'd every dish—
Now, Richard, now, I stalk around and look
Upon the dress and title of a book,
Try half a page, and then can taste no more,
But the dull volume to its place restore;
Begin a second slowly to peruse,
Then cast it by, and look about for news;
The news itself grows dull in long debates,—
I skip, and see what the conclusion states;
And many a speech, with zeal and study made
Cold and resisting spirits to persuade,
Is lost on mine; alone, we cease to feel
What crowds admire, and wonder at their zeal.
'But how the day? No fairer will it be?
Walk you? Alas! 'tis requisite for me—
Nay, let me not prescribe—my friends and guests are free.'

* * *

It was a fair and mild autumnal sky,
And earth's ripe treasures met th' admiring eye,
As a rich beauty, when her bloom is lost,
Appears with more magnificence and cost:
The wet and heavy grass, where feet had stray'd,
Not yet erect, the wanderer's way betray'd;
Showers of the night had swell'd the deep'ning rill,
The morning breeze had urged the quick'ning mill;
Assembled rooks had wing'd their sea-ward flight,
By the same passage to return at night,
While proudly o'er them hung the steady kite,

Then turn'd him back, and left the noisy throng,
Nor deign'd to know them as he sail'd along.
Long yellow leaves, from oziers, strew'd around,
Choked the small stream, and hush'd the feeble sound;
While the dead foliage dropt from loftier trees
Our squire beheld not with his wonted ease,
But to his own reflections made reply,
And said aloud, 'Yes! doubtless we must die.'
'We must;' said Richard, 'and we would not live
To feel what dotage and decay will give;
But we yet taste whatever we beheld,
The morn is lovely, though the air is cold:
There is delicious quiet in this scene,
At once so rich, so varied, so serene;
Sounds too delight us,—each discordant tone
Thus mingled please, that fail to please alone;
This hollow wind, this rustling of the brook,
The farm-yard noise, the woodman at yon oak—
See, the axe falls!—now listen to the stroke!
That gun itself, that murders all this peace,
Adds to the charm, because it soon must cease.'
'No doubt,' said George, 'the country has its charms!
My farm behold! the model for all farms!
Look at that land—you find not there a weed,
We grub the roots, and suffer none to seed.
To land like this no botanist will come,
To seek the precious ware he hides at home;
Pressing the leaves and flowers with effort nice,
As if they came from herbs in Paradise;
Let them their favourites with my neighbours see,
They have no—what?—no *habitat* with me.
  'Now see my flock, and hear its glory;—none
Have that vast body and that slender bone;
They are the village boast, the dealer's theme,
Fleece of such staple! flesh in such esteem!'
  'Brother,' said Richard, 'do I hear aright?
Does the land truly give so much delight?'
  'So says my bailiff: sometimes I have tried
To catch the joy, but nature has denied;
It will not be—the mind has had a store
Laid up for life, and will admit no more:

Worn out in trials, and about to die,
In vain to these we for amusement fly;
We farm, we garden, we our poor employ,
And much command, though little we enjoy;
Or, if ambitious, we employ our pen,
We plant a desert, or we drain a fen;
And—here, behold my medal!—this will show
What men may merit when they nothing know.'
'Yet reason here,' said Richard, 'joins with pride:—'
'I did not ask th' alliance,' George replied—
'I grant it true, such trifle may induce
A dull, proud man to wake and be of use;
And there are purer pleasures, that a mind
Calm and uninjured may in villas find;
But where th' affections have been deeply tried,
With other food that mind must be supplied:
'Tis not in trees or medals to impart
The powerful medicine for an aching heart;
The agitation dies, but there is still
The backward spirit, the resisting will.
Man takes his body to a country seat,
But minds, dear Richard, have their own retreat;
Oft when the feet are pacing o'er the green
The mind is gone where never grass was seen,
And never thinks of hill, or vale, or plain,
Till want of rest creates a sense of pain,
That calls that wandering mind, and brings it home again.
No more of farms: but here I boast of minds
That makes a friend the richer when he finds;
These shalt thou see;—but, Richard, be it known,
Who thinks to see must in his turn be shown:—
But now farewell! to thee will I resign
Woods, walks, and valleys! take them till we dine.'

* * *

The Brothers dined, and with that plenteous fare
That seldom fails to dissipate our care,
At least the lighter kind; and oft prevails
When reason, duty, nay, when kindness fails.
Yet food and wine, and all that mortals bless,
Lead them to think of peril and distress;

Cold, hunger, danger, solitude, and pain,
That men in life's adventurous ways sustain.
'Thou hast sail'd far, dear brother,' said the 'squire—
'Permit me of these unknown lands t' inquire,
Lands never till'd, where thou hast wondering been,
And all the marvels thou hast heard and seen:
Do tell me something of the miseries felt
In climes where travellers freeze, and where they melt;
And be not nice,—we know 'tis not in men,
Who travel far, to hold a steady pen:
Some will, 'tis true, a bolder freedom take,
And keep our wonder always wide awake;
We know of those whose dangers far exceed
Our frail belief, that trembles as we read;
Such as in deserts burn, and thirst, and die,
Save a last gasp that they recover by:
Then, too, their hazard from a tyrant's arms,
A tiger's fury, or a lady's charms;
Beside th' accumulated evils borne
From the bold outset to the safe return.
These men abuse; but thou hast fair pretence
To modest dealing, and to mild good sense;
Then let me hear thy struggles and escapes
In the far lands of crocodiles and apes:
Say, hast thou. Bruce-like, knelt upon the bed
Where the young Nile uplifts his branchy head?
Or been partaker of th' unhallow'd feast,
Where beast-like man devours his fellow beast,
And churn'd the bleeding life? while each great dame
And sovereign beauty bade adieu to shame?
Or did the storm, that thy wreck'd pinnace bore,
Impel thee gasping on some unknown shore;
Where, when thy beard and nails were savage grown,
Some swarthy princess took thee for her own,
Some danger-dreading Yarico, who, kind,
Sent thee away, and, prudent, staid behind?
'Come—I am ready wonders to receive,
Prone to assent, and willing to believe.'
Richard replied: 'It must be known to you,
That tales improbable may yet be true;
And yet it is a foolish thing to tell

A tale that shall be judged improbable;
While some impossibilities appear
So like the truth, that we assenting hear:
Yet, with your leave, I venture to relate
A chance-affair, and fact alone will state;
Though, I confess, it may suspicion breed,
And you may cry, "improbable, indeed!"

* * *

'When first I tried the sea, I took a trip,
But duty none, in a relation's ship;
Thus, unengaged, I felt my spirits light,
Kept care at distance, and put fear to flight;
Oft this same spirit in my friends prevail'd,
Buoyant in dangers, rising when assail'd;
When, as the gale at evening died away,
And die it will with the retiring day,
Impatient then, and sick of very ease,
We loudly whistled for the slumbering breeze.
'One eve it came; and, frantic in my joy,
I rose and danced, as idle as a boy:
The cabin-lights were down, that we might learn
A trifling something from the ship astern;
The stiffening gale bore up the growing wave,
And wilder motion to my madness gave:
Oft have I since, when thoughtful and at rest,
Believed some maddening power my mind possess'd;
For, in an instant, as the stern sank low,
(How moved I knew not—What can madness know?)
Chance that direction to my motion gave,
And plunged me headlong in the roaring wave:
Swift flew the parting ship,—the fainter light
Withdrew,—or horror took them from my sight.
'All was confused above, beneath, around;
All sounds of terror; no distinguish'd sound
Could reach me, now on sweeping surges tost,
And then between the rising billows lost;
An undefined sensation stopp'd my breath;
Disorder'd views and threat'ning signs of death
Met in one moment, and a terror gave—
I cannot paint it—to the moving grave.
My thoughts were all distressing, hurried, mix'd,

On all things fixing, not a moment fix'd:
Vague thoughts of instant danger brought their pain,
New hopes of safety banish'd them again;
Then the swoln billow all these hopes destroy'd,
And left me sinking in the mighty void:
Weaker I grew, and grew the more dismay'd,
Of aid all hopeless, yet in search of aid;
Struggling awhile upon the wave to keep,
Then, languid, sinking in the yawning deep:
So tost, so lost, so sinking in despair,
I pray'd in heart an indirected prayer,
And then once more I gave my eyes to view
The ship now lost, and bade the light adieu!
From my chill'd frame th' enfeebled spirit fled,
Rose the tall billows round my deep'ning bed,
Cold seized my heart, thought ceased, and I was dead.
 'Brother, I have not,—man has not the power
To paint the horrors of that life-long hour;
Hour!—but of time I knew not—when I found
Hope, youth, life, love, and all they promised, drown'd;
When all so indistinct, so undefined,
So dark and dreadful, overcame the mind;
When such confusion, on the spirit dwelt,
That, feeling much, it knew not what it felt.
 'Can I, my brother—ought I to forget
That night of terror? No! it threatens yet.
Shall I days, months—nay, years, indeed, neglect,
Who then could feel what moments must effect
Were aught effected? who, in that wild storm,
Found there was nothing I could well perform;
For what to us are moments, what are hours,
If lost our judgment, and confused our powers?
 'Oft in the times when passion strives to reign,
When duty feebly holds the slacken'd chain,
When reason slumbers, then remembrance draws
This view of death, and folly makes a pause—
The view o'ercomes the vice, the fear the frenzy awes.
 'I know there wants not this to make it true,
What danger bids be done, in safety do;
Yet such escapes may make our purpose sure,
Who slights such warning may be too secure.'

'But the escape!'—'Whate'er they judged might save
Their sinking friend they cast upon the wave;
Something of these my heaven-directed arm
Unconscious seized, and held as by a charm:
The crew astern beheld me as I swam,
And I am saved—O! let me say I am.'

* * *

'Brother,' said George, 'I have neglected long
To think of all thy perils:—it was wrong;
But do forgive me; for I could not be
Than of myself more negligent of thee.
Now tell me, Richard, from the boyish years
Of thy young mind, that now so rich appears,
How was it stored? 'twas told me, thou wert wild,
A truant urchin,—a neglected child.
I heard of this escape, and sat supine
Amid the danger that exceeded thine;
Thou couldst but die—the waves could but infold
Thy warm gay heart, and make that bosom cold—
While I——but no! Proceed, and give me truth;
How past the years of thy unguided youth?
Thy father left thee to the care of one
Who could not teach, could ill support a son;
Yet time and trouble feeble minds have stay'd,
And fit for long-neglected duties made:
I see thee struggling in the world, as late
Within the waves, and with an equal fate,
By Heaven preserved—but tell me, whence and how
Thy gleaning came?—a dexterous gleaner thou!'

'Left by that father, who was known to few,
And to that mother, who has not her due
Of honest fame,' said Richard, 'our retreat
Was a small cottage, for our station meet,
On Barford Downs: that mother, fond and poor,
There taught some truths, and bade me seek for more,
Such as our village-school and books a few
Supplied; but such I cared not to pursue;
I sought the town, and to the ocean gave
My mind and thoughts, as restless as the wave:
Where crowds assembled, I was sure to run,
Hear what was said, and mused on what was done;

Attentive listening in the moving scene,
And often wondering what the men could mean.
When ships at sea made signals of their need,
I watch'd on shore the sailors, and their speed:
Mix'd in their act, nor rested till I knew
Why they were call'd, and what they were to do.
'Whatever business in the port was done,
I, without call, was with the busy one;
Not daring question, but with open ear
And greedy spirit, ever bent to hear.
'To me the wives of seamen loved to tell
What storms endanger'd men esteem'd so well;
What wond'rous things in foreign parts they saw,
Lands without bounds, and people without law.
'No ships were wreck'd upon that fatal beach,
But I could give the luckless tale of each;
Eager I look'd, till I beheld a face
Of one disposed to paint their dismal case;
Who gave the sad survivors' doleful tale,
From the first brushing of the mighty gale
Until they struck; and, suffering in their fate,
I long'd the more they should its horrors state;
While some, the fond of pity, would enjoy
The earnest sorrows of the feeling boy.
I sought the men return'd from regions cold,
The frozen straits, where icy mountains roll'd;
Some I could win to tell me serious tales
Of boats uplifted by enormous whales,
Or, when harpoon'd, how swiftly through the sea
The wounded monsters with the cordage flee;
Yet some uneasy thoughts assail'd me then,
The monsters warr'd not with, nor wounded men:
The smaller fry we take, with scales and fins,
Who gasp and die—this adds not to our sins;
But so much blood! warm life, and frames so large
To strike, to murder—seem'd an heavy charge.
'They told of days, where many goes to one—
Such days as ours; and how a larger sun,
Red, but not flaming, roll'd, with motion slow,
On the world's edge, and never dropt below.
'There were fond girls, who took me to their side

To tell the story how their lovers died;
They praised my tender heart, and bade me prove
Both kind and constant when I came to love.
In fact, I lived for many an idle year
In fond pursuit of agitations dear;
For ever seeking, ever pleased to find,
The food I loved, I thought not of its kind;
It gave affliction while it brought delight,
And joy and anguish could at once excite.
'One gusty day, now stormy and now still,
I stood apart upon the western hill,
And saw a race at sea: a gun was heard,
And two contending boats in sail appear'd:
Equal awhile; then one was left behind,
And for a moment had her chance resign'd,
When, in that moment, up a sail they drew—
Not used before—their rivals to pursue.
Strong was the gale! in hurry now there came
Men from the town, their thoughts, their fears the same;
And women too! affrighted maids and wives,
All deeply feeling for their sailors' lives.
'The strife continued; in a glass we saw
The desperate efforts, and we stood in awe,
When the last boat shot suddenly before,
Then fill'd, and sank—and could be seen no more!
'Then were those piercing shrieks, that frantic flight,
All hurried! all in tumult and affright!
A gathering crowd from different streets drew near,
All ask, all answer—none attend, none hear!
'One boat is safe; and see! she backs her sail
To save the sinking—Will her care avail?
'O! how impatient on the sands we tread,
And the winds roaring, and the women led,
As up and down they pace with frantic air,
And scorn a comforter, and will despair;
They know not who in either boat is gone,
But think the father, husband, lover, one.
'And who is she apart? She dares not come
To join the crowd, yet cannot rest at home:
With what strong interest looks she at the waves,
Meeting and clashing o'er the seamen's graves:

'Tis a poor girl betroth'd—a few hours more,
And *he* will lie a corpse upon the shore.
'Strange, that a boy could love these scenes, and cry
In very pity—but that boy was I.
With pain my mother would my tales receive,
And say, "my Richard, do not learn to grieve."
One wretched hour had past before we knew
Whom they had saved! Alas! they were but two,
An orphan'd lad and widow'd man—no more!
And they unnoticed stood upon the shore,
With scarce a friend to greet them—widows view'd
This man and boy, and then their cries renew'd:—
'Twas long before the signs of wo gave place
To joy again; grief sat on every face.
'Sure of my mother's kindness, and the joy
She felt in meeting her rebellious boy,
I at my pleasure our new seat forsook,
And, undirected, these excursions took:
I often rambled to the noisy quay,
Strange sounds to hear, and business strange to me;
Seamen and carmen, and I know not who,
A lewd, amphibious, rude, contentious crew—
Confused as bees appear about their hive,
Yet all alert to keep their work alive.
'Here, unobserved as weed upon the wave,
My whole attention to the scene I gave;
I saw their tasks, their toil, their care, their skill,
Led by their own and by a master-will;
And though contending, toiling, tugging on,
The purposed business of the day was done.
'The open shops of craftsmen caught my eye,
And there my questions met the kind reply:
Men, when alone, will teach; but, in a crowd,
The child is silent, or the man is proud;
But, by themselves, there is attention paid
To a mild boy, so forward, yet afraid.
'I made me interest at the inn's fire-side,
Amid the scenes to bolder boys denied;
For I had patrons there, and I was one,
They judged, who noticed nothing that was done.
"A quiet lad!" would my protector say;

"To him, now, this is better than his play:
Boys are as men; some active, shrewd, and keen,
They look about if aught is to be seen;
And some, like Richard here, have not a mind
That takes a notice—but the lad is kind."
'I loved in summer on the heath to walk,
And seek the shepherd—shepherds love to talk:
His superstition was of ranker kind,
And he with tales of wonder stored my mind;
Wonders that he in many a lonely eve
Had seen, himself, and therefore must believe.
His boy, his Joe, he said, from duty ran,
Took to the sea, and grew a fearless man:
"On yonder knoll—the sheep were in the fold—
His spirit past me, shivering-like and cold!
I felt a fluttering, but I knew not how,
And heard him utter, like a whisper, 'now!'
Soon came a letter from a friend—to tell
That he had fallen, and the time he fell."
'Even to the smugglers' hut the rocks between,
I have, adventurous in my wandering, been:
Poor, pious Martha served the lawless tribe,
And could their merits and their faults describe;
Adding her thoughts; "I talk, my child, to you,
Who little think of what such wretches do."
'I loved to walk where none had walk'd before,
About the rocks that ran along the shore;
Or far beyond the sight of men to stray,
And take my pleasure when I lost my way;
For then 'twas mine to trace the hilly heath,
And all the mossy moor that lies beneath:
Here had I favourite stations, where I stood
And heard the murmurs of the ocean-flood,
With not a sound beside, except when flew
Aloft the lapwing, or the gray curlew,
Who with wild notes my fancied power defied,
And mock'd the dreams of solitary pride.
'I loved to stop at every creek and bay
Made by the river in its winding way,
And call to memory—not by marks they bare,
But by the thoughts that were created there.

4. *Adventures of Richard*

'Pleasant it was to view the sea-gulls strive
Against the storm, or in the ocean dive,
With eager scream, or when they dropping gave
Their closing wings to sail upon the wave:
Then as the winds and waters raged around,
And breaking billows mix'd their deafening sound,
They on the rolling deep securely hung,
And calmly rode the restless waves among.
Nor pleased it less around me to behold,
Far up the beach, the yesty sea-foam roll'd;
Or from the shore upborn, to see on high,
Its frothy flakes in wild confusion fly:
While the salt spray that clashing billows form,
Gave to the taste a feeling of the storm.
'Thus, with my favourite views, for many an hour
Have I indulged the dreams of princely power;
When the mind, wearied by excursions bold,
The fancy jaded, and the bosom cold,
Or when those wants, that will on kings intrude,
Or evening-fears, broke in on solitude;
When I no more my fancy could employ,
I left in haste what I could not enjoy,
And was my gentle mother's welcome boy.
'But now thy walk,—this soft autumnal gloom
Bids no delay—at night I will resume
My subject, showing, not how I improved
In my strange school, but what the things I loved,
My first-born friendships, ties by form uncheck'd,
And all that boys acquire whom men neglect.'

9. THE PRECEPTOR HUSBAND

'Whom pass'd we musing near the woodman's shed,
Whose horse not only carried him but led,
That his grave rider might have slept the time,
Or solved a problem, or composed a rhyme?
A more abstracted man within my view
Has never come—He recollected you.'
'Yes,—he was thoughtful—thinks the whole day long,
Deeply, and chiefly that he once thought wrong;

He thought a strong and kindred mind to trace
In the soft outlines of a trifler's face.
'Poor Finch! I knew him when at school,—a boy
Who might be said his labours to enjoy;
So young a pedant that he always took
The girl to dance who most admired her book;
And would the butler and the cook surprise,
Who listen'd to his Latin exercise;
The matron's self the praise of Finch avow'd,
He was so serious, and he read so loud:
But yet, with all this folly and conceit,
The lines he wrote were elegant and neat;
And early promise in his mind appear'd
Of noble efforts when by reason clear'd.
'And when he spoke of wives, the boy would say,
His should be skill'd in Greek and algebra;
For who would talk with one to whom his themes,
And favourite studies, were no more than dreams?
For this, though courteous, gentle, and humane,
The boys contemn'd and hated him as vain,
Stiff and pedantic.—'
'Did the man enjoy,
In after life, the visions of the boy?'
'At least they form'd his wishes, they were yet
The favourite views on which his mind was set:
He quaintly said, how happy must they prove,
Who, loving, study—or who, studious, love;
Who feel their minds with sciences imbued,
And their warm hearts by beauty's force subdued.
'His widow'd mother, who the world had seen,
And better judge of either sex had been,
Told him that just as their affairs were placed,
In some respects, he must forego his taste;
That every beauty, both of form and mind,
Must be by him, if unendow'd, resign'd;
That wealth was wanted for their joint affairs;
His sisters' portions, and the Hall's repairs.
'The son assented—and the wife must bring
Wealth, learning, beauty, ere he gave the ring;
But as these merits, when they all unite,
Are not produced in every soil and site;

And when produced are not the certain gain
Of him who would these precious things obtain;
Our patient student waited many a year,
Nor saw this phœnix in his walks appear;
But as views mended in the joint estate,
He would a something in his points abate;
Give him but learning, beauty, temper, sense,
And he would then the happy state commence.
The mother sigh'd, but she at last agreed,
And now the son was likely to succeed;
Wealth is substantial good the fates allot,
We know we have it, or we have it not;
But all those graces, which men highly rate,
Their minds themselves imagine and create;
And therefore Finch was in a way to find
A good that much depended on his mind.
  'He look'd around, observing, till he saw
Augusta Dallas! when he felt an awe
Of so much beauty and commanding grace,
That well became the honours of her race:
  'This lady never boasted of the trash
That commerce brings: she never spoke of cash;
The gentle blood that ran in every vein
At all such notions blush'd in pure disdain.—
  'Wealth once relinquish'd, there was all beside,
As Finch believed, that could adorn a bride;
He could not gaze upon the form and air,
Without concluding all was right and fair;
Her mild but dignified reserve suprest
All free inquiry—but his mind could rest,
Assured that all was well, and in that view was blest.
  'And now he asked, "am I the happy man
Who can deserve her? is there one who can?"
His mother told him, he possess'd the land
That puts a man in heart to ask a hand;
All who possess it feel they bear about
A spell that puts a speedy end to doubt;
But Finch was modest—"May it then be thought
That she can be so gained?"—"She may be sought:"
"Can love with land be won?" "By land is beauty
  bought.

Do not, dear Charles, with indignation glow,
All value that the want of which they know;
Nor do I blame her; none that worth denies:
But can my son be sure of what he buys?
Beauty she has, but with it can you find
The inquiring spirit, or the studious mind?
This wilt thou need who art to thinking prone,
And minds unpair'd had better think alone;
Then now unhappy will the husband be,
Whose sole associate spoils his company?"
This he would try; but all such trials prove
Too mighty for a man disposed to love;
He whom the magic of a face enchains
But little knowledge of the mind obtains;
If by his tender heart the man is led,
He finds how erring is the soundest head.
'The lady saw his purpose; she could meet
The man's inquiry, and his aim defeat;
She had a studied flattery in her look,
She could be seen retiring with a book;
She by attending to his speech could prove,
That she for learning had a fervent love;
Yet love alone she modestly declared,
She must be spared inquiry, and was spared;
Of her poor studies she was not so weak,
As in his presence, or at all, to speak;
But to discourse with him—who, all agreed,
Had read so much, would be absurd indeed;
Ask what he might, she was so much a dunce
She would confess her ignorance at once.
'All this the man believed not,—doom'd to grieve
For this belief, he this would not believe:
No! he was quite in raptures to discern
That love, and that avidity to learn.
"Could she have found," she said, "a friend, a guide,
Like him, to study had been all her pride;
But, doom'd so long to frivolous employ,
How could she those superior views enjoy?
The day might come—a happy day for her,
When she might choose the ways she should prefer."
'Then too he learn'd, in accidental way,

How much she grieved to lose the given day
In dissipation wild, in visitation gay.
Happy, most happy, must the woman prove
Who proudly looks on him she vows to love;
Who can her humble acquisitions state,
That he will praise, at least will tolerate.
'Still the cool mother sundry doubts express'd,—
"How! is Augusta graver than the rest?
There are three others: they are not inclined
To feed with precious food the empty mind:
Whence this strong relish?" "It is very strong,"
Replied the son, "and has possess'd her long,
Increased indeed, I may presume, by views,—
We may suppose—ah! may she not refuse?"
"Fear not!—I see the question must be tried,
Nay, is determined—let us to your bride."
'They soon were wedded, and the nymph appear'd
By all her promised excellence endear'd:
Her words were kind, were cautious, and were few,
And she was proud—of what her husband knew.
'Weeks pass'd away, some five or six, before,
Bless'd in the present, Finch could think of more:
A month was next upon a journey spent,
When to the Lakes the fond companions went;
Then the gay town received them, and, at last,
Home to their mansion, man and wife, they pass'd.
'And now in quiet way they came to live
On what their fortune, love, and hopes would give:
The honied moon had nought but silver rays,
And shone benignly on their early days;
The second moon a light less vivid shed,
And now the silver rays were tinged with lead.
They now began to look beyond the Hall,
And think what friends would make a morning-call;
Their former appetites return'd, and now
Both could their wishes and their tastes avow;
'Twas now no longer "just what you approve,"
But "let the wild fowl be to-day, my love."
In fact the senses, drawn aside by force
Of a strong passion, sought their usual course.
'Now to her music would the wife repair,

To which he listen'd once with eager air;
When there was so much harmony within,
That any note was sure its way to win;
But now the sweet melodious tones were sent
From the struck chords, and none cared where
they went.
Full well we know that many a favourite air,
That charms a party, fails to charm a pair;
And as Augusta play'd she look'd around,
To see if one was dying at the sound:
But all were gone—a husband, wrapt in gloom,
Stalk'd careless, listless, up and down the room.
'And now 'tis time to fill that ductile mind
With knowledge, from his stores of various kind:
His mother, in a peevish mood, had ask'd,
"Does your Augusta profit? is she task'd?"
'"Madam!" he cried, offended with her looks,
"There's time for all things, and not all for books:
Just on one's marriage to sit down, and prate
On points of learning, is a thing I hate.—"
'"'Tis right, my son, and it appears to me
If deep your hatred, you must well agree."
'Finch was too angry for a man so wise,
And said, "Insinuation I despise!
Nor do I wish to have a mind so full
Of learned trash—it makes a woman dull:
Let it suffice, that I in her discern
An aptitude, and a desire to learn.—"
'The matron smiled, but she observed a frown
On her son's brow, and calmly sat her down;
Leaving the truth to Time, who solves our doubts,
By bringing his all-glorious daughter out—
Truth! for whose beauty all their love profess,
And yet how many think it ugliness!
'"Augusta, love," said Finch, "while you engage
In that embroidery, let me read a page;
Suppose it Hume's; indeed he takes a side,
But still an author need not be our guide;
And as he writes with elegance and ease,
Do now attend—he will be sure to please.
Here at the Revolution we commence,—

We date, you know, our liberties from hence."
  '"Yes, sure," Augusta answer'd with a smile,
"Our teacher always talk'd about his style;
When we about the Revolution read,
And how the martyrs to the flames were led;
The good old bishops, I forget their names,
But they were all committed to the flames;
Maidens and widows, bachelors and wives,—
The very babes and sucklings lost their lives.
I read it all in Guthrie at the school,—
What now!—I know you took me for a fool;
There were five bishops taken from the stall,
And twenty widows, I remember all;
And by this token, that our teacher tried
To cry for pity, till she howl'd and cried."
  '"True, true, my love, but you mistake the thing,—
The Revolution that made William King
Is what I mean; the Reformation you,
In Edward and Elizabeth."—"'Tis true:
But the nice reading is the love between
The brave Lord Essex and the cruel queen;
And how he sent the ring to save his head,
Which the false lady kept till he was dead.
  '"That is all true: now read, and I'll attend:
But was not she a most deceitful friend?
It was a monstrous, vile, and treacherous thing,
To show no pity, and to keep the ring;
But the queen shook her in her dying bed,
And 'God forgive you!' was the word she said;
'Not I for certain:'——Come, I will attend,
So read the Revolutions to an end."
  'Finch, with a timid, strange, inquiring look,
Softly and slowly laid aside the book
With sigh inaudible——"Come, never heed,"
Said he, recovering, "now I cannot read."
  'They walk'd at leisure through their wood and groves,
In fields and lanes, and talk'd of plants and loves,
And loves of plants.—Said Finch, "Augusta, dear,
You said you loved to learn,—were you sincere?
Do you remember that you told me once
How much you grieved, and said you were a dunce?

That is, you wanted information. Say,
What would you learn? I will direct your way."
'"Goodness!" said she, "what meanings you discern
In a few words! I said I wish'd to learn,
And so I think I did; and you replied,
The wish was good: what would you now beside?
Did not you say it show'd an ardent mind;
And pray what more do you expect to find?"
'"My dear Augusta, could you wish indeed
For any knowledge, and not then proceed?
That is not wishing——"
"Mercy! how you tease!
You knew I said it with a view to please;
A compliment to you, and quite enough,—
You would not kill me with that puzzling stuff!
Sure I might say I wish'd; but that is still
Far from a promise: it is not,—'I will.'
'"But come, to show you that I will not hide
My proper talents, you shall be my guide;
And lady Boothby, when we meet, shall cry,
She's quite as good a botanist as I."
'"Right, my Augusta;" and, in manner grave,
Finch his first lecture on the science gave;
An introduction,—and he said, "My dear,
Your thought was happy,—let us persevere;
And let no trifling cause our work retard,—"
Agreed the lady, but she fear'd it hard.
'Now o'er the grounds they rambled many a mile;
He show'd the flowers, the stamina, the style,
Calix and corol, pericarp and fruit,
And all the plant produces, branch and root;
Of these he treated, every varying shape,
Till poor Augusta panted to escape:
He show'd the various foliage plants produce,
Lunate and lyrate, runcinate, retuse;
Long were the learned words, and urged with force,
Panduriform, pinnatifid, premorse,
Latent, and patent, papulous, and plane,—
"Oh!" said the pupil, "it will turn my brain."
"Fear not," he answer'd, and again, intent
To fill that mind, o'er class and order went;

And stopping, "Now," said he, "my love, attend."
"I do," said she, "but when will be an end?"
"When we have made some progress,—now begin,
Which is the stigma, show me with the pin:
Come, I have told you, dearest, let me see,
Times very many,—tell it now to me."
'"Stigma! I know,—the things with yellow heads,
That shed the dust, and grow upon the threads;
You call them wives and husbands, but you know
That is a joke—here, look, and I will show
All I remember."—Doleful was the look
Of the preceptor, when he shut his book,
(The system brought to aid them in their view,)
And now with sighs return'd—"It will not do."
'A handsome face first led him to suppose,
There must be talent with such looks as those;
The want of talent taught him now to find
The face less handsome with so poor a mind;
And half the beauty faded, when he found
His cherish'd hopes were falling to the ground.
'Finch lost his spirit; but e'en then he sought
For fancied powers: she might in time be taught.
Sure there was nothing in that mind to fear;
The favourite study did not yet appear.—
'Once he express'd a doubt if she could look
For five succeeding minutes on a book;
When, with awaken'd spirit, she replied,
"He was mistaken, and she would be tried."
'With this delighted, he new hopes express'd,—
"How do I know?—She may abide the test?
Men I have known, and famous in their day,
Who were by chance directed in their way:
I have been hasty.—Well, Augusta, well,
What is your favourite reading? prithee tell;
Our different tastes may different books require,—
Yours I may not peruse, and yet admire:
Do then explain"—"Good Heaven!" said she, in haste,
"How do I hate these lectures upon taste!"
'"I lecture not, my love; but do declare,—
You read you say—what your attainments are."
'"Oh! you believe," said she, "that other things

Are read as well as histories of kings,
And loves of plants, with all that simple stuff
About their sex, of which I know enough.
Well, if I must, I will my studies name,
Blame if you please—I know you love to blame.
When all our childish books were set apart,
The first I read was 'Wanderings of the Heart:'
It was a story, where was done a deed
So dreadful, that alone I fear'd to read."
'"The next was 'The Confessions of a Nun,—'
'Twas quite a shame such evil should be done;
Nun of—no matter for the creature's name,
For there are girls no nunnery can tame:
Then there was the story of the Haunted Hall,
Where the huge picture nodded from the wall
When the old lord look'd up with trembling dread,
And I grew pale, and shudder'd as I read:
Then came the tales of Winters, Summers, Springs,
At Bath and Brighton,—they were pretty things!
No ghosts nor spectres there were heard or seen,
But all was love and flight to Gretna-green.
Perhaps your greater learning may despise
What others like, and there your wisdom lies,—
Well! do not frown,—I read the tender tales
Of lonely cots, retreats in silent vales
For maids forsaken, and suspected wives,
Against whose peace some foe his plot contrives;
With all the hidden schemes that none can clear
Till the last book, and then the ghosts appear.
'"I read all plays that on the boards succeed,
And all the works, that ladies ever read,—
Shakespeare, and all the rest,—I did, indeed,—
Ay! you may stare; but, sir, believe it true
That we can read and learn, as well as you.
'"I would not boast,—but I could act a scene
In any play, before I was fifteen.
'"Nor is this all; for many are the times
I read in Pope and Milton, prose and rhymes;
They were our lessons, and, at ten years old,
I could repeat——but now enough is told.
Sir, I can tell you I my mind applied

To all my studies, and was not denied
Praise for my progress——Are you satisfied?"
'"Entirely, madam! else were I possess'd
By a strong spirit who could never rest.
Yes! yes, no more I question,—here I close
The theme for ever—let us to repose."'

13. DELAY HAS DANGER

Three weeks had past, and Richard rambles now
Far as the dinners of the day allow;
He rode to Farley Grange and Finley Mere,
That house so ancient, and that lake so clear:
He rode to Ripley through that river gay,
Where in the shallow stream the loaches play,
And stony fragments stay the winding stream,
And gilded pebbles at the bottom gleam,
Giving their yellow surface to the sun,
And making proud the waters as they run:
It is a lovely place, and at the side
Rises a mountain-rock in rugged pride;
And in that rock are shapes of shells, and forms
Of creatures in old worlds, of nameless worms,
Whose generations lived and died ere man,
A worm of other class, to crawl began.
There is a town call'd Silford, where his steed
Our traveller rested—He the while would feed
His mind by walking to and fro, to meet,
He knew not what adventure, in the street:
A stranger there, but yet a window-view
Gave him a face that he conceived he knew;
He saw a tall, fair, lovely lady, dress'd
As one whom taste and wealth had jointly bless'd;
He gazed, but soon a footman at the door
Thundering, alarm'd her, who was seen no more.
'This was the lady whom her lover bound
In solemn contract, and then proved unsound:
Of this affair I have a clouded view,
And should be glad to have it clear'd by you.'
So Richard spake, and instant George replied,

'I had the story from the injured side,
But when resentment and regret were gone,
And pity (shaded by contempt) came on.
Frail was the hero of my tale, but still
Was rather drawn by accident than will;
Some without meaning, into guilt advance
From want of guard, from vanity, from chance;
Man's weakness flies his more immediate pain,
A little respite from his fears to gain;
And takes the part that he would gladly fly,
If he had strength and courage to deny.
  'But now my tale, and let the moral say,
When hope can sleep, there's danger in delay.
Not that for rashness, Richard, I would plead,
For unadvised alliance: No, indeed:
Think ere the contract—but, contracted, stand
No more debating, take the ready hand:
When hearts are willing, and when fears subside,
Trust not to time, but let the knot be tied;
For when a lover has no more to do,
He thinks in leisure, what shall I pursue?
And then who knows what objects come in view?
For when, assured, the man has nought to keep
His wishes warm and active, then they sleep:
Hopes die with fears; and then a man must lose
All the gay visions, and delicious views,
Once his mind's wealth! He travels at his ease,
Nor horrors now nor fairy-beauty sees;
When the kind goddess gives the wish'd assent,
No mortal business should the deed prevent;
But the blest youth should legal sanction seek
Ere yet th' assenting blush has fled the cheek.
  'And—hear me, Richard,—man has reptile-pride
That often rises when his fears subside;
When, like a trader feeling rich, he now
Neglects his former smile, his humble bow,
And, conscious of his hoarded wealth, assumes
New airs, nor thinks how odious he becomes.
  'There is a wandering, wavering train of thought
That something seeks where nothing should be
    sought,

And will a self-delighted spirit move
To dare the danger of pernicious love.
 'First be it granted all was duly said
By the fond youth to the believing maid;
Let us suppose with many a sigh there came
The declaration of the deathless flame;—
And so her answer—"She was happy then,
Blest in herself, and did not think of men;
And with such comforts in her present state,
A wish to change it was to tempt her fate;
That she would not; but yet she would confess
With him she thought her hazard would be less;
Nay, more, she would esteem, she would regard express:
But to be brief—if he could wait and see
In a few years what his desires would be."'
 Henry for years read months, then weeks, nor found
The lady thought his judgment was unsound;
'For months read weeks,' she read it to his praise,
And had some thoughts of changing it to *days*.
 And here a short excursion let me make,
A lover tried, I think, for lovers' sake;
And teach the meaning in a lady's mind
When you can none in her expressions find:
Words are design'd that meaning to convey,
But often *Yea* is hidden in a *Nay!*
And what the charmer wills, some gentle hints betray.
Then, too, when ladies mean to yield at length,
They match their reasons with the lover's strength,
And, kindly cautious, will no force employ
But such as he can baffle or destroy.
 As when heroic lovers beauty woo'd,
And were by magic's mighty art withstood,
The kind historian, for the dame afraid,
Gave to the faithful knight the stronger aid.
 A downright *No!* would make a man despair,
Or leave for kinder nymph the cruel fair;
But '*No!* because I'm very happy now,
Because I dread th' irrevocable vow,
Because I fear papa will not approve,
Because I love not—No, I cannot love;
Because you men of Cupid make a jest,

Because——in short, a single life is best.'
A *No!* when back'd by reasons of such force,
Invites approach, and will recede of course.
  Ladies, like towns besieged, for honour's sake,
Will some defence or its appearance make;
On first approach there's much resistance made,
And conscious weakness hides in bold parade;
With lofty looks, and threat'nings stern and proud,
'Come, if you dare,' is said in language loud,
But if th' attack be made with care and skill,
'Come,' says the yielding party, 'if you will;'
Then each the other's valiant acts approve,
And twine their laurels in a wreath of love.—
  We now retrace our tale, and forward go,—
Thus Henry rightly read Cecilia's No!
His prudent father, who had duly weigh'd,
And well approved the fortune of the maid,
Not much resisted, just enough to show
He knew his power, and would his son should know.
  'Harry, I will, while I your bargain make,
That you a journey to our patron take:
I know her guardian; care will not become
A lad when courting; as you must be dumb,
You may be absent; I for you will speak,
And ask what you are not supposed to seek.'
  Then came the parting hour, and what arise
When lovers part! expressive looks and eyes,
Tender and tear-full,—many a fond adieu,
And many a call the sorrow to renew;
Sighs such as lovers only can explain,
And words that they might undertake in vain.
  Cecilia liked it not; she had, in truth,
No mind to part with her enamour'd youth;
But thought it foolish thus themselves to cheat,
And part for nothing but again to meet.
  Now Henry's father was a man whose heart
Took with his interest a decided part;
He knew his lordship, and was known for acts
That I omit,—they were acknowledged facts;
An interest somewhere; I the place forget,
And the good deed—no matter—'twas a debt:

Thither must Henry, and in vain the maid
Express'd dissent—the father was obey'd.
  But though the maid was by her fears assail'd,
Her reason rose against them, and prevail'd;
Fear saw him hunting, leaping, falling—led,
Maim'd and disfigured, groaning to his bed;
Saw him in perils, duels,—dying,—dead.
But Prudence answer'd, 'Is not every maid
With equal cause for him she loves afraid?'
And from her guarded mind Cecilia threw
The groundless terrors that will love pursue.
  She had no doubts, and her reliance strong
Upon the honour that she would not wrong:
Firm in herself, she doubted not the truth
Of him, the chosen, the selected youth;
Trust of herself a trust in him supplied,
And she believed him faithful, though untried:
On her he might depend, in him she would confide.
  If some fond girl express'd a tender pain
Lest some fair rival should allure her swain,
To such she answer'd, with a look severe,
'Can one you doubt be worthy of your fear?'
  My lord was kind,—a month had pass'd away,
And Henry stay'd,—he sometimes named a day;
But still my lord was kind, and Henry still must stay:
His father's words to him were words of fate—
'Wait, 'tis your duty; 'tis my pleasure, wait!'
In all his walks, in hilly heath or wood,
Cecilia's form the pensive youth pursued;
In the gray morning, in the silent noon,
In the soft twilight, by the sober moon,
In those forsaken rooms, in that immense saloon;
And he, now fond of that seclusion grown,
There reads her letters, and there writes his own.
  'Here none approach,' said he, 'to interfere,
But I can think of my Cecilia here!'
  But there did come—and how it came to pass
Who shall explain?—a mild and blue-eyed lass;—
It was the work of accident, no doubt—
The cause unknown—we say, 'as things fall out;'—
The damsel enter'd there, in wand'ring round about:

At first she saw not Henry; and she ran,
As from a ghost, when she beheld a man.
She was esteem'd a beauty through the hall,
And so admitted, with consent of all;
And, like a treasure, was her beauty kept
From every guest who in the mansion slept;
Whether as friends who join'd the noble pair,
Or those invited by the steward there.
She was the daughter of a priest, whose life
Was brief and sad: he lost a darling wife,
And Fanny then her father, who could save
But a small portion; but his all he gave,
With the fair orphan, to a sister's care,
And her good spouse: they were the ruling pair—
Steward and steward's lady—o'er a tribe,
Each under each, whom I shall not describe.
This grave old couple, childless and alone,
Would, by their care, for Fanny's loss atone:
She had been taught in schools of honest fame;
And to the hall, as to a home, she came,
My lord assenting: yet, as meet and right,
Fanny was held from every hero's sight,
Who might in youthful error cast his eyes
On one so gentle as a lawful prize,
On border land, whom, as their right or prey,
A youth from either side might bear away.
Some handsome lover of th' inferior class
Might as a wife approve the lovely lass;
Or some invader from the class above,
Who, more presuming, would his passion prove
By asking less—love only for his love.
This much experienced aunt her fear express'd,
And dread of old and young, of host and guest.
'Go not, my Fanny, in their way,' she cried,
'It is not right that virtue should be tried;
So, to be safe, be ever at my side.'
She was not ever at that side; but still
Observed her precepts, and obey'd her will.
But in the morning's dawn and evening's gloom
She could not lock the damsel in her room;
And Fanny thought, 'I will ascend these stairs

To see the chapel,—there are none at prayers;
None,' she believed, 'had yet to dress return'd,
By whom a timid girl might be discern'd:'
In her slow motion, looking, as she glides,
On pictures, busts, and what she met besides,
And speaking softly to herself alone,
Or singing low in melancholy tone;
And thus she rambled through the still domain,
Room after room, again, and yet again.
  But, to retrace our story, still we say,
To this saloon the maiden took her way;
Where she beheld our youth, and frighten'd ran,
And so their friendship in her fear began.
  But dare she thither once again advance,
And still suppose the man will think it chance?
Nay, yet again, and what has chance to do
With this?—I know not: doubtless Fanny knew.
  Now, of the meeting of a modest maid
And sober youth why need we be afraid?
And when a girl's amusements are so few
As Fanny's were, what would you have her do?
Reserved herself, a decent youth to find,
And just be civil, sociable, and kind,
And look together at the setting sun,
Then at each other—What the evil done?
  Then Fanny took my little lord to play,
And bade him not intrude on Henry's way:
'O, he intrudes not!' said the youth, and grew
Fond of the child, and would amuse him too;
Would make such faces, and assume such looks—
He loved it better than his gayest books.
  When man with man would an acquaintance seek,
He will his thoughts in chosen language speak;
And they converse on divers themes, to find
If they possess a corresponding mind;
But man with woman has foundation laid,
And built up friendship ere a word is said:
'Tis not with words that they their wishes tell,
But with a language answering quite as well;
And thus they find, when they begin t' explore
Their way by speech, they knew it all before.

And now it chanced again the pair, when dark,
Met in their way, when wandering in the park;
Not in the common path, for so they might,
Without a wonder, wander day or night;
But, when in pathless ways their chance will bring
A musing pair, we do admire the thing.
The youth in meeting read the damsel's face,
As if he meant her inmost thoughts to trace;
On which her colour changed, as if she meant
To give her aid, and help his kind intent.
Both smiled and parted, but they did not speak—
The smile implied, 'Do tell me what you seek:'
They took their different ways with erring feet,
And met again, surprised that they could meet;
Then must they speak—and something of the air
Is always ready—''Tis extremely fair!'
'It was so pleasant!' Henry said; 'the beam
Of that sweet light so brilliant on the stream;
And chiefly yonder, where that old cascade
Has for an age its simple music made;
All so delightful, soothing, and serene!
Do you not feel it? not enjoy the scene?
Something it has that words will not express,
But rather hide, and make th' enjoyment less:
'Tis what our souls conceive, 'tis what our hearts confess.'
Poor Fanny's heart at these same words confess'd
How well he painted, and how rightly guess'd;
And, while they stood admiring their retreat,
Henry found something like a mossy seat;
But Fanny sat not; no, she rather pray'd
That she might leave him, she was so afraid.
'Not, sir, of you; your goodness I can trust,
But folks are so censorious and unjust,
They make no difference, they pay no regard
To our true meaning, which is very hard
And very cruel; great the pain it cost
To lose such pleasure, but it must be lost:
Did people know how free from thought of ill
One's meaning is, their malice would be still.'
At this she wept; at least a glittering gem

Shone in each eye, and there was fire in them,
For as they fell, the sparkles, at his feet,
He felt emotions very warm and sweet.
'A lovely creature! not more fair than good,
By all admired, by some, it seems, pursued,
Yet self-protected by her virtue's force
And conscious truth—What evil in discourse
With one so guarded, who is pleased to trust
Herself with me, reliance strong and just?'
Our lover then believed he must not seem
Cold to the maid who gave him her esteem;
Not manly this; Cecilia had his heart,
But it was lawful with his time to part;
It would be wrong in her to take amiss
A virtuous friendship for a girl like this;
False or disloyal he would never prove,
But kindness here took nothing from his love:
Soldiers to serve a foreign prince are known,
When not on present duty to their own;
So, though our bosom's queen we still prefer,
We are not always on our knees to her.
'Cecilia present, witness yon fair moon,
And yon bright orbs, that fate would change as soon
As my devotion; but the absent sun
Cheers us no longer when his course is run;
And then those starry twinklers may obtain
A little worship till he shines again.'
The father still commanded 'Wait awhile,'
And the son answer'd in submissive style,
Grieved, but obedient; and obedience teased
His lady's spirit more than grieving pleased:
That he should grieve in absence was most fit,
But not that he to absence should submit;
And in her letters might be traced reproof,
Distant indeed, but visible enough;
This should the wandering of his heart have stay'd;
Alas! the wanderer was the vainer made.
The parties daily met, as by consent,
And yet it always seem'd by accident;
Till in the nymph the shepherd had been blind
If he had fail'd to see a manner kind,

With that expressive look, that seem'd to say,
'You do not speak, and yet you see you may.'
O! yes, he saw, and he resolved to fly,
And blamed his heart, unwilling to comply:
He sometimes wonder'd how it came to pass,
That he had all this freedom with the lass;
Reserved herself, with strict attention kept,
And care and vigilance that never slept:
'How is it thus that they a beauty trust
With me, who feel the confidence is just?
And they, too, feel it; yes, they may confide,'—
He said in folly, and he smiled in pride.
'Tis thus our secret passions work their way,
And the poor victims know not they obey.
Familiar now became the wandering pair,
And there was pride and joy in Fanny's air;
For though his silence did not please the maid,
She judged him only modest and afraid;
The gentle dames are ever pleased to find
Their lovers dreading they should prove unkind;
So, blind by hope, and pleased with prospects gay,
The generous beauty gave her heart away
Before he said, 'I love!'—alas! he dared not say.
Cecilia yet was mistress of his mind,
But oft he wish'd her, like his Fanny, kind;
Her fondness sooth'd him, for the man was vain,
And he perceived that he could give her pain:
Cecilia liked not to profess her love,
But Fanny ever was the yielding dove;
Tender and trusting, waiting for the word,
And then prepared to hail her bosom's lord.
Cecilia once her honest love avow'd,
To make him happy, not to make him proud;
But she would not, for every asking sigh,
Confess the flame that waked his vanity;
But this poor maiden, every day and hour,
Would, by fresh kindness, feed the growing power;
And he indulged, vain being! in the joy,
That he alone could raise it, or destroy;
A present good, from which he dared not fly,
Cecilia absent, and his Fanny by.

O! vain desire of youth, that in the hour
Of strong temptation, when he feels the power,
And knows how daily his desires increase,
Yet will he wait, and sacrifice his peace,
Will trust to chance to free him from the snare,
Of which, long since, his conscience said, beware!
Or look for strange deliverance from that ill,
That he might fly, could he command the will!
How can he freedom from the future seek,
Who feels already that he grows too weak?
And thus refuses to resist, till time
Removes the power, and makes the way for crime:
Yet thoughts he had, and he would think, 'Forego
My dear Cecilia? not for kingdoms! No!
But may I, ought I not the friend to be
Of one who feels this fond regard for me?
I wrong no creature by a kindness lent
To one so gentle, mild, and innocent;
And for that fair one, whom I still adore,
By feeling thus I think of her the more;'
And not unlikely, for our thoughts will tend
To those whom we are conscious we offend.
Had Reason whisper'd, 'Has Cecilia leave
Some gentle youth in friendship to receive,
And be to him the friend that you appear
To this soft girl?—would not some jealous fear
Proclaim your thoughts, that he approach'd too near?'
But Henry, blinded still, presumed to write
Of one in whom Cecilia would delight;
A mild and modest girl, a gentle friend,
If, as he hoped, her kindness would descend—
But what he fear'd to lose or hoped to gain
By writing thus, he had been ask'd in vain.
It was his purpose, every morn he rose,
The dangerous friendship he had made to close;
It was his torment nightly, ere he slept,
To feel his prudent purpose was not kept.
True, he has wonder'd why the timid maid
Meets him so often, and is not afraid;
And why that female dragon, fierce and keen,

Has never in their private walks been seen;
And often he has thought, 'What can their silence
mean?
'They can have no design, or plot, or plan,—
In fact, I know not how the thing began,—
'Tis their dependence on my credit here,
And fear not, nor, in fact, have cause to fear.'
But did that pair, who seem'd to think that all
Unwatch'd will wander and unguarded fall,
Did they permit a youth and maid to meet
Both unreproved? were they so indiscreet?
This sometimes enter'd Henry's mind, and then,
'Who shall account for women or for men?'
He said, 'or who their secret thoughts explore?
Why do I vex me? I will think no more.'
My lord of late had said, in manner kind,
'My good friend Harry, do not think us blind!'
Letters had past, though he had nothing seen,
His careful father and my lord between;
But to what purpose was to him unknown—
It might be borough business, or their own.
Fanny, it seem'd, was now no more in dread,
If one approach'd, she neither fear'd nor fled:
He mused on this,—'But wherefore her alarm?
She knows me better, and she dreads no harm.'
Something his father wrote that gave him pain:
'I know not, son, if you should yet remain;—
Be cautious, Harry, favours to procure
We strain a point, but we must first be sure:
Love is a folly,—that, indeed, is true,—
But something still is to our honour due,
So I must leave the thing to my good lord and you.'
But from Cecilia came remonstrance strong:
'You write too darkly, and you stay too long;
We hear reports; and, Henry,—mark me well,—
I heed not every tale that triflers tell;—
Be you no trifler; dare not to believe
That I am one whom words and vows deceive:
You know your heart, your hazard you will learn,
And this your trial——instantly return.'
'Unjust, injurious, jealous, cruel maid!

Am I a slave, of haughty words afraid?
Can she who thus commands expect to be obey'd?
O! how unlike this dear assenting soul,
Whose heart a man might at his will control!'
Uneasy, anxious, fill'd with self-reproof,
He now resolved to quit his patron's roof;
And then again his vacillating mind
To stay resolved, and that her pride should find:
Debating thus, his pen the lover took,
And chose the words of anger and rebuke.
Again, yet once again, the conscious pair
Met, and 'O, speak!' was Fanny's silent prayer;
And, 'I must speak,' said the embarrass'd youth,
'Must save my honour, must confess the truth:
Then I must lose her; but, by slow degrees,
She will regain her peace, and I my ease.'
Ah! foolish man! to virtue true nor vice,
He buys distress, and self-esteem the price;
And what his gain?—a tender smile and sigh
From a fond girl to feed his vanity.
Thus, every day they lived, and every time
They met, increased his anguish and his crime.
Still in their meetings they were ofttimes nigh
The darling theme, and then past trembling by;
On those occasions Henry often tried
For the sad truth—and then his heart denied
The utterance due: thus daily he became
The prey of weakness, vanity, and shame.
But soon a day, that was their doubts to close,
On the fond maid and thoughtless youth arose.
Within the park, beside the bounding brook,
The social pair their usual ramble took;
And there the steward found them: they could trace
News in his look, and gladness in his face.
He was a man of riches, bluff and big,
With clean brown broad-cloth, and with white cut wig:
He bore a cane of price, with riband tied,
And a fat spaniel waddled at his side:
To every being whom he met he gave
His looks expressive; civil, gay, or grave,

But condescending all; and each declared
How much he govern'd, and how well he fared.
  This great man bow'd, not humbly, but his bow
Appear'd familiar converse to allow:
The trembling Fanny, as he came in view,
Within the chestnut grove in fear withdrew;
While Henry wonder'd, not without a fear,
Of that which brought th' important man so near:
Doubt was dispersed by—'My esteem'd young man!'
As he with condescending grace began——
  'Though you with youthful frankness nobly trust
Your Fanny's friends, and doubtless think them just;
Though you have not, with craving soul, applied
To us, and ask'd the fortune of your bride,
Be it our care that you shall not lament
That love has made you so improvident.
  'An orphan maid——Your patience! you shall have
Your time to speak, I now attention crave;—
Fanny, dear girl! has in my spouse and me
Friends of a kind we wish our friends to be,
None of the poorest——nay, sir, no reply,
You shall not need——and we are born to die:
And one yet crawls on earth, of whom, I say,
That what he has he cannot take away;
Her mother's father, one who has a store
Of this world's good, and always looks for more;
But, next his money, loves the girl at heart,
And she will have it when they come to part.'
  'Sir,' said the youth, his terrors all awake,
'Hear me, I pray, I beg,—for mercy's sake!
Sir, were the secrets of my soul confess'd,
Would you admit the truths that I protest
Are such——your pardon'——
                    'Pardon! good, my friend,
I not alone will pardon, I commend:
Think you that I have no remembrance left
Of youthful love, and Cupid's cunning theft?
How nymphs will listen when their swains persuade,
How hearts are gain'd, and how exchange is made?—
Come, sir, your hand'——
                    'In mercy, hear me now!'

'I cannot hear you, time will not allow:
You know my station, what on me depends,
For ever needed—but we part as friends;
And here comes one who will the whole explain,
My better self—and we shall meet again.'
'Sir, I entreat'——
'Then be entreaty made
To her, a woman, one you may persuade;
A little teasing, but she will comply,
And loves her niece too fondly to deny.'
'O! he is mad, and miserable I!'
Exclaim'd the youth; 'But let me now collect
My scatter'd thoughts, I something must effect.'
Hurrying she came—'Now, what has he confess'd,
Ere I could come to set your heart at rest?
What! he has grieved you! Yet he, too, approves
The thing! but man will tease you, if he loves.
'But now for business: tell me, did you think
That we should always at your meetings wink?
Think you, you walk'd unseen? There are who bring
To me all secrets—O, you wicked thing!
Poor Fanny! now I think I see her blush,
All red and rosy, when I beat the bush;
And hide your secret, said I, if you dare!
So out it came, like an affrighten'd hare.
'Miss! said I, gravely; and the trembling maid
Pleased me at heart to see her so afraid;
And then she wept;—now, do remember this,
Never to chide her when she does amiss;
For she is tender as the callow bird,
And cannot bear to have her temper stirr'd;—
Fanny, I said, then whisper'd her the name,
And caused such looks—Yes, yours are just the same;
But hear my story—When your love was known
For this our child—she is, in fact, our own—
Then, first debating, we agreed at last
To seek my lord, and tell him what had past.'
'To tell the earl?'
'Yes, truly, and why not?
And then together we contrived our plot.'

'Eternal God!'
'Nay, be not so surprised,—
In all the matter we were well advised;
We saw my lord, and Lady Jane was there,
And said to Johnson, "Johnson, take a chair:"
True, we are servants in a certain way,
But in the higher places so are they;
We are obey'd in ours, and they in theirs obey—
So Johnson bow'd, for that was right and fit,
And had no scruple with the earl to sit—
Why look you so impatient while I tell
What they debated?—you must like it well.
'"Let them go on," our gracious earl began;
"They will go off," said, joking, my good man:
"Well!" said the countess,—she's a lover's friend,—
"What if they do, they make the speedier end"——
But be you more composed, for that dear child
Is with her joy and apprehension wild:
O! we have watch'd you on from day to day,
"There go the lovers!" we were wont to say—
But why that look?'—
'Dear madam, I implore
A single moment!'
'I can give no more:
Here are your letters—that's a female pen,
Said I to Fanny—"'tis his sister's, then,"
Replied the maid.—No! never must you stray;
Or hide your wanderings, if you should, I pray;
I know, at least I fear, the best may err,
But keep the by-walks of your life from her:
That youth should stray is nothing to be told,
When they have sanction in the grave and old,
Who have no call to wander and transgress,
But very love of change and wantonness.
'I prattle idly, while your letters wait,
And then my lord has much that he would state,
All good to you—do clear that clouded face,
And with good looks your lucky lot embrace.
'Now, mind that none with her divide your heart,
For she would die ere lose the smallest part;
And I rejoice that all has gone so well,

For who th' effect of Johnson's rage can tell?
He had his fears when you began to meet,
But I assured him there was no deceit:
He is a man who kindness will requite,
But injured once, revenge is his delight;
And he would spend the best of his estates
To ruin, goods and body, them he hates;
While he is kind enough when he approves
A deed that's done, and serves the man he loves:
Come, read your letters—I must now be gone,
And think of matters that are coming on.'

Henry was lost,—his brain confused, his soul
Dismay'd and sunk, his thoughts beyond control;
Borne on by terror, he foreboding read
Cecilia's letter! and his courage fled;
All was a gloomy, dark, and dreadful view,
He felt him guilty, but indignant too:—
And as he read, he felt the high disdain
Of injured men—'She may repent, in vain.'

Cecilia much had heard, and told him all
That scandal taught—'A servant at the hall,
Or servant's daughter, in the kitchen bred,
Whose father would not with her mother wed,
Was now his choice! a blushing fool, the toy,
Or the attempted, both of man and boy;
More than suspected, but without the wit
Or the allurements for such creatures fit;
Not virtuous though unfeeling, cold as ice
And yet not chaste, the weeping fool of vice;
Yielding, not tender; feeble, not refined;
Her form insipid, and without a mind.

'Rival! she spurn'd the word; but let him stay,
Warn'd as he was! beyond the present day,
Whate'er his patron might object to this,
The uncle-butler, or the weeping miss—
Let him from this one single day remain,
And then return! he would to her, in vain;
There let him then abide, to earn, or crave
Food undeserved! and be with slaves a slave.'

Had reason guided anger, govern'd zeal,
Or chosen words to make a lover feel,

She might have saved him—anger and abuse
Will but defiance and revenge produce.
'Unjust and cruel, insolent and proud!'
He said, indignant, and he spoke aloud.
'Butler! and servant! Gentlest of thy sex,
Thou wouldst not thus a man who loved thee vex;
Thou wouldst not thus to vile report give ear,
Nor thus enraged for fancied crimes appear;
I know not what, dear maid!—if thy soft smiles were here.'
And then, that instant, there appear'd the maid,
By his sad looks in her approach dismay'd;
Such timid sweetness, and so wrong'd, did more
Than all her pleading tenderness before.
In that weak moment, when disdain and pride,
And fear and fondness, drew the man aside,
In this weak moment—'Wilt thou,' he began,
'Be mine?' and joy o'er all her features ran;
'I will!' she softly whisper'd; but the roar
Of cannon would not strike his spirit more;
Ev'n as his lips the lawless contract seal'd
He felt that conscience lost her seven-fold shield,
And honour fled; but still he spoke of love,
And all was joy in the consenting dove.
That evening all in fond discourse was spent,
When the sad lover to his chamber went,
To think on what had past, to grieve and to repent:
Early he rose, and look'd with many a sigh
On the red light that fill'd the eastern sky;
Oft had he stood before, alert and gay,
To hail the glories of the new-born day:
But now dejected, languid, listless, low,
He saw the wind upon the water blow,
And the cold stream curl'd onward as the gale
From the pine-hill blew harshly down the dale;
On the right side the youth a wood survey'd,
With all its dark intensity of shade;
Where the rough wind alone was heard to move,
In this, the pause of nature and of love,
When now the young are rear'd, and when the old,
Lost to the tie, grow negligent and cold—
Far to the left he saw the huts of men,

Half hid in mist, that hung upon the fen;
Before him swallows, gathering for the sea,
Took their short flights, and twitter'd on the lea;
And near the bean-sheaf stood, the harvest done,
And slowly blacken'd in the sickly sun;
All these were sad in nature, or they took
Sadness from him, the likeness of his look,
And of his mind—he ponder'd for a while,
Then met his Fanny with a borrow'd smile.
  Not much remain'd; for money and my lord
Soon made the father of the youth accord;
His prudence half resisted, half obey'd,
And scorn kept still the guardians of the maid:
Cecilia never on the subject spoke,
She seem'd as one who from a dream awoke;
So all was peace, and soon the married pair
Fix'd with fair fortune in a mansion fair.
  Five years had past, and what was Henry then?
The most repining of repenting men;
With a fond, teasing, anxious wife, afraid
Of all attention to another paid;
Yet powerless she her husband to amuse,
Lives but t' entreat, implore, resent, accuse;
Jealous and tender, conscious of defects,
She merits little, and yet much expects;
She looks for love that now she cannot see,
And sighs for joy that never more can be;
On his retirements her complaints intrude,
And fond reproof endears his solitude:
While he her weakness (once her kindness) sees,
And his affections in her languor freeze;
Regret, uncheck'd by hope, devours his mind,
He feels unhappy, and he grows unkind.
  'Fool! to be taken by a rosy cheek,
And eyes that cease to sparkle or to speak;
Fool! for this child my freedom to resign,
When one the glory of her sex was mine;
While from this burthen to my soul I hide,
To think what Fate has dealt, and what denied.
  'What fiend possess'd me when I tamely gave
My forced assent to be an idiot's slave?

Her beauty vanish'd, what for me remains?
Th' eternal clicking of the galling chains:
Her person truly I may think my own,
Seen without pleasure, without triumph shown:
Doleful she sits, her children at her knees,
And gives up all her feeble powers to please;
Whom I, unmoved, or moved with scorn, behold,
Melting as ice, as vapid and as cold.'
  Such was his fate, and he must yet endure
The self-contempt that no self-love can cure:
Some business call'd him to a wealthy town
When unprepared for more than Fortune's frown;
There at a house he gave his luckless name,
The master absent, and Cecilia came;
Unhappy man! he could not, dared not speak,
But look'd around, as if retreat to seek:
This she allow'd not; but, with brow severe,
Ask'd him his business, sternly bent to hear;
He had no courage, but he view'd that face
As if he sought for sympathy and grace;
As if some kind returning thought to trace:
In vain; not long he waited, but with air,
That of all grace compell'd him to despair,
She rang the bell, and, when a servant came,
Left the repentant traitor to his shame;
But, going, spoke, 'Attend this person out,
And if he speaks, hear what he comes about!'
Then, with cool courtesy, from the room withdrew,
That seem'd to say, 'Unhappy man, adieu!'
  Thus will it be when man permits a vice
First to invade his heart, and then entice;
When wishes vain and undefined arise,
And that weak heart deceive, seduce, surprise;
When evil Fortune works on Folly's side,
And rash Resentment adds a spur to Pride;
Then life's long troubles from those actions come,
In which a moment may decide our doom.

22. THE VISIT CONCLUDED

'No letters, Tom?' said Richard—'None to-day.'
'Excuse me, Brother, I must now away;
Matilda never in her life so long
Deferr'd—Alas! there must be something wrong!'
  'Comfort!' said George, and all he could he lent;
'Wait till your promised day, and I consent;
Two days, and those of hope, may cheerfully be spent.
  'And keep your purpose, to review the place,
My choice; and I beseech you do it grace:
Mark each apartment, their proportions learn,
And either use or elegance discern;
Look o'er the land, the gardens, and their wall,
Find out the something to admire in all:
And should you praise them in a knowing style,
I'll take it kindly—it is well—a smile.'

* * *

  Richard must now his morning visits pay,
And bid farewell! for he must go away.
  He sought the Rector first, not lately seen,
For he had absent from his parish been;
'Farewell!' the younger man with feeling cried,
'Farewell!' the cold but worthy priest replied;
'When do you leave us?'—'I have days but two:'
''Tis a short time—but, well—Adieu, adieu!'
  'Now here is one,' said Richard, as he went
To the next friend in pensive discontent,
'With whom I sate in social, friendly ease,
Whom I respected, whom I wish'd to please;
Whose love profess'd, I question'd not was true,
And now to hear his heartless, "Well! adieu!"
  'But 'tis not well—and he a man of sense,
Grave, but yet looking strong benevolence;
Whose slight acerbity and roughness told
To his advantage; yet the man is cold;
Nor will he know, when rising in the morn,
That such a being to the world was born.
  'Are such the friendships we contract in life?
O! give me then the friendship of a wife!

Adieus, nay, parting-pains to us are sweet,
They make so glad the moments when we meet.
'For though we look not for regard intense,
Or warm professions in a man of sense,
Yet in the daily intercourse of mind
I thought that found which I desired to find,
Feeling and frankness—thus it seem'd to me,
And such farewell!—Well, Rector, let it be!'
Of the fair sisters then he took his leave,
Forget he could not, he must think and grieve,
Must the impression of their wrongs retain,
Their very patience adding to his pain;
And still the better they their sorrows bore,
His friendly nature made him feel them more.
He judged they must have many a heavy hour
When the mind suffers from a want of power;
When troubled long we find our strength decay'd,
And cannot then recall our better aid;
For to the mind, ere yet that aid has flown,
Grief has possess'd, and made it all his own;
And patience suffers, till, with gather'd might,
The scatter'd forces of the soul unite.
But few and short such times of suffering were
In Lucy's mind, and brief the reign of care.
Jane had, indeed, her flights, but had in them
What we could pity but must not condemn;
For they were always pure and oft sublime,
And such as triumph'd over earth and time,
Thoughts of eternal love that souls possess,
Foretaste divine of Heaven's own happiness.
Oft had he seen them, and esteem had sprung
In his free mind for maids so sad and young,
So good and grieving, and his place was high
In their esteem, his friendly brother's nigh,
But yet beneath; and when he said adieu!
Their tone was kind, and was responsive too.
Parting was painful; when adieu he cried,
'You will return?' the gentle girls replied;
'You must return! your Brother knows you now,
But to exist without you knows not how;
Has he not told us of the lively joy

He takes—forgive us—in the Brother-boy?
He is alone and pensive; you can give
Pleasure to one by whom a number live
In daily comfort—sure for this you met,
That for his debtors you might pay a debt—
The poor are call'd ungrateful, but you still
Will have their thanks for this—indeed you will.'
  Richard but little said, for he of late
Held with himself contention and debate.
  'My Brother loves me, his regard I know,
But will not such affection weary grow?
He kindly says "defer the parting day,"
But yet may wish me in his heart away;
Nothing but kindness I in him perceive,
In me 'tis kindness then to take my leave;
Why should I grieve if he should weary be?
There have been visitors who wearied me;
He yet may love, and we may part in peace,
Nay, in affection—novelty must cease—
Man is but man; the thing he most desires
Pleases awhile—then pleases not—then tires;
George to his former habits and his friends
Will now return, and so my visit ends.'
  Thus Richard communed with his heart; but still
He found opposed his reason and his will,
Found that his thoughts were busy in this train,
And he was striving to be calm in vain.
  These thoughts were passing while he yet forbore
To leave the friends whom he might see no more.
  Then came a chubby child and sought relief,
Sobbing in all the impotence of grief;
A full fed girl she was, with ruddy cheek,
And features coarse, that grosser feelings speak,
To whom another miss, with passions strong,
And slender fist, had done some baby-wrong.
On Lucy's gentle mind had Barlow wrought
To teach this child, whom she had labouring taught
With unpaid love—this unproductive brain
Would little comprehend, and less retain.
  A farmer's daughter, with redundant health,
And double Lucy's weight and Lucy's wealth,

Had won the man's regard, and he with her
Possess'd the treasure vulgar minds prefer;
A man of thrift, and thriving, he possess'd
What he esteem'd of earthly good the best;
And Lucy's well-stored mind had not a charm
For this true lover of the well-stock'd farm,
This slave to petty wealth and rustic toil,
This earth-devoted wooer of the soil:—
But she with meekness took the wayward child,
And sought to make the savage nature mild.
  But Jane her judgment with decision gave—
'Train not an idiot to oblige a slave.'
  'And where is Bloomer?' Richard would have said,
But he was cautious, feeling, and afraid;
And little either of the hero knew,
And little sought—he might be married too.
Now to his home, the morning visits past,
Return'd the guest—that evening was his last.
  He met his Brother, and they spoke of those
From whom his comforts in the village rose;
Spoke of the favourites, whom so good and kind
It was peculiar happiness to find:
Then for the sisters in their griefs they felt,
And, sad themselves, on saddening subjects dwelt.
  But George was willing all this woe to spare,
And let to-morrow be to-morrow's care:
He of his purchase talk'd—a thing of course,
As men will boldly praise a new-bought horse.
  Richard was not to all its beauty blind,
And promised still to seek, with hope to find:
'The price indeed——'
                    'Yes, that,' said George, 'is high:
But if I bought not, one was sure to buy,
Who might the social comforts we enjoy,
And every comfort lessen or destroy.
  'We must not always reckon what we give,
But think how precious 'tis in peace to live;
Some neighbour Nimrod might in very pride
Have stirr'd my anger, and have then defied;
Or worse, have loved, and teased me to excess
By his kind care to give me happiness;

Or might his lady and her daughters bring
To raise my spirits, to converse, and sing:
'Twas not the benefit alone I view'd,
But thought what horrid things I might exclude.
 'Some party man might here have sat him down,
Some country champion, railing at the crown,
Or some true courtier, both prepared to prove,
Who loved not them, could not their country love:
If we have value for our health and ease,
Should we not buy off enemies like these?'
 So pass'd the evening in a quiet way,
When, lo! the morning of the parting day.
 Each to the table went with clouded look,
And George in silence gazed upon a book;
Something that chance had offer'd to his view,—
He knew not what, or cared not, if he knew.
Richard his hand upon a paper laid,—
His vacant eye upon the carpet stray'd;
His tongue was talking something of the day,
And his vex'd mind was wandering on his way.
 They spake by fits,—but neither had concern
In the replies,—they nothing wish'd to learn,
Nor to relate; each sat as one who tries
To baffle sadnesses and sympathies:
Each of his Brother took a steady view,—
As actor he, and as observer too.
 Richard, whose heart was ever free and frank,
Had now a trial, and before it sank:
He thought his Brother—parting now so near—
Appear'd not as his Brother should appear;
He could as much of tenderness remark
When parting for a ramble in the park.
 'Yet, is it just?' he thought; 'and would I see
My Brother wretched but to part with me?
What can he further in my mind explore?
He saw enough, and he would see no more:
Happy himself, he wishes now to slide
Back to his habits——He is satisfied;
But I am not—this cannot be denied.
 'He has been kind,—so let me think him still;
Yet he expresses not a wish, a will

To meet again!'——And thus affection strove
With pride, and petulance made war on love:
He thought his Brother cool—he knew him kind—
And there was sore division in his mind.
'Hours yet remain,—'tis misery to sit
With minds for conversation all unfit;
No evil can from change of place arise,
And good will spring from air and exercise:
Suppose I take the purposed ride with you,
And guide your jaded praise to objects new,
That buyers see?'——
And Richard gave assent
Without resistance, and without intent:
He liked not nor declined,—and forth the Brothers went.
'Come, my dear Richard! let us cast away
All evil thoughts,—let us forget the day,
And fight like men with grief till we like boys are gay.'
Thus George,—and even this in Richard's mind
Was judged an effort rather wise than kind;
This flow'd from something he observed of late,
And he could feel it, but he could not state;
He thought some change appear'd,—yet fail'd to prove,
Even as he tried, abatement in the love;
But in his Brother's manner was restraint
That he could feel, and yet he could not paint.
That they should part in peace full well he knew,
But much he fear'd to part with coolness too:
George had been peevish when the subject rose,
And never fail'd the parting to oppose:
Name it, and straight his features cloudy grew
To stop the journey as the clouds will do;—
And thus they rode along in pensive mood,
Their thoughts pursuing, by their cares pursued.
'Richard,' said George, 'I see it is in vain
By love or prayer my Brother to retain;
And, truth to tell, it was a foolish thing
A man like thee from thy repose to bring
Ours to disturb——Say, how am I to live
Without the comforts thou art wont to give?
How will the heavy hours my mind afflict,—
No one t' agree, no one to contradict,

None to awake, excite me, or prevent,
To hear a tale, or hold an argument,
To help my worship in a case of doubt,
And bring me in my blunders fairly out.
 'Who now by manners lively or serene
Comes between me and sorrow like a screen,
And giving, what I look'd not to have found,
A care, an interest in the world around?'
 Silent was Richard, striving to adjust
His thoughts for speech,—for speak, he thought, he must:
Something like war within his bosom strove—
His mild, kind nature, and his proud self-love:
Grateful he was, and with his courage meek,—
But he was hurt, and he resolved to speak.
 'Yes, my dear Brother! from my soul I grieve
Thee and the proofs of thy regard to leave:
Thou hast been all that I could wish,—my pride
Exults to find that I am thus allied:
Yet to express a feeling, how it came,
The pain it gives, its nature and its name,
I know not,—but of late, I will confess,
Not that thy love is little, but is less.
 'Hadst thou received me in thy present mood,
Sure I had held thee to be kind and good;
But thou wert all the warmest heart could state,
Affection dream, or hope anticipate;
I must have wearied thee yet day by day,—
"Stay!" said my Brother, and 'twas good to stay;
But now, forgive me, thinking I perceive
Change undefined, and as I think I grieve.
 'Have I offended?—Proud although I be,
I will be humble, and concede to thee:
Have I intruded on thee when thy mind
Was vex'd, and then to solitude inclined?
O! there are times when all things will molest
Minds so disposed, so heavy, so oppress'd;
And thine, I know, is delicate and nice,
Sickening at folly, and at war with vice:
Then, at a time when thou wert vex'd with these,
I have intruded, let affection tease,

And so offended.'——
'Richard, if thou hast,
'Tis at this instant, nothing in the past:
No, thou art all a Brother's love would choose;
And, having lost thee, I shall interest lose
In all that I possess: I pray thee tell
Wherein thy host has fail'd to please thee well,—
Do I neglect thy comforts?'—
'O! not thou,
But art thyself uncomfortable now,
And 'tis from thee and from thy looks I gain
This painful knowledge—'tis my Brother's pain;
And yet that something in my spirit lives,
Something that spleen excites and sorrow gives,
I may confess,—for not in thee I trace
Alone this change, it is in all the place:
Smile if thou wilt in scorn, for I am glad
A smile at any rate is to be had.
'But there is Jacques, who ever seem'd to treat
Thy Brother kindly as we chanced to meet;
Nor with thee only pleased our worthy guide,
But in the hedge-row path and green-wood side,
There he would speak with that familiar ease
That makes a trifle, makes a nothing please.
'But now to my farewell,—and that I spoke
With honest sorrow,—with a careless look,
Gazing unalter'd on some stupid prose—
His sermon for the Sunday I suppose,—
"Going?" said he: "why then the 'Squire and you
Will part at last—You're going?—Well, adieu!"
'True, we were not in friendship bound like those
Who will adopt each other's friends and foes,
Without esteem or hatred of their own,—
But still we were to intimacy grown;
And sure of Jacques when I had taken leave
It would have grieved me,—and it ought to grieve;
But I in him could not affection trace,—
Careless he put his sermons in their place,
With no more feeling than his sermon-case.
'Not so those generous girls beyond the brook,—
It quite unmann'd me as my leave I took.

'But my dear Brother! when I take at night,
In my own home, and in their mother's sight,
By turns my children, or together see
A pair contending for the vacant knee,
When to Matilda I begin to tell
What in my visit first and last befell—
Of this your village, of her tower and spire,
And, above all, her Rector and her 'Squire,
How will the tale be marr'd when I shall end—
I left displeased the Brother and the friend?'

'Nay, Jacques is honest—Marry, he was then
Engaged—What! part an author and his pen?
Just in the fit, and when th' inspiring ray
Shot on his brain, t' arrest it in its way!
Come, thou shalt see him in an easier vein,
Nor of his looks nor of his words complain:
Art thou content?'

If Richard had replied,
'I am,' his manner had his words belied:
Even from his Brother's cheerfulness he drew
Something to vex him—what, he scarcely knew:
So he evading said, 'My evil fate
Upon my comforts throws a gloom of late:
Matilda writes not; and, when last she wrote,
I read no letter—'twas a trader's note,—
"Yours I received," and all that formal prate
That is so hateful, that she knows I hate.

'Dejection reigns, I feel, but cannot tell
Why upon me the dire infection fell:
Madmen may say that they alone are sane,
And all beside have a distemper'd brain;
Something like this I feel,—and I include
Myself among the frantic multitude:
But, come, Matilda writes, although but ill,
And home has health, and that is comfort still.'

George stopt his horse, and with the kindest look
Spoke to his Brother,—earnestly he spoke,
As one who to his friend his heart reveals,
And all the hazard with the comfort feels.

'Soon as I loved thee, Richard,—and I loved
Before my reason had the will approved,

Who yet right early had her sanction lent,
And with affection in her verdict went,—
So soon I felt, that thus a friend to gain,
And then to lose, is but to purchase pain:
Daily the pleasure grew, then sad the day
That takes it all in its increase away!
'Patient thou wert, and kind,—but well I knew
The husband's wishes, and the father's too;
I saw how check'd they were, and yet in secret grew:
Once and again, I urged thee to delay
Thy purposed journey, still deferr'd the day,
And still on its approach the pain increased
Till my request and thy compliance ceased;
I could not further thy affection task,
Nor more of one so self-resisting ask;
But yet to lose thee, Richard, and with thee
All hope of social joys—it cannot be.
Nor could I bear to meet thee as a boy
From school, his parents, to obtain a joy,
That lessens day by day, and one will soon destroy.
'No! I would have thee, Brother, all my own,
To grow beside me as my trees have grown;
For ever near me, pleasant in my sight,
And in my mind, my pride and my delight.
'Yet will I tell thee, Richard; had I found
Thy mind dependent and thy heart unsound,
Hadst thou been poor, obsequious, and disposed
With any wish or measure to have closed,
Willing on me and gladly to attend,
The younger brother, the convenient friend;
Thy speculation its reward had made
Like other ventures—thou hadst gain'd in trade;
What reason urged, or Jacques esteem'd thy due,
Thine had it been, and I, a trader too,
Had paid my debt, and home my Brother sent,
Nor glad nor sorry that he came or went;
Who to his wife and children would have told,
They had an uncle, and the man was old;
Till every girl and boy had learn'd to prate
Of uncle George, his gout, and his estate.
'Thus had we parted; but as now thou art,

I must not lose thee—No! I cannot part;
Is it in human nature to consent,
To give up all the good that heaven has lent,
All social ease and comfort to forego,
And live again the solitary? No!
  'We part no more, dear Richard! thou wilt need
Thy Brother's help to teach thy boys to read;
And I should love to hear Matilda's psalm,
To keep my spirit in a morning calm,
And feel the soft devotion that prepares
The soul to rise above its earthly cares;
Then thou and I, an independent two,
May have our parties, and defend them too;
Thy liberal notions, and my loyal fears,
Will give us subjects for our future years;
We will for truth alone contend and read,
And our good Jacques shall oversee our creed.
  'Such were my views; and I had quickly made
Some bold attempts my Brother to persuade
To think as I did; but I knew too well
Whose now thou wert, with whom thou wert to dwell,
And why, I said, return him doubtful home,
Six months to argue if he then would come
Some six months after? and, beside, I know
That all the happy are of course the slow;
And thou at home art happy, there wilt stay,
Dallying 'twixt will and will-not many a day,
And fret the gloss of hope, and hope itself away.
  'Jacques is my friend; to him I gave my heart,
You see my Brother, see I would not part;
Wilt thou an embassy of love disdain?
Go to this sister, and my views explain;
Gloss o'er my failings, paint me with a grace
That Love beholds, put meaning in my face;
Describe that dwelling; talk how well we live,
And all its glory to our village give;
Praise the kind sisters whom we love so much,
And thine own virtues like an artist touch.
  'Tell her, and here my secret purpose show,
That no dependence shall my sister know;
Hers all the freedom that she loves shall be,

And mine the debt,—then press her to agree;
Say, that my Brother's wishes wait on hers,
And his affection what she wills prefers.
  'Forgive me, Brother,—these my words and more
Our friendly Rector to Matilda bore;
At large, at length, were all my views explain'd,
And to my joy my wishes I obtain'd.
  'Dwell in that house, and we shall still be near,
Absence and parting I no more shall fear;
Dwell in thy home, and at thy will exclude
All who shall dare upon thee to intrude.
  'Again thy pardon,—'twas not my design
To give surprise; a better view was mine;
But let it pass—and yet I wish'd to see
That meeting too: and happy may it be!'
Thus George had spoken, and then look'd around,
And smiled as one who then his road had found;
'Follow!' he cried, and briskly urged his horse:
Richard was puzzled, but obey'd of course:
He was affected like a man astray,
Lost, but yet knowing something of the way;
Till a wood clear'd, that still conceal'd the view,
Richard the purchase of his Brother knew;
And something flash'd upon his mind not clear,
But much with pleasure mix'd, in part with fear;
As one who wandering through a stormy night
Sees his own home, and gladdens at the sight,
Yet feels some doubt if fortune had decreed
That lively pleasure in such time of need;
So Richard felt—but now the mansion came
In view direct,—he knew it for the same;
There too the garden walk, the elms design'd
To guard the peaches from the eastern wind;
And there the sloping glass, that when he shines
Gives the sun's vigour to the ripening vines.—
  'It is my Brother's!'—
                    'No!' he answers, 'No!
'Tis to thy own possession that we go;
It is thy wife's, and will thy children's be,
Earth, wood, and water!—all for thine and thee;
Bought in thy name—Alight, my friend, and come,

I do beseech thee, to thy proper home;
There wilt thou soon thy own Matilda view,
She knows our deed, and she approves it too;
Before her all our views and plans were laid,
And Jacques was there t' explain and to persuade.
Here, on this lawn, thy boys and girls shall run,
And play their gambols when their tasks are done;
There, from that window, shall their mother view
The happy tribe, and smile at all they do;
While thou, more gravely, hiding thy delight,
Shalt cry "O! childish!" and enjoy the sight.
'Well, my dear Richard, there's no more to say—
Stay, as you will—do any thing—but stay;
Be, I dispute not, steward—what you will,
Take your own name, but be my Brother still.
'And hear me, Richard! if I should offend,
Assume the patron, and forget the friend;
If aught in word or manner I express
That only touches on thy happiness;
If I be peevish, humoursome, unkind,
Spoil'd as I am by each subservient mind;
For I am humour'd by a tribe who make
Me more capricious for the pains they take
To make me quiet; shouldst thou ever feel
A wound from this, this leave not time to heal,
But let thy wife her cheerful smile withhold,
Let her be civil, distant, cautious, cold;
Then shall I woo forgiveness, and repent,
Nor bear to lose the blessings Heaven has lent.'
But this was needless—there was joy of heart,
All felt the good that all desired t' impart;
Respect, affection, and esteem combined,
In sundry portions ruled in every mind;
And o'er the whole an unobtrusive air
Of pious joy, that urged the silent prayer,
And bless'd the new-born feelings——Here we close
Our Tale of Tales!—Health, reader, and repose!

IN A NEAT COTTAGE

In a neat cottage hid from public view,
Within a vally bounded by a wood,
Near to the coast, but distant from a town,
With the kind sister of a mother dead
Dwelt a fair damsel named Elizabeth.
  From an expiring mother's feeble hand,
In holy confidence, a sacred trust
The aunt receiv'd, and bore her to this place.
There as a parent, governess and friend,
She nurst and trained and led the little maid,
In peace to virtue, and in love to knowledge;
Gave to her mind the riches of her own,
Corrected all that she perceiv'd amiss,
Implanted every truth that she believed,
Fostered the new-born virtue, and in time
Spoke of God's grace and taught the soul to pray.
But of the ways of social life, the good
And evil, dangers and delights, the charm
And fascination of society,
Save with that mind whose stores were made
    her own,
She nothing knew; The world was yet a book
In a strange language written, and the guide,
When the niece, eager and inquisitive,
Begged for one page, said tenderly: 'Forbear:
Ask me not, love, I read it not myself.'
  The persons whom Elizabeth beheld
Were a few peasants from the neighbouring green,
Farmers of occupations small, and wives
Of these small farmers who in modest pride
Looked kindly down upon the cottage dames,
Wives to the lads who laboured for the farm.
  To these we add the vicar and his wife,
A man of Cambridge, but of him unseen
These forty years; and he would sometimes say,
Vapoured perhaps, or troubled for a tax,
Or forced to take a twentieth for a tithe,

Or when his brother cast upon his coat
A look contemptuous, but with pity blent,
Pride's tenderness: 'I wish I had not seen.'—
He was an elder son, whose father sent
The boy to Cambridge, and kept John at home.
And John in time was tenant in the farm,
And of its stock the owner. Dick must pay
For what it cost at college, and has paid,
For he is vicar in the place, where John
Is lord, and governs as an overseer.
But still he makes his bow, and gives his seat,
And says: 'My Brother is a learned man;
'Twas my poor father's pride, but he could not
Afford to make his John a gentleman.
Brother, my service, we are getting poor;
Come now, abate a little of your tithe.'
　Such the companions of Elizabeth.
Here she resided, of the world she knew
What these could give—no more. Some pious books
Of solid practical divinity,
Laid in a quiet case; the vicar lent
Monthly a magazine, and Farmer John
A weekly paper fraught with country news.
But not this reading, tho' she often read
And try'd to make another's thoughts her own;
Not conversation with her village friends,
Nor closer converse with the dearer one,
Not the good vicar's piety or pride,
When dwelling on the sermon of the day;
Nor song of morning bird nor, sweeter yet,
The varied sweetness of the bird of night,
Nor these, nor aught of Nature she [?removed]
On earth or in the waters, nor the tribes
Of sportive insects on the wing, at eve,
Soft but not silent, satisfied the heart
That ever sought for that it never found.
　It wanted something that was like itself,
But not itself, and in her devious walks,
Or on the heath, or by the rapid brook,
Not in the path way, not within the wood,
Nor where a bound was fixt, nor where the feet

Of numbers marked the way; she chose her own,
But in her own she mus'd, and dared to think
Of forms and minds that she should love to know.—
The forms majestic with the noblest mind,
Beauty and courage, tenderness and grace,
Not without splendour in the very garb
And grandeur in the mein; and she would suit
Deeds to the man; Elizabeth was young.
While thus she lived, and thought, and wish'd, and dreamt,
Her aunt died suddenly—
A large, lone house
Between the river and the sea was named
'The Dolphin's Wreck'; Some sixty years had past,
Since that good ship 'The Dolphin' on the sand
Of that wild shore was stranded, and the plank
First formed a shepherd's lodge, and hence the name.
Strange place for one who tended flocks; yet there
Were marshes all around, from that rude sea
To that wide river; and in time one man
Was the sole tenant. In the narrow farm
Between the wasty bounds for many a mile
Bit the small hardy breed. And then arose
A more commodious building, but the name
Was yet 'The Dolphin's Wreck'. Within was heard,
In the soft summer night, the rimpled waves
Roll on the sanded shore; in winter, floods.
When the full moon upon the billowy tide
Shone in her splendor fearfully, and the wind
Changed from the south unto the dread north-west,
Then from her window looked Elizabeth,
For 'twas her father's house, and she at home
Had found a melancholy mishap there.
There she beheld the troubled waters rise,
And from her bow-formed window on the west
Saw the broad stream for many a rood engulph
The salt short herbage. Wider yet became
The watry-waste, and billowy like the sea!
So thought the maid, but, turning to the sea,
Thought that no likeness to that dreadful sight

Could the sad world present; above the ridge
Stoney and steep, the giant billows threw
Their foaming [?force], and dreadful was the sight
Of clashing waves as far as eye could reach,
And sounds of blended horror, as they raked
The rolling fleet far down the lengthen'd shore.
  How trembled then the maid; it could not be
But those wild waters in their strength would meet!
All would be sea, and like a stranded ship
Their house a wreck, and all it held a prey.
  Eastward and westward as she turned, the moon,
As parting clouds admitted, now appear'd
Refulgent, riding in her cloudless way,
Smiling at horror in [the] storm beneath.
There was a strong enchantment in the scene:
It gave the maiden-mind a strange delight,
Made up by terror and astonishment,
And admiration and religious awe,
That strove with fear, and made divine the event.
Unsated by the views, not unalarmed,
From east to west still turning, the mid space
Seem'd ever less'ning to Elizabeth.
She had observed, beside the path that led
To the low water's mark, the river made,
But distant more than half that pebbly way,
And near the house, a chalky, hilly heap,
By none regarded till the damsel now,
Trac'd the broad stream encroaching, till it reach'd
The scatter'd stones, then washed the hillock's
    base;
Then turning to the sea, awhile she staid
Watching the froathy foam that from the sea
Arose and fell upon the river's tide—
The tide, that since her last alarming look
Had covered all the heap. 'And what is there
Bourne by the flood along?—it has a form,
And struggles as it rolls! Good heaven, it lives,
And feels its fate—'tis of my father's flock!
And where my father?'—
                Here the maiden joined
Her two domestic damsels, for the men

Were all abroad, to pen the fright'n'd flocks,
Save the poor strays, that, like to men astray,
Disdain'd the power that saved them; and so fled,
And perished in their search for liberty.
For not the tyger nor the pard can share
Freedom and safety both; nor sheep nor men!
 'Where is my father?', said the fearful maid.
'Master is safe,' was said as Nature bade,
Nor reason knew what better to reply,
Master was safe, but 'twas a dreadful night!
In it the river and the ocean met—
Not like the Thames and Medway, in their pomp
And pride of lawful wedlock, but in force,
Tumult and wrath, and with a voice that said:
'To meet is to destroy!' But they did meet,
And parted as a pair who should not meet,
Save in that place where they can part no more.
The season chang'd, and our young heroine
Had view'd the waters in their various forms,
The calm and storm, the day and moonlight make,
Summer and winter; she had seen the fleets,
Warlike, or fraught with merchandise, had seen
Men in distress, and in distress had seen them
Crowd on the deck, and clinging to the shrouds
For momentary safety, and then part,
Never to meet again. Strong pity seized
The gentle breast, and she would millions give
That she might save a sailor—
 To the house
At morn or night a rude amphibious crew
Would come, her father's visitors, not hers,
For she was then permitted to retire,
But not compelled; for they were coarse and loud,
Their subjects puzzled and disgusted her.
Fairly they bought, they said, and fairly sold,
And yet they dealt in darkness, and they fled
When none persued; and they were sore afraid
Of law, and poor Elizabeth of them.
Save this, the farm had little to offend,
But, to be just, yet less to edify,
And nothing to amuse, as said the maid,

When she had picked her pebbles from the beach,
And, sighing, ask'd: 'What is the worth of these?
Comes there no being to my father's house
But those who, being come, I wish away?
I've dreamt of men who could have made this seat,
Where strive the bittern and the cormorant,
Which should describe it in the vilest tone,
As one where patience might abide, and joy
Make frequent stay; but O! the bitter fate,
Ev'n patience sickens here, and hope must die.'
Such were the breathings of Elizabeth,
When a youth saw her in her seat at church,
Made his proposals, and the fathers saw
No cause nor just impediment—How then?
The lady loves not, and she will not wed.
And what her reason? That she will not give,
But he is not the very being formed
In her imagination. 'Leave her, Dick,'
His father counsel'd: 'That I cannot do,'
The young man answer'd. Richard was in love!
The summer past away with little change,
With its small cares and pleasures; roughly kind
Her father's voice; and Richard fond and true.
With many a thought where they had not a place,
The maiden sat, and gazed for many an hour
On the bright surface of the summer sea,
Not without memory of the winter's storm.
And once again it came, more dreadful still,
For fear had now its object.
In the dawn
Of a December day Elizabeth
Had fixt the eye upon a ship at sea,
That was all day in sight. Her father said
It was a ship he knew not; yet he knew
Our various kinds, from her whose hundred guns
Bore Britain's thunder, thro' the subject sea
To the small craft that from the foreign shore
Lands the clandestine freight and trades by night.
It was a ship he knew not, homeward bound;
But in her sailing there was something strange;
All was not right. Alas! but he was so,

For there had been a kind of mutiny,
Not yet appeased; the men would not obey,
And whom the superior few could not controul,
Nor would [?]—and so the ship remain'd
Upon the coast of danger. Night came on
And with it came a storm, when, terror-calm'd,
The disobedient crew with one consent
Returned to duty, penitent too late—
To the far shore, where stretch'd the dangerous
  sands,
Raged the strong wind full east, and trembling hope
Upon the weak anchor rested now,
And [?] to hear the full stretch'd cable strain'd
And groaning in the storm;
    A gathering crowd
Beneath the now deserted lodge indulged
Vain curiosity and strong surprise.
Sole at her window stood Elizabeth;
She saw the ship, how tost by every wave,
For ever moving, but for ever fixed—
O! not for ever! hold the corded strength
For a few hours, and let the winds be still,
Or the tide turn, and all may yet be well.
To sailors, as they walked the window by,
She said: 'When will it be that they are sav'd?'
One answer'd: 'What o'clock?', and she replied:
'Eleven!' 'Good! and yesternight the moon
Was in her second quarter; wind at east.'
'But is there safety?'—'If they ride it out.'
'But will they ride it out?' 'Perhaps they may,'
He answered careless, and the pitying maid
Felt some concern, and not without reproof:
'How feel you for men in such distress?'
'In my distress as such would feel for me:
Let him that is watchman keep the ward,
And take his turn for perils and for play.'—
  What is that cry? the cable holds not now,
The ship is drifting! Every eye is bent
Upon her crowded deck; she answers not,
The helm but drifts, a victim to the wind.
  How silent every man, and every wave

Falls unobserved! The soul and all its powers,
And every sense and every heart is there;
And there all hearts are trembling to that shore,
Where they behold so many gaze on them.
They have small chance to rest as living men,
But they approach; Elizabeth can see,
As she stands shivering, in a ague-fit. . . .